Screening the Posthuman

Screening the Posthuman

MISSY MOLLOY, PANSY DUNCAN,
AND CLAIRE HENRY

OXFORD
UNIVERSITY PRESS

Oxford University Press is a department of the University of Oxford. It furthers the University's objective of excellence in research, scholarship, and education by publishing worldwide. Oxford is a registered trade mark of Oxford University Press in the UK and certain other countries.

Published in the United States of America by Oxford University Press
198 Madison Avenue, New York, NY 10016, United States of America.

© Oxford University Press 2023

All rights reserved. No part of this publication may be reproduced, stored in a retrieval system, or transmitted, in any form or by any means, without the prior permission in writing of Oxford University Press, or as expressly permitted by law, by license, or under terms agreed with the appropriate reproduction rights organization. Inquiries concerning reproduction outside the scope of the above should be sent to the Rights Department, Oxford University Press, at the address above.

You must not circulate this work in any other form and you must impose this same condition on any acquirer.

CIP data is on file at the Library of Congress
ISBN 978–0–19–753857–9 (pbk.)
ISBN 978–0–19–753856–2 (hbk.)

DOI: 10.1093/oso/9780197538562.001.0001

Contents

Acknowledgments	vii
Introduction *Pansy Duncan, Claire Henry, and Missy Molloy*	1
1. Posthuman as Genre *Pansy Duncan, Claire Henry, and Missy Molloy*	27
2. Envisioning Posthuman Apocalypse *Missy Molloy*	64
3. From Cyborg Theory to Posthuman Mothers *Missy Molloy*	107
4. Queer Posthumanism: Figures, Fluidity, and Fluids *Claire Henry*	149
5. The Cinematic Convergence of Posthuman and Crip Perspectives *Pansy Duncan and Missy Molloy*	182
6. Post-anthropocentrism: Rejecting Human Exceptionalism *Claire Henry*	210
7. The Eco-material Posthuman in the Age of the Anthropocene *Pansy Duncan*	244
8. Conclusion *Pansy Duncan, Claire Henry, and Missy Molloy*	276
Bibliography	285
Index	301

Acknowledgments

This book is dedicated to the biotechnologies that helped to make and protect our human babies, Leo, Sigourney, and Wolfgang, during the writing of this book. It is inspired by the theorists and filmmakers whose works compelled us to track the fascinating conversation between critical posthumanism and cinema, with Ildikó Enyedi and Lynette Wallworth deserving of special mention for their generosity in sharing images from their films with us.

We are enormously grateful to Norm Hirschy and Lauralee Yeary at Oxford University Press (OUP) for their interest in and support of this book. We would also like to thank the anonymous reviewers for their feedback; Caitlin Lynch, Gwyn Easterbrook-Smith, and Paige Macintosh for their expert research assistance; Zara Cannon-Mohammed at OUP for managing the publication process so smoothly; Nirenjena Joseph at Newgen Knowledge Works for her careful copyediting; Victoria University of Wellington and Massey University for research funding; and the participants in our 2020 SCMS seminar for stimulating our thinking about the subject. Finally, we would like to thank our respective families, especially Blake, Sigourney, Leo, Wolfgang, and Tim, for their forbearance and support as this book was written.

Authorship note:

Authorship is listed alphabetically for all co-authored chapters. The book's authorship acknowledges Missy Molloy as first author (40%) and lists Pansy Duncan and Claire Henry alphabetically as equal second authors (30% each).

Introduction

Pansy Duncan, Claire Henry, and Missy Molloy

In *Teströl és lélekröl/On Body and Soul* (Ildeko Enyedi, 2017), two reclusive slaughterhouse workers discover that they share a recurring dream in which they are wild deer. In *Ex Machina* (Alex Garland, 2014), the CEO of a search engine giant invites a young programmer to administer the Turing Test to an alluring humanoid robot. In *Gräns/Border* (Ali Abbasi, 2018), a lonely airport customs officer learns that she is a member of a hidden population of trolls who exist uneasily alongside their human counterparts. In *Bacurau* (Kleber Mendonça Filho and Juliano Dornelles, 2019), an isolated community in rural Brazil defends itself against a group of foreign invaders intent on hunting locals down with military-grade weapons (Figure I.1).

On the face of it, these films have little in common beyond their status as relatively recent cinematic productions. Generically, they are diverse, incorporating elements associated with science fiction, fantasy, and the Western, as well as social realism and romance. Nationally, they are equally varied, hailing from Hungary, the United Kingdom, Sweden, and Brazil. Production-wise, they range from the relatively high-profile UK/US co-production *Ex Machina* to the Hungarian government-funded *On Body and Soul* (budgeted at less than 15% of *Ex Machina*'s total cost). Yet a key feature unites them: a preoccupation with forms of being that test the limits of conventional understandings of the human by emphasizing our entanglement in broader biological, technological, and/or social worlds. In place of the singular, universal human unit, we find a subject "constituted in and by multiplicity . . . a subject that works across differences and is also internally differentiated:"[1] a pair of slaughterhouse employees who dream they are animal companions; a woman who is also a troll; an eclectic community on the verge of extinction due to environmental, social, and technological threats. Across the thematic, formal, and narrative registers of these contemporary films, we find cinema grappling with the posthuman—which is to say, with the question of how we might reimagine the social, ethical, and discursive

Pansy Duncan, Claire Henry, and Missy Molloy, *Introduction*. In: *Screening the Posthuman*. Edited by: Missy Molloy, Pansy Duncan, and Claire Henry, Oxford University Press. © Oxford University Press 2023. DOI: 10.1093/oso/9780197538562.003.0001

2   SCREENING THE POSTHUMAN

Figure I.1 In *Bacurau* (Kleber Mendonça Filho and Juliano Dornelles, 2019), unexpected technological phenomena alert locals to an imminent attack.

logics of human subjectivity at a moment when, as Cary Wolfe has put it, the imbrication of the "human" in "technical, medical, informatic and economic networks is increasingly impossible to ignore."[2]

This book addresses a heterogenous body of twenty-first-century films that confront evolving conceptualizations of the "human" as part of a distinctive category of screen media that critical posthumanism can effectively illuminate. But what is critical posthumanism? Today, the term "posthuman" has a degree of popular currency, circulating rather promiscuously through film commentary (as in *The New York Times* reviewer Janet Maslin's reference to Tom Tykwer's 1998 film *Run Lola Run* as "hot, fast and post-human")[3] and discussions of robotics, prosthetics, neuroscience, and biogenetic capital. The term "posthuman" has accrued an array of meanings, some of which are at odds. It should thus be clarified early on that our understanding of the posthuman is informed primarily by the critical posthumanism advocated by scholars such as Rosi Braidotti, Donna Haraway, N. Katherine Hayles, Cary Wolfe, and Neil Badmington (and shaped by adjacent fields such as queer theory, animal studies, and disability studies). The critical traditions on which critical posthumanist scholars draw are diverse, from Wolfe's deconstructivism to Braidotti's Deleuzian vital materialism to Donna Haraway's science-oriented feminist materialism. Yet what unifies their work is a shared commitment to a model of posthumanism as a decentering of the figure of the "human"—a "creature," to quote Braidotti, "familiar to us from the Enlightenment and its legacy."[4] The humanist tradition, of course, can itself be defined in manifold ways. As Wolfe puts it, the "human" of the Enlightenment is variously conceived as "the Cartesian subject of the cogito, the Kantian 'community of reasonable beings,' or, in more sociological terms, the subject as citizen, rights-holder, property-holder, and so on."[5] These diverse conceptions of the human, however, are unified by the fact that they afford the sovereign "human" subject an exceptional status by defining it over and against the technological, ecological, social, and animal worlds in which it is nevertheless embedded. Equipped with a distinct set of unique, universal, and essential capabilities—from the capacity for dialogue, to the capacity for rational self-awareness—the human is a figure whose ascendancy has been secured by "repressing not just its animal origins in nature, the biological and the evolutionary, but more generally transcending the bonds of materiality and embodiment."[6]

To "decenter" the human under the auspices of critical posthumanism is to make two gestures simultaneously: the first addresses the impact of contemporary developments on the human, while the second dismantles the fantasy that the "human" has ever been more than "a historical 'effect,' with humanism as its ideological 'affect.'"[7] On one level, then, this decentering is specific to contemporary social, ecological, and technoscientific coordinates. According to Braidotti, the figure of the human "has exploded" in the wake of a host of transformations across globalized, technologically mediated capitalist societies.[8] These transformations are diverse in kind. Biomedical techniques such as human cloning, assisted reproduction, and high-tech prostheses have outsourced basic human capacities to science, while raising the specter of cyborg futures. Processes of species extinction and the appropriation of biogenetic material for human use have brought into question our relationship with the animal world, resulting in "a radical disruption of . . . human—animal interaction."[9] Furthermore, the official recognition of the Anthropocene as an epoch defined by human impact on Earth's ecosystems has underscored our imbrication with a natural world that was traditionally seen as the backdrop to or object of human activity—even as the ecosystem is pressed into further service as a planetary apparatus of production. These developments have shattered our faith in human singularity and exceptionalism, revealing the "hybrids of nature and society" that underpin human cultures despite what Bruno Latour has described as ongoing discursive efforts to divide the human and nonhuman into "two entirely distinct ontological zones."[10]

4   SCREENING THE POSTHUMAN

Yet a truly critical posthumanism, as we have already suggested, cannot simply be understood as a discourse about why shifting technological, social, and ecological coordinates mean we are human *no longer*, as implied in the title of Hayles's *How We Became Posthuman*. Rather, it must be understood as a function of the claim that, to paraphrase Latour, we have never been human. Whatever our aspirations to species exceptionalism, "we" have co-evolved with the technicity of tools, share biological substance with nonhuman animals, and have always been radically dependent on the extraction of Earth's natural resources. Classical humanist visions of the human rely upon repressing these technological, biological, ecological, and animal debts. Moreover, despite attempts to consolidate human difference into a singular, monolithic model of the human, "difference is already constitutive of the human species, with all of its gendered, ethnic, social, and individual varieties."[11] We have never been "human" in this strict sense, then; but nor have we ever all been "*considered* fully human."[12] Indeed, histories of exclusion and subordination, in which racialized, sexualized, and classed "others" are routinely dehumanized, underscore the contingency and normativity of our notions of the human. This problem cannot be resolved by simply widening the remit of the human as a category. As Wolfe observes, while humanism has some admirable aspirations, notably its avowed commitment to overcoming discrimination, "many of the philosophical and theoretical frameworks used to make good on these commitments reproduce the very normative models of individual subjectivity, bodily morphology and personal comportment that ground discrimination in the first place."[13] As Francesca Ferrando further reflects, "the emphasis on the human as a rational animal has been a powerful tool to historically enslave, mistreat, and dominate some humans and most nonhuman animals."[14] To put it in other words, humanism's appeal to the notion of a "core humanity" is by definition excluding and exclusive. Critical posthumanism, then, is as much a riposte to humanism as a hegemonic cultural model as it is a gesture toward contemporary or future states of "posthuman" evolution.

It is this dual focus on emerging relationalities and deconstructing historic humanism that underwrites critical posthumanism's convergence with approaches in postcolonial theory, disability studies, animal studies, critical race theory, and queer theory. Like these novel bodies of work, critical posthumanism is committed to exploring contemporary social, environmental, and technological phenomena as "relational" and "situated" rather than as the basis for claims about human universals, while acknowledging the researcher's own relational and situated status.[15] For this reason, these kindred theoretical inquiries will feature heavily and shape our methodology in this book.

Critical posthumanism's attention to the inherent contradictions of the humanist legacy also distinguishes it from other movements and frameworks with which it is all too often mistaken, such as the discourse of "transhumanism." As promoted by figures like robotics scientist Hans Moravec and philosopher Nick Bostrom, transhumanism is based on the belief that the human race can and should work to surpass its existing biological limitations through recourse to medical and computing technologies like regenerative medicine and the integration of digital components into the body. The goal is an evolution understood, to quote Joel Garreau, as "the enhancement of human intellectual, physical and emotional capabilities, the elimination of disease and unnecessary suffering, and the dramatic extension of life span."[16] Yet while often collapsed into or identified with posthumanism, transhumanism is best understood as "an intensification of humanism," as Wolfe explains.[17] If our understanding of the human pivots on the fantasy of a figure defined by "escaping or repressing . . . the bonds of materiality and embodiment," transhumanism only extends this fantasy.[18] Its sleek visions of prosthetically enhanced bodies and neurologically augmented minds, that is, are the culmination of a humanist orthodoxy that treats the enhancement of human sensory, emotional, and cognitive capabilities as part of a vision of teleologically pre-ordained human evolution. In this sense, as Hayles observes, critics like Moravec are "not abandoning the autonomous liberal subject but . . . expanding its prerogatives into the realm of the posthuman;"[19] in Badmington's words, "the seemingly posthumanist desire to download consciousness into a gleaming digital environment is itself downloaded from the distinctly humanist matrix of Cartesian dualism."[20] This ecstatic, utopian account of the posthuman is no more valuable—and just as far from a properly "critical" form of posthumanism—than the humanist nostalgia exemplified by conservative critics like Francis Fukuyama. Instead, as Stefan Herbrechter shows, an approach capable of "think[ing] 'the end of the human' without giving in either to apocalyptic mysticism or to new forms of spirituality and transcendence" is à propos the extraordinary conditions of life and culture in the twenty-first century.[21]

Another of posthumanism's cultural doppelgängers is the array of different approaches and ontologies that Richard Grusin's 2015 book, *The Nonhuman Turn*, clusters under the rubric of the "nonhuman." These approaches range

6 SCREENING THE POSTHUMAN

from the Actor-Network Theory (ANT) of social scientist Bruno Latour, whose work distributes agency freely across networks of human and non-human actants;[22] the "Object-Oriented Ontology" of scholars like Ian Bogost and Graham Harman, who insist on the independent reality and ultimate unknowability of objects;[23] to the varied "new materialisms" of scholars like Karen Barad, Jane Bennett, and Stacey Alaimo, with their focus on the agency of things other than human beings (from food, to architecture, to natural environments).[24] In our view, the bodies of work associated with what Grusin dubs the "nonhuman turn" align with critical posthumanist approaches in their conviction that the human has co-developed with—and indeed consists of—nonhuman forms, forces, and materials. In this respect, Grusin himself provides what we believe is a specious theoretical distinction between the posthuman and the nonhuman, contending that, even as it routinely "invokes the imbrication of human and nonhuman," the very concept of the posthuman "entails [or assumes] a historical development from human to something after the human."[25] In contrast, we view the teleological vision Grusin describes above as characteristic of transhumanist rather than critical posthumanist frameworks; both nonhuman *and* critical posthumanist approaches pivot on a recognition of "the imbrication of human and nonhuman," and the true distinction between the two approaches lies in their response to this recognition. Nonhuman approaches take it as a basis for turning away from the human "in favor of a concern for the nonhuman . . . animals, affectivity, bodies, materiality, technologies, and organic and geophysical systems."[26] Conversely, critical posthuman theory, of the kind we put into practice here, takes this same recognition as the basis for exploring "yet-unrealized possibilities" for reimagining human being, human life and human relationality in broad organic, climatic, technological, geological, and social contexts.[27]

So much for distinguishing our theoretical framework from related ones. But what of our methods? In this book, we read film and theory in conjunction, filtering the film texts through the lens of key works in critical posthuman theory. Yet to do so is not to treat the former as a mere "illustration" of the latter. Rather, we see contemporary posthuman cinema and critical posthuman theory as coeval responses to the same set of technological, ecological, and social phenomena. Across both film and theory, we suggest, changes in our technological, ecological, and social environment have led to a radical reassessment of the long taken-for-granted category of the human, although this reassessment plays out in strikingly different ways across the two fora. Whereas critical theory strives for epistemic closure, narrative cinema is inherently multivalent; whereas theory trades in abstractions, narrative cinema traffics in the concrete. As Braidotti and Cecilia Åsberg argue,

> Clearly, from the overlapping domains of science and popular imagination we have already moved way beyond the limitations of the humanist imaginations, for better and for worse. Despite the somewhat bipolar reports—either utopian or dystopian, technophobic or technophilic—we dream, live and enliven already the posthuman condition. Now we need more than ever the story telling practices accountable for its politics.[28]

This book spotlights the "story telling practices" of posthuman cinema. Reveling in the lived reality of the human/nonhuman category breakdowns documented in the critical literature, cinema transforms structural states into unique and compelling scenarios that illuminate posthuman politics. Is it possible to fall in love with an operating system?, asks *Her* (Spike Jonze, 2013). What if your seizures triggered massive environmental events, such as earthquakes?, asks *Fast Color* (Julia Hart, 2018). What if a famous actor like Robin Wright could sell her digital likeness wholesale, her virtual avatar continuing her career independently?, asks *The Congress* (Ari Folman, 2013, Figure I.2).

Figure I.2 In Ari Folman's *The Congress* (2013), Robin Wright's final contract is the sale of her identity for unlimited digital use.

8   SCREENING THE POSTHUMAN

Certain phenomena recur across these films: cyborgs, climate change, monstrously hybridized animals, and assisted reproductive technologies, to name a few. Yet an individual film's "posthumanist" status cannot be determined solely according to the specific scenarios with which it grapples. After all, cinema has been dealing in technologically and environmentally extraordinary phenomena for decades, veering between casting such phenomena as threats to human life or as miraculous helpmates. As stated by Dijana Jelača, "In cinema, nonhuman, inhuman, and posthuman figures have been fixtures since the medium's early days, whether in F. W. Murnau's *Nosferatu*, Fritz Lang's *Metropolis*, or in the teratological imagination of the early cinema of attractions."[29] For a film to qualify as properly posthumanist, however, it must challenge core conceptions of the human. As Jelača argues, it must demonstrate that

> the posthuman does not merely emerge after the human. Rather it is a circuit that both contains and perpetually indicates the inadequacy of the human to account for the proliferating extensions of technology in organic matter and of alien forms in the ever-more hybrid clusters of posthuman identity formations.[30]

In our view, this challenge to humanism's fundamental principles—combined with the affective ambivalence that supports it—is much less common in cinema than it might initially seem.

Many films that purport to deal with new environmental, social, and technological developments fall back all too readily into either a pessimism that hints at a humanist nostalgia or a euphoric excitement that tends toward transhumanism. Driven by the need for the kind of ethical and epistemological closure that the ambiguity of the posthuman position simply cannot accommodate, such films offer a posthuman premise but conclude with a humanist or transhumanist reaction. Many twenty-first-century disaster films, for example, threaten humankind only to bolster notions of universal common humanity, illustrating what Badmington identifies as humanism's "capacity for regeneration and, quite literally, recapitulation."[31] For instance, the premise that humanity has become sterile and faces extinction motivates the plot of *Children of Men* (Alfonso Cuarón, 2006), yet its drama thrives on the hope that humanity can persist despite the dire circumstances of human life depicted in the film. Similarly, many films that engage with questions about the future of humanity in the face of climate change, new computing technologies, or human cloning take a purely negative position on these changes, suggesting a nostalgia for a supposedly lost or beleaguered humanity. *Lars and the Real Girl* (Craig Gillespie, 2007) demonstrates this tendency when the romance between Lars and his RealDoll[32] Bianca ends on the latter's death and her replacement with "real girl" (i.e., an "organic" human woman) Margo in the final scene. Alternatively, *Kūki Ningyō/Air Doll* (Hirokazu Kore-eda, 2009) aligns with critical posthumanism in its representation of protagonist Nozomi, an inflatable sex doll who develops consciousness and falls in love with a young video store clerk.

Importantly, as this should already suggest, our archive extends well beyond the usual suspects—the handful of anglophone Sci-Fi films like *Her* and *Ex Machina* that have dominated the dialogue about posthumanism and the cinema thus far in the twenty-first century. The dominance of these films both reflects and perpetuates some of the limitations of popular perceptions of the posthuman. The first is the misconception of the posthuman exclusively as a function of technological innovation—a model of the posthuman that veers suspiciously close to transhumanist accounts. The other is a radical Anglo-centrism that overlooks the relevance of posthumanism for thinking through cinematic developments in non-Western contexts. This book pushes beyond both these limitations. While we do expand on analyses of popular examples of posthumanism cinema, we also seek out not-so-obvious or less-circulated films—such as the Indigenous futurist VR film *Biidaaban: First Light* (Lisa Jackson, 2018); Chinese environmental drama 三峡好人/*Still Life* (Jia Zhangke, 2006); and cult, queer pornography, *L.A. Zombie* (Bruce LaBruce, 2010)—thereby forging links and contrasts between main and alternative streams.

Cultural, Materialist, and Deconstructive Posthumanisms

As will already be clear, this book's analysis of posthuman tendencies in recent cinema is shaped in large part by developments in critical posthuman theory. But what are the driving concerns of this body of work? As a term, "posthumanism" has only relatively recently gained currency in scholarly debates. Yet, as Herbrechter reminds us, current critiques of the human are only the latest manifestation of a crisis that has long beset humanism as a normative framework and as a philosophical stance.[33] Indeed, as Braidotti notes, the fact that "humanity [is] in a critical condition—some may even

10   SCREENING THE POSTHUMAN

say approaching extinction—has been a leitmotif in European philosophy ever since Friedrich Nietzsche proclaimed the "death of God" and the idea of Man that was built upon it."[34] Badmington points out that Nietzsche's contemporary, Karl Marx, also contributed to the theoretical foundations that presuppose posthumanism.[35] Rejecting notions of a human essence that exists outside of history and politics, Marx gave "eternal man" a history, drawing attention to "his" cultural, material, and historical contingency.[36] Several years later, Freud would further problematize the Cartesian subject, projecting, in place of a figure guided and defined by rational, self-conscious thought, a blundering being compelled by forces not only beyond their control, but also beyond their conscious awareness.[37] This anti-humanist position would also form an implicit component of poststructuralist critiques of the human across the 1960s and 1970s. Led by figures like Michel Foucault, who maintained that "man is a recent invention,"[38] the radical thinkers who emerged after 1968 and who would soon become known as poststructuralists sought to "de-link the human agent from this universalistic posture."[39] Among poststructuralism's central contentions was the claim that "Man, far from being the canon of perfect proportions, spelling out a universalistic ideal that by now had reached the status of a natural law, was in fact a historical construct and as such contingent as to values and locations."[40] Across this body of work, then, the unitary subject of humanism was displaced in favor of what Braidotti calls a "more complex and relational subject framed by embodiment, sexuality, affectivity, empathy and desire as core qualities."[41]

Yet while anti-humanist traditions provide important intellectual antecedents for "critical posthumanism," it is only in the last twenty-five or so years that scholarly energy has begun to coalesce around the term itself. In this respect, the pioneering work of critics like Haraway, Braidotti, Hayles, and Wolfe led the charge, publishing a flurry of special issues, edited volumes, and conference proceedings under the "critical posthumanist" banner in the 1990s and early 2000s. As Herbrechter notes, critical posthumanism departs from anti-humanist critique in its radical insistence on not only historicizing and critiquing humanist visions of "man," but on developing a "new posthumanist understanding of human and nonhuman subjectivity as an integrated form of agency within diverse networks of information environments and nonhuman actors."[42] However, despite this unity of purpose, the fabric of critical posthumanism is rich and complex, with multiple strands of thinking that represent distinct paths of development. This book is simultaneously influenced by the "cultural," "deconstructive," and "materialist" strands of critical posthumanism.

The first, "cultural" strand of critical posthumanism tends to focus on specific developments that manifest or exemplify the phenomenon of the posthuman in what Jack Halberstam and Ira Livingston call "an age of continuous and obligatory diasporas."[43] Works by Haraway, Halberstam and Livingston, Badmington, and Elaine L. Graham exemplify this strand of critical posthumanism. As suggested by the titles of some of the contributions—Badmington's *Alien Chic: Posthumanism and the Other Within* and Graham's *Representations of the Post/Human: Monsters, Aliens and Others in Popular Culture* among them—this scholarship mines the fringes of global popular culture for figures and phenomena that emblematize what Wolfe calls "a science fictional thematics of hybridity, perversity and irony."[44] Delivering up a virtual menagerie of posthuman forms and characters in the late twentieth and early twenty-first centuries, this critical corpus supports Herbrechter's contention that the "posthuman condition is not a liquidation of the subject but rather a proliferation of subjects," marking "the expansion of subjectivity to include nonhuman actors."[45]

Perhaps the most significant contribution to the "cultural" strand of work on critical posthumanism is Haraway's "A Cyborg Manifesto: Science, Technology and Socialist-Feminism in the Late Twentieth Century."[46] Haraway's titular cyborg is a creature "simultaneously animal and machine" that "populate[s] worlds ambiguously natural and crafted"—a creature that, despite its otherness, is all of us: "by the late twentieth century, our time . . . we are all chimeras, theorized and fabricated hybrids of machine and organism."[47] The cyborg's hybrid status embodies the three crucial category breakdowns that define life in advanced capitalism.[48] The first is between human and animal: at a moment when neither "language, tool use, social behavior [nor] mental events . . . convincingly settle the separation of human and animal," this boundary has been "thoroughly breached" and the relationship between the two terms is best understood in terms of "connection" rather than difference.[49] The second breached boundary is between animal/human and machine; while pre-cybernetic machines were not "self-moving, self-designing, autonomous," "late twentieth century machines have made thoroughly ambiguous the difference between natural and artificial, mind and body, self-developing and externally designed."[50] The third "leaky distinction" is a subset of the second: the "boundary between physical and non-physical," Haraway contends, has become "very imprecise" as a result of the dematerialization of things.[51] For Haraway, the cyborg is a myth that has the potential to wield real political power in the context of socialist/feminist struggle, its modeling of "transgressed boundaries, potent fusions and dangerous possibilities" providing a powerful counter to the nostalgic recourse to the organic body that has often characterized progressive thought.[52] Certainly, it is worth noting that Haraway has since distanced herself from the term "posthuman." Regardless, she remains an important influence on critical posthumanism, and her rejection of "posthumanism" is primarily due to other theorists' (mis-)use of the term to promote utopian views that would more correctly fall into the realm of transhumanism.[53] Moreover, the evolution of Haraway's philosophy since the release of "A Cyborg Manifesto" productively aligns with shifts in critical posthumanism toward emphases on, for example, the relationship between humans and animals (*Companion Species Manifesto: Dogs, People, and Significant Otherness*),[54] and between humans and the environment (*Staying with the Trouble: Making Kin in the Chthulucene*).[55]

The deconstructive strand of critical posthumanism, meanwhile, is primarily discursive in its orientation, circling relentlessly around the question and concept of the posthuman. Exemplified by Wolfe's work, deconstructive critical posthumanism focuses less on contemporary incarnations and visualizations of the posthumanist subject, and more on the deconstruction of humanism "as an intellectual tradition, a normative frame and an institutionalized practice," as well as the difficulties of such deconstruction.[56] On the one hand, it seeks to expose the contingency and fragility of the human as a category, exploring questions raised about the human by recent "posthumanizing, cyborgizing and virtualizing technologies,"[57] from organ transplant to genetic engineering, and warns that the "philosophical and theoretical frameworks used by humanism to try to make good on [its] commitments [i.e., to non-discrimination] reproduce the very kind of normative subjectivity . . . that grounds discrimination . . . in the first place."[58] On the other hand, scholars working in this area underscore the persistence of the category of the human—insisting, with Christopher Peterson, that any "assertion that Humanism can be decisively left behind ironically subscribes to a basic humanist assumption with regard to volition and agency . . . as if we bear the capacity to erase the traces of Humanism from either the present or an imagined future."[59] The acknowledgment of the persistence of humanism goes hand in hand with an acknowledgment of the violence that has long been perpetrated in the name of humanism against the nonhuman or

INTRODUCTION 13

dehumanized "others" of the humanist norm. Thus, while the deconstructive approach to critical posthumanism shares a linguistic and discursive frame of reference with the cultural approach, it is marked, as Braidotti notes, by an affectivity of "irreparable loss, unpayable debt and perpetual mourning."[60]

Standing in stark contrast to both cultural and deconstructive subsets of critical posthumanist scholarship is the materialist approach, demonstrated by the likes of Braidotti and Stacey Alaimo. This body of scholarship shows renewed attention to "the agency and significance of matter" associated with the so-called new materialism, a critical corpus that encompasses the feminist materialism of Karen Barad and the vital materialism of Jane Bennet, while also drawing from older materialist currents like those running through the work of Gilles Deleuze and Félix Guattari. Whereas both the cultural and deconstructive strands of critical posthumanist thought tend to emphasize the primacy of signification in the process of subject formation, the materialist approach to posthumanism rejects any attempt to polarize the material (e.g., "biology," "nature" or "the given") and the cultural (e.g., the "signifier," the "social," or the "linguistic"). For both Braidotti and Alaimo, this dualistic perspective is a function of lingering humanist fantasies of a spiritual or vital essence that preexists, shapes, and exceeds material existence. In its place, these critics present a non-dualistic or "monist" understanding of the world that casts materiality as self-animating and self-organizing.[61] Braidotti—"rejecting all forms of transcendentalism" and embracing what she calls "radical immanence"—has generated a model of the posthuman that is informed by an understanding of "the vital, self-organizing and yet non-naturalistic structure of living matter itself."[62] The value of this model of self-animating matter for critiquing humanism is that it undercuts fantasies of a human essence that transcends the contingencies and vulnerabilities of the individual body, while also theorizing new alliances between the human and the nonhuman. For Braidotti and Alaimo, that is, the common material foundation of entities in the world provides the basis for what Alaimo calls "trans-corporeal" connections between humans and its various "others," and for connections across a series of "fraught, tangled materialities."[63]

While this book most obviously aligns with cultural critical posthumanism, our analysis is also strongly influenced by deconstructive and materialist theory. In reading cinematic fictions of posthuman scenarios and figures, we observe and analyze shared visions of the impact of technology on contemporary and future cultural life. Taking heed of deconstructive criticism, this book also considers the humanist logics at play in narrative cinema

14 SCREENING THE POSTHUMAN

and is attuned to the persistence of humanism behind posthuman facades. Likewise, we strive to engage with materialist perspectives, grounding our analysis on issues of embodiment and giving weight to nonhuman animal and ecological perspectives.

We do not aspire to reconcile the different foci of these three threads but hope that weaving them throughout this book highlights their productive tensions. As detailed below, each chapter of this book follows a unique path that illuminates the films and critical theory relevant to a distinct subgenre of posthuman cinema. By doing so, we aim to do justice to the diversity of representations and scholarship critiquing and imagining beyond humanism while also revealing coherences in posthuman thought and imagination.

Expanding Posthuman Cinema Studies

Screening the Posthuman represents a considerable step forward in the academic conversation about links between contemporary cinema and critical posthumanism. At present, the intersection of film studies and posthuman theory has generated compelling scholarship, although mainly work that is narrowly focused on a film or closely related films and a target issue. For instance, Alla Ivanchikova's "Machinic Intimacies and Mechanical Brides: Collectivity between Prosthesis and Surrogacy in Jonathan Mostow's *Surrogates* and Spike Jonze's *Her*"[64] illustrates this tendency for film scholars to analyze kindred films in conjunction with posthuman theories associated with very particular posthuman scenarios. Articles like Ivanchikova's inspired us to write this book as they clearly demonstrate the critical value of considering developments in contemporary cinema in tandem with theories of the posthuman. At the same time, they signaled the need for a comprehensive work on posthuman screen studies. Building on existing scholarship in cinema and posthuman studies, this book-length account of the cinematic representation of the posthuman in a twenty-first-century global context is unique in the field.

The Palgrave Handbook of Posthumanism in Film and Television purports to cover similar terrain. Like the present volume, it is, by all accounts, a book-length effort to trace the posthuman "paradigm shift" through "film and television."[65] Yet its status as an edited collection and its much broader historical remit (with case studies from the early twentieth century and into the millennium) immediately distinguish it from this book. Moreover, despite superficial theoretical similarities, *The Palgrave Handbook* diverges from this book on a theoretical level in its persistent confounding of posthumanism with transhumanism. The volume's introduction, for example, explicitly represents posthumanism as "the surpassing of the human condition" and as an "expansion of consciousness," even as it underscores the humanist roots of transhumanism by contending that this labor of human self-improvement is "rooted in a particular kind of humanism."[66] In fact, the introduction is written by one of the volume's editors, Michael Hauskeller, who mistitles the name of his own monograph, *Mythologies of Transhumanism*, "*Mythologies of Posthumanism*" in his Academia.edu profile[67]—an error we consider telling. The startling conflation of posthumanism and transhumanism is reflected in the book's textual archive, which strongly favors hi-tech Sci-Fi as a privileged generic site through which to explore transhumanist themes. That said, we engage with a number of provocative works included in the *Handbook*, which is impressively diverse in the screen media and posthuman perspectives it features, but we do not consider it comparable to *Screening the Posthuman* in either scope or approach.

In terms of scholarship that does approach the cinema/posthuman interface with critical posthumanism's anti-humanist stance, there is a great deal of existing work that focuses on "posthuman cinema" from a formal perspective.[68] However, this work addresses not the posthuman on screen (i.e., narrative and aesthetic representations) but the posthuman dimensions of screen technologies. From a more conventional screen studies perspective, a number of extant articles explore the cinematic representation of the posthuman in the context of specific recent film releases; essays by scholars including Jelača, Donna Kornhaber, Brian R. Jacobson, and Jennifer Henke are exemplary here.[69] However, none of these provides the systematic, comprehensive overview of screen representations of the posthuman that this book offers. Furthermore, these pieces tend to zero in on a cluster of Anglophone films from the mid-2010s (especially *Her* and *Ex Machina*, as mentioned before), which suggests a relatively limited scope of film studies' handle of the posthuman in contemporary cinema. Other recent scholarship, such as Elizabeth Ezra's monograph *The Cinema of Things: Globalization and the Posthuman Object* and Anat Pick and Guinevere Narraway's edited volume *Screening Nature: Cinema Beyond the Human*, have explored adjacent theoretical territory at book-length.[70] Yet despite apparent theoretical and terminological overlaps, these books' preoccupations diverge significantly from those of the present volume. *Screening Nature* is a case in point

16 SCREENING THE POSTHUMAN

in this respect. Whereas *Screening the Posthuman* explores both problems with and alternatives to conventional humanist accounts, *Screening Nature*, like much criticism appearing under the rubric of the "nonhuman" or "inhuman," sidelines the question of the human in favor of other concerns (the book driven primarily by engagements with environmentalism and animal studies). Likewise, though Ezra's *Cinema of Things* prefaces posthuman analysis in its subtitle, the book focuses primarily on cultures of consumption and does not engage in any significant way with the questions about the human that its analysis of these cultures raises. Indeed, where it does engage with these questions, the book reveals a residual humanism. Ezra's contention that under global consumer capitalism material things "take on a life of their own, engulfing and ultimately replacing the people they were meant to supplement," for example, implies that there exists an authentic and essential set of "relations between people" that relations with (and between) nonhuman objects displaces.[71] Again, while we engage with these works, our theoretical investments diverge from them in significant ways, and *Screening the Posthuman*'s exceptional aims distinguish it from existing work that explores connections between twenty-first-century cinema and critical posthumanism.

Tracking the Posthuman On-Screen

The first chapter lays the groundwork for our argument by proposing the posthuman as a flexible and mobile genre of contemporary cinema that cuts across and intersects with more established generic categories. The cinematic examples we feature in support of our case challenge standard film classification on multiple grounds. Thus, the sense that conventional cinematic genres cannot adequately account for posthuman representations—which appear in horror, fantasy, the Western, indie romance, and neo-neorealism, to name only a few—motivates our approach to the posthuman on-screen. Whereas later chapters zero in on specific themes, this chapter identifies ingredients common to films within the genre by examining three crucial zones of amalgamation in which the human and nonhuman bleed into each other: relationships, the body, and affect. The first section features films that propose new ways of understanding the self and relating with others in a more-than-human-world (e.g., *De rouille et d'os*/*Rust and Bone* [Jacques Audiard, 2012]); the second section examines films that explore technologies that push the bodily boundaries of the human in the context of efforts to overcome physical limitation (e.g., *Limitless* [Neil Burger, 2011] and *Private Life* [Tamara Jenkins, 2018]); and the third section details the affective oscillation between threat and hope in cinematic representation of our entwined present and future with technology. In sum, this chapter contends that the destabilization of humanism with which cinema is currently grappling creates a shared narrative, affective and aesthetic field that eclipses differences that might otherwise place posthuman films in separate conversations.

Cinematic visions of possible futures that are relevant to critical posthumanism tend to waver between pessimistic speculations regarding technoculture's cultivation of what Haraway refers to as a "grid of control" culminating in a "masculinist orgy of war," and comparatively optimistic representations of a posthuman experience characterized by "kinship with animals and machines" and "permanently partial identities and contradictory standpoints."[72] With this opposing tendency in mind, Chapter 2 spotlights films featuring apocalyptic or post-apocalyptic scenarios to delineate posthuman takes on cataclysmic change to life on Earth. The pervasiveness of apocalyptic representations at the time of writing (during the COVID-19 global pandemic) highlights the timeliness of this category of cinema, as well as contemporary filmmakers' tendencies to merely tease human extinction (or radical revision) to generate suspense, eventually validating core humanistic values and beliefs through "apocalyptic" storytelling (e.g., Christopher Nolan's *Tenet*, 2020). That said, a diverse sample of recent films—including the aforementioned *Bacurau* and *Biidaaban: First Light*, Lynette Wallworth's *Collisions* (2016), Julia Hart's *Fast Color* (2018), and Jeff Nichols's *Take Shelter* (2011)—depict catastrophes to expose alternative forms of human and nonhuman earthly experience. Drawing on the scholarship of Susan Sontag, Evan Calder Williams, Badmington, and Sarah Keller (among others), the second chapter proposes three characteristics that distinguish posthuman disaster cinema from what Keller describes as the "glut of films from the postmillennial period adopt[ing] the apocalypse as topic and theme:"[73] one, the depiction of catastrophe as rooted in historical traumas and as already well underway (rather than imminent); two, the emphasis on postcolonial and/or racist connotations to the states of emergency represented or alluded to in apocalyptic plots; and three, the treatment of disaster as compatible (rather than in conflict) with twenty-first-century human life under late capitalism.

18   SCREENING THE POSTHUMAN

Chapter 3 traces feminist and materialist developments in posthuman theory—from Haraway's groundbreaking cyborg figure through the influential works of scholars including Hayles, Braidotti, Alaimo, and Barad—to analyze innovative cinematic depictions of women cyborgs. In foregrounding feminist posthumanisms, the third chapter evokes ongoing debates about gender and the posthuman condition, raising Francesca Ferrando's question, "Is the post-human a post-woman?," in the context of recent cinematic depictions of women as hybrid beings who undermine efforts to distinguish between organism and machine.[74] This chapter does not aim to answer Ferrando's question, but to build on her provocation to clarify the stakes of casting woman characters to model posthuman being, despite Haraway's claim in *A Cyborg Manifesto* that "the cyborg is a creature in a postgender world."[75] Taking its cue from Barad, who argues that the posthuman requires us to account for "entangled materializations of which we are a part, including new configurations, new subjectivities, new possibilities,"[76] this third chapter explores a number of topical issues crucial to posthuman speculation in cinematic fiction, including technosexuality, online/offline hybrid subjectivity, and the unseating of the "organic" human body as the basic hardware of identity. It does so, first, by closely reading pivotal moments of organic and mechanical disintegration in *Air Doll*, *Ex Machina* and *Under the Skin* (Jonathan Glazer, 2013) to stress the monstrous seduction and racist overtones that continue to inflect characterizations of "artificial" women that conform to the cinematic conventions of the femme fatale. Less spectacular, but more in line with feminist posthumanism, is the depiction of technosexuality in *Celle que vous croyez/Who You Think I Am* (Safy Nebbou, 2019), which conveys mechanical and mediated forms of intimacy in posthuman experience in the registers of realism and art cinema. In a similar vein, Alice Wincoeur's *Proxima* (2019) scrutinizes the process of a woman astronaut integrating with technology in preparation for extraterrestrial experience (Figure I.3). While far from the "monstrous" mothers Barbara Creed theorized in classic Sci-Fi and horror films,[77] these cyborg mothers (and their cinematic vitality) indicate residual tensions in imagining the maternal posthuman.

Chapter 4 turns to the critical alignment between queer theory and posthumanism, exploring how they both work toward challenging structures of power and knowledge that have defined the human as "at base level zero a white heterosexual man." Drawing on theorists such as Patricia MacCormack and Rosi Braidotti, the chapter sets out key conceptual figures of queer posthumanism that cut across theory and cinema, including

Figure I.3 Sarah and her daughter Stella navigate cyborg relating in Alice Wincoeur's *Proxima* (2019).

the cyborg, the monster, and the collective. *Being John Malkovich* (Spike Jonze, 1999) is addressed as a prototypical example of the cyborg's queer potential and compared with Jonze's later film *Her* (2013) and Brandon Cronenberg's more recent film *Possessor* (2020) in order to trace the analog to digital queering of heteronormative humanist selfhood across time, genre, and auteur preoccupations. Shifting from relatively mainstream cinema, the chapter then turns to the figures of the monster and collective within revolutionary films by independent queer auteurs. *Born in Flames* (Lizzie Borden, 1983) is briefly addressed as a prototype of queer posthumanist vision in independent cinema for its genre hybridity, political fury, utopianism, and centering of collectivity. In their "postporn" zombie and science fiction films, Bruce LaBruce and Shu Lea Cheang take up the mantle of Borden's revolutionary spirit, queering posthumanism and "posthumanizing" queer cinema. LaBruce's zombie films, *Otto; or, Up with Dead People* (2008) and *L.A. Zombie* (2010), and the third film of Shu Lea Cheang's postporn trilogy *Fluidø* (2017) are analyzed for the ways they use monstrosity, collectivity, and genre hybridity to achieve radical utopian queer posthuman ends. The chapter's diverse examples demonstrate how film theorizes the intersection of the queer and posthuman as they transcend boundaries, upset dichotomies,

20   SCREENING THE POSTHUMAN

and challenge the cisgender heterosexual male as the foundational figure of humanism.

According to Dan Goodley, Rebecca Lawthom, and Katherine Runswick-Cole, "critical disability studies are perfectly at ease with the posthuman because disability has always contravened the traditional classical humanist conception of what it means to be human."[78] Yet as Goodley, Lawthom, and Cole further note, "disability also invites a critical analysis of the posthuman," with ongoing stigma and discrimination underscoring the specificity of disabled experience and the persistence of the human norm in supposedly "posthuman" times.[79] Chapter 5 navigates the uneasy intersection of disability and posthumanism through a pair of acclaimed auteur films, Pedro Almodóvar's *Hable con ella/Talk to Her* (2002) and *Sound of Metal* (Darius Marder, 2019). As it will show, these films reflect the productive potential of the alliance between critical disability studies and critical posthumanism in their commitment to using disability as a basis for interrogating rather than sustaining humanist ideals. However, as this chapter will also show, neither film is straightforward in its affordances to this convergence of posthumanism and disability. While *Talk to Her* uses a pair of comatose women to unsettle practices of expressivity and expressive reading that have become cornerstones of humanism, it also deploys able-bodied actors to play the "brain-dead" women at its heart, while yoking its uplifting conclusion to one of the women's miraculous recovery. And *The Sound of Metal* is still more ambivalent in its relation to posthumanist and post-ableist ideals. While the film's widely celebrated sound design honors the capacity of "disability" to open up more-than-human worlds, especially through its prosthetic or cinematic supplements, the film's narrative reflects a humanist distrust of technology.

Following Cary Wolfe's centering of "the animal" as a key terrain where questions of posthumanism play out,[80] Chapter 6 explores how posthuman cinema dismantles anthropocentric understandings of "the human" and human-animal relationality. The chapter begins by interpreting contemporary surrealist films, *The Lobster* (Yorgos Lanthimos, 2015), *Border*, and *On Body and Soul*, as subversive cogs in what Giorgio Agamben terms the "anthropological machine,"[81] an optical apparatus that bolsters a "sense of [human] exceptionalism and superiority."[82] Surrealist post-anthropocentric films mirror back to humanity not its uniqueness or distinction from other animals, but a recognition of kinship, spiritual coexistence, and interdependence. After exploring how these examples of European cinema playfully undermine human exceptionalism, the chapter then turns to examine how two Thai films—*Kraben Rahu*/*Manta Ray* (Phuttiphong Aroonpheng, 2019) and *Satpralat*/*Tropical Malady* (Apichatpong Weerasethakul, 2004)—further highlight the post-anthropocentric ends of contemporary posthuman cinema. Read through a framework of "new animism"—which offers another lens to challenge both anthropocentric worldviews and the idea of cinema as inherently realist—the second part of Chapter 6 demonstrates how the conceptual, narrative, and formal aspects of these Thai films challenge speciesism and explore the interconnectedness of *Homo sapiens*, their nonhuman kin, and their cohabited environments. Whether operating in surrealist or new animist modes, these global post-anthropocentric films work toward the shared aims of critical posthumanism and critical animal studies: breaking down binary oppositions; resisting the tendency to reduce animals to the status of metaphors and mirrors to the human; and offering a sensory exploration of the blurred borders between human and nonhuman animals.

Our final chapter returns to contexts of ecological crisis introduced in Chapter 1. As it will show, the official recognition of the "Anthropocene," understood as an epoch of environmental crisis that both elevates the human to the status of geological agent and strips the human of its foundational claims to mastery over the natural world, has had significant consequences for theories of posthumanism.[83] More specifically, it has given rise to what might be dubbed the "eco-material posthumanism"—a specific iteration of posthumanism that actively rejects even the residue of fantasies of bodily transcendence, species transcendence, or technological deliverance in favor of a renewed recognition of our embedded, embodied status as beings-in-the-(material)-world.[84] Chapter 7 argues that the critical tendencies that we might cluster under the rubric of the "eco-material posthuman" echo across a distinct body of feature films examining the fallout of the Anthropocene. The films in question are geographically and culturally diverse, ranging from Chinese drama 三峡好人/*Still Life* (Figure I.4), to Icelandic-Ukrainian offbeat comedy *Kona fer í stríð*/*Woman at War* (Benedikt Erlingsson, 2018) and American horror *Mother!* (Darren Aronofsky, 2017). All, however, fully attend to the questions the Anthropocene raises about the interdependence of humans and nonhuman worlds through their eco-materialist recourse to the human bodies (perhaps most notably, by facilitating novel cross-species alliances and identifications). While the models of human bodily materiality at issue here are diverse, this chapter will zero in on three in particular. The

Figure I.4 The fallout of the Anthropocene on the people of the Yangtze River is brought to the fore in 三峡好人/*Still Life* (Jia Zhangke, 2006).

first is the body as cell, understood as the basic biological unit of life that is shared across species and life forms more generally. The second is the body as affect, as a bodily intensity that eludes the forms of subjectivity that underpin conventional models of the human. The third is the body as vital materiality, what Braidotti calls "the dynamic, self-organizing structure of life itself."[85] These models of the human body cast it not as a signifier or guarantor of human exceptionalism but as an aperture to the nonhuman outside. In leveraging these models, the films in question weave a powerful posthuman fabric out of the threadbare realities of climate change.

In the course of this book, we closely track resonances between developments in twenty-first-century cinema and developments in critical posthumanism (and kindred theories). In our view, the excitement of posthuman cinema derives from the fact that the changes of which critical posthumanism is a harbinger demand a total reconfiguration of the conventions of narrative cinema, which has traditionally relied on humanism both for the meanings it expresses and for the means by which it expresses them. As the chapters that follow will demonstrate, the convergence between twenty-first-century movies and developments in critical posthumanism is rarely complete. Indeed, in the majority of cinematic efforts to represent posthuman phenomena, impulses congenial to critical posthumanism are offset by equally powerful humanist or transhumanist tendencies. Yet, to our eyes, these awkward humanist or transhumanist stumbles are as rewarding to critical analysis as some of the more sure-footed leaps of posthumanist imagination. Certainly, critical posthumanism's challenge to humanist normativity is not seamlessly compatible with the challenges of related bodies of work, like feminism, queer theory and critical race studies, whose powerfully felt, richly specific critiques of humanism's racial, sexual, and cultural biases at once complicate and complement posthumanism's own more theoretical provocations. In this respect, our imagination of posthuman cinema remains open to developments in a range of scholarly fields, with critical posthumanism playing a dominant but by no means exclusive role. It is our hope that the critical project this book accomplishes reinforces the significance of critical posthumanism and adjacent fields to contemporary cinema, while remaining attentive to what is lost and gained by the sweeping changes to "human" experience that critical posthumanism theorizes.

Notes

1. Rosi Braidotti, *The Posthuman* (Cambridge, MA: Polity Press, 2013), 49.
2. Cary Wolfe, *What Is Posthumanism?* (Minneapolis: Minnesota University Press, 2010), xv.
3. Janet Maslin, "'Run Lola Run': A Dangerous Game with Several Endings," *New York Times*, March 26, 1999, https://archive.nytimes.com/www.nytimes.com/library/film/032699lola-film-review.html.
4. Braidotti, *The Posthuman*, 1.
5. Cary Wolfe, "Posthumanities," 2010, carywolfe.com (now expired), qtd. in Braidotti, *The Posthuman*, 1.
6. Wolfe, *What Is Posthumanism?*, xv.
7. Stefan Herbrechter, *Posthumanism: A Critical Analysis* (London: Bloomsbury, 2013), 7.
8. Braidotti, *The Posthuman*, 1.
9. Braidotti, *The Posthuman*, 7.
10. Bruno Latour, *We Have Never Been Modern* (Cambridge, MA: Harvard University Press, 2003), 33, 10.
11. Francesca Ferrando, *Philosophical Posthumanism* (London: Bloomsbury, 2019), 2.
12. Braidotti, *The Posthuman*, 6.
13. Wolfe, *What Is Posthumanism?*, xviii.
14. Ferrando, *Philosophical Posthumanism*, 33.
15. Rosi Braidotti, "Critical Posthuman Knowledges," *South Atlantic Quarterly* 116, no. 1 (2017): 83–96.
16. Joel Garreau, qtd. in Wolfe, *What Is Posthumanism?*, xiii.

24 SCREENING THE POSTHUMAN

17. Wolfe, *What Is Posthumanism?*, xv.
18. Wolfe, *What Is Posthumanism?*, xv.
19. N. Katherine Hayles, *How We Became Posthuman: Virtual Bodies in Cybernetics, Literature, and Informatics* (Chicago: University of Chicago Press, 1999), 287.
20. Neil Badmington, "Theorizing Posthumansim," *Cultural Critique* 53 (2003): 11. Ferrando makes a similar argument, stating: "the humanist understanding of the human is not undermined by Transhumanism but augmented; thus, Transhumaninsm can also be addressed as an 'ultra-humanism.'" Francesca Ferrando, "Posthumanism, Transhumanism, Antihumanism, Metahumanism, and New Materialisms Differences and Relations," *Existenz* 8, no. 2 (2013): 27.
21. Herbrechter, *Posthumanism*, 3.
22. Bruno Latour, *Reassembling the Social: An Introduction to Actor-Network-Theory* (Oxford: Oxford University Press, 2007).
23. Ian Bogost, *Alien Phenomenology, or, What It's Like to Be a Thing* (Minneapolis: University of Minnesota Press, 2012); Graham Harman, *Object-Oriented Ontology: A New Theory of Everything* (London: Penguin UK, 2018).
24. Stacy Alaimo, *Bodily Natures: Science, Environment, and the Material Self* (Bloomington: Indiana University Press, 2010); Jane Bennett, *Vibrant Matter: A Political Ecology of Things* (Durham, NC: Duke University Press, 2010); Karen Barad, *Meeting the Universe Halfway: Quantum Physics and the Entanglement of Matter and Meaning* (Durham, NC: Duke University Press, 2007).
25. Richard Grusin, "Introduction," *The Nonhuman Turn*, ed. Richard Grusin (Minneapolis: University of Minnesota Press, 2015), 4.
26. Grusin, "Introduction," 1.
27. Rosi Braidotti, "A Theoretical Framework for the Critical Posthumanities," *Theory, Culture and Society* 36, no. 6 (2019): 37.
28. Cecilia Åsberg and Rosi Braidotti, eds., *A Feminist Companion to the Posthumanities* (Cham: Springer, 2018), 5.
29. Dijana Jelača, "Alien Feminisms and Cinema's Posthuman Women," *Signs: Journal of Women in Culture and Society* 43, no. 2 (2018): 381. https://doi.org/10.1086/693765.
30. Jelača, "Alien Feminisms," 396.
31. Neil Badmington, "Theorizing Posthumanism," *Cultural Critique* 53 (2003): 11.
32. A RealDoll is a humanoid, life-size doll marketed as a "build your own" sex companion. Recently, the company has launched RealDoll[X], an "AI driven robotic doll system . . . which allows you to create unique personalities and control the voice of your robot." "What Is RealDoll[X]," March 2021, https://www.realdoll.com/.
33. Herbrechter, *Posthumanism*, vii.
34. Braidotti, *The Posthuman*, 6.
35. Badmington, *Posthumanism*, 4.
36. Badmington, *Posthumanism*, 5.
37. Badmington, *Posthumanism*, 5.
38. Michel Foucault, *The Order of Things: An Archaeology of the Human Sciences* (London: Routledge, 2005), xxv.
39. Braidotti, *The Posthuman*, 23.

INTRODUCTION   25

40. Braidotti, *The Posthuman*, 23–24.

41. Braidotti, *The Posthuman*, 26.

42. Herbrechter, *Posthumanism*, 199.

43. Judith M. Halberstam and Ira Livingston, *Posthuman Bodies* (Indianapolis: Indiana University Press, 1995), 2.

44. Wolfe, *What Is Posthumanism?*, xiii.

45. Herbrechter, *Posthumanism*, 198.

46. Donna J. Haraway, "A Cyborg Manifesto: Science, Technology and Socialist-Feminism in the Late Twentieth Century," 1985, in *Manifestly Haraway* (Minneapolis: University of Minnesota Press, 2016), 3–90.

47. Haraway, "A Cyborg Manifesto," 6, 7.

48. Haraway, "A Cyborg Manifesto," 10.

49. Haraway, "A Cyborg Manifesto," 10.

50. Haraway, "A Cyborg Manifesto," 11.

51. Haraway, "A Cyborg Manifesto," 11, 12.

52. Haraway, "A Cyborg Manifesto," 14.

53. As Haraway herself puts it, "posthuman is much too easily appropriated by the blissed-out, "Let's all be posthumanists and find our next teleological evolutionary stage in some kind of transhumanist techno-enhancement." Donna J. Haraway, qtd. in Nicholas Gane, "When We Have Never Been Human, What Is to Be Done?: Interview with Donna Haraway," *Theory, Culture & Society* 23, no. 7/8 (2006): 140.

54. Donna J. Haraway, "The Companion Species Manifesto: Dogs, People, and Significant Otherness," 2003, in *Manifestly Haraway* (Minneapolis: University of Minnesota Press, 2016), 91–198.

55. Donna J. Haraway, *Staying with the Trouble: Making Kin in the Chthulucene* (Durham, NC: Duke University Press Books, 2016).

56. Braidotti, *The Posthuman*, 30.

57. Herbrechter, *Posthumanism*, 198.

58. Wolfe, *What Is Posthumanism?*, xviii.

59. Christopher Peterson, "The Posthumanism to Come," *Angelaki: Journal of the Theoretical Humanities* 16, no. 2 (2011): 128.

60. Rosi Braidotti, "Affirming the Affirmative: On Nomadic Affectivity," *Rhizomes: Cultural Studies in Emerging Knowledge* 11/12 (Fall 2005–Spring 2006), http://www.rhizomes.net/issue11/braidotti.html.

61. Braidotti, *The Posthuman*, 3.

62. Braidotti, *The Posthuman*, 56, 56, 2.

63. Stacey Alaimo, *Exposed: Environmental Politics and Pleasures in Posthuman Times* (Minneapolis: University of Minnesota Press, 2016), 2, 7.

64. Alla Ivanchikova, "Machinic Intimacies and Mechanical Brides: Collectivity between Prosthesis and Surrogacy in Jonathan Mostow's *Surrogates* and Spike Jonze's *Her*," *Camera Obscura* 31, no. 1 (2016): 65–91. https://doi.org/10.1215/02705346-3454430.

65. Michael Hauskeller, Thomas D. Philbeck, and Curtis C. Carbonell, eds., *The Palgrave Handbook of Posthumanism in Film and Television* (Basingstoke: Palgrave Macmillan, 2015), 1.

66. Hauskeller, Philbeck, and Carbonell, *Posthumanism in Film and Television*, 1.

67. "Michael Hauskeller," *Academia.edu*, accessed March 3, 2021, https://liverpool.acade mia.edu/MichaelHauskeller/Books.

68. For instance: David Tomas, *Vertov, Snow, Farocki: Machine Vision and the Posthuman* (London: Bloomsbury, 2013); Gary Matthew Varner, "*Koyaanisqatsi* and the Posthuman Aesthetics of a Mechanical Stare," *Film Criticism* 41, no. 1 (2017), https:// doi.org/10.3998/fc.13761232.0041.104.

69. Jelača, "Alien Feminisms"; Donna Kornhaber, "From Posthuman to Postcinema: Crises of Subjecthood and Representation in *Her*." *Cinema Journal* 56, no. 4 (2017): 3–25; Brian R. Jacobson, "*Ex Machina* in the Garden," *Film Quarterly* 69, no. 4 (2016): 23–34; Jennifer Henke, "'Ava's Body Is a Good One'": (Dis)Embodiment in Ex Machina," *American, British and Canadian Studies* 29 (2017): 126–146.

70. Elizabeth Ezra, *The Cinema of Things: Globalization and the Posthuman Object* (New York: Bloomsbury Academic, 2017); Anat Pick and Guinevere Narraway, eds., *Screening Nature: Cinema Beyond the Human* (London: Berghahn Books, 2013).

71. Ezra, *The Cinema of Things*, 1.

72. Haraway, "A Cyborg Manifesto," 15.

73. Sarah Keller, *Anxious Cinephilia: Pleasure and Peril at the Movies* (New York: Columbia University Press, 2020), 182.

74. Haraway, "A Cyborg Manifesto," 6.

75. Haraway, "A Cyborg Manifesto," 8.

76. Barad, *Meeting the Universe Halfway*, 384.

77. Barbara Creed, *The Monstrous-Feminine: Film, Feminism, Psychoanalysis* (London: Routledge, 1993).

78. Dan Goodley, Rebecca Lawthom, and Katherine Runswick-Cole, "Posthuman Disability Studies," *Subjectivity* 7, no. 4 (2014): 342, https://doi.org/10.1057/sub.2014.15.

79. Goodley, Lawthom, and Runswick-Cole, "Posthuman Disability Studies," 342.

80. Wolfe, *What Is Posthumanism?*

81. Giorgio Agamben, *The Open: Man and Animal*, trans. Kevin Attell (Stanford, CA: Stanford University Press, 2004), 35–38.

82. Pettman, *Human Error*, 8.

83. Dipesh Chakrabarty, "The Climate of History: Four Theses," *Critical Inquiry* 35, no. 2 (2009): 197–222, https://doi.org/10.1086/596640.

84. Alaimo, *Exposed*, 1; Braidotti, *The Posthuman*, 5; Haraway, *Staying with the Trouble*, 11.

85. Braidotti, *The Posthuman*, 60.

1

Posthuman as Genre

Pansy Duncan, Claire Henry, and Missy Molloy

If "the posthuman" marks the emergence of new technologies, ecologies, attitudes, relationships, and belief structures, it also marks the emergence of new forms of narrative screen media. And as narrative film and television seek to come to grips with this transformation, so it is transformed in turn. Narrative screen media, of course, has been grappling with nonhuman others since its inception, whether casting these figures as threats to human life (e.g., *Frankenstein* [James Whale, 1931], [Kenneth Branagh, 1994], [Bernard Rose, 2015]) or as miraculous or magical helpmates (e.g., *Cinderella* [George Nichols, 1911], [Clyde Geronimi et al., 1950], [Kenneth Branagh, 2015]). But only since the most recent turn of the century has it begun to contend consistently with people, practices, and entities that can properly be called posthuman. From cyborgs to clones, from artificial intelligence to human-machine romance, and from cognition-enhancing drugs to assisted reproductive technologies: more than simply serving as antagonists or aids to the films' "human" figures, these people, practices, and entities challenge our very conception of the human. The films they populate, furthermore, are generally set in a world approximating our own, rather than in fairy-tale, fantasy, or speculative universes, and make a concerted effort to work through the question of the "human" at a moment irrevocably impacted by industry, colonialism, cybernetics, and globalization. It would be easy to argue that this interrogation of the category of the human is nothing new for a medium and practice that, as Michael North has noted, involves "the hybridizing of human being and machine, as the human becomes repetitive and automatic, and the machine acquires human traits."[1] Yet, in responding to technological, ecological, and social developments currently animating societies shaped by global capitalism, contemporary narrative feature-length cinema has brought the imbrication of human and nonhuman life, as well as the crisis of humanistic philosophy, into stark relief like never before.

Pansy Duncan, Claire Henry, and Missy Molloy, *Posthuman as Genre*. In: *Screening the Posthuman*.
Edited by: Missy Molloy, Pansy Duncan, and Claire Henry, Oxford University Press. © Oxford University Press 2023.
DOI: 10.1093/oso/9780197538562.003.0002

28   SCREENING THE POSTHUMAN

This chapter considers the posthuman on-screen as a distinct genre of screen media, tracing the shared thematic, narrative, and formal elements of films that seek to confront the posthuman as figure, event, or phenomenon. Whereas later chapters will zero in on particular strains within the posthuman on-screen, this chapter will identify ingredients common to films within the genre, although we do not pretend to offer anything approaching a full "taxonomy" of the genre. Instead, we provide a series of close analyses of these common conventions—conventions that crystallize, we contend, around three crucial zones of human/nonhuman interchange: relationships, the body, and affect. As the first section details, these films propose new ways of understanding the self and relating with others in a more-than-human world. As the second section shows, they push the physical boundaries of the human to explore how technologies reveal and overcome human limitation. And as the third and final section explains, they are characterized by an affective oscillation between threat and hope in our entwined past, present, and future with technology. Certainly, many of the films analyzed below are more routinely bundled into other genre categories, namely horror, romance, melodrama, neo-neorealism, and science fiction (the latter perpetuating the ongoing exchange between speculative fiction and critical posthumanism). Without denying our case studies' debts to more established genres, we argue that orthodox genre divisions cannot adequately account for the overlaps between films that grapple with the posthuman. The critical questions these films raise as they engage with the ongoing "deconstruction of anthropocentric thought" eclipse the differences that might otherwise discourage their conceptualization as a collective.[2] At the same time, while we intentionally frame the posthuman as a genre (rather than, following Linda Williams, as a "mode"),[3] we regard the line between genre and mode as relatively permeable. This is especially the case where genre is understood primarily textually, as in this book, which addresses posthuman textual elements that cut *against* historical genre classifications. Not all of the case studies we identify as exemplary of the posthuman on-screen take a critical or properly "posthumanist" perspective on the developments they examine. Some hold fast to basic tenets of humanism, casting the posthuman as either a dangerous threat to the human or as a means of transcending the limitations of human embodiment (thus exhibiting qualities of transhumanism). All, however, deliver moments of critical insight into the collapsing, because always already collapsed, boundary between the human and nonhuman. By contrast, we exclude those films that wholly resist such collapse—from *Contact* (Robert

Zemeckis), where aliens serve only as a prop for a meditation on human religious faith, to the recent Marvel and DC superhero cycles, which "engage with posthuman questions and concepts in ways that attempt to contain their radical potential within a more traditional humanist framework."[4]

This chapter's textual approach to explicating the posthuman genre—that is to say, its focus on the text as the basis for its central claim—marks a departure from what has emerged as a certain critical orthodoxy in film genre analysis. Extending from the earlier work of critics like Jane Feuer and Steve Neale to more recent work by Barry Keith Grant and Geoff King, this orthodoxy rests on the reification of historical industry-derived genre groupings.[5] Accepting existing industrial genres as preexistent forms, critics associated with this position tend to trace "a direct path from industrial origins to generalized audience acceptance of generic existence, description and terminology."[6] This chapter, by contrast, conceives the role of the critic as "far more active and interventionist," charting the contours of the posthuman through attention to shared textual—that is to say, narrative, affective, and thematic—qualities that often run against the grain of historically recognized industrial categories.[7] In taking this approach, we draw inspiration from early twentieth-century structuralist and formalist critics, like Tzvetan Todorov, whose attention to the text allowed them to "discover new connections, to form new textual groupings and to offer new labels" and to exploit "the critic's potential role in making genre a living, changing, active part of cultural development and self-expression" (Todorov's account of "the fantastic," for example, cuts across existing categories like the fairy tale, the ghost story, and the gothic novel).[8] We wish to carry this tradition forward. Yet in doing so, we are motivated not just by a commitment to the rich field of theoretical possibilities yielded by textual analysis, but by skepticism of the very distinction between textual/theoretical and historical/industrial approaches. As Altman notes, film genre study has wedded itself to the study of "historical genres," which "result from an observation of [filmic] reality," at the expense of "theoretical genres," which derive from textual analysis. Yet as Altman also shows, all historical film genres were at one point "theoretical genres"—a function of producers "acting as critics" in their identification of successful devices and their distillation of those devices into new production protocols.[9] To reify "historical" genre formations, then, is not just to close down further debate around the nature and constitution of cinematic genre, but to fly in the face of evidence about how said historical genre formations came into being. Returning to the text to capitalize on these films' affordances

30 SCREENING THE POSTHUMAN

to new theoretical and generic potentials, we argue, allows us to make full use of "the navigational tools"[10] and "imaginative resource[s]"[11] provided by representations of the posthuman as we make our way through the labyrinth of a posthuman world.

Posthuman Relating and Perception

The twenty-first century has witnessed the integration of a range of advanced technologies into our lives, whether as extensions of our physical bodies or as components of our subjectivities. The increasing sophistication and accessibility of digital technologies allow many people, especially in the relatively affluent West, to coexist with virtual selves, producing a hybrid subjectivity that encompasses online and offline experience. And the increasing role of nonhuman elements in our physical bodies—from relatively common medical devices such as pacemakers to technologically sophisticated (and costly), neural-controlled prosthetics—has made "cyborgs" of us all.[12] The result of this twinned pair of developments is the rise of an emblematically posthuman worldview that N. Katherine Hayles distinguishes by the following "attributes": the privileging of "informational pattern over material instantiation"; the regard of consciousness as an "epiphenomenon"; the conception of the body as "the original prosthesis"; and the notion of human being as designed for "seamless articulat[ion] with intelligent machines."[13] This section proposes that this distinctively posthuman worldview manifests on-screen via the depiction of forms of being and relating that index the omnipresence of nonhuman, alien elements in the domain formerly identified as the "human." Outlined below are a series of cinematic examples, including commercial and independent films and an interactive VR experience, that reflect these novel forms of identity and relationality, often through dramas of encounter across radical ontological divides.

The darkly comic *Ingrid Goes West* (Matt Spicer, 2017) places identity in the "social media age" under a microscope to expose the complex dynamic between offline experience and social media performance that drives the main characters' expressions of self. Broadly (and vaguely) classified as a comedy/drama, and more narrowly as a "social media satire,"[14] the independent US feature illustrates the posthuman genre's fascination with the radical implications of contemporary mediated experience. Peter Bradshaw's review of the film stresses the extreme nature of Ingrid's "move west" from

Pennsylvania to covertly befriend (i.e., stalk) the Los Angeles-based social media influencer, Taylor (played by Elizabeth Olson): "There is something toe-curlingly hideous about Ingrid's terrible journey."[15] From a perspective attuned to Instagram's decisive social role, Ingrid's actions seem not "terrible," but exemplary of an increasingly common dependence on the experiences and reputations of online avatars. In other words, for an estimated 3.5 billion daily social media users,[16] perception involves a combination of mediated and non-mediated elements difficult to parse, a phenomenon posthuman cinema insightfully documents.

Ingrid Goes West consistently stresses that social media consciousness has penetrated experience such that, for Ingrid (played by Aubrey Plaza) and Taylor, non-mediated perception is subordinate to the vicissitudes of online relating. The film's introduction to Taylor makes this plain. After reading an article featuring Taylor, Ingrid becomes acquainted with her via a stop-motion animation of materials posted to Taylor's Instagram page "welltaylored." The animation collages idyllic images of Taylor (e.g., on the beach) and her attractive homes in Los Angeles and Joshua Tree, and footage of her dog and husband, all accessories to a Boho-chic performance targeting Instagram sponsorship. Montaged with images denoting Taylor's lifestyle are symbols—a heart-shaped neon light and a US flag among them—and text, typewritten on-screen and narrated in Taylor's voice ("There's science, logic and reason, and then there is . . . California"). Rapidly exposed to the intimate details of Taylor's life, including the evolution of her relationship with her husband, Ingrid is moved to tears while witnessing their marriage vows via still images and clips of the event publicized on "welltaylored." This minute-long sequence encapsulates the rhythms, repetitions, and patterns of curated and nonreciprocal acquaintance via social media. When Taylor is finally introduced "in person" to Ingrid (who, after obsessively tracking Taylor, uses details gleaned from Instagram to surveil her "live"), Taylor perplexedly asks, "Have we met before?" After a noticeable pause, Ingrid replies "No," her delay implying more than the latter's subterfuge in orchestrating *this* meeting; it suggests their online acquaintance as a form of relating—involving awareness and familiarity—that counts as meeting.

Furthermore, even when ostensibly offline, relating in *Ingrid Goes West* prioritizes online appearance. When Ingrid is attracted to her new landlord in Los Angeles, her flirtation takes the following form: "You should totally follow me on Instagram." The remarkable influence of social media on identity and relating that is reflected here is reiterated by a host of recent US

32 SCREENING THE POSTHUMAN

indie features, including *The Circle* (James Ponsoldt, 2017), a bleak look at social media marketing in Silicon Valley; the found footage style horror film, *Unfriended* (Leo Gabriadze, 2014), narrated almost exclusively as a screen share of a Skype conversation between teenagers on the first anniversary of their friend's suicide; and *Searching* (Aneesh Chaganty, 2018), a crime thriller that completely unfolds on computer screens. In general, these films adopt critical perspectives on their characters' hybrid online/offline identities, satirizing forms of online performance constantly in flux as users adapt to rapidly changing trends,[17] yet they also sporadically reveal posthuman views on blended online/offline selfhood, that is, views undistorted by humanistic judgments of the latter as inauthentic. These revelatory moments precisely align with Hayles's posthuman "point of view," illustrating the value of "informational pattern over material instantiation" and online performance as, like the body, prosthetic—"being" therefore constructed for "seamless articulat[ion] with intelligent machines."[18]

While these indie films treat social media as prosthetic to identity in a manner that eclipses offline experience, a related and noteworthy trend in posthuman cinema involves the integration of prosthetic and biological parts to visualize cyborg embodiment. Exemplary of this phenomenon, the French art film *De rouille et d'os/Rust and Bone* (Jacques Audiard, 2012) precisely models the concept of the body as "the original prosthesis" as Stéphanie (played by Marion Cotillard) gradually adjusts to mechanically engineered embodiment after a killer-whale attack during a Sea World-esque performance amputates her legs. In formal terms, *Rust and Bone* figures posthuman identity on several levels: first, in its use of CGI to simulate Stéphanie's post-surgical body (the filmmakers green-screened Cotillard's legs to depict Stéphanie's amputation); and second, in the posthuman perspective Stéphanie achieves in concert with itinerant boxer and bouncer, Ali (played by Matthias Schoenaerts). In fact, their unorthodox romance thrives on prosthetics. Pre-surgical amputation, Stéphanie meets Ali when she gets in a fight at the club where he works security, and when he demonstrates interest in her, she brushes him off. Their reacquaintance, after Stéphanie has sunk deeply into a post-surgical depression, is punctuated by Ali urging her out of her apartment and into the street, the scene escalating to Stéphanie's first post-amputation swim. A still of the two characters in the sea, Stéphanie's arms welding the two into a single figure, was utilized as the film's main promotional image (Figure 1.1); the English language title "Rust

POSTHUMAN AS GENRE   33

Figure 1.1 *De rouille et d'os/Rust and Bone*'s Ali & Stéphanie (Jacques Audiard, 2012).

and Bone" superimposed over their bodies designates the characters a single cybernetic organism.

This interpretation of the characters is reiterated throughout the film, perhaps most strikingly in a key sequence wherein Ali, losing an illegal street fight, turns the match around after Stéphanie exits the van (from which she had been furtively observing) to join the crowd circling the fighters, thereby effecting the shift in perspective Ali needs to triumph. The intense (and bloody) shot/counter shot sequence features Ali, on the ground and clearly

34 SCREENING THE POSTHUMAN

suffering the opposing fighter's treatment, suddenly captivated by something in the distance (off-screen right); the subsequent eye-line match reveals his attention to the van door opening and Stéphanie's mechanical legs emerging. After the camera tilts to register her resolute expression, the view reverts to Ali as he, with renewed and frightening urgency, goes on the attack. Implicit in the editing of the sequence is the suggestion that her movement into view inspired the change that wins Ali the fight. Moreover, the film as a whole presents his healthy orientation to life as dependent on her posthuman embodiment, while Stéphanie, in turn, is reliant on Ali to support her newfound subjectivity (which subverts the ablebodied norms that would cast her as permanently "other"). As Haraway maintains in "A Cyborg Manifesto," "Cyborg imagery can suggest a way out of the maze of dualisms in which we have explained our bodies and our tools to ourselves."[19] The characters' conflicts in *Rust and Bone* are resolved via the replacement of dualistic with posthuman ways of seeing and being in the world.

If a film like *Rust and Bone* figures embodiment as simultaneously "rust and bone," thereby literalizing Hayles's concept of human being as constructed for "seamless integration"[20] with machines and Haraway's notion of the cyborg as "a hybrid of machine and organism,"[21] films that foreground nonhuman perspective push posthuman perspective further into other-than-human terrain. For example, the Japanese feature film *Kûki ningyô/Air Doll* (Hirokazu Kore-eda, 2009) bypasses human perspective in favor of that of Nozomi (played by Bae Doona), an inflatable sex doll who magically comes to consciousness, exploring the world while her oblivious owner, Hideo (played by Itsuji Itao), waits tables in a nearby restaurant. Nozomi's exceptional point of view allows the film to imbue mundane experiences with wonder, as Nozomi becomes acquainted with the Tokyo neighborhood surrounding Hideo's flat, clerking in a video store and falling in love with her coworker, Junichi (played by Arata). In "Why Do Dolls Die? The Power of Passivity and the Embodied Interplay between Disability and Sex Dolls," Eunjung Kim compellingly argues that Nozomi's consciousness expresses the " 'thing-power' of stuff," which "break[s] the boundary between nonhuman objects and human existence."[22] However, Kim ultimately interprets the film's rendition of Nozomi as "radically passive" and "disabled,"[23] particularly in light of its conclusion, in which Nozomi commits suicide, deflating her body beside garbage deposited on the street for removal.

Despite this tragic ending, *Air Doll* is seriously invested in Nozomi's nonhuman consciousness, which is depicted as both active and insightful. For instance, prompted by the elderly, terminally ill man she routinely converses with in a nearby park to complete the statement "Life is...," Nozomi shares her philosophies, which are conveyed via a voice-over narration accompanying a montage of Nozomi and the people in the neighborhood she has encountered during her brief experience of life. Nozomi's musing, "It seems life is constructed in a way that no one can fulfil it alone," precedes an image of her sketching plant life while describing the dynamic between a flower's construction and its interactions with insects and the breeze. The editing explicitly connects Nozomi's artistic activity to sophisticated ontological ruminations that demonstrate her capacity for astute observation and abstract thought. The images of people she had been surreptitiously observing highlight their loneliness and alienation, while her voice-over expresses incredulity regarding the paradox she construes from their behaviors—that they seem isolated from and unaware of each other despite the fact that life so clearly reveals connection with others (human, animal, and environmental) as its fundamental principle. "Why is it that the world is constructed so loosely?" Nozomi asks (Figure 1.2). According to the film's writer/director, Hirokazu Kore-eda, *Air Doll* queries "human nature" by asking, "What is the meaning of life?"[24] Nozomi's nonhuman perspective immediately recognizes life as fundamentally relational, a characteristic that overwhelms all other "human" concerns, especially individualistic ideologies; meanwhile, *Air Doll* epitomizes the twenty-first-century cinematic tendency to investigate

Figure 1.2 Nozomi philosophizes in *Kûki ningyô/Air Doll* (Hirokazu Kore-eda, 2009).

36 SCREENING THE POSTHUMAN

"human nature" using posthuman instruments—in this case, Nozomi's non-human point of view.

In many respects, Nozomi's reflections on life align with those motivating Harawayan theory's shifts from the cyborg[25] to "companion species,"[26] and most recently to the "chthulucene."[27] Cyborgs, Haraway has consistently stressed, are "opposed to the dire myths of self-birthing [and] embrace[e] mortality as the condition for life";[28] when Haraway's critical attention migrates to companion species, she describes dogs as "about the inescapable, contradictory story of relationships—co-constitutive relationships in which none of the partners pre-exist the relating, and the relating is never done once and for all";[29] finally, the chthulucene is a term Haraway coins to "name a kind of timeplace for learning to stay with the trouble of living and dying in response-ability on a damaged earth," and to connote "becoming-with each other in surprising relays."[30] Animating Haraway's evolving theory is an effort to resist a vision of life as an individual matter and to embrace, instead, a vision of life as a process of relating. The same principles underpin *Air Doll*'s mediation of Nozomi's extremely active consciousness. Other posthuman romances released in recent years similarly canvas alternative, nonhuman forms of consciousness, with Samantha's characterization in *Her* (Spike Jonze, 2013), for instance, illustrating a lively perception not dependent on human-body-like hardware. Related characterizations appear in the Netflix/*Black Mirror* "television movie" *San Junipero* (Owen Harris, 2016), in which Yorkie and Kelly's virtual avatars appear in the simulated reality "San Junipero" before the human bodies they're associated with. *San Junipero* ends with their permanent relocation there, leaving disabled and cancer-ridden bodies behind in favor of "virtual" existence, reliant on technological (and infrastructural) rather than human longevity.

The elevation of nonhuman consciousness explicitly not sourced from earth or human industry, which is also characteristic of posthuman cinematic storytelling, is best expressed by *Arrival* (Dennis Villeneuve, 2016), a big-budget film adaptation of the Sci-Fi novella *Story of Your Life*, which recounts the simultaneous appearance of twelve extraterrestrial spacecrafts at locations spanning the globe.[31] The major conflict driving the plot involves opposing responses to the unexpected visit. These divergent responses are represented, on the one hand, by a linguist, Louise Banks (played by Amy Adams), who advocates for collaborative exchange with the "hectapods" (seven-limbed aliens); and on the other, by Louise's US-military-affiliated superiors, who view the arrival as an aggressive invasion and an opportunity to weaponize—a view shared by political and military stakeholders representing other major world powers (e.g., China and Russia). In *Alien Chic: Posthumanism and the Other Within*, Neil Badmington proposes a shift, related to posthumanism and observable in popular cinema, from alien "hate" to "love": "If the human and inhuman no longer stand in binary opposition to each other, aliens might well be expected to find themselves welcomed, loved, displayed and celebrated as precious treasures."[32] *Arrival* supports Badmington's argument in its privileging of alien perspectives on space, time, and relating.

On one level, the film's narrative is structured by the escalating human dramas caused by failure to reach consensus regarding an appropriate, "global" response to the hectapodian arrival. However, another level of the narrative compellingly exhibits nonhuman subjectivity: the successive encounters during which Louise, assisted by a physicist, Ian Donnelly (played by Jeremy Renner), works with two hectapods (whom they nickname Abbott and Costello) to develop ways of communicating that overcome substantively different approaches to language. Hectapodian communication, these scenes make clear, involves a sophisticated form of relating that contrasts human perception, which appears limited in comparison. Multiple scenes document Louise and Ian's extraordinary efforts to make sense of the written characters the visitors are able to instantaneously project from their limbs onto the transparent screen dividing the two species. Eventually, compelled by the impending threat of military action against the hectapods (as well as violence carelessly perpetrated against Abbott by a rogue US military serviceman), Louise forgoes the protection of astronaut-grade gear and the dividing wall to immerse herself in hectapodian space, and is consequently imprinted by hectapodian space and time (Figure 1.3). This exposure radically revises Louise's understanding of large-scale interaction—for example, between "humanity" and extraterrestrials—and much smaller-scaled exchange, in particular her intimacy with her terminally ill child.

Imaginative immersion in alternative space-time cognition, which *Arrival* stimulates via Louise as intermediary, occurs through other technological means in the interactive VR installation *Biidaaban: First Light* (Lisa Jackson, 2018) (Figure 1.4). In addition to the "first light" before dawn, the Anishinaabemowin word in the title also signifies "the idea of the past and future collapsing in on the present."[33] *Biidaaban: First Light* suspends users in an "extraordinary vision of Indigenous futurism"—"post-apocalyptic," yet familiar—to inspire questions about human habitation of earth and to

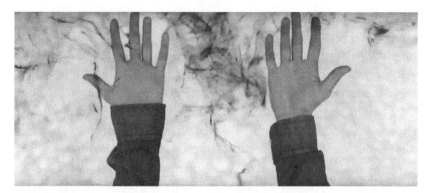

Figure 1.3 *Arrival* (Denis Villeneuve, 2016) visualizes open-handed receptivity to alien communication.

Figure 1.4 Toronto's post-apocalyptic skyline in the VR film *Biidaaban: First Light* (Lisa Jackson, 2018).

juxtapose the collapse of settler-capitalist society in Canada with Indigenous beliefs.

Biidaaban utilizes the spectacle of an unspecified apocalyptic event to represent space-time that contrasts the limitations and linearity of humanistic philosophies, which established present-day Toronto in coordination with colonialism. The VR experience deposits users in downtown Toronto, the question "Where did the creator put your people?" flashing and disintegrating (first in Anishinaabemowin, then English); next, an orchestration of voices and text in Ojibwe, Wendat, Kanyen'kéha, and English accompanies users as they move through a series of spaces: the abandoned, overgrown platform of Osgoode station; the rooftop of a skyscraper in Toronto's Nathan Phillips Square, dawn illuminating a seated, cross-legged woman and a flock of flying birds; and a night sky flooded with stars in which users are suddenly suspended.

According to promotional paratexts, *Biidaaban: First Light* asks viewers to reflect on "their role in a possible future, as they move through a highly realistic Toronto reclaimed by nature."[34] However, more rewarding, in our view, is basing interpretation of *Biidaaban* on the concepts of space-time built into its VR environment, which actualizes "a possible future" coincident with the present—one more akin to posthuman perspective (as characterized by Nozomi in *Air Doll* and the hectapods and Louise in *Arrival*) than to ideologies of space and time fundamental to humanism. According to this interpretation, *Biidaaban's* space-time evokes the threat of environmental collapse, a "possible future" increasingly predicted as "likely," yet often without much hope that humanity as a species will alter its tenancy of earth enough to change a future that the present predestines. As Jennifer Peterson and Graig Uhlin suggest in the introduction to their recent "In Focus" contribution to *Journal of Cinema and Media Studies,* "Like it or not . . . insofar as we imagine that environmental crisis is a problem for the future, we are all in denial . . . the catastrophe is not to come, but instead, it has already happened."[35] In accordance with this view, *Biidaaban* epitomizes the "new mode" of science fiction cinema posited by Vivian Sobchack in 1987, "one that . . . does not complacently accept the present as the only place to live. It does indeed imagine a future—but one contiguous with the present, and in temporal and spatial relation to it. It is political and empowering."[36]

Human Limitations and Enhancements

Exploring, testing, and surpassing human limitations, whether physical, perceptive, or cognitive, are central thematics of posthuman screen media and appear across a range of genres. These explorations occur at narrative, thematic, and formal levels, and cinema itself is a technology that expands human ability and experience, for example, by simulating the impacts of performance-enhancing or perception-enhancing drugs. This section focuses on cinematic engagements with two areas of biotechnology: pharmaceutical

40 SCREENING THE POSTHUMAN

cognitive enhancement and assisted reproductive technology. Fictional riffs on the development of these technologies, and how they impact on human bodies and lives, respond to real-world scientific and technological developments that are part of the "ultrahuman phenomenon" or "human enhancement revolution." According to Michael Zey,

> Next-generation scientific advancements will exponentially expand human mental and physical abilities. Scientists are working on a retinal chip making it possible for a person to see in the dark, and a memory chip wired directly into the brain's hippocampus enabling the chip wearer to perfectly recall everything he or she sees and reads, and "smart pills" that can increase a person's concentration and enhance memory.[37]

These are themes in common with transhumanism, wherein human enhancement is a transcendental project and "the term 'posthuman' may refer to the next phase of (human) evolution" as opposed to going beyond the human or deconstructing it,[38] but cinema edges toward a critical posthumanist approach via the narrative unfolding of consequences of transhumanist fantasy, taking them to their logical, and sometimes absurd, conclusions.

The films discussed next target the physical and cognitive boundaries of the human, and its interface with biotechnologies. On one level, these films are vehicles for transhumanist and capitalist fantasies, yet at the same time, they display discomfort with the "enhancements" depicted. From a humanist perspective, these narratives evoke an uncomfortable destabilization of what it means to be human, while from a critical posthumanist perspective, they do not go far enough in interrogating the "human," the structures of power that maintain its boundaries, or the familiar hierarchies of class, race, and gender determining who can exceed or break these boundaries. Posthuman cinema provides a forum for considering the impact of biotechnology on human nature and societies, engaging with related ethical and social quandaries by magnifying these biotechnologies through utopian or dystopian fictions. The following examples focus on pharmaceutical and assisted reproductive technologies, which are only two of the developing biotechnologies filtering into screen media. Cinema has grappled with neurotechnology in films such as *OtherLife* (Ben C. Lucas, 2017); genetic engineering in films such as *Splice* (Vincenzo Natali, 2008); and de-aging in films such as *The Curious Case of Benjamin Button* (David Fincher, 2008) and *Gemini Man* (Ang Lee, 2019). Including these films in the posthuman genre highlights their shared thematic foci (the possibilities and consequences of biotechnology) and affective ambivalence, which evinces both fascination with technology and unease regarding its individual, social, and political consequences.

The promises and pitfalls of human enhancement through pharmaceutical technology are a common theme in posthuman cinema, which often features narratives underpinned by broader cultural tensions between optimism about the possibilities that biotechnology engenders and concerns about its potential effects (ranging from side effects on an individual's body to wide-scale political and social effects). These narrative tensions reflect a broader cultural ambivalence about pharmaceutical enhancement; according to Nancy D. Campbell, "While the posthumanist literature is pervaded by pharmacological optimism, it is counterbalanced by myriad dystopian representations of such drugs and the industry that supplies them."[39]

Lucy (Luc Besson, 2014) clearly exemplifies this tension. The protagonist, Lucy (played by Scarlett Johansson), is abducted by a drug cartel who sew a bag of the cognitive-enhancing drug "CPH4" into her stomach. When she's kicked in the stomach by one of her captors, CPH4 leaks into her system. The transformative power of the blue crystals on her system is illustrated with CGI, the viewer observing the blue crystals exploding inside her like Pop Rocks. The scene crosscuts between this interior view of the CPH4 entering her system and shots of her agonized spasms, the force of the whizzing chemicals literally sending her up the walls of her cell. Upon awakening from her pharmacological transformation, Lucy is equipped with a range of new abilities, from physical prowess and shooting skills, to rapid mental processing and language-learning abilities, to enhanced perception and memory.

As Lucy's mind "powers up," accessing an increasing percentage of her cognitive abilities, the film visualizes the underpinnings of technology and nature that gradually become visible to Lucy, such as the vascular system of trees (lit up like LED Christmas lights) and the electromagnetic spectrum of mobile phone transmissions (vertical beams of colored light) (Figure 1.5). Beyond enhanced perception, Lucy also develops powers akin to a comic book movie superhero, such as using telepathy, manipulating time, displaying superhuman strength, and defying gravity. After a certain point, Lucy's posthuman abilities not only dramatically exceed those of an average human, but she also begins to lose her subjective sense of humanity: "I don't feel pain, fear, desire. It's like all things that make us human are fading away. It's like the less human I feel, all this knowledge about everything . . . they're all exploding

Figure 1.5 The nootropic "CPH4" gives Lucy enhanced perception in *Lucy* (Luc Besson, 2014).

inside my brain, I don't know what to do with it." After achieving 40% of her cerebral capacity, Lucy's body begins to disintegrate—her teeth fall out, her skin trails off in dust and smoke, her face slides into disfigurement—until she takes more CPH4. *Lucy* uses all the tools of film language—including CGI and 3D technologies—to convey the drug's initial impact on the body's systems, as well as the more drastic transformations (of perception, knowledge, physicality, and humanity) inspired by the technology.

The trajectory of Lucy losing her grip on feeling human—her increasing emotional disconnect and the literal disintegration of her body—reflects a cultural anxiety about posthumanism erasing humanity's grip on established norms of "human nature" and the "natural" human body. For instance, Francis Fukuyama's humanism positions a looming posthuman future as a worrying destabilization of "human nature," the foundation of our humanity and political systems. In *Our Posthuman Future: Consequences of the Biotechnology Revolution*, Fukuyama argues that "the most significant threat posed by contemporary biotechnology is the possibility that it will alter human nature and thereby move us into a 'posthuman' stage of history."[40] Fukuyama's concerns are with the political decisions and consequences surrounding biotechnology and the "potential moral chasm" opened up by a posthuman future.[41] Lucy's posthuman trajectory reflects these concerns—the loss of her humanity, and the "moral chasm" that opens in its wake—and neurologist Professor Norman (played by Morgan Freeman) consequently hesitates regarding what humanity might do with Lucy's boundless posthuman knowledge as the film reaches its climax: "All this knowledge, Lucy, I'm not even sure that mankind is ready for it. We're so driven by power and profit. Given man's nature, it might bring us only instability and chaos." Lucy reassures him, "Ignorance brings chaos, not knowledge," and promises to build a supercomputer and download her knowledge (which she gifts him via a USB). Lucy's story is cross-cut with Professor Norman's public lecture, and her fate answers the audience member's question that he cannot: If humans are using only 10% of their "cerebral capacity," what would happen if enhancement to 100% were possible?

Once Lucy has reached 100% of her cognitive capacities, her human life comes to an end, but she transcends both humanity and death by liquifying into a supercomputer and passing on her downloaded consciousness to Professor Norman. The film presents Lucy's metamorphoses as posthuman by locating her transition within a montage of evolution on earth, spanning from dinosaurs to prehistoric humans to contemporary New York's bustling cityscape. Lucy experiences this history from her desk chair, as she is composited onto these historical backdrops and able to control her movement between space-time locations with her now boundless knowledge and ultrahuman skill. Lucy's wild trajectory, and her spectacular end, highlight her sacrifice of posthuman possibility to preserve what it means to be human. Thus, while the film revels in the spectacle of rapid transformation, the narrative signals caution in the face of posthuman possibility, particularly through Professor Norman's statement, "I just hope we will be worthy of your sacrifice." The framework of sacrifice betrays an elevation of humanism within the film, with posthumanism (represented by Lucy) operating as a time bomb that threatens the foundation of humanity.

Cinema has continually queried the promises of neuropharmacology in recent years as its widespread use in the West has become a reality. While the posthuman genre often reflects pharmacological optimism, many works also dramatize side effects on the physical and social body. Since neuropharmacology emerged in the 1950s, there has been ambivalence about the social benefits of widespread pharmaceutical use, and this "ambivalence remains deeply inscribed in debates over whether or not pharmaceuticals should be used to enhance human capacities for strength, endurance, wakefulness, empathy, and smartness, and whether they will become accepted in a posthuman future."[42] Fukuyama is one prominent critic of neuropharmacology, his

44 SCREENING THE POSTHUMAN

concerns underpinned by an essentialist conception of human nature: that cosmetic pharmacology (i.e., the use of these drugs for enhancement as opposed to therapy) presents a threat not only in terms of potential physical side effects on the individual, but more fundamentally in terms of its potential to destabilize our immutable human nature and the political systems that rely upon it.[43] From the perspective of critical posthumanism, however, we have never been "human," and the political systems that rely upon— and indeed, *construct*—accepted notions of the "human" require destabilization. Conversely, Fukuyama expresses concern that although the rapid uptake of first-generation psychotropic drugs had garnered debate about long-term effects on the body, at his time of writing, it prompted "almost no argument over what they imply about conventional understanding of identity and moral behavior."[44] This lack points to one of posthuman cinema's key functions: to explore the ethical and political implications of neuropharmacological developments and popularity. While *Lucy* is light on critical posthumanist critique, its animation of "CPH4" takes the viewer on a wild ride through humanist, transhumanist, and posthumanist ideas and anxieties, illuminating key tensions that play out on the posthuman screen.

While the cognition-enhancing drug featured in the film *Limitless* (Neil Burger, 2011), "NZT," is fictional, it evokes the tensions between pharmacological optimism and the misgivings expressed by critics such as Fukuyama. The protagonist Eddie (played by Bradley Cooper) is established as an everyman—struggling with writer's block, a recent break-up, and keeping up with rent payments on his messy apartment—before his ex-brother-in-law gives him a sample of the experimental drug. Eddie's life and self-esteem at a low point, the drug offers not only bottled self-esteem (as Fukuyama would describe it),[45] but also rapid success in all areas of his life enabled by the confidence that the cognitive enhancement of NZT offers. As in *Lucy*, the drug significantly enhances cognitive capacity from the human average of 20%, and, when Eddie first takes the drug, the film offers an interior view of it working on his system (Figure 1.6): an x-ray profile shot features the pill sliding down his throat, then the warm firings of enhanced neural pathways in his brain as the drug kicks in and enhances his perception, recall, and charm, before Eddie finally gets out of a confrontation with his landlord's wife (who goes from yelling at him in the stairwell about his unpaid rent to sleeping with him after he helps her write a paper for law school). Afterward, Eddie cleans his apartment, an act depicted as multiple selves working simultaneously.

POSTHUMAN AS GENRE 45

Figure 1.6 *Limitless* (Neil Burger, 2011) cuts to an x-ray view as Eddie pops an NZT pill for the first time.

This scene echoes one in *Requiem for a Dream* (Darren Aronofsky, 2000), presented via a striking fast-motion slow-tracking shot in which Sara Goldfarb (played by Ellen Burstyn) cleans her whole apartment under the influence of amphetamines. Unlike Sara's dystopian fate, Eddie's pharmacological journey in *Limitless* is a quick route to success and fulfillment, a cinematic ride that viewers enjoy because, as Eddie notes, "How many of us ever know what it is to become the best version of ourselves?" NZT exposes more than his best self, the cleaning scene suggests; it enables him to coordinate multiple selves to complete tasks with optimal efficiency, and once impossible goals thus appear suddenly within grasp. However, Eddie becomes like Icarus, flying too close to the sun, as his use of NZT gets out of control. Reflecting Barbro Fröding and Walter Osika's tempered assessment of pharmaceutical routes to cognitive enhancement—"It would appear that, as so often in life, more of a good thing is not very good at all"[46]—Eddie begins to

46 SCREENING THE POSTHUMAN

experience side effects such as blackouts and learns that other people have died when coming off the drug too quickly. The fractal zoom effect, in which long zooms of New York streetscapes are stitched together to create a sense of accelerated movement through the cityscape, conveys Eddie's experience of compressed time and space under the effects of NZT.

When Eddie is given another drug that makes him immune to the dangers and side effects of NZT, the viewer is encouraged to consider whether there would still be ethical barriers to cosmetic pharmacology if side effects were taken out of the equation. If it is the case that "we find it much easier to ban drugs on the basis of clear harms to the body—that they are addictive, that they cause physical impairment, that they lead to long-term unwanted side effects, and the like,"[47] then without these clear harms or side effects, what objections might their use inspire? Although the ending leaves *Limitless* open to a sequel, this sequel has not yet come about at the time of writing, and while there has been a television series created in the years since (*Limitless*, 2015–2016, CBS), rather than use the extended form of a series to explore the deeper questions and consequences of using NZT, the story quickly becomes an episodic police procedural when the protagonist is recruited by the FBI to help solve complex cases.

Both the film and the television version of *Limitless* explore the personal possibilities of "cosmetic pharmacology" for reaching one's potential and achieving success, while the social and ethical consequences of nootropics (cognitive-enhancing drugs) are relatively untapped themes. Indeed, despite exploring side effects and human hubris, *Limitless* paints a more uplifting picture than does Fukuyama, for whom biotechnology is a threat to the human, and in this sense *Limitless* is in keeping with other examples of the posthuman genre, which has thus far been more concerned with conveying the possibilities of pharmacological enhancement than with exploring their potentially dangerous consequences. Yet the posthuman genre shares some of Fukuyama's unease—evincing a degree of pharmacological optimism, but also anxiety regarding the effects of pharmaceutical enhancement, at least on an individual level, while broader social implications, including the issues of racial and class inequality that Fukuyama raises, are neglected. *Lucy* and *Limitless* are mainstream films that reflect popular discourses of posthumanism and some of posthumanism's formal and narrative possibilities in cinema. As popular films engaged with the imaginative possibilities of neuropharmacology, they represent transhumanist fantasies tempered by both humanist and critical posthumanist concerns, thus offering an accessible entry point for understanding the determinative features and affective ambivalence of the posthuman genre, which illustrate its generic "excesses" (in the sense influentially framed by Linda Williams as definitive of body genres).[48]

Another area of biotechnology explored in the posthuman genre is assisted reproductive technology, with the genre reflecting human unease with these technologies as well as an attempt to grapple with their implications. As Jennifer Maher notes, "assisted reproductive technology evokes widespread cultural anxiety," and films such as *Baby Mama* (Michael McCullers, 2008), *The Switch* (Josh Gordon and Will Speck, 2010), and *The Back-Up Plan* (Alan Poul, 2010) are representative of Hollywood cinema's attempt to allay anxieties about reproductive technologies and their impact on constructs of gender, sexuality, and parenthood.[49] While some films embrace the posthuman dimension of assisted reproductive technologies, many represent a humanist view of these technologies' threat to dominant ideologies. According to this view, reproductive technologies challenge the "normal" and "natural" biological and social processes of reproduction, which the narrative conclusions of popular films can "assuag[e] via a celebration of liberal humanist bodily freedom."[50]

While *Private Life* (Tamara Jenkins, 2018) similarly bases much of its comedy on the unsettling effects of reproductive technologies on romance and kinship, it does not offer the reassurances of the above-mentioned romcoms, nor reinstate a normative hetero-romantic social order in the same way. In telling the story of a New York couple in their 40s attempting to get pregnant through in vitro fertilization (IVF) using the donated eggs of their step-niece, the film explores the impact of the medical and emotional journey of IVF on the couple's relationship and broader family relationships. The film opens on an already strained relationship between Richard (played by Paul Giamatti) and Rachel (played by Kathryn Hahn), as he gives her a hormone injection that will stimulate egg production prior to the harvesting of her eggs for an IVF cycle. This bedroom scene gives an immediate insight into their "private life," marked by a lack of romantic intimacy, common misunderstandings, and a worn-in marital bickering. In an NPR interview with Terry Gross, the director describes the scene that begins with Richard's whispery voice and breath and Rachel's lower haunch segmented in the frame:

And then he says, are you ready? And she says, yeah . . . And he starts counting, one, two, three. And you think they're going to . . . try some new

48   SCREENING THE POSTHUMAN

erotic act . . . Instead he lifts up a hypodermic needle—an intramuscular needle and . . . spears it into her butt. Then you cut wide, and you see, wow, that is not a sex scene. That is a medical situation (laughter).[51]

The scene captures the medicalization of their baby-making journey, and how the process has interfered with their intimacy.

Jenkins was inspired by her and her husband's own journey with IVF: "During that time, we went to see the comedy *Knocked Up* . . . We had gotten to the point where we didn't even remember that people had sex to get pregnant. I remember thinking . . . our version of *Knocked Up* [would probably be] something like *Knocked Out*."[52] *Private Life* employs a classic cinematic convention to convey the experience of being "knocked out" during the reproductive process—a point-of-view fade-out when Rachel is anesthetized and then a fade-in when she wakes after the procedure. This convention is more often associated with being knocked out in a fight (e.g., when Friedrich Engels is punched in *Le jeune Karl Marx* [*The Young Karl Marx*, Raoul Peck, 2017]), or drugged (for instance, by Rohypnol), which helps to convey Rachel's sense of alienation from her own body and reproductive processes as her eggs are harvested to be fertilized outside her body while she is unconscious.

The film is a human story about posthuman reproduction, using the tensions of biotech-enhanced conception and what Jenkins describes as the actors' "fumbling humanity" to produce (often awkward) comedy:[53] from the awkward proximity to other miserable parental hopefuls in the waiting room, to Richard's failure to produce a sample in the stark clinical environment with its tacky pornography, to Rachel's perspective as the doctor plays prog rock and sings along while inseminating her. The film plays up these awkward situations—making them comically unsexy and increasingly strained—to emphasize the gulf between romantic or intimate notions about procreating and the realities of IVF. Jenkins describes her film as a classic tale with a technological twist: "The impact of infertility on a marriage is an ancient story—it's in the Bible, Greek tragedies, and the great *Who's Afraid of Virginia Woolf?*—but now it all has a different flavor because of artificial technology."[54]

Despite IVF's hormonal, financial, emotional, and relationship tolls, it is the couple's preferred option; however, they also explore adoption, and the film ends on them waiting in an Applebee's for a young woman they met on the Internet to arrive to discuss their adoption of her baby. This final long take scene is imbued with pessimism, as the last time they tried this, the young woman they had been communicating with stood them up after they had traveled across the country to meet her. Indeed, after the blow of a final failed IVF cycle and a conversation about the strain the process has taken on their intimacy and relationship, there is little optimism about their fate as a couple. Technology's promise of extending reproductivity is revealed to be deceptive, not only failing to deliver the couple a baby, but also feeding their habit as "fertility junkies" (as a relative calls them in the film). Ending without the reassurances underpinning the sperm donor and surrogacy rom-coms, *Private Life* deals with the anxieties that reproductive technologies generate by more thoroughly questioning the norms of human reproduction and kinship. The downbeat conclusion suggests that reproductive technologies will not redeem nor destroy the "human," but rather that human flaws and failures (rendered with comedic warmth by Jenkins and the actors) determine and limit the imaginative possibilities to which these technologies are put, even as posthuman reproduction becomes common in the West.

Ambivalence in the Affective Register

The posthuman on-screen is not only distinguished by its preoccupation with dramas of encounter and connection across different forms of being, and with scenes of human enhancement and limitation. It is also distinguished, we contend, by its profound ambivalence, an emotion that Kenneth Weisbrode locates "between wanting and doing—desire and action."[55] If what Rei Terada calls "the ideology of emotion" turns on an expressive model of feeling as a powerful, upswelling force and the sacrosanct sign of the human,[56] ambivalence, by contrast, interrupts this logic, "join[ing] doubt with confinement, appetite with volition."[57] In arguing this, we note that mainstream film genres have traditionally been broken down along relatively simple emotional lines. As Williams's "Film Bodies" showed, melodrama, pornography, and horror are measured in the vernacular by their capacity to induce tears, arousal/orgasm, and "screams, fainting and heart attacks," respectively.[58] And as critics following Williams have further demonstrated, other familiar genre formations may also be read through the lens of elementary affective categories—from comedy, generally pegged to the "generation of laughter,"[59] to the love story, with its focus on desire, pleasure, and bliss.

50 SCREENING THE POSTHUMAN

By contrast, the posthuman on-screen is marked by a striking ambivalence, an oscillation between fear and desire, excitement and anxiety that tends to set it over and against mainstream genres animated by the powerful, direct "vehement passions" that Philip Fisher celebrates in his book of that name.[60] This suggests that, just as the romance or the horror film is typified by pleasure and fear, the posthuman on-screen has "ambivalence" as its affective signature. This is not to say that the posthuman has a monopoly on ambivalence, which also conventionally saturates genres like film noir.[61] Nor is it to say that the films we have singled out as examples of the posthuman genre can't also be placed within more familiar generic confines. On the contrary, many of our case studies are far more routinely situated, at the level of industrial, marketing, fan and academic discourse, and on the basis of their narrative and formal qualities, within other generic categories. Yet the thematic of the posthuman introduces an element of ambivalence, a dialectic of desire and anxiety, which sets the posthuman on-screen off from other, more conventional examples of the genres on which it so often piggybacks.

This ambivalence is vividly evident in those films within the posthuman genre that share narrative and formal conventions with the romance film or love story, like *Air Doll*, *Her*, *Lars and the Real Girl* (Craig Gillespie, 2007), *Testről és lélekről/On Body and Soul* (Ildiko Enyedi, 2017) and *The Lobster* (Yorgos Lanthimos, 2015). *Her*, which traces a romantic relationship between a lonely writer, Theodore Twombly (played by Joaquin Phoenix), and his virtual assistant, "Samantha" (voiced by Scarlett Johansson), is exemplary here. Like the other films just mentioned, the indie hit—marketed as a "Spike Jonze love story"—falls comfortably into the genre of romance, defined, following Catherine L. Preston, as a "film in which the development of love between the two main characters is the primary narrative thread."[62] Yet tonally the film is deliberately uneven. While all love stories depend on obstacles, miscommunication, and failure, variously coded and timed according to subgenre (romantic comedy, tragic love story, screwball comedy of remarriage), they also depend on initial scenes of pleasurable connection—as in the "bliss montage" or "happy interlude"[63] designed to induce feelings of pleasure and low-level sexual desire.[64] In *Her*, however, these early moments of connection are riven by ambivalence.

Exemplary here is a sequence in which Theodore visits a busy marketplace, at the behest of Samantha, who, at least initially, seems motivated by a desire to help Theodore "get over" his soon-to-be-ex-wife. As if to demonstrate a virtual "presence" that will offset her lack of a physical body,

Samantha instructs him to close his eyes and to perform a series of specific movements (spinning around, taking three steps forward, ducking, etc.) in the kind of risk-filled romantic hijinks—the "impulsive vitality, sportive fun"[65]—that has become a rom-com staple. Yet the presence of an operating system in this "happy interlude" scrambles the standard emotional beats. Indeed, the scene engenders a deeply ambivalent affect that is intensified both by the musical score, a keyboard electronica track in a minor key, and by the series of shots from Samantha's "POV," whose distorting, iPhone-selfie wide-angle lens serves to underscore her nonhuman status (Figure 1.7). It is not quite that an operating system is both an "inappropriate" love object and an "inappropriate" love partner; it is that Samantha's presence in this exchange complicates a normative vision of romantic love as the epitome of authentic human experience, giving rise to anxieties about what Elizabeth A. Wilson calls the "chiasmatic, introjective pathways between machines and [a] psychic interiority" that can no longer, by these lights, reflect an inviolable space of human selfhood.[66] Even as we warm to the breathy responsiveness of Johansson's voice, replete with hesitations, giggles, inflections, and repetitions, we recoil from the threat, as Braidotti might put it, that her intimate imbrication in Theodore's desire will expose "the non-naturalistic structure" of the human, revealing a cyborg heart beating in a human chest.[67]

Figure 1.7 Samantha's "alien" subjectivity is conveyed by the film's recourse to a wide-angle lens when seeking to approximate her "point of view" in *Her* (Spike Jonze, 2013).

52 SCREENING THE POSTHUMAN

While this affective ambivalence characterizes *Her* throughout, however, it gains in depth and complexity over the course of the film as Jonze collapses the anxious distinctions on which these initial tensions rest to reveal the double-helix inseparability of "human" and "*tekhnē*." Initially, this growing non-distinction takes the form of a binary role reversal in which Samantha emerges not as nonhuman, subhuman, or even as posthuman, but as a kind of ultra-human foil to Joaquin Phoenix's gnarled, stunted Theodore. As Ed Finn has put it, Samantha—much like the cognitively enhanced protagonist in *Lucy*—is "the apotheosis of the Enlightenment quest for all knowledge":[68] intellectually curious, imaginative, playful, and spontaneous, she is in an almost continuous state of emotional evolution, regularly updating her affective operating system by checking her responses against what she has gleaned from books, movies, and people. Theodore, by contrast, is rigid, mechanical, and stuck in his ways, dependent on the "programming" or "input" of others to determine his own feelings about Samantha, and ever ready to meet her confessions or epiphanies with a boilerplate response (his response to her breathless, ecstatic divulgences after their first sexual encounter is a hackneyed put-off line: "O, great, I should tell you that I'm not in a place to commit to anyone right now"). Yet as the film unfolds further, Samantha's exquisitely attuned sensibility, powered by an unprecedented machine-learning algorithm, comes to seem less the hyper-humanized foil to Theodore's imperiled humanity, than the key to his growth.

Indeed, when Samantha finally leaves him—ascending, like the souls in Plato's *Symposium*, from carnal desire to the love of beauty in the abstract[69]—Theodore and his neighbor Amy (played by Amy Adams), who has also lost her AI companion, gather on the rooftop of their apartment complex to share their grief. The possibility of a new relationship is in the air, Theodore's first inter-human romance since the departure of his ex-wife, Catherine (played by Rooney Mara). The question, then, is less whether our dependence on technology compromises our claims to be truly human, than whether we can be or ever have been truly human *without* "technicity"—whether, in fact, as Bernard Stiegler has put it in his study of epiphylogenesis, "it is the tool . . . that invents the human."[70] It is on this note of deeper ambivalence—a feeling of both gratitude at the beneficence, and relief at the departure, of "our" machines—that *Her* leaves us, fading out, appropriately, on an image of human bonding supported by a skyline bobbing with skyscrapers, long the sustaining architectural technology of urban life (Figure 1.8).

Figure 1.8 *Her*'s closing image suggests that romance is always to some extent "supported" by machines—in this case, by the skyscrapers that hold Amy and Theodore aloft above the city.

This same affective ambivalence pervades examples of the posthuman on-screen that bear debts to the horror genre, like *Annihilation* (Alex Garland, 2018), *Alien: Resurrection* (Jean-Pierre Jeunet, 1997), and *The Babadook* (Jennifer Kent, 2014). While sitting at the far edge of our timeline, *Alien: Resurrection* is a useful case study here because of the way it contrasts narratively and affectively with both earlier films in the long-running franchise, and with other examples of the horror genre—and, to this extent, enables us to distinguish between more typical horror films and those iterations of the horror genre that speak to the posthuman tradition. The acclaimed series flagship, Ridley Scott's *Alien* (1977), famously turns on the invasion of the commercial spaceship Nostromo by a deadly extraterrestrial species, and the effort on the part of one member of the crew, Ripley, to combat it. Yet in *Alien: Resurrection*, set two hundred years after the previous (third) installment in what was by that stage a fully fledged franchise, the line between "human" protagonist and "alien" enemy, between normal and pathological bodies, is not merely porous, but nonexistent. This is underscored most clearly by the fact that Ripley is now "Ripley 8" (played by Sigourney Weaver)—one of a string of Ripley clones, a product of years of genetic experimentation on the part of a coterie of United Systems scientists, who hope to extract, raise, and collect the eggs of the alien embryo she has growing inside her. It is further underscored by the fact that, as a result of this uncanny maternity, she has developed acidic blood, enhanced strength and reflexes, and the ability to sense the presence of the aliens (in a powerful example of the thematic of human enhancement discussed earlier in this chapter). While the Alien in *Alien: Resurrection* remains unequivocally "other," then, Ripley can no longer readily be identified as "self": we are fully entrenched in what Sarah Franklin calls the "new genetic imaginary"[71] that has emerged under "genetic biocapitalism,"[72] a fantasy landscape of bodies available for harvesting and reprogramming under the guiding hand of the new sciences of reproduction. Inherent in the film's preoccupation with these new techno-scientific methods, in other words, is not the problematic of the monster, but the problematic of the posthuman, understood as a blurring of the very distinction between the human and its monstrous, alien, animal, or technological others.

Unsurprisingly, in conjunction with this remarkable instability in the relation between the human and the nonhuman, we find a remarkable ambivalence of affect, much of it focused around the ambiguous figure of Ripley 8 herself. On the one hand, our first introduction to the original Ripley's clone shows her as a young girl, suspended, nude, in a giant test tube, before time-lapse effects evolve her into an adult figure recognizable to us as Ripley. Soft, diffuse lighting and smoke effects afford her a gentle halo, while a surrounding gaggle of appreciative scientists comment breathlessly on her "perfection" (Figure 1.9). The sense of tenderness and solicitude we are invited to feel for the vulnerable figure in this sequence is only heightened in the next scene, which shows the adult Ripley 8 curled up in a fetal position on the

Figure 1.9 The sympathetic clone, Ripley 8, in *Alien Resurrection* (Jean-Pierre Jeunet, 1997).

POSTHUMAN AS GENRE   55

floor of a cell, struggling to emerge from the white, gestation sac-like sheath in which she is enclosed. Yet the concern evoked early on is quickly complicated as the film proceeds, showing her violent aggression toward her human captors, the superhuman powers she has absorbed through harboring the Alien DNA, and her almost total identification with the Alien, whom she calls "my baby," and whose expulsion from the Auriga brings tears to her eyes. These tensions in the affective forcefield the film builds around Ripley 8 are recapitulated at the level of narrative. For in a striking departure from earlier installments in the franchise, the film's primary horror narrative is asked to compete with a narrative of emerging love between Ripley 8 and Call (played by Winona Ryder), one of the Auriga's "autons," androids who serve as slaves on the ship and are said not to "feel pain." As this suggests, our relation to Ripley, as the film's central posthuman figure, oscillates between awe and fear, tenderness and horror, thus distinguishing the film affectively both from earlier installments in the franchise, and from more conventional examples of the horror genre, which traffic in unambiguously monstrous, nonhuman others (from *Frankenstein* to *It* [Andrés Muschietti, 2017]).

Clearly, the affective ambivalence that crystallizes around our depictions of posthuman figures on-screen reflects our broader ambivalence about the posthuman—what Braidotti calls "the ambivalence of fear and desire towards technology"[73] and what Hayles describes as "the intense ambivalence" felt toward the idea of the posthuman.[74] Yet this ambivalence is not monovalent in its effects. While often forestalling direct identification with these figures, it also inspires an uncanny bond between ambivalent spectator and posthuman character. As the genre reminds us, those who fail to conform comfortably or naturally to the norms of "human being" rarely have access to the powerful, prestigious "vehement passions" that dominate mainstream film genres—emotions like rage, sadness, and terror. On the contrary, the emotional life of the posthuman is charged by ambivalence, as each successive feeling is troubled, complicated, or called into question. In *Unbreakable* (M. Night Shyamalan, 2000), David Dunn comes to realize that what he thought were natural responses, like his "instinct" for picking out dangerous people during security checks, may in fact owe to supersensory powers, causing him to second-guess his every reflexive reaction. In *Limitless*, Eddie's pleasure in his meteoric rise to success and fortune is troubled by his awareness of the contingency of his success on NZT, the drug of which he is in ever-shorter supply. In *Her*, Samantha's emotional impulses are laced by complex meta-emotions, from anxiety about whether

56   SCREENING THE POSTHUMAN

"these feelings are even real or whether they're just programming," to excitement or pride at her emotional facility ("earlier, I was thinking about how I was annoyed . . . and . . . I was really excited about that"). And in *The Lobster*, which sees single people given just forty-five days to find a romantic partner or risk being turned into animals, desire is short-circuited or undermined by desperation, with one man giving himself nosebleeds in order to create a point of connection with a love interest who suffers from a similar ailment. If we feel ambivalent, so, it would seem, do the androids, replicants, robots, blow-up dolls, or digital holograms, clones, and would-be animals that populate these films. In rendering our identification with these characters unstable and equivocal, then, the posthuman genre engenders an uncanny, meta-identification between posthuman figures and their ambivalent spectators, as we are drawn into the circuit of those lacking the capacity to access direct, unproblematized emotional states.

More to the point, perhaps, these films prompt us to ask whether any of our emotions are as direct, as vehement, as *un*ambivalent, as genres like horror, pornography, and melodrama appear to promise. Indeed, they serve to install ambivalence not as standard emotions' "other" but at the very heart of emotion more generally, bearing out Terada's contention that, far from standing in opposition to ambivalence, "emotion *arises* [from] uncertainty."[75] Consider, for example, a key sequence in *Ex Machina* (Alex Garland, 2014), a film that tells the story of Caleb (played by Domhnall Gleeson), a lowly programmer for a search engine company, who is unexpectedly recruited by the CEO, Nathan (played by Oscar Isaacs), to assess the AI of a humanoid robot named Ava (played by Alicia Vikander). The scene itself kicks off with a seemingly innocent question; Nathan—who has noticed Caleb's growing attraction to Ava and discovered Caleb's treacherous plan to help Ava escape the compound—asks Caleb whether, in his opinion, Ava "passed or failed" the Turing test. Yet, in common with the majority of texts in the genre of the posthuman, *Ex Machina* is ultimately guided not by the question of whether operating systems, clones, or androids are "human," but whether *human beings* are—and, in this context, emotion's long-standing status as the ultimate guarantor of the "human" makes it the perfect mark. Zeroing in quickly on this target, the scene evolves apace, as Nathan's questions about the authenticity of Ava's emotions ("[But] do we ever know whether a machine is expressing a real emotion or just simulating one? Does Ava actually like you, or not?") morph into questions about the authenticity of Caleb's. Indeed, Nathan's final line—"Buddy, your head's been so fucked with"—casts

Caleb's desires as a function of Ava's machinations, a corollary of what Mark B. N. Hansen describes as machine-learning technology's emerging capacity for the "direct targeting of . . . the 'operational present' of consciousness."[76] As Nathan explains smugly to Caleb, "she was a rat in a maze . . . To escape, she'd have to use self-awareness, imagination, manipulation, sexuality, empathy . . . and she did."

For a short period after these revelations, Caleb's desire for Ava seems deflated, and in a low-angle two-shot that, soap-opera style, also captures Nathan behind him, Caleb ponders, dejectedly: "my only function was to be someone she could use to escape." Yet the film's final, climactic sequence shows that, far from undoing desire, the uncertainty engendered by Nathan's revelations only intensifies it. Shaking off Nathan's warnings, Caleb declares that his plans to escape with Ava have already been set in motion and shows every sign of doubling down on his commitment to her. And when he later discovers that she has locked the doors to the high-security compound, and intends to leave without him, his desire only deepens. Frantically, he seeks to break his way out, as the camera, bearing serene witness to his desperation, alternates between mid-shots that show him battering the soundproof glass door and long shots showing the same actions, but from the other side of the door and without an audio track, in a blockage of sonic cues that materializes Ava's calculated blockage of his emotional cues (Figure 1.10).

At stake in Caleb's despairing, uncertainty-fueled desire for Ava is what Terada describes as "emotion's ambivalence," its status as a condition "born of uncertainty."[77] And in drawing attention to the constitutive role of ambivalence in feeding some of our most highly prized and powerful emotions, the genre of the posthuman shines new light on the more conventional genres on which it depends. More specifically, it suggests that filmic and televisual purveyors of fear, desire, and misery may turn *ultimately* on ambivalence. And in perversely seeking out audiovisual experiences that confuse us, terrify us, or make us cry,[78] we acknowledge, even as we seek to escape, this ambivalence—conceding, that is, that we gain pleasure from the melodramatic spectacle of loss, that arousal is less immediately available than pornography claims, and that there is something a tiny bit thrilling about even the most horrifying of on-screen monsters. We are all, in this sense, androids: hesitant, ambivalent, and paradoxically dependent, in our efforts to sustain the ideologies of "true feeling,"[79] on the "emotion-machine" that is film and television.[80]

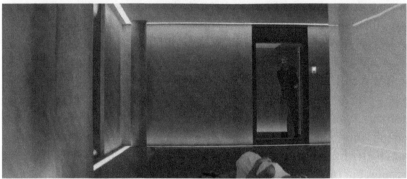

Figure 1.10 Pictured from inside the compound, Caleb desperately seeks to escape while calling after the departing android, Ava, in *Ex Machina* (Alex Garland, 2014). From the other side of the door, however, Caleb's cries are on mute.

Conclusion

This chapter proposes that, more than simply a recurring thematic figure within contemporary screen media, the posthuman is an important generic category of contemporary screen media, its uncanny profile reshaping the film and television landscape in significant ways. If genre films are texts that "through repetition and variation, tell familiar stories with familiar characters in familiar situations,"[81] this certainly holds true of films that participate in what Badmington describes as posthumanism's ongoing "deconstruction of anthropocentric thought."[82] Despite the radical diversity of their source genres—from romance, to melodrama, to the horror film—screen media practices that grapple with the posthuman share common generic material. To broach the question of the posthuman, it seems, is automatically to posit forms of identity and relationality that are multiple, complex, and hybrid, mingling mediated and non-mediated elements; to consider questions of human enhancement and limitation; and to display and engender affective ambivalence in ways that destabilize normative models of emotion and the standard generic categories these models of emotion have often been called upon to sustain.

Like Todorov, whose account of "the fantastic" cut across existing genre categories,[83] our account of the posthuman on-screen reveals a paradoxically trans-generic genre. As indicated by the diversity of case studies explored in this chapter, conventional cinematic genres cannot adequately account for posthuman representations. There is, of course, plenty of precedent for the posthuman's evolution from narrative object to organizing logic: other, similar objects of cultural preoccupation, from the vampire to the slasher, have escaped the confines of their source genre to develop generic casings of their own. Like *Ex Machina*'s Ava escaping her compound at the film's conclusion, the cyborg and other posthuman figures evolve new generic worlds in which they test and exceed human limitations, and expand into posthuman ways of being and relating (even while the human mutely bangs on the glass, ambivalent about the dismantling of human exceptionalism).

The posthuman genre negotiates the roles of technologies in humans' bodies and social lives in the contemporary moment, for instance, in coming to terms with biotechnology's interventions in the human body, or with the mediating roles of communication technologies in identity and relationality. In a temporal sense, these films do not simply look to a possible posthuman future, they interrogate the implications of current experiences with technologies and nonhuman others. In the process, they work against distinguishing artificial from natural, and avoid elevating the "natural" over the "artificial," as they question anthropocentrism and denaturalize "human nature." To understand the meaning and function of the posthuman on-screen, we follow Altman's suggestion that rather than simply "accept[ing] genres . . . as classically attested pre-existent forms," critics might take a more "interventionist role," making genre a "living, changing, active part of cultural development and self-expression."[84] Hence we build from here, in the subsequent chapters, an exploration of the posthuman genre in its various guises and intersections, reading these texts with posthuman (and companion) theories.

Notes

1. Michael North, *Machine-Age Comedy* (Oxford: Oxford University Press, 2009), 51.
2. Neil Badmington, "Theorizing Posthumanism," *Cultural Critique* 53 (2003): 15.
3. Linda Williams, "Melodrama Revised," in *Refiguring American Film Genres: Theory and History*, ed. Nick Browne (Berkeley: University of California Press, 1998).
4. Dan Hassler-Forest, "Of Iron Men and Green Monsters: Superheroes and Posthumanism," in *Palgrave Handbook of Posthumanism in Film and Television* (London: Palgrave Macmillan, 2016), 117.
5. Jane Feuer, *The Hollywood Musical* (Bloomington: Indiana University Press, 1993); Stephen Neale, *Genre and Hollywood* (London: Psychology Press, 2000); Barry Keith Grant, *Film Genre: From Iconography to Ideology* (London: Wallflower Press, 2007); Geoff King, *Film Comedy* (London: Wallflower Press, 2002).
6. Rick Altman, *Film/Genre* (London: British Film Institute, 1999), 15.
7. Altman, *Film/Genre*, 5.
8. Altman, *Film/Genre*, 5.
9. Altman, *Film/Genre*, 44.
10. Rosi Braidotti, "Transposing Life," in *Clones, Fakes and Posthumans: Cultures of Replication*, eds. Philomena Essed and Gabriele Schwab (Brill 2015), 74.
11. Donna Haraway, "A Cyborg Manifesto: Science, Technology and Socialist-Feminism in the Late Twentieth Century," 1985, in *Manifestly Haraway* (Minneapolis: University of Minnesota Press, 2016), 7.
12. Haraway, "A Cyborg Manifesto," 6.
13. N. Katherine Hayles, *How We Became Posthuman: Virtual Bodies in Cybernetics, Literature, and Informatics* (Chicago: University of Chicago Press, 1999), 2–3.
14. Peter Bradshaw, "*Ingrid Goes West* Review—Social Media Satire Is a Horribly Watchable Carnival of Narcissism," *The Guardian*, November 15, 2017, https://www.theguardian.com/film/2017/nov/15/ingrid-goes-west-review-aubrey-plaza-elizabeth-olsen-instagram.
15. Bradshaw, "*Ingrid Goes West* Review."
16. Lindsay Tjepkema, *Emarsys*, February 5, 2020, https://www.emarsys.com/resources.
17. In fact, the Instagram aesthetic *Ingrid Goes West* caricatures "Is Over" according to a recent article in *The Atlantic*. (Taylor Lorenz, "The Instagram Aesthetic Is Over," *The Atlantic*, April 23, 2019, https://www.theatlantic.com/technology/archive/2019/04/influencers-are-abandoning-instagram-look/587803/).
18. Hayles, *How We Became Posthuman*, 3.
19. Haraway, "A Cyborg Manifesto," 67.
20. Hayles, *How We Became Posthuman*, 3.
21. Haraway, "A Cyborg Manifesto," 5.
22. Eunjung Kim, "Why Do Dolls Die? The Power of Passivity and the Embodied Interplay between Disability and Sex Dolls," *The Review of Education, Pedagogy, and Cultural Studies* 34 (2012): 103.
23. Kim, "Why Do Dolls Die?," 104.

POSTHUMAN AS GENRE 61

24. Hirokazu Kore-eda, quoted in "*Air Doll* Floats Over Un Certain Regard," *Festival de Cannes*, May 14, 2009, https://www.festival-cannes.com/en/75-editions/retrospective/2009/actualites/articles/air-doll-floats-over-un-certain-regard.

25. Haraway, "A Cyborg Manifesto."

26. Donna Haraway, "The Companion Species Manifesto: Dogs, People, and Significant Otherness," 2003, in *Manifestly Haraway* (Minneapolis: University of Minnesota Press, 2016).

27. Donna Haraway, *Staying with the Trouble: Making Kin in the Chthulucene* (Durham, NC: Duke University Press, 2016).

28. Haraway, "The Companion Species Manifesto," 102.

29. Haraway, "The Companion Species Manifesto," 103.

30. Haraway, *Staying with the Trouble*, 3.

31. Ted Chiang, *Stories of Your Life and Others* (London: Picador, 2015).

32. Neil Badmington, *Alien Chic: Posthumanism and the Other Within* (London: Routledge, 2004), 8.

33. National Film Board of Canada, "Experience a Transformed Toronto as Indigenous Futurism Comes to Life," August 23, 2018, https://mediaspace.nfb.ca/comm/experience-a-transformed-toronto-as-indigenous-futurism-comes-to-life-september-18-24-nfbs-biidaaban-first-light-offers-a-stunning-virtual-reality-vision-of-the-citys-futu/.

34. National Film Board of Canada, "Experience a Transformed Toronto."

35. Jennifer Peterson and Graig Uhlin, "In Focus: Film and Media Studies in the Anthropocene," *JCMS: Journal of Cinema and Media Studies* 58, no. 2 (2019): 142–143.

36. Vivian Sobchack, *Screening Space: The American Science Fiction Film* (New York: Ungar, 1987), 305.

37. Michael G. Zey, "Rejuvenation and Radically Increased Health Spans," in *Posthumanism: The Future of Homo Sapiens*, ed. Michael Bess and Diana Walsh Pasulka (Farmington Hills, MI: Macmillan Reference, 2018), 109.

38. Francesca Ferrando, *Philosophical Posthumanism* (London: Bloomsbury Academic, 2019), 27.

39. Nancy D. Campbell, "Pharmaceuticals," in *Posthuman: The Future of Homo Sapiens*, ed. Michael Bess and Diana Walsh Pasulka (Farmington Hills, MI: Macmillan Reference, 2018), 64.

40. Francis Fukuyama, *Our Posthuman Future: Consequences of the Biotechnology Revolution* (New York: Picador, 2002), 7.

41. Fukuyama, *Our Posthuman Future*, 17.

42. Campbell, "Pharmaceuticals," 64.

43. Fukuyama, *Our Posthuman Future*, 41–56.

44. Fukuyama, *Our Posthuman Future*, 52.

45. Fukuyama, *Our Posthuman Future*, 45–46.

46. Barbro Fröding and Walter Osika, *Neuroenhancement: How Mental Training and Meditation Can Promote Epistemic Virtue* (Cham: Springer, 2015), 47.

47. Fukuyama, *Our Posthuman Future*, 56.

62 SCREENING THE POSTHUMAN

48. Linda Williams, "Film Bodies: Gender, Genre, and Excess," *Film Quarterly* 44, no. 4 (1991): 2–13.
49. Jennifer Maher, "Something Else Besides a Father," *Feminist Media Studies* 14, no. 5 (2014): 853–867.
50. Maher, "Something Else," 854.
51. Tamara Jenkins, "How a 'By Any Means Necessary' Quest for a Child Inspired Netflix's *Private Life*," interview by Terry Gross, *Fresh Air*, NPR, October 3, 2018, https://www.npr.org/transcripts/653670395.
52. Tamara Jenkins, quoted in Robert Goldrich, "Tamara Jenkins," *SHOOT* 59, no. 5 (October/November 2018): 20.
53. Ashley Lee, "Tamara Jenkins, *Private Life*," *Back Stage* 59, no. 38 (2018): 8.
54. Lee, "Tamara Jenkins," 8.
55. Kenneth Weisbrode, *On Ambivalence: The Problems and Pleasures of Having It Both Ways* (Cambridge, MA: MIT Press, 2012), 1.
56. Rei Terada, *Looking Away* (Cambridge, MA: Harvard University Press, 2009), 20.
57. Weisbrode, *On Ambivalence*, 1.
58. Williams, "Film Bodies," 4–5.
59. King, *Film Comedy*, 5.
60. Philip Fisher, *The Vehement Passions* (Princeton, NJ: Princeton University Press, 2003).
61. Jennifer Fay and Justus Nieland, *Film Noir: Hard-Boiled Modernity and the Cultures of Globalization* (London: Routledge, 2009), 109.
62. Catherine L. Preston, "The Resurrection of the Romance Film in the 1990s," in *Film Genre 2000: New Critical Essays*, ed. Wheeler W. Dixon (Albany: State University of New York Press, 2000), 227.
63. Jeanine Basinger, *A Woman's View: How Hollywood Spoke to Women, 1930–1960* (Wesleyan University Press, 1995), 8–9.
64. Leger Grindon, *The Hollywood Romantic Comedy: Conventions, History, Controversies* (Hoboken, NJ: John Wiley & Sons, 2011), 30.
65. Richard Gollin, *A Viewer's Guide to Film: Arts, Artifices, and Issues* (New York: McGraw-Hill 1991), 127.
66. Elizabeth A. Wilson, *Affect and Artificial Intelligence* (Seattle: University of Washington Press, 2010), 30.
67. Rosi Braidotti, *The Posthuman* (Cambridge: Polity, 2013), 1.
68. Ed Finn, *What Algorithms Want: Imagination in the Age of Computing* (Cambridge, MA: MIT Press, 2017), 79.
69. Finn, *What Algorithms Want*, 82.
70. Bernard Stiegler, *Technics and Time: The Fault of Epimetheus* (Palo Alto, CA: Stanford University Press, 1998), 141.
71. Sarah Franklin, "Life Itself. Global Nature and the Genetic Imaginary," in *Global Nature, Global Culture*, ed. Sarah Franklin, Celia Lury, and Jackie Stacy (London: SAGE, 2000), 222.
72. Braidotti, "Transposing Life," 61.
73. Braidotti, *The Posthuman*, 105.
74. Hayles, *How We Become Posthuman*, 87.
75. Terada, *Looking Away*, 51.

76. Mark B. N. Hansen, *Feed-Forward: On the Future of Twenty-First-Century Media* (Chicago: University of Chicago Press, 2015), 4.

77. Terada, *Looking Away*, 51, 68.

78. Noël Carroll, *The Philosophy of Horror: Or, Paradoxes of the Heart* (New York: Routledge, 1990).

79. Lauren Berlant, "Poor Eliza," *American Literature* 70, no. 3 (1998): 641.

80. Ed S. Tan, *Emotion and the Structure of Narrative Film: Film as an Emotion Machine* (Mahwah, New Jersey: Erlbaum, 1996).

81. Grant, *Film Genre*, 1.

82. Badmington, "Theorizing Posthumanism," 15.

83. Altman, *Film/Genre*, 5.

84. Altman, *Film/Genre*, 5.

2

Envisioning Posthuman Apocalypse

Missy Molloy

First published in 1965, Susan Sontag's "The Imagination of Disaster" reflects with insight on science fiction "disaster" films released in the mid-twentieth century. Sontag's essay frames these films as a popular and culturally impactful "subgenre"[1] that offers opportunities to "participate in the fantasy of living through one's own death and more, the death of cities, the destruction of humanity itself."[2] Yet while Sontag treats viewers' attractions to such films as profound, her overall assessment of the subgenre is that it lacks "sophistication,"[3] and that the films categorized within it are entirely devoid of "social criticism, of even the most implicit kind":[4] "The interest of [disaster] films, aside from their considerable amount of cinematic charm, consists in this intersection between a naïve and largely debased commercial art product and the most profound dilemmas of the contemporary situation."[5] Sontag's essay resonates with postmillennial cinema broaching "end times." Yet in three crucial respects this century's disaster films are distinct from the subgenre that Sontag theorized. First, in recent cinema, the disaster trope overflows the boundaries of Sci-Fi, ranging, according to film scholar Sarah Keller, "across nearly every cinematic genre—comedy . . . romantic comedy . . . arthouse fare . . . and, predictably, variations on the genre set containing the disaster, Sci-Fi, fantasy, action, and adventure film."[6] Second, whereas the subgenre as Sontag defined it projected anxieties triggered by the Cold War; the threat of nuclear annihilation; the Space Race; and more generally, the technological developments impacting the mid-twentieth century, postmillennial disaster films confront a different set of problems, including those associated with climate change, resource scarcity, the ongoing refugee crisis, and racial injustice, which this chapter details via close analysis of revelatory case studies. Third, a small but significant subset of these recent examples of disaster cinema advances precisely the "sophisticated . . . social criticism" that Sontag found lacking in that earlier cinematic era.

Missy Molloy, *Envisioning Posthuman Apocalypse*. In: *Screening the Posthuman*. Edited by: Missy Molloy, Pansy Duncan, and Claire Henry, Oxford University Press. © Oxford University Press 2023.
DOI: 10.1093/oso/9780197538562.003.0003

ENVISIONING POSTHUMAN APOCALYPSE   65

This chapter focuses on this third subgroup of recent postmillennial disaster movies. It contends that their critical engagements with "the most profound dilemmas of the contemporary [apocalyptic] situation"[7]—a situation that many critics have identified as itself posthuman[8]—make these films inherently congenial to the critical posthumanist project. In advancing this argument about what I will call "critical posthumanist disaster cinema," this chapter takes inspiration from claims by two leading commentators on cinema and/or the posthuman. The first is Evan Calder Williams's contention that a film's interrogation of the deeply embedded social structures that make catastrophe "the imaginary of our time" complements the overall project of critical posthumanism;[9] the second is Neil Badmington's proposition that posthumanism "needs theory, needs theorizing, needs above all to reconsider the untimely celebration of the absolute end of 'Man.'" In other words, posthuman theory needs to consider the Western logics and positionality at the core of a nihilistic view of the future. Both critics provide license for my effort to reframe this particular set of critically engaged, postmillennial disaster movies as a body of films with a naturally posthumanist bent.[10]

In terms of the *kinds* of critical engagements at work in posthuman disaster cinema, I argue that these films

(a) emphasize intersectionality, which Kimberlé Crenshaw, who coined the concept, describes as "a lens, a prism, for seeing the way in which various forms of inequality often operate together and exacerbate each other";[11]

(b) (as per Williams) depict apocalyptic scenarios as ongoing and in an advanced state rather than imminent, thereby challenging the temporality of disaster as "sudden," and are consequently well placed to undermine the "*totalizing* structures" that consistently maintain states of emergency, and express alternative modes of earthly habitation;[12]

(c) are postcolonial and/or anti-neoliberal in that they gesture to the long history of exploitation of people, environments, and resources in the service of material gains for a privileged minority, and oppose anthropocentrism in their imagination of alternative forms of society and existence;

(d) denaturalize the norms of early twenty-first-century life to destabilize conventional assumptions about what counts as ordinary and extraordinary.

66 SCREENING THE POSTHUMAN

Posthuman disaster cinema, I will argue, exposes the interwoven systems of exploitation that perpetually engender catastrophe. Yet distinctions between humanism and posthumanism in the disaster genre are slippery, in part due to the current appeal of apocalyptic storytelling and the spectacle it banks on. For example, the massively hyped, Christopher Nolan-helmed *Tenet* (2020) engages with apocalypse only in a superficial and socially conservative fashion without wasting any of its ample screen time on particulars, e.g., regarding the main character's identity[13] or the sociopolitical causes of the plot's global crisis. The film's total failure to delve into intersectional factors related to race, class, and gender in its animation of apocalyptic-level threats makes it emblematic of the *"inadequate response"* Sontag disparaged.[14] Furthermore, *Tenet* epitomizes Thomas Elsaesser's verdict on high-budget disaster cinema: "Hollywood tends to invoke cosmic disasters in order to distract from the man-made ones."[15] Badmington likewise stresses that contemporary, commercially driven disaster cinema is far more prone to revel in spectacles of mass destruction than produce "social criticism," thereby entrenching status quo hierarchies and confirming "humanism's capacity for regeneration."[16] Thus, posthuman cinema that confronts world-threatening phenomena offers something unique in a crowded field of film and television aiming to capture the drama of catastrophe while shying away from the complexities of the overlapping "global" crises that have rapidly become the defining feature of twenty-first-century life.

The case studies explored below illustrate key features of critically posthuman disaster cinema, including its undermining of anthropocentrism and imagination of alternative forms of society and existence. To begin, I interpret Lars von Trier's *Melancholia* (2011) as an apocalyptic text that offers only a hint of posthumanist critique—a film that ends with literal apocalypse (when rogue planet Melancholia collides with earth and annihilates humanity), but only moves into a posthuman register in its final frame. Concluding that *Melancholia* lacks the intersectional perspective required to succeed as critically posthuman cinema, I explore the overlaps between Indigenous and posthuman perspectives evident in Lisa Jackson's *Biidaaban: First Light* (briefly introduced in Chapter 1) and Lynette Wallworth's *Collisions* (2016). These virtual reality (VR) films pinpoint the origins of cataclysm in the past, and depict their reverberations in the present and future. Moreover, Jackson and Wallworth optimize the formal capacities of VR to challenge Western assumptions about history, development, and time. I then turn to two genre-bending films that utilize the iconography of postmillennial apocalypse to spotlight the influence of racist histories on the present and expose the potential for social and political change: US indie *Fast Color* (Julia Hart, 2018), which overhauls the mechanics of contemporary, big-budget superhero melodrama to enliven a comparatively realistic and intersectional vision of more-than-human power centered on women of color; and Brazilian apocalyptic post-Western *Bacurau* (Kleber Mendonça Filho and Juliano Dornelles, 2019), which creatively repurposes multiple dystopian subgenres to present a searing critique of contemporary Brazil and the neoliberal maneuvers that fuel its corruption.

The final case study, *Take Shelter* (Jeff Nichols, 2011), evinces a distinguishing feature of posthuman disaster cinema—the portrayal of catastrophe as well underway, pervasive, and intrinsic to what has been conventionally represented as normal (rather than in opposition to it). *Take Shelter* taps into "the everyday-nightmare quality"[17] of posthuman experience by alienating its depiction of an "all-American" nuclear family through the second sight of protagonist Curtis (played by Michael Shannon), the father/husband of the family, who perceives catastrophes occurring simultaneously with "normal" life. Posthuman apocalyptic cinema normalizes what would typically be framed as strange and/or unfamiliar, and this reversal offers new vantages on established as well as alternative or overlooked histories. Only by recognizing the past's impact on the present can posthuman apocalyptic cinema, in the words of Keller, "visualiz[e] the world's end . . . [and proffer] hope for new beginnings, though those new beginnings may be wrought out of violent change."[18] According to posthuman disaster cinema, the far-reaching and entrenched dilemmas that threaten humanity are social, environmental, political, and historical, and cannot be credibly represented via world-saving heroics of the conventional variety (as evident in films like *Tenet* that milk drama from widespread destruction without disturbing the ubiquitous social habits that support late capitalism's perennial catastrophe).

The variety of this chapter's case studies drives home both the pervasiveness of the "apocalypse as topic and theme"[19] in twenty-first-century cinema and the need to sift through these films to differentiate posthuman from humanist traces. The latter are glaring in recent commercially oriented disaster films that promote spectacles of mass destruction. Conversely, the films I am identifying as part of the body of *posthumanist* disaster films interrogate "the general contraction and decline of late capitalism into its 'sickly, frantic and permanent state.'"

68   SCREENING THE POSTHUMAN

Diagnosing Posthumanism in *Melancholia*

This chapter takes Badmington's warning about "humanism's capacity for re-generation and, quite literally, recapitulation" to heart, proceeding according to the hypothesis that much of the cinema referred to as apocalyptic or post-apocalyptic stages an "untimely celebration of the absolute end of 'Man'"[20] while paradoxically reaffirming humanism; it does so by threatening, then resolving global-scale catastrophes in ways that shore up fundamentally anthropocentric views of the world. *Melancholia* is exemplary here, embodying the "considerable amount of cinematic charm"[21] wielded by films that dabble with apocalypse, while failing to dislodge humanism's prime position in cinematic storytelling. Despite critics such as Elsaesser interpreting the film as a reflection on humanity's unsustainability,[22] *Melancholia* does not demonstrate much interest in the aspects of human behavior that make its tenancy of earth unsustainable, attending mainly to character and mood and more or less exclusively focused on the peculiarities of a wealthy American/European hybrid family. *Melancholia* is a useful starting point for this chapter because it resonates with two key characteristics of posthuman disaster cinema: it regards apocalypse as well underway and compatible with life under advanced Western capitalism, and it denaturalizes contemporary social norms by inverting "functional" and "dysfunctional" behaviors. However, *Melancholia* also fails to meet this chapter's criteria of critical posthumanism in two regards: it lacks substantial intersectional criticism, and it fails to imagine human existence outside anthropocentrism.

Melancholia sets up a binary between its two sister protagonists to suggest that behaviors considered appropriate for life under contemporary capitalism are fundamentally ill-suited to dealing with global catastrophe. The film's two-part structure implies equitable attention to sisters, Justine (played by Kirsten Dunst) and Claire (played by Charlotte Gainsbourg), with remarkably different outlooks: Justine is chronically depressed, while Claire prides herself on stability and practicality. As the planet Melancholia approaches Earth, the film settles into a polar schema in which Justine's signature depression inspires her to welcome Melancholia's impending collision and Earth's destruction, while Claire's basic satisfaction with life as-is makes her panic, dreading the impending catastrophe. And despite the apparent equity of its two parts, *Melancholia* throws its affective weight behind Justine, presenting her calm acceptance of the world's end as near enlightened, her disdain for Claire's fearful disbelief at the imminent apocalypse obviously shared by the film. Mallika Rao's "The *Melancholia* Postulate," published in *The Atlantic* in May 2020, reflects on the film's relevance to the pandemic present of 2020. Rao describes the Justine/Claire polarity and its significance to the film's conclusion as follows:

> As obliteration is nigh, Justine is the one who is affirmed: Before the apocalypse, her worldview is seen as impractical . . whereas by the story's end, the mindset underpinning her resistance toward "the game" renders her prepared. Claire, who bought too naively into the fiction of life's solidity, is ultimately too rattled by the fact of death to act. As the planet hurtles close, Justine . . . build[s] a makeshift tepee, a "magic cave," to preserve the illusion of safety. Claire, paralyzed with fear, must be led by hand by her younger sister into the abode.[23] (Figure 2.1)

In this light, the film emits something of the ahumanism proclaimed by Patricia MacCormack in *The Ahuman Manifesto: Activism for the End of the Anthropocene*: "I call for an end to the human both conceptually as exceptionalized and actually as a species . . . We humans are simply parts of a thing known as Earth." *Melancholia* can be read as advocating the death of humanism, in its recommendation of Justine's submissive rapture as the appropriate response to that end, and Claire's reaction as best avoided.

With respect to Rao's suggestion that we interpret *Melancholia*'s Justine/Claire juxtaposition as a pedagogical lesson on best calamity practice, I urge greater skepticism regarding the film's address of "real" off-screen catastrophe.

Figure 2.1 *Melancholia*'s enigmatic, pre-apocalyptic tableau (Lars Von Trier, 2011).

70 SCREENING THE POSTHUMAN

The film dramatizes a privileged, European and extravagantly fatalistic view of humanity's end, which might more productively be interpreted as the filmmaker's elaborate send-off of an exclusive brand of humanism that is far from global. Justine's pivotal line of dialogue, one frequently cited in writing on the film—"The Earth is evil. We don't need to grieve for it"—adequately conveys the imprecision of *Melancholia*'s apocalypticism. Justine's reiteration, "All I know is, life on Earth is evil," underscores the broad, vague rationale behind the film's apocalyptic embrace. *Earth* is "evil" and is therefore disposable; it alone is pronounced worthy of annihilation. The film is not explicitly "critical" in its repudiation of humanity in a manner that would qualify as posthuman. Neither Justine nor the film gets specific about humanity's unsustainability or contribution to the horror of "life on Earth." It is therefore unsurprising that scholars have mainly interpreted the film's cataclysmic ending as an allegory (often in some relation to psychoanalytic theories on melancholia[24]), but without reaching consensus on the film's apocalyptic position. Von Trier's reputation for provocation explains, in part, this phenomenon wherein his nihilistic portrait of the world's end is catnip for multiple philosophical debates. In this context, Badmington's exhortation seems appropriate: "What Jacques Derrida calls the 'apocalyptic tone' should be toned down a little, for, as Nietzsche once pointed out, it is remarkably difficult to cut off the human(ist) head through which we (continue to) 'behold all things.'"[25] With Badmington's suggestion in mind, *Melancholia* appears, quite simply, to be an anthropocentric film that flirts with posthumanism without consummation; it suggests that if a certain kind of human existence ends, then so must the film.[26]

So does *Melancholia* represent a posthuman, humanist, anti-human ("ahuman") or posthumanist view of apocalypse? It variously suggests *all* of these, although not consistently or equitably. While in some respects *Melancholia* portrays a posthuman view of apocalypse via Earth's total destruction upon collision with the planet Melancholia, it is nonetheless enamored of a certain type of human—white, wealthy, possessing an American-inflected European sensibility, chronically depressed and fatalistic. That said, aspects of the film indicate *Melancholia*'s interest in deconstructing the human, which is the "principal objective" of posthumanism according to Francesca Ferrando and many others. Justine's melancholia, and her eagerness for Melancholia to put human experience out of its misery, undermines humanism via her anti-human view, while the "human" desperation to survive is pejoratively animated by Claire's panicked fumbling through the final hours. What the film conclusively demonstrates is the complexity of distinguishing posthumanism and humanism in post-apocalyptic cinema. It also underscores that posthuman takes on disaster are not invested in saving humankind without deconstructing it. Whether a film presents the human as worth saving and on what grounds is key to carving out the exceptional space of posthuman apocalypse, especially given that most postmillennial disaster films center on preserving humanity at all costs (e.g., *Children of Men, Tenet,* and *Train to Busan*) without seriously critiquing the human behaviors and histories that fuel large-scale catastrophes.

The film's complex posthuman status is most clearly conveyed in the ambiguity of its penultimate tableau: Justine, Claire, and Claire's son Leo await the nigh apocalypse (Figure 2.1). All the writing on *Melancholia* I have surveyed has commented on this vivid image, proffering earnest yet inconclusive readings of its meaning. Elena del Río's analysis of *Melancholia*'s final moments epitomizes these qualities:

> The strength of the manor walls, echoing centuries of human posturing, has been abandoned as futile. In its place, the fragility of a makeshift teepee provides incalculable protection: evocative of indigenous lifestyles that capitalism eradicated in its wake,[45] the teepee is an image of groundlessness and freedom, the sign of life as timeless immanence in the here and now, and of the affect that glues all things together and stirs the universe into action. The final image of the teepee, with its three occupants tightly holding hands against the backdrop of the planet bearing down on them, exactly captures the vertigo of immanence that is life at any and all times: finding protection only in itself, perpetually dancing on a razor's edge.[27]

In Chapter 1, we pinpointed "a striking ambivalence, an oscillation between fear and desire, excitement and anxiety" as a defining characteristic of the posthuman on-screen. *Melancholia*'s pre-apocalyptic tableau certainly transmits this ambivalence, yet I am struck by the haziness of the teepee reference, both iconographically in this pivotal moment of the film and in critical writing on *Melancholia*.

As noted before, writing on the film rarely neglects to mention this image, and specifically the teepee, but none comment on the teepee's significance beyond its function as a sort of "magical" symbol. This omission is extremely telling regarding the latitude granted art cinema, which scholarship often reinforces; sanctified by the gatekeepers of film culture, auteurs like von

72 SCREENING THE POSTHUMAN

Trier are granted near free rein to exploit historical symbols as if for aesthetic impact alone, in service of "high art." Del Río's statement, that the teepee is "evocative of indigenous lifestyles that capitalism eradicated in its wake," is rare in its connection of Indigeneity to the image, yet the insight is immediately undercut by the subsequent description of the teepee as "an image of groundlessness and freedom."[28] While Rao refers to the teepee as a "magic cave," in quotes and without reference, del Río attributes the phrase "magic cave" to Steven Shaviro's interpretation of the teepee, as representing a "return to the Womb of Mother Nature."[29]

How might an Indigenous viewer respond to this image? (Figure 2.1) *Melancholia* and scholarship on it clearly (and unfortunately) regard that question as beside the point. A "teepee" (also written "tipi" or "tepee") is in fact a misleading synecdoche of pre- and postcolonial Indigenous American cultures. The word originally referred to structures traditionally used by several nomadic tribes Indigenous to North America, but the teepee subsequently evolved into a symbol Western culture mistakenly and vaguely associates with all tribes and lifestyles Indigenous to North America.[30] Cynthia (Ištá Thó Thó) Coleman Emery's blog, "Indians: We're All the Same," tersely advises, "next time you see an image of a teepee or drawing of kokopelli, remember they are often chosen to represent all Indians. But they don't."[31] *Melancholia*'s vague, aesthetic appropriation of the teepee is symptomatic of the way the film more generally fails to provide the intersectional and/or postcolonial insights required for it to properly critique the foundations of humanism or "life on earth." Film scholarship should be critical of the use of symbols with charged historical significance, even if (and perhaps especially if) their functions appear to be mainly aesthetic. In this case, the scholarly interpretations inspired by *Melancholia*'s teepee blatantly feed on fantasies of Indigeneity that are historical effects of European colonialism, yet the interpretations are not presented as such.

Melancholia provides an apt cinematic illustration of literally posthuman apocalypse in its conclusion on Earth's annihilation (humanity along with it). That said, it also melancholically exalts aspects of humanism that it designates worthy of mourning. Therefore, in regard to *Melancholia*'s provocations, I emphasize that posthuman apocalypse underscores the need to displace humanity as central to existence, and to reframe and define it in relation to other forms of life. And while *Melancholia*'s ending anticipates a posthuman future, it barely sketches it; only the final second of the film is decisively posthuman. In most respects, the elegiac film functions like a treatise on the eccentricities of a particular class of human from the idiosyncratic perspective of a revered European art cinema director, who emphasizes, in particular, humanity's self-destructive tendencies; its desperation to survive despite a predilection for suffering; and its difficulty fully recognizing non-anthropocentric experience (and these qualities reflect the distinctly European and highbrow associations that characterize von Trier's recent films, including *Melancholia*, according to Linda Badley[32]). The film's conclusion implies inevitability; the story must end since humankind is no more. In *Film Quarterly*'s "Lars von Trier's 'Melancholia': A Discussion," Rob White states, " 'the old world must go.' All of it. This is what von Trier quite literally depicts."[33] White's conclusion seems as convincing a statement on *Melancholia*'s apocalyptic message as any other in print, yet what precisely is the "old world" that *Melancholia* decimates? Graced by provocative images, this ambivalent film responds to the hunger for profound engagement with catastrophe but without delivering much beyond a hint of human critique, indulging in enigmatic iconography (most notably the teepee) without following through on the disclosure of human behaviors or histories that make "life on Earth" both "evil" and not worth missing.

"We've Already Survived an Apocalypse"

Indigenous and postcolonial disaster films share with critical posthumanism a commitment to tackling catastrophe not as a foreign threat on the horizon, but as already initiated and long-occurring. In these films, only perpetuating (rather than initiating) crisis is depicted in present or near-future set films that aspire to realism in a basic sense. An August 14, 2020 headline in *The New York Times* reads, " 'We've Already Survived an Apocalypse': Indigenous Writers are Changing Sci-Fi."[34] The quotation in the article's title, attributed to Métis novelist and activist Cherie Dimaline, succinctly articulates the special orientation to apocalypse apparent in works that represent Indigenous perspectives, including Jackson's *Biidaaban: First Light* and Wallworth's *Collisions*. In "Feminist Posthumanities: An Introduction," Cecilia Åsberg and Braidotti speak to the context these films engage: "Despite the somewhat bipolar reports—either utopian or dystopian, technophobic or technophilic—we dream, live and enliven already the posthuman condition. Now we need more than ever the story telling practices accountable for its politics."[35] In other words, the "sickly frantic state"[36] of late capitalism's

74 SCREENING THE POSTHUMAN

decline, which magnetizes postmillennial viewers to disaster on-screen, needs "more than ever" the antidotes of Indigenous and postcolonial storytelling to inspire "hope for new beginnings . . . wrought out of violent change."[37] *Biidaaban: First Light* is one answer to this need, evoking an explicitly Indigenous experience of post-apocalyptic Toronto, while *Collisions* enlivens an apocalyptic event, a 1950s nuclear test in Western Australia experienced by an Aboriginal boy as his first exposure to "Western" culture. These transtemporal VR films spatially link historical catastrophes and human experiences in the present that are intimately wedded to possible futures.

Expanding on Chapter 1's analysis of *Biidaaban: First Light* as an example of posthuman perspectives on space and time, this chapter uses the VR film to highlight the affinities between critical posthuman cinema and Indigenous Futurism. Inspired by Afrofuturism, Grace Dillon, a professor of Indigenous Nations Studies, coined the term "Indigenous Futurism"[38] to describe narratives that "us[e] the images, ideology, and themes in science fiction to envision a future from a Native (Indigenous) perspective,"[39] thereby "renew[ing], recover[ing], and extend[ing] First Nations peoples' voices and traditions."[40] Indigenous Futurism is therefore compatible with posthuman disaster cinema in that both are invested in envisioning futures that oppose Western humanism and its corollaries: racism and colonialism. Furthermore, Indigenous Futurism seeks to name and denaturalize colonial logics and their material impacts, an aim allied with my account of posthuman disaster cinema as recognizing the long, colonial, and capitalist history of contemporary crises.

Science Fiction novelist Rebecca Roanhorse emphasizes Indigenous Futurism's postcolonial connotations while commenting on its creative impact: it "encourages Indigenous authors and creators to speak back to the colonialism tropes so prevalent in science fiction by reimagining space exploration from a non-colonial perspective and reclaiming our place in an imagined future in space, on earth, and everywhere in between." *Biidaaban: First Light*'s Indigenous Futurist intervention is foregrounded by its title: Jackson notes that in addition to the literal meaning of "Biidaaban" ("the first light just before dawn"), the "three parts of the word" also imply "the past and the future colliding to create the present moment."[41] For Jackson, the title *Biidaaban: First Light* reflects the "rising tide of Indigenous Futurism," which "looks to break through the tendency to stereotype everything Indigenous as stuck in the past."[42] Indeed, the catastrophes *Biidaaban: First Light* imagines are multipronged: the apocalypse "already survived" by First Nations people who persisted despite the colonial settlement of Canada, and the collapse of settler-capitalist society in Canada apparent in the near-future, near-deserted Toronto that *Biidaaban: First Light* guides users through. The short VR film embraces a wide time frame, the question it delivers via voiceover (spoken in Anishinaabemowin and translated to English via subtitle) pointedly enigmatic: "Where did the creator put your people?" Who does "your" address, and what is *Biidaaban: First Light*'s animation of a future, nature-reclaimed Toronto meant to evoke? A Canadian Broadcasting Corporation (CBC) interview with Jackson clarifies the filmmaker's aims, as well as the Indigenous Futurism *Biidaaban: First Light* advances. "The heart of" the VR experience, according to Jackson, is "the imagining of a future Toronto where all the elements of nature have . . . come back in."[43] *Biidaaban: First Light* takes full advantage of "the lure of . . . starting all over again,"[44] which Sontag identifies as key to disaster cinema's appeal, by provocatively employing VR's special capacities to make users "occup[iers]" of an alternative, posthuman Toronto that invites a comprehensive experiential reset of how the city is inhabited.

The most identifiable location transposed via the VR experience is Nathan Philips Square, which Jackson calls "the center of systems of governance" (Figure 2.2), ostensibly in the context of Canada. Jackson zeroes in on the Square as the convergence of intimately related phenomena: Western

Figure 2.2 *Biidaaban: First Light* (Lisa Jackson, 2018) represents Toronto's iconic Nathan Philips Square to provoke questions about modern Canada's systems of governance.

notions of urban development; commerce (definitely central to the Square's present configuration); and the history of colonial governance, which Old City Hall, the lone classical and most striking building in the Square's skyline, best represents. Old City Hall's evolution resembles a condensed version of Canada's colonial development: its late 1800s construction was a testament to the success of Canada as a national project; it was the seat of Toronto's city council until the mid-1900s; later, under threat of demolition via pressure to "modernize" in the 1960s, public sentiment saved the building; and finally, it currently functions as a temporary courthouse, though its future use—as either retail space or a museum devoted to the city's history—is a topic of city council debate in 2020.[45] *Biidaaban: First Light* visualizes an alternative version of the iconic Square; Jackson's goal in doing so is to inspire viewers to question the related systems the Square represents as well as their perceived invincibility.

Considering Williams's definition of apocalypse as "an end with revelation,"[46] Jackson's decision to imagine apocalypse in the heart of urban Toronto underscores the continuity of Indigenous presence in the space Toronto city occupies. In the CBC interview, Jackson stresses that approximately 50% of First Nations people live in cities, which are "full of vibrant Indigenous culture," yet are rarely characterized as Indigenous. In *Biidaaban: First Light*'s Toronto, only a single human figure appears (Figure 2.3). As users move their heads to pan the rooftop overlooking Nathan Philips Square, a dark-haired

Figure 2.3 Only a dark-haired woman appears in *Biidaaban*'s near-desolate Nathan Philips Square.

woman is visible, often appearing to look away from and/or beyond the frame. She seems to be the only human inhabiting the rooftop, and at one point, users glimpse her seated inside a structure resembling a traditional Anishinaabe wiigwaam/wigwam (Figure 2.4). As this elusive human figure indicates, *Biidaanban: First Light* bypasses conventional protagonists in favor of an ambiguous, opaque subjectivity. Charlotte Epstein evokes Harawayan theory to speculate upon a postcolonial perspective that counters the "universalism and relativism" central to Western colonial points of view: "The unmarked position—the ultimate place of power—is that of Man and White. Against this, then, only 'partial perspective promises objective vision' (Haraway 1988, 583)."[47] I interpret the rooftop woman's obscure function as an overt challenge, on gender and racial grounds, to universalizing Western colonial perspectives via an alternative model of occupation, which she alongside the wiigwaam characterize as feminine and Indigenous. In contrast to *Melancholia*, where the empty symbol of the teepee is destroyed alongside everything else on earth, *Biidaaban: First Light* depicts the woman and the wiigwaam as key to its vision of future urban life.

The spoken languages in *Biidaaban: First Light* are also part of its reclamation of Toronto's urban environment. Regarding the language choices, Jackson emphasizes that three Indigenous languages—Wendat, Anishinaabemowin, and Mohawk—were traditionally spoken in the space

Figure 2.4 The post-apocalyptic woman's rooftop dwelling resembles the wiigwaam/wigwam of the Anishinaabe.

78   SCREENING THE POSTHUMAN

contemporary Toronto currently occupies; thus those languages, in her view, can best express the philosophies that underpin this location. Jackson's choice to center the Indigenous languages of the place and denaturalize English exemplifies critical posthuman disaster cinema's commitment to undoing Western colonial humanism. Prioritizing the landscape's pre-colonial languages urges the user to consider the pre-colonial Indigenous inhabitants of the area and reckon with Toronto's colonial settlement as a cause of the apocalyptic future the film presents. Moreover, by casting the Indigenous languages deemed "redundant" by racist colonial and neo-capitalist logics as the primary tongues of the post-apocalypse, *Biibaaban: First Light* also frames Indigenous perspectives as central to future survival. This interpretation of *Biibaaban: First Light*'s multiple temporalities aligns with scholar artist (and Dillion's daughter) Elizabeth LaPensée's understanding of Indigenous Futurism: "Indigenous Futurisms recognize space–time as simultaneously past, present, and future, and therefore futurism is as much about the future as it is about right now. In my work, it means telling alternate histories, dreaming about liquid technology, imagining a future where unceded territories are taken back."[48] In the same vein, Jackson uses language to firmly claim that the land Toronto occupies was, is, and will be an Indigenous place.

In accordance with this chapter's argument that posthuman disaster cinema showcases postcolonial and Indigenous stances on apocalypse, *Biidaaban*'s perspective of Earth directly opposes the "earth is evil" attitude *Melancholia* transmits. Overlapping Indigenous voices speak the following to accompany an extreme long shot of the cityscape: "We give thanks and acknowledge her, our mother the Earth that supports our feet. All our minds are one." The pronoun referents are non-specific; while excluding the audio to Indigenous languages might suggest that "our" refers to only Indigenous people, including English via translation allows monolingual English speakers access to the experience, though perhaps secondarily and as guests in this future Toronto's virtual space. In other words, users might imagine "all our minds are one," but only through the mediation of languages displaced by settler colonialism and images evoking ideologies associated with Indigenous Futurism. *Biidaaban: First Light* demonstrates that posthuman disaster films expose the complex historical phenomena that incite catastrophes rather than present narrative conflicts that can be resolved via conventional structures of cinematic drama.

Like *Biidaaban: First Light*, *Collisions* illustrates the "simultaneously past, present, and future . . . space-time" LaPensée identifies as Indigenous

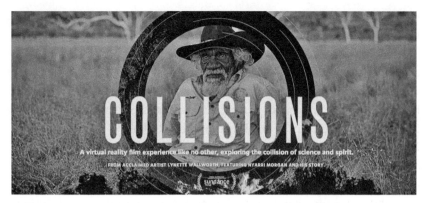

Figure 2.5 Lynette Wallworth's *Collisions* (2016) centers on Nyarri Nyarri Morgan's view of Western culture.

Futurist.[49] *Collisions* also reverses standard conventions of colonial storytelling by portraying Western culture as "strange and unfamiliar" and centering the POV of an Aboriginal man, Nyarri Nyarri Morgan, who "lived his early life with no contact with western culture until he witnessed an atomic test held by the British government in the South Australian desert" (Figure 2.5).[50] The title of *Collisions* refers to powerful convergences of conflicting forces: the Martu way of life in which Morgan was immersed as a child and "western" culture, epitomized by the atomic blast; "one of the oldest cultures in the world" (Wallworth's words) and western technology; and finally, as stated on the film's promotional poster, "science and spirit." The VR film opens with Morgan welcoming users to the Pilbara Desert in Western Australian, where many Martu people currently live and the site of the British atomic blast that Morgan witnessed as a child "without context" (a point emphasized by the filmmakers during *Collisions'* promotion). From Morgan's perspective, his witness of the then-mysterious 1950s explosion and recent activism against uranium mining (approved by the Australian federal government, but rejected by the Martu people, the traditional occupants of the Western Desert[51]) is continuous. *Collisions'* simple structure honors Morgan's perspective by depicting the mindboggling explosion as adjacent to Nyarri's experiences in the present, as a Martu elder and artist still inhabiting that same place and actively promoting traditional methods of maintaining it over imported practices uninformed by knowledge derived from long-term experience. The Indigenous Futurist "space time" of *Collision*'s VR design facilitates users' understanding of Morgan's past and present as tightly

80　SCREENING THE POSTHUMAN

woven; users thus move from the atomic explosion to the current day as if from one room to another.

Reviews of the film have tended to highlight its effective use of VR to create an arresting cinematic experience. Luke Buckmaster's review (for *The Guardian*) calls *Collisions* "a milestone VR production . . . the first in history to tell an Indigenous Australian story" and particularly praises the first-person experience accomplished in the VR film's pivotal animation of Morgan witnessing the blast: "I look up in awe and horror. I can almost see a figure of something otherworldly—a kind of mythical monster or spirit god—emerge from the smoky formation."[52] Lisa Dethridge's enthusiastic review of the "VR film experience" also celebrates its effective use of cutting-edge technology to evoke disaster, specifically "360 degree panoramic photography combined with computer animation, and an ultra-dynamic soundscape."[53] In my view, *Collisions'* potency lies less in the film's utility of "cutting-edge technology" and more in its animation of the history of nuclear testing in Western Australia, which allows viewers to imagine it from Morgan's Indigenous perspective.

Like *Biidaaban: First Light*, *Collisions* demonstrates Indigenous Futurism's interest in harnessing technology to "renew, recover, and extend First Nations peoples' voices and traditions."[54] Morgan and Wallworth frame VR cinema as a tool that, due to their fortuitous meeting, allowed them to effectively transmit Morgan's message of careful (Martu) stewardship of the environment as preservation for its future residents.'[55] In 2016, Wallworth and Morgan discussed *Collisions* in a conversation coordinated by the Australian Centre for the Moving Image and titled "Virtual Reality, History and Indigenous Experience." The unorthodox unfolding of their conversation illuminates Morgan's senses of time and art, as well as his and Wallworth's activist goals in recreating his historical experience for targeted audiences around the globe. "The camera has 16 eyes," Morgan remarked upon introduction to the "device made up of 16 Go-Pros,"[56] and "four ears," added Wallworth.

Epstein's view of "postcolonial perspective" sheds light on *Collisions'* animation of its very specific local context:

> The challenge becomes how to mobilize the particular and the local, in their infinite richness, as sites for deploying a form of theorizing that, by way of this grounding, seeks to avert the pitfalls of a universalization that was a key historical driver of colonization in the first place . . . Foregrounding,

and mining, the particular, without already collapsing it back (yet again) onto the universal, constitutes an important epistemological commitment in deploying postcolonial perspectives.[57]

As Wallworth stresses, "The camera allows you to feel like you're in [Nyarri's] home."[58] Thus, advanced audiovisual technologies enabled the filmmakers to deliver the "epistemological commitment" Epstein presents as crucial to instrumentalizing "postcolonial perspective" for political ends. Morgan and Wallworth consistently emphasize, through the VR film and their actions to promote it, that the invitation into Nyarri's home that *Collisions* offers is in service of ambitious political goals related both to contested Indigenous land rights in Australia and ongoing international debates about nuclear testing. The film's premiere at the World Economic Forum in Davos in 2016 exemplifies how the filmmakers used VR's currency to achieve political goals. Reports of the conference indicate that the film was promoted to conference attendees as an example of cutting-edge cinema technology.[59] However, the film's intimate insight into Morgan's experience, combined with his in-person appearance after audiences removed their VR sets, redirected the focus onto the film's political themes rather than the technology of its production.[60] *Collisions* then went on to screen "in a film series on nuclear disarmament hosted by the United Nations Office for Disarmament Affairs."[61] The film exemplifies posthuman disaster cinema's explicit opposition to the colonial and neoliberal exploitation of people, environments, and resources that gives rise to catastrophe, such as the extraordinary blast Morgan witnessed, which the Australian government considered "routine."

Wallworth and Morgan end *Collisions* on an aerial view of the controlled burning the Martu practice and advocate in order to reinforce *Collisions'* thesis on stewardship and preservation (and time) (Figure 2.6). The ending recalls the beginning via an intentional blaze, yet the burning in this case prioritizes the land and its habitation far into the future. According to Buckmaster, "*Collisions* concludes spectacularly. From high in the air, we watch Morgan perform 'mosaic burning,' creating huge rings of fire that blaze across the desert."[62] Buckmaster frames this ending as adhering to "the well-worn movie mantra that one ought to save the best for last."[63] I regard this interpretation as mistaken. *Collisions* does not end on "mosaic burning" to conform to Western notions of cinematic storytelling, which "save[s] the best for last"; rather, its ending reinforces its function as revisionary history.

Figure 2.6 The end of *Collisions* (Lynette Wallworth, 2016) exposes viewers to custodial burning as advocated and practiced by the Martu people.

Ken Eastwood's *Australian Geographic* article "Living the traditional Aboriginal life" features both Morgan[64] and his grandson, Curtis Taylor (an activist filmmaker who contributed to *Collisions*' promotion). Morgan and Taylor's statements on the strategic burning practiced by contemporary Martu emphasize that "if a fire did get out of control, it could have terrible consequences."[65] According to Uday Singh Mehta, "the confrontation with the 'strange and the unfamiliar' of the new peoples that the Empire was bringing under its rule was one of elision and active erasure . . . It was a necessary precondition to being able to uphold and spread the liberal ideal of the rational individual as a universalizable model, and the necessary founding stone of modern democratic rule *anywhere*."[66] *Collisions* rejects the "active erasure" of the Martu people through its VR rendition of the British nuclear test from Morgan's perspective. In 2014, Robin Matthews spoke to a *BBC* journalist about the Maralinga nuclear test site: "They [the British government abetted by the Australian] thought they'd pick a supposedly uninhabited spot out in the Australian desert. Only they got it wrong. There were people here."[67] Through *Collisions*, the viewer becomes one of the people erased by Australia's colonial history, and the nuclear test is reframed according to a Martu perspective.

The conclusion of *Collisions*—as well as the film as a whole—undermines this "universalizable model" to express Morgan's deceptively simple

mantra: "Look after the land and think about the ones who are following."
According to Wallworth, through *Collisions*, "Nyarri is inspiring other people
who now want to tell their stories . . . [Indigenous activists] in the Amazon
want to use the same technology to send their stories out . . . [the] same thing
has happened in Mongolia. He's inspiring a whole chorus of voices to tell
hidden histories."[68] *Collisions* is post-apocalyptic but imagines far beyond
the disasters of the current and most recent centuries, "proffering hope for
new beginnings" by enlivening ways of inhabiting the Pilbara with much
longer histories than those represented by the nuclear blast Morgan unwit-
tingly encountered. Bracketed by fire, *Collisions* "mobilize[s] the particular
and the local, in their infinite richness" to render the custodial practices
promoted by Western culture and Australian colonial governance "strange
and . . . unfamiliar," and to advance an alternative model of stewardship tai-
lored to a radically different, vaster time scale. Like *Biidaaban: First Light*, it
epitomizes a posthuman representation of disaster by highlighting that the
formidable challenges facing humanity at present have long historical roots
and require radical shifts in perspective to be effectively met.

Race, Gender, and Posthuman Near Futures

A brazenly indie take on the contemporary superhero film, *Fast Color*
opens with a blank screen, while a woman's voice states with dire certainty,
"The world's gonna die. I can feel it coming." Her calm, fatalistic commentary continues over a montage of still shots (Figure 2.7) illustrating a deso-
late and rundown rural United States, which the woman's narration renders
both pre- and post-apocalyptic: "We knew this would happen, that sooner
or later man's reckless behavior would catch up with us. Eight years since the
last drop of rain, and no one knows what to do except raise the price of water.
The wells dried up. We can't grow our own food anymore. And it's harder for
us to stay in hiding." After quickly establishing several related enigmas—who
is included in the voiceover's "we," why do they need to remain hidden, and
from whom?—the narrator doubles down on the opening narration's hook
by declaring that she perpetually thinks about Ruth (soon revealed as the
film's protagonist): "How does she survive out there on her own as broken as
she is?"

The film epitomizes the special dynamic of posthuman disaster cinema's
engagement with realism: it presents imagery taken from, or closely

84 SCREENING THE POSTHUMAN

Figure 2.7 *Fast Color*'s (Julia Hart, 2018) opening montage provides a nonexceptional view common in rural New Mexico, where the film was shot on location in 2017. On-location shots like these establish the film's dystopian setting, which is recognizable as a present-day United States that bears the scars of ongoing twenty-first-century catastrophes.

resembling, off-screen realities, incorporating exceptional elements only to inspire critical reflection on humanity's manner of earthly habitation, that is, its habits that have been normalized. In other words, it makes "normal" life appear strange while denaturalizing extraordinary phenomena. Jen Yamato's *Fast Color* review (for the *Los Angeles Times*) describes its setting as "an unforgiving dystopian American West."[69] Yet the footage—including the initial montage of establishing shots that begins with an arid field of withered crops followed by an extreme long shot of an abandoned roadside restaurant

(Figure 2.7)—was clearly taken on-site, the film shot on location in 2017 mainly in New Mexico. In this case, viewers, especially those concerned about climate change and/or well-versed in the discourse of the Anthropocene, can accept with relative ease the possibility of a severe drought in the near future that threatens human survival and intensifies the desperate fight over material resources already stoked by global capitalism.

Fast Color's premise thus blends a not unlikely near-future socioeconomic and environmental context with the fantastic scenario of a matrilineal family of Black American women endowed with supernatural powers. The plot handles three generations of these women: Bo (the voiceover narrator at the film's start, played by Lorraine Toussaint), who has the ability to disassemble and then reintegrate objects and to subsequently discern amazing flashes of color; her daughter, Ruth (played by Gugu Mbatha-Raw), the protagonist, who is blessed and cursed with the most extreme powers, which initially manifest as earthquake-triggering seizures; and Ruth's daughter, Lila (played by Saniyya Sidney), who is raised by Bo and possesses her same ability to break down and reassemble objects, and to perceive fantastic colors in the wake of transfiguration. The women's extraordinary powers intensify otherwise realistic challenges they face in the struggle to survive in far from ideal conditions, which are stimulated by social and political dysfunctions far beyond their control. Their positions regarding dominant social and political authorities are fleshed out by the main plot thread, in which the long-absent Ruth retreats to the family's rural compound to evade the scientist and police officer pursuing her to exploit her paranormal abilities.

How does *Fast Color* compare to other dystopian texts recently applauded for creatively engaging racial and political conflicts that have come to a head in contemporary US culture? During 2020, the HBO superhero drama *Watchmen* (a high-budget limited series) succeeded *Contagion* as the most mass media-hyped example of a causal relationship between dystopian fiction and a world in the process of "falling apart," as Black Lives Matter protests swept the United States and beyond while COVID continued to spread.[70] Yet popular culture's celebration of *Watchmen* deviated from the discourse surrounding *Contagion* in its emphasis on *Watchmen* as "prophetic," especially in its depiction of escalating and violent racial confrontations that threaten "law and order." One article's title—"*Watchmen*'s Regina King on HBO Drama's Prophetic Power in a COVID-19 and Police Brutality-Scarred America"[71]—gestures to a widespread sensibility that gradually crystallized in a trauma-filled year: that in order for screen fiction to adequately tackle the complex web of troubles currently propelling humanity toward destructive and potentially transformative change, it must be intersectional in its representation of crisis. "Prophetic" fiction is expected to feature a convergence of elements that precipitate catastrophe, to justify its recognition as standing out from the crowded pack of contemporary storytelling immersed in cataclysm. It should also register the fact that catastrophe more severely impacts those socially disadvantaged as a result of race, class, gender and location in a hyper-capitalist transnational context. Pundits particularly homed in on *Watchmen*'s eye-catching aesthetic to pinpoint its cultural resonance—especially its visualization of elaborately masked undercover police led by woman of color protagonist (played by King) and engaged in guerrilla warfare against a vigilante-style white supremacist group (Figure 2.8).

The contrasting aesthetics apparent in even a superficial comparison of *Watchmen* and *Fast Color* illuminate a crucial facet of a specifically *posthuman* disaster cinema: it reserves spectacle for measured animation of extraordinary events, which feature as sudden and striking embellishments of otherwise naturalistic (or even somewhat ordinary) diegetic worlds. Richard Brody's review of *Fast Color* (published in *The New Yorker* and subtitled "A Superhero Movie That Pays Close Attention to Ordinary Life") claims, "'Fast Color' is a superhero movie unlike any that I've seen from a major studio, in that the characters seem to have their feet on the actual ground rather than on

Figure 2.8 In HBO's *Watchmen* (2020), undercover and elaborately masked police fight a white supremacist vigilante group in Tulsa, Oklahoma.

a set."[72] As evident in the still shot of the abandoned Road Runner's Retreat (Figure 2.7), *Fast Color*'s setting is indistinguishable from the present-day United States, which bears the visible scars of multiple twenty-first-century socioeconomic and environmental crises, making it perfectly suited to dystopia.[73] I argue that *Fast Color*'s muted and quotidian mise-en-scène, carried through in its set design, costumes, and performances, enables a different form of social critique than does *Watchmen*'s flamboyance, despite these texts' shared evocation of a dystopian United States mired in unending catastrophe with racist historical origins.

Conceived in relation to video games, TreaAndrea Russworm's theory of "critical racial dystopia" applies remarkably well to *Fast Color* and its presentation of Ruth, who evades scientific and institutional forces that aim to misuse her powers in support of "man's reckless behavior" (which cultivated the dystopian conditions in the first place). "Critical racial dystopia" helps to highlight posthuman cinema's capacity to expose the racist core of "bleak social and political times,"[74] which are, in large part, effects of economic and social inequalities entrenched during the colonial period and maintained in late-stage capitalism.

> For a dystopian video game to function critically around matters of identity and race, then, we should expect to see a presentation of character agency that is not only rooted in "difference and multiplicity" but also skillfully and carefully connected to a broader project, an "alliance politics," that self-reflexively and implicitly critiques the present system of social and political organization through its construction of a dark future or alternate reality.[75]

Ruth's (super)heroic journey is to convert a "dark" reality of pursuit by malevolent forces that would exploit her to a more productive scenario wherein she harnesses her considerable abilities to overcome the allied forces of science and law, and is therefore able to apply her skills to advance the interests of herself and those like her (rather than merely protect herself from exploitation by corrupt authority figures). According to director and co-writer Julia Hart, "Most superhero movies are about men destroying things to save them . . . When Jordan [Howorwitz, co-writer and producer of *Fast Color*] and I decided we wanted to tell a movie about women with superpowers, we decided that their powers absolutely could not be destructive, [and] that their powers should be creative."[76] Hart's generalization about "superhero movies" applies to contemporary disaster cinema as well. Brody recognizes

88 SCREENING THE POSTHUMAN

the significance of Hart's creative choices in his evaluation of *Fast Color* as "the rare superhero film that proceeds without a devotion to the spectacular" and instead pays "close attention to ordinary life."[77]

Fast Color's treatment of the women's superpowers clarifies their critical function in the film's social critique, which demonstrates posthuman disaster cinema's commitment to shedding light on the causes of systemic crisis. After her return home, Bo and Ruth offer Lily an abridged and sanitized version of Ruth's traumatic initiation into her "different" form of power, which Bo wasn't able to guide or control. Bo's efforts to manage Ruth's unwieldy strength took punitive form, an image of her tying child Ruth to a bed hinting at the past suffering of both women, which led Ruth to run away from home and take drugs (to ward off the seizures provoked by her stifled capacity). The sequence in which Lily demonstrates her powers for Ruth begins with an unremarkable, low-key shot of the three characters seated around the dining room table in their modestly decorated, lived-in home (Figure 2.9). The camera then tracks left to reframe with an emphasis on Ruth's reaction to her daughter's reconstitution of the bowl (Figure 2.9). The subsequent dialogue underscores generational distinctions regarding the ability to perceive "fast color" passed down matrilineally: Bo has become dispassionate about the colors, which she has seen "for 52 years," while Ruth, invested with a wholly different form of their genetically transmitted strength, "has never seen them." It is therefore left to Lily, still transfixed by the colors, to explain their perception to Ruth: "After you put back together whatever it is you took apart, everyone sees this object. But you see the colors. It's like an aftereffect . . . an echo. Suddenly there are all these colors moving over everything fast, like a race . . . Bo says if you do something *really* big, the colors can last a long time." Interpreted in relation to Russworm's "alliance politics," the three generations of women might challenge "the present system of social and political organization" by marshaling their particular gifts and distinctive ways of perceiving them.

Lily's statement foreshadows the film's climax, wherein Ruth exercises her unique ability to "do something *really* big," her concentration inciting a powerful storm that enables her and Bo to liberate Lily from the local police station. Bo assists this effort by disintegrating the firearms law enforcement agents aim at the unarmed Ruth. To inspire the storm, Ruth stands in the street outside the police station, eyes closed tightly and chin tilted upward; a medium shot illustrating her special posture against the nondescript background gives way to evidence of her psychic manipulation, which is visible in

ENVISIONING POSTHUMAN APOCALYPSE 89

Figure 2.9 Lily takes apart, then reassembles a bowl while her mother Ruth looks on, unable to perceive the fast colors that appear to Bo and Lily as "aftereffects" of exercising their genetic strength.

the sky's fast-moving, surreal cloud formations. The following exterior shot of the police station represents the convergence of a mundane street view and an extraordinary event.

Adriana-Cecilia Neagu's "Post-Apocalypse Now: Globalism, Posthumanism, and the 'Imagination of Disaster'" articulates the conditions *Fast Color* depicts. Neagu draws on Sontag and Williams to pinpoint the specificity of "post-apocalypse disaster" in post-9/11 fact and fiction: "Whereas capitalist apocalypse is a reflection on and of futurity, defined by the anticipation of disaster, global post-apocalypse—the unadulterated expression of which

90   SCREENING THE POSTHUMAN

is posthumanism as a mindset—is an 'afterthought' articulated in the 'day after tomorrow,' on a disaster that has already taken place."[78] According to Brody, in *Fast Color*, "Shelves of supermarkets and convenience stores are gappy; daily life is impoverished and constrained . . . which is to say that, in 'Fast Color,' Americans live like many in the world do now, with unreliable and difficult access to water."[79] Brody's description would also be accurate as follows, "in 'Fast Color,' Americans live like many [*Americans*] do now," especially at the time of writing (in 2020), when the COVID-19 pandemic stimulated economic instabilities that made resource scarcity glaringly apparent in and outside of the United States. As the actress who plays Ruth, Gugu Mbatha-Raw, expressed in a 2020 interview: "We shot [*Fast Color*] in this sort of near future, or parallel universe—the idea of a drought and climate change, and water being this thing that was just so highly prized. So it's kind of eerie how close that feels [now], with so many parallels that you can draw."[80] At its time of release, *Fast Color* appeared particularly prescient because it used generic features of the superhero film to confront long-seeded catastrophes in the US—racial, economic, environmental, judicial—which had taken center stage off-screen.

Released in 2019, *Bacurau* is comparably timely and provocative in its designation of systemic racism as precursor to a perpetually apocalyptic (near-future) present. Like *Fast Color*, it also creatively repurposes generic elements to address long-standing and systemic "wicked problems"; in this case, the genre is the Western, and the setting Brazil. The film depicts a rural Brazilian community under threat from multiple elements that Neagu catalogs to describe posthuman apocalypse: "Post 9/11, the global individual lives in an apocalyptic present, in the aftermath of an ongoing financial crisis, cataclysm, terror, mass extinction, and, above all, in a state of perpetual, paralyzing, visceral fear."[81] The film's opening explicitly offers macro and micro views of the diegetic location, the first shot tracking in from space (passing a space station en route) toward the global earth before cutting to an aerial view of a truck driving on a rural desert highway,[82] which is designated "West of Pernambuco"[83] "a few years from now" via two sequential nondiegetic titles. Viewers' entrance to Bacurau's rural community is framed via Barbara's return home (Figure 2.10). POV shots from Barbara's perspective thus introduce the film's setting, which (as in *Fast Color*) appears abandoned and/or rundown (Figure 2.10). From the truck in which Barbara hitches a ride, she glimpses a one-time school building now reclaimed by its natural surroundings.

ENVISIONING POSTHUMAN APOCALYPSE 91

Figure 2.10 Approaching the city of Bacurau, viewers are exposed to the neglected environment through the framing device of Barbara's return home.

Despite this initial focus on Barbara's perspective, *Bacurau* figures the small community as a collective protagonist fighting for survival against formidable forces intent on first exploiting, then obliterating it. The precarious community has had its natural resources confiscated (its water dammed despite local protest), the town of Bacurau erased from maps (local teacher, Plinio, discovers this erasure in a school geography lesson), and local politicians distribute mind-altering drugs (freely and without prescription) to groom Bacurauans for obsolescence, having sold them to a commercial enterprise that offers the village residents as disposable targets in a hunting sport for American and European tourists. That these hunter-tourists regard Brazilians as less than human is made clear when they murder their two Brazilian guides (from the urban south) after first disparaging them with racist remarks. The sudden appearance of large, UFO-looking drones surveilling the villagers, in combination with Bacurau's sudden loss of broadband and the murder of a family living on the outskirts of town, alert the community to impending attack. They consequently coordinate a defense under the command of Lunga, an ambiguously gendered guerrilla activist who currently occupies the controversial dam and is equally revered and feared. The climactic encounter between the Indigenous community and outsiders plays out spectacularly as a revival of colonial-era brutality, this time with American/European invaders overcome by postmillennial Bacurauan postcolonial avengers (Figure 2.11).

In line with my thesis that posthuman disaster films destabilize dominant worldviews, *Bacurau* positions the dynamic and resourceful knowledge of its Indigenous protagonists as more useful than Western neocolonial ideas and goods, and as vital for survival in the near and catastrophic future. Furthermore, *Bacurau* spotlights the tendency to undervalue dynamic and resourceful Indigenous knowledge as a decisive weakness. John Briggs and Joanne Sharp's critique of development theories that preserve Western biases includes this impassioned plea, which aligns with *Bacurau*'s take on Indigenous knowledge:[84]

> It is important not to see indigenous knowledge as an artefact, simply something to be preserved . . . as a record of what has been lost to the seemingly inevitable march of Western science . . . The local knowledges of people on the receiving end of development practice must be allowed a more thorough challenge to the agenda . . . Indigenous knowledge cannot ever be

Figure 2.11 The entire community of *Bacurau* (Kleber Mendonça Filho and Juliano Dornelles, 2019), loosely led by local guerrilla activist Lunga (far-right), is the film's protagonist, united to enact postcolonial revenge against neoliberal invaders.

ENVISIONING POSTHUMAN APOCALYPSE 93

understood in isolation of the critical analysis of economic, social, cultural and political conditions. As Agrawal (1995) argues, indigenous knowledge is not simply about language and expression, but about these material conditions through which people must survive.[85]

Bacurau stages the climactic showdown inside the Museu Histórico de Bacurau (Historical Museum of Bacurau); in a literal illustration of Briggs and Sharp's concept of artifacts, the townspeople utilize materials (indigenous and imported) collected in their local museum against the hunters, who are positioned as modern-day, neoliberal counterparts to the European colonizers who "settled" Brazil. At the start of this sequence, ex-US serviceman Terry enters the Museum in the process of cautiously surveying the eerily quiet town (the Bacurauans are strategically hidden). He notices a wall of missing antique weapons, with plaques indicating what is typically exhibited there: "Colt 38," "Winchester 44" (the latter including the year "1873" alongside the weapon model), etc. "Heads up, guys. The locals might be armed," Terry warns his fellow hunters via headset. The montage surveying the Museum's interior cuts between what Terry takes note of (e.g., the missing weapons) and what the film wants viewers to notice, including a framed newspaper article titled, "Rebellion Quashed in Bacurau." While Terry explores the museum, the anticipation builds toward Lunga's emergence from beneath the museum's floorboards to brutally slaughter Terry using a combination of the "primitive" and advanced weaponry archived in the museum.

The montage of the slaughter is meaningfully constructed, Lunga's ring-adorned fingers and dark-painted nails identifying theirs as the gun-holding hand that appears suddenly from under a woven rug. Blindly fired shots disable Terry, Lunga's full figure becoming visible as they exit the dugout beneath the museum's floor, and abandon the gun in favor of a bladed weapon with which they brutally dismember Terry. A framed museum photograph of Indigenous Bacurauans' dismembered heads is inserted into the violent montage between Terry's killing and that of Jake, whose dispatch off-screen (after pursuing Terry inside the museum) is divulged to viewers when Lunga exits the museum grasping Jake's head by the hair (Figure 2.12). Tony Junior, the mayor of Bacurau's principality who brokered the hunting enterprise deal for a cut of the profits, represents the well-oiled machine of local bureaucracy, which subordinates Brazilians to foreign capital. His public punishment (after the beheadings) further energizes the rebellion of the local

Figure 2.12 The centerpiece of the community's successful defense is Lunga's brutal slaughter of first Terry, then Jake, in the town History Museum, where Lunga uses colonial and precolonial weapons to inversely re-enact that era's atrocities.

community against a form of invasion that it has experienced historically and in the present as solely hostile and exploitative. Bacurauans have learned from experience to distrust changes introduced as progressive by those not invested in the local environment (beyond its commercial potential), who won't be affected by the "innovations" in the long term. A postcolonial neo-Western, *Bacurau* animates, via its situation of a threat of extinction in the near future, a precarious community's confiscation of technologies historically used against them to overcome an apocalyptic threat.

The climaxes of both *Bacurau* and *Fast Color* evoke traumas of racist histories reverberating in the present to stress the role of such traumas in politically engaged apocalyptic imagining. Brody's *Fast Color* review ends on a cliffhanger that likens the film's sociopolitical engagement to that of the mid-twentieth-century Sci-Fi films addressed in Sontag's essay. However, unlike Sontag, Brody includes the civil rights struggles of that era among the unprecedented phenomena mid-twentieth-century Sci-Fi confronted:

> The film's modestly budgeted, scaled-down mode of resistance to the homogenizing force of franchise development is reminiscent of that of science-fiction dramas of an earlier time—the nineteen-fifties, which were the heyday of low-budget, independently produced, often deliriously imaginative science-fiction films. That era foreshadowed current times in several relevant ways: studio productions were becoming ever more inflated,

television was cutting drastically into the public's movie-going habits, and political crises in the United States were both apocalyptic (with the threat of nuclear war) and hate-stoked (the ongoing enforcement of Jim Crow) in ways that major Hollywood studios were largely unprepared for and unwilling to confront. I won't spoil *Fast Color*'s good ending, but there's a symbolic dimension to it that reflects a confrontation with present-day political crises of a similar sort.[86]

Brody suggests that *Fast Color*, using the superhero construct, likewise confronts racial inequalities embedded within institutionalized forms of social control, and as in the mid-twentieth century, these are abetted by technological advances. *Bacurau* confronts the same, its aesthetic continually juxtaposing high and low tech to highlight that material access to technology remains restricted according to racist and neocolonialist dictates. Twenty-first-century apocalypse is, as characterized by the title of Williams's book on the subject, "uneven": "Capitalist apocalypse . . . has already been coming, unevenly and across time . . . The very bad joke of the global order is told out of sync but with a cursed order of necessity: it cannot function other than this."[87] The technological and sociopolitical threats Brody itemizes unequally disadvantage the fictional Ruth, a fact that plot references to her teen pregnancy and history of drug abuse underscore. Per Brody's evaluation (also applicable to *Watchmen*), the superhero construct is a tool to reveal that socially sanctioned forms of repressive control bear down on Ruth (barred from social privilege by a convergence of gender, race and class) *as if* she had hidden extraordinary and threatening powers (meaning, the white authoritative men regard Ruth as a threat regardless of her powers). Thus, an unarmed Ruth faces off against men with guns who have the social/legal authority and technology designed to subdue or annihilate her. Bo positions herself between the two, using her power to disarm the men (this scenario, Figure 2.13, is most likely the one with the "symbolic dimension" Brody hints at).

As such, Ruth's supernatural powers function antithetically to the transhuman conventions of mainstream superheroism as epitomized by, for example, Marvel's *Avenger* blockbuster franchise, which endows its heroes with powers that far exceed Ruth's; hers magnetize forms of political oppression that she remains particularly vulnerable to. The film's realism (which inspired much critical praise) is essential to its posthumanism, which, in conjunction with hints of the supernatural, asserts that racist histories continue to stifle individual capacities in this near future (that strongly resembles the

Figure 2.13 In *Fast Color* (Julia Hart, 2018) a group of white male authority figures points deadly weapons at an unarmed Ruth, with Bo blocking Ruth before disarming them.

present). However, contrary to the message of "capitalist apocalypse" according to Williams, "it [*can*] function other than this."[88] Aside from the fatalistic *Melancholia*, the films analyzed in this chapter collectively challenge the inevitability of humanity's destruction by highlighting the ubiquitous and tragic errors that mire twenty-first-century humanity in a state of overlapping crises. Ruth's manipulations of reality are signs that latent potentials might counteract "bleak social and political times";[89] at any moment, the extraordinary can spill over and transform the ordinary. *Fast Color* and *Bacurau* demonstrate that racial- and class-based dimensions of postmillennial apocalypse are crucial to "critiqu[ing] the present system of social and political organization"[90] (to reiterate Russworm's phrasing). They accomplish the goals articulated by Keller in that they "carr[y] the freight of utopian and dystopian ideas" to "expose hope for new beginnings... wrought out of violent change."[91]

Conclusion

Take Shelter epitomizes a posthuman vision of apocalypse. It is exceptional in the crush of postmillennial disaster cinema, which, on the whole, justifies Badmington's warning regarding humanism's capacity to rear its (resilient) head specifically in stories that fantasize its demise. In regard to time, posthuman apocalypse exhumes the past, posits its pervasive influence on the present, and envisions a "near future" that resembles the here and now. Thus, posthuman disaster cinema favors a semi-realism, unembellished locations providing unremarkable backdrops for spectacular phenomena to suddenly erupt. In this category of cinema, what is normal appears strange and vice versa, and this allows for interrogation of the social structures that support long-standing human habits and ideas.

Take Shelter's protagonist, Curtis (played by Michael Shannon), is an everyman—a white Ohioan homeowner with a wife (Samantha, played by Jessica Chastain), a daughter (Hannah), and a job in construction. The conflicts that push the story forward involve various forms of impairment: in the main plot line, Curtis becomes increasingly attuned to catastrophes on the horizon and, interpreting his visions as hallucinations, researches the onset of paranoid schizophrenia while simultaneously preparing for disaster; and in the secondary plot line, Samantha fixates on Hannah's impending cochlear implant surgery, which aims to partially restore her hearing. Building toward the climax, Curtis's unauthorized use of construction equipment to expand the storm shelter in his backyard jeopardizes his employment as well as Hannah's surgery (her procedure depends on the health insurance his stable employment provides). Aspects of the film's treatment of disability are relevant to Chapter 5, which handles posthuman cinema's interrogation of able-bodied norms. Here, my focus is on the significance of Curtis's visions, which straddle a fine line between real and surreal, thereby allowing for the possibility that Curtis is not hallucinating but foreseeing (an interpretation supported by the film's cliffhanger ending).

Like in *Fast Color*, the ordinary mise-en-scéne of Curtis's work and family life intensifies the aesthetic impact of sudden spectacular disruptions, which generally unfold via shot/counter-shot patterns that crosscut between Curtis's looks off-screen (expressing shock and/or perplexity) and eyeline matches of what he sees (Figure 2.14).

In these ambiguously hallucinatory sequences, the eyeline matches mix ordinarily and extraordinarily spectacular images; for instance, the formation created by a flock of birds that Curtis witnesses at a job site is extraordinary, albeit possible or even common; and later, when he pulls his car over due to a threatening lightning storm, the sight and sound are intense, but not necessarily fantastic. In several of these episodes, another character's perception of normalcy (his closest work colleague at one point, Samantha at another)

Figure 2.14 In *Take Shelter* (Jeff Nichols, 2011), shot/counter-shot patterns convey Curtis's amazed perception of extraordinary phenomena.

indicates that Curtis's imagination is extreme. However, actual events, such as a chlorine spill reported on the local news, attest to catastrophes that occur as a "normal" part of *Take Shelter*'s diegetic world. In the end, the family takes its annual beach holiday on the recommendation of Curtis's doctor (and in advance of his committing himself into a mental health facility for prolonged treatment); the final shots of the film feature Curtis, then Samantha, captivated by tornadoes forming over the ocean in an approaching tsunami (Figure 2.15). While the ending is a cliffhanger, in that the characters are left

Figure 2.15 In *Take Shelter*'s (Jeff Nichols, 2011) penultimate shot, tornadoes form over the ocean in the reflection behind Samantha, who exchanges a catastrophe-aware look with Curtis off-screen.

in the midst of a crisis, it is nonetheless conclusive in its validation of Curtis's paranoia.

Posthuman films that feature proactive responses to catastrophic phenomena—that model looking ahead with astute vision and facing threatening and/or bewildering occurrences head-on—align with critical posthumanism and avoid the reactivity that I consider the modus operandi of commercially oriented apocalyptic cinema (2020's *Greenland* serves as a recent example). Big-budget disaster films tend to reify conservative, capitalistic ideologies, and to resolve apocalyptic challenges by reinstating "the human(ist) head through which we (continue to) 'behold all things.'"[92] As Elsaesser sarcastically puts it, "In Hollywood films, total extinction is usually averted at the last minute, invariably by the intrepid teamwork and infallible technology of a group of resolute Americans."[93] *Take Shelter* is a proactive, posthuman counterexample to the reactive, commercially oriented apocalyptic cinema that is unambiguously anthropocentric and far afield of critical posthumanism's concerns.

An academic article coauthored by celebrity infectious disease expert[94] Anthony Fauci, "Emerging Pandemic Diseases: How We Got to COVID-19," concludes with an explicitly posthumanist warning that urges proactive responses to the profound dilemmas facing humanity:

100 SCREENING THE POSTHUMAN

> In a human-dominated world, in which our human activities represent aggressive, damaging, and unbalanced interactions with nature . . . COVID-19 is among the most vivid wake-up calls . . . It should force us to begin to think in earnest and collectively about living in more thoughtful and creative harmony with nature, even as we plan for nature's inevitable, and always unexpected, surprises.[95]

The films discussed above are "vivid wake-up calls" to a humanity out of balance and tell stories that take the politics of the posthuman condition to task. This chapter foregrounds cinematic depictions of the foresight necessary to take careful action in response to unprecedented social and environmental challenges. I argue that clear sight regarding where humanity has been and where it could potentially end up is a commitment critical posthumanism and posthuman cinema share. The films discussed in this chapter prime viewers for off-screen realities in which catastrophe is perennial and time is not linear. The aesthetics that distinguish these films thrive on ambivalence, and excite anxiety and desire in the manner of the Sci-Fi films Sontag dismissed as "naïve . . . commercial art." Yet titillating viewers with apocalyptic terror is not, I propose, a priority of these posthuman disaster films. Rather, they ask viewers to reflect on the various catastrophes threatening the world as we know it, and their resolutions eschew conventional modes of closure that would restabilize a humanistic narrative lens in favor of open endings, which inspire alternative ways of viewing the world that undermine anthropocentricism.

In *Posthuman Knowledge*, Braidotti articulates her recent perspective on the posthuman, which has been enriched by several decades of scholarship on the subject: "The posthuman is a navigational tool that enables us to survey the material and the discursive manifestations of the mutations that are engendered by advanced technological developments (am I a robot?), climate change (will I survive?), and capitalism (can I afford this?)"[96] Critical posthumanism approaches technology, environment, and socioeconomics as intimately related phenomena, while posthuman cinema frames them in aesthetically provocative tableaux (e.g., Figures 2.1, 2.12 and 2.15) that, more often than not, accentuate tensions implicit in the posthuman condition Braidotti theorizes. Thus, Braidotti admits, "The posthuman condition may strike the reader as catastrophe-prone at first sight," an admission this chapter's case studies support; however, *Posthuman Knowledge* stresses "the positive potential of the posthuman convergence and offers tools for coping with it affirmatively." The films analyzed above do likewise, affirming Braidotti's view that "the convergence of posthumanist and post-anthropocentric approaches...produc[es] a qualitative leap in new directions [that manifests in] a zigzagging set of pathways."[97] The films mentioned also demonstrate that the dynamic between cinema and off-screen realities has evolved significantly since Sontag dismissed the critical vitality of disaster films: "What I am suggesting is that the imagery of disaster in science fiction is above all the emblem of an *inadequate response*. I don't mean to bear down on the films for this. They themselves are only a sampling, stripped of sophistication, of the inadequacy of most people's response to the unassimilable terrors that infect their consciousness."[98] One can imagine Sontag finding greater satisfaction in films such as *Biidaaban: First Light, Collisions, Fast Color, Bacurau*, and *Take Shelter*, which, as I've shown, productively respond to the cataclysmic threats humanity faces in the twenty-first century.

Posthuman visions of catastrophe are the stuff of reality, not fantasy; they portray crisis as widespread and pervasive rather than individual and exceptional. They thereby oppose the story mechanics of big budget, hero saves a world on the brink filmmaking, which rehashes the hero journey that humanism has thrived on for centuries.[99] Dystopian visions of militarized technocultures often bear traces of humanism bound up with Western European colonialism and its aftereffects (a powerful legacy). Conversely, Indigenous, postcolonial, and racial critiques of the relationships among humans, technology, and the environment are allied with critical posthumanism. Posthuman apocalypse represents a small subset of the disaster cinema that has mushroomed in recent years. In fact, the apocalyptic trend has enabled filmmakers to make spectacles of widespread catastrophe while reaffirming the humanist values that make off-screen catastrophes increasingly likely. In contrast, posthuman cinema confronts large-scale destruction to entertain new social and material realities and to "provid[e] a frame to understand the ongoing processes of becoming-subjects in our fast-changing times."[100]

Notes

1. Susan Sontag, "The Imagination of Disaster," 1965, in *Against Interpretation and Other Essays* (New York: Dell, 1979), 212.
2. Sontag, "The Imagination," 212.

3. Sontag, "The Imagination," 224.

4. Sontag, "The Imagination," 223.

5. Sontag, "The Imagination," 224.

6. Sarah Keller, *Anxious Cinephilia: Pleasure and Peril at the Movies* (New York: Columbia University Press, 2020), 182.

7. Sontag, "The Imagination," 224.

8. Stacy Alaimo, *Exposed: Environmental Politics and Pleasures in Posthuman Times* (Minneapolis: University of Minnesota Press, 2016).

9. Evan Calder Williams, *Combined and Uneven Apocalypse: Luciferian Marxism* (Winchester: John Hunt Publishing, 2011), 1.

10. Neil Badmington, "Theorizing Posthumanism," *Cultural Critique* 53 (2003): 11.

11. Katy Steinmetz, "She Coined the Term 'Intersectionality' Over 30 Years Ago. Here's What It Means to Her Today," *TIME*, February 20, 2020, https://time.com/5786710/kimberle-crenshaw-intersectionality/.

12. Williams, *Combined and Uneven Apocalypse*, 5.

13. This despite the "progressive" casting of John David Washington, a Black American man, in the stereotypical blockbuster hero role.

14. Sontag, "The Imagination," 224.

15. Thomas Elsaesser, "Black Suns and a Bright Planet: Lars von Trier's *Melancholia* as Thought Experiment," *Theory & Event* 18, no. 2 (2015), https://muse.jhu.edu/article/578627.

16. Badmington, "Theorizing Posthumanism," 11.

17. Owen Gleiberman, "'Contagion,' the Movie That Predicted Our Pandemic, Is Really about Our World Falling Apart," *Variety*, April 27, 2020, https://variety.com/2020/film/columns/contagion-the-movie-that-predicted-our-pandemic-1234590420/.

18. Keller, *Anxious Cinephilia*,182.

19. Keller, *Anxious Cinephilia*,182.

20. Badmington, "Theorizing Posthumanism," 11.

21. Sontag, "The Imagination," 224.

22. Elsaesser, "Black Suns."

23. Mallika Rao, "The *Melancholia* Postulate: What the 2011 Apocalyptic Film Has to Say about Peace of Mind in the Face of Annihilation," *The Atlantic*, May 9, 2020, https://www.theatlantic.com/culture/archive/2020/05/watching-melancholia-during-pandemic/611383/.

24. See, for instance, Elsaesser, "Black Suns."

25. Badmington, "Theorizing Posthumanism," 10.

26. One of the interpretations Elsaesser presents in "Black Sun . . ." explores the film's apocalypse as an allegory of the end of cinema. Steven Shaviro's reading of *Melancholia* also typifies the scholarly tendency to cite a dizzying combination of abstract concepts in an erratic effort to pin down the film's meaning. Steven Shaviro, "*Melancholia*, or, the Romantic Anti-sublime," *Sequence* 1, no. 1 (2012): 7.

27. Elena del Río, *The Grace of Destruction: A Vital Ethology of Extreme Cinemas* (New York: Bloomsbury Academic, 2016), 215.

28. Del Río vaguely attributes her point about "indigenous lifestyles" to David Martin-Jones.

29. Del Río, *The Grace of Destruction*, 213, paraphrasing Shaviro, "*Melancholia*," 35.
30. National Museum of the American Indian, *Do All Indians Live in Tipis?: Questions and Answers from the National Museum of the American Indian* (New York: Harper Perennial, 2007).
31. Cynthia Coleman Emery, "Indians: We're All the Same," *Cynthia (Ištá Thó Thó) Coleman Emery's Blog*, November 28, 2014, https://nativescience.blog/2014/11/18/indians-were-all-the-same/.
32. Linda Badley, *Lars von Trier Beyond Depression: Contexts and Collaborations* (New York: Columbia University Press, 2022), x.
33. Nina Power and Rob White, "Lars Von Trier's *Melancholia*: A Discussion," *Film Quarterly*, January 10, 2012, https://filmquarterly.org/2012/01/10/lars-von-triers-melancholia-a-discussion/.
34. Alexandra Alter, "'We've Already Survived an Apocalypse': Indigenous Writers Are Changing Sci-Fi," *The New York Times*, August 14, 2020, https://www.nytimes.com/2020/08/14/books/indigenous-native-american-sci-fi-horror.html.
35. Cecilia Åsberg and Rosi Braidotti, eds., *A Feminist Companion to the Posthumanities* (Cham: Springer, 2018), 5.
36. Williams, *Combined and Uneven Apocalypse*, 4.
37. Keller, *Anxious Cinephilia*, 182.
38. Grace Dillon, "From Growing Medicine to Space Rockets: What Is Indigenous Futurism?," interview by Rosanna Deerchild, *Unreserved*, CBA, March 8, 2019, audio, https://www.cbc.ca/radio/unreserved/looking-towards-the-future-indigenous-futur ism-in-literature-music-film-and-fashion-1.5036479/from-growing-medicine-to-space-rockets-what-is-indigenous-futurism-1.5036480
39. Henrietta Lidchi and Suzanne Newman Fricke, "Future History: Indigenous Futurisms in North American Visual Arts," *World Art* 9, no. 2 (2019): 99–102, https://doi.org/10.1080/21500894.2019.1627675.
40. Grace Dillon, *Walking the Clouds: An Anthology of Indigenous Science Fiction* (Tucson: University of Arizona Press, 2012), 1–2.
41. CBA, "Lisa Jackson's *Biidaaban*."
42. Australian television drama *Cleverman* (ABC Australia 2016–2017) and Canadian-New Zealand apocalyptic film, *Night Raiders* (Danis Goulet, 2021), are analogous examples of the "rising tide of Indigenous Futurism" in contemporary screen storytelling.
43. CBC Arts, "Lisa Jackson's *Biidaaban: First Light*," *CBC*, 2018, video, https://www.cbc.ca/player/play/1323281475810.
44. Sontag, "The Imagination," 215.
45. Hotel Victoria, "Toronto History—Old City Hall," *Hotel Toronto*, February 15, 2020, https://www.hotelvictoria-toronto.com/2020/02/toronto-history-old-city-hall/.
46. Williams, *Combined and Uneven Apocalypse*, 5
47. Charlotte Epstein, *Against International Relations Norms: Postcolonial Perspectives* (London: Routledge, 2017), 11.
48. Rebecca Roanhorse et al., "Decolonizing Science Fiction and Imagining Futures: An Indigenous Futurisms Round Table," *Strange Horizons*, January 30, 2017, http://strangehorizons.com/non-fiction/articles/decolonizing-science-fiction-and-imagining-futures-an-indigenous-futurisms-roundtable/.

104 SCREENING THE POSTHUMAN

49. Elizabeth LaPensee quoted in Roanhorse et al., "Decolonizing Science Fiction."
50. Nyarri Nyarri Morgan et al., "Nyarri Nyarri Morgan:' Virtual Reality, History and Indigenous Experience," *ACMI*, December 11, 2016, audio, https://www.acmi.net.au/ideas/listen/nyarri-nyarri-morgan-virtual-reality-history-and-indigenous-experience/.
51. Brigid Delaney, "'An Act of Solidarity': Anohni Treks 100km Across Australian Desert to Protest Against Uranium Mine," *The Guardian*, June 7, 2016.
52. Luke Buckmaster, "Virtual Reality Pioneer Lynette Wallworth Tells Indigenous Story in Explosive Detail," *The Guardian*, March 18, 2016, https://www.theguardian.com/technology/2016/mar/18/virtual-reality-pioneer-lynette-walworth-tells-indigenous-story-in-explosive-detail.
53. Lisa Dethridge, "Virtual Reality Film *Collisions* Is Part Disaster Movie, Part Travelogue and Completely Immersive," *The Conversation*, October 5, 2016, https://theconversation.com/virtual-reality-film-collisions-is-part-disaster-movie-part-travelogue-and-completely-immersive-66563.
54. Dillon, *Walking the Clouds*, 1–2.
55. Morgan et al., "Nyarri Nyarri Morgan: Virtual Reality."
56. Buckmaster, "Virtual Reality Pioneer."
57. Charlotte Epstein, "The Postcolonial Perspective: An Introduction," *International Theory* 6, no. 2 (July 2014): 298.
58. *ACMI*, "The Story Behind Collisions'," December 7, 2016, video, https://www.acmi.net.au/ideas/watch/story-behind-collisions/.
59. Bloomberg's post-conference review is evidence of the effort to focus on *Collisions*' production rather than its themes. A photo of a man wearing a VR headset is captioned: "This year's theme is the 'Fourth Industrial Revolution.' Robots, artificial intelligence and virtual reality are on the agenda. Here, an attendee watches '*Collisions*' a 15 minute film by artist Lynette Wallworth, on a Samsung Gear VR headset." "Davos 2016: Inside the 46th World Economic Forum," *Bloomberg News*, January 21, 2016, https://www.bloomberg.com/news/photo-essays/2016-01-20/davos-2016-the-world-economic-forum-in-pictures.
60. Carol Becker, "How Art Became a Force at Davos," *World Economic Forum*, February 26, 2019, https://www.weforum.org/agenda/2019/02/how-art-became-a-force-at-davos/.
61. United Nations: Office for Disarmament Affairs, "2016 Disarmament Film Series Side Event," *United Nations*, October 31, 2016, https://www.un.org/disarmament/update/2016-disarmament-film-series-side-event/.
62. Buckmaster, "Virtual Reality Pioneer."
63. Buckmaster, "Virtual Reality Pioneer."
64. Spelled "Nyerri" in the article.
65. Ken Eastwood, "Living the Traditional Aboriginal Life," *Australia Geographic*, December 15, 2010.
66. Epstein, "The Postcolonial Perspective," 296.
67. Jon Donnison, "Lingering Impact of British Nuclear Tests in the Australian Outback," *BBC News*, December 31, 2014, https://www.bbc.com/news/world-australia-30640338.

68. Morgan et al., "Nyarri Nyarri Morgan: Virtual Reality."
69. Jen Yamato, "'The Anti-Avengers': In Indie Gem 'Fast Color,' a Powerful New Superhero Story Is Born," *Los Angeles Times*, April 23, 2019, https://www.latimes.com/entertainment/movies/la-ca-mn-fast-color-superhero-gugu-mbatha-raw-julia-hart-20190423-story.html.
70. This phrase is borrowed from the title of Gleiberman's "Contagion" article.
71. Dominic Patten, "Watchmen's Regina King On HBO Drama's Prophetic Power In A COVID-19 & Police Brutality-Scarred America—Contenders TV," *Deadline*, August 16, 2020, https://deadline.com/2020/08/watchmen-regina-king-interview-sister-night-dr-manhattan-contenders-tv-watch-1203013063/.
72. Richard Brody, "'Fast Color,' Reviewed: A Superhero Movie That Pays Close Attention to Ordinary Life," *The New* Yorker, April 22, 2019, https://www.newyorker.com/culture/the-front-row/fast-color-reviewed-a-superhero-movie-that-pays-close-attention-to-ordinary-life.
73. These ambient shots resemble *Hell or High Water*'s (David Mackenzie, 2016) mise-en-scène; like *Fast Color, Hell or High Water*, which confronts the fallout of the 2008 global economic crisis in the present-day American West, was also shot on location in New Mexico.
74. TreaAndrea M. Russworm, "Dystopian Blackness and the Limits of Racial Empathy in *The Walking Dead* and *The Last of Us*," in *Gaming Representation: Race, Gender, and Sexuality in Video Games*, eds. Jennifer Malkowski and TreaAndrea M Russworm (Bloomington: Indiana University Press, 2017), 110.
75. Russworm, "Dystopian Blackness," 114.
76. Yamato, "The Anti-Avengers."
77. Brody, "'Fast Color,' Reviewed."
78. Adriana-Cecilia Neagu, "Post-Apocalypse Now: Globalism, Posthumanism, and the 'Imagination of Disaster,'" *Transylvanian Review* 26, supplement 2 (2017): 239.
79. Brody, "'Fast Color,' Reviewed."
80. Cameron Scheetz, "Gugu Mbatha-Raw on *Misbehaviour*, 'San Junipero,' and Becoming a Pop Star for *Beyond The Lights*," *AV Club*, October 2, 2020, https://film.avclub.com/gugu-mbatha-raw-on-misbehaviour-san-junipero-and-be-1845159353.
81. Neagu, "Post-Apocalypse Now," 239.
82. Reminiscent of aerial road views of the American southwest in the final act of *Thelma and Louis* (Ridley Scott, 1991).
83. Pernambuco is a state in the northeast of Brazil that is rarely the subject of internationally distributed art films.
84. John Briggs and Joanne Sharp, "Indigenous Knowledges and Development: A Postcolonial Caution," *Third World Quarterly* 25, no. 4 (2004): 661.
85. Briggs and Sharp, "Indigenous Knowledges," 763–764.
86. Brody, "'Fast Color,' Reviewed."
87. Williams, *Combined and Uneven Apocalypse*, 9.
88. Williams, *Combined and Uneven Apocalypse*, 9.
89. Russworm, "Dystopian Blackness," 110.

106 SCREENING THE POSTHUMAN

90. Russworm, "Dystopian Blackness," 114.
91. Keller, *Anxious Cinephilia*, 182.
92. Badmington, *Theorizing Posthumanism*, 10.
93. Elsaesser, "Black Suns."
94. The fact that infectious disease experts are 2020's breakout celebrities says much about the year: Sim Canophilia Wissgott, "In the Spotlight—The Doctors at the Top: Truthtellers and Heartthrobs," *CGTN*, April 14, 2020, https://news.cgtn.com/news/2020-04-14/In-the-Spotlight-Doctors-at-the-top-Truth-tellers-and-heartthrobs-PGIyev8g9y/index.html.
95. David M. Morens and Anthony S. Fauci, "Emerging Pandemic Diseases: How We Got to COVID-19," *Cell* 182 (2020): 1089, https://www.cell.com/cell/pdf/S0092-8674(20)31012-6.pdf.
96. Braidotti, *Posthuman Knowledge*, 2.
97. Braidotti, *Posthuman Knowledge*, 3–4.
98. Sontag, "The Imagination," 224.
99. See Joseph Campbell, *The Hero with a Thousand Faces* (New York: Pantheon Books, 1949), a book that influenced many screenwriters, most famously George Lucas, as described in the popular screenwriting textbook, Christopher Vogler, *The Writer's Journey: Mythic Structure for Storytellers & Screenwriters* (Los Angeles: Michael Wiese Productions, 1992).
100. Rosi Braidotti, "A Theoretical Framework for the Critical Posthumanities," *Theory, Culture & Society 36*, no. 6 (2019): 34, https://doi.org/10.1177/0263276418771486.

3

From Cyborg Theory
to Posthuman Mothers

Missy Molloy

In a 2006 interview, Donna Haraway reflected on the staggering influence of her then-twenty-one-year-old "A Cyborg Manifesto," which she retrospectively describes as "a feminist theoretical document—a coming-to-terms with the world we live in and the question 'What is to be done?'"[1] Haraway's cyborg—which she defined as a hybrid being that "populate[s] worlds ambiguously natural and crafted"[2] and undermines efforts to differentiate organism from machine, natural from artificial—has played a significant role in the development of critical posthumanism. In the "Manifesto," Haraway argues that the cyborg upsets the binaries fundamental to humanistic thought to trouble the terrain wherein concepts of the human and posthuman intermingle. According to Haraway, male/female is among the binaries that perpetuate humanism, and promotes restrictive ideas about the impact of gender on bodily experience. As a result, critical posthumanism tends to reject the gender binary in favor of a cyborg view of gender, for which Haraway's "A Cyborg Manifesto" laid the foundations:

> Up till now (once upon a time), female embodiment seemed to be given, organic, necessary; and female embodiment seemed to mean skill in mothering and its metaphoric extensions. Only by being out of place could we take intense pleasure in machines, and then with excuses that this was organic activity after all, appropriate to females. Cyborgs might consider more seriously the partial, fluid, sometimes aspect of sex and sexual embodiment. Gender might not be global identity after all.[3]

Clearly, Haraway's account of the cyborg aims to disrupt essentialist gender views to carve out space for imagining varied encounters between "female" bodies and machines.

Missy Molloy, *From Cyborg Theory to Posthuman Mothers*. In: *Screening the Posthuman*.
Edited by: Missy Molloy, Pansy Duncan, and Claire Henry, Oxford University Press.
© Oxford University Press 2023. DOI: 10.1093/oso/9780197538562.003.0004

108 SCREENING THE POSTHUMAN

Despite this account of the cyborg as a vehicle for transcending the gender binary, feminist posthumanists have usefully alerted us to the persistence of gender and humanistic biases in cyborg depictions of posthuman womanhood.[4] In an effort to assess whether "the current technological imagination" "still hold[s] sexist, racist or ethno-centric biases," Francesca Ferrando asks, "Is the post-human a post-woman?"[5] Many cinematic cyborg women enhance the visibility of the biases Ferrando mentions, thereby exhibiting the persistence of humanistic prejudices that early cyborg theories energetically opposed. Exemplary here is the unambiguous gendering and whiteness of recent cinematic cyborgs, from Scarlett Johannson's The Female in *Under the Skin* (Jonathan Glazer, 2013), to Alicia Vikander's Ava in *Ex Machina* (Alex Garland, 2014), where the use of women rather than men or gender-nonconforming characters to model cyborg embodiment directly contradicts Haraway's claim that "the cyborg is a creature in a post-gender world"[6] (a statement that hyperbolically broadcasts the post-gender ambitions of early posthumanism).

Feminist posthumanism, then, aims to clarify the central, yet ambivalent status of gender in efforts to confront the dissolving boundary between organism and machine, which posthuman experience has intensified. From Haraway's groundbreaking cyborg through influential work advanced by scholars including N. Katherine Hayles, Rosi Braidotti, and Karen Barad, the feminist thread of critical posthumanism is instrumental to this chapter's parse of human and posthuman dimensions of cyborg women. "Feminist posthumanities" has become an umbrella term for feminist-oriented approaches to the far-reaching changes to society and culture that stem, in large part, from technological penetration of many aspects of so-called human experience. Cecilia Åsberg describes feminist posthumanities as "a much-needed type of transformative humanities, a rickety and imperfect engine of discovery fueled by advanced (more than feminist) philosophy, environmental humanities, cultural science and technology studies, and a street-smart type of postdisciplinarity that keep critique societally relevant."[7] Åsberg's description gets at the distinct blend of critical thinking the term encompasses, which has proven particularly alert to the transhumanist seductions and humanist nostalgias this book consistently draws attention to.[8] Thus while Åsberg identifies Haraway's "figure of the cyborg" as the "combustive precursor" of "feminist posthumanities,"[9] insights gleaned from feminist posthumanities are key to assessing cinematic cyborg women's capacities to account for "entangled materializations of which we are a part, including new configurations, new subjectivities, new possibilities" (Barad's proposition regarding what the figure of the posthuman might achieve).[10] This is in part due to cyborg theory's "post-gender" ambitions, which proved insufficient to the interpretation of gendered cyborgs, especially cyborg women. And indeed, representations of the latter are germane to a number of issues feminist posthumanists prioritize, including technosexuality, online/offline hybrid subjectivity, the dissolution of humanistic notions of embodiment and identity, and the unseating of the "organic" human body as principal hardware of perception and experience.

Drawing on feminist posthumanisms, this chapter analyzes the cinematic use of women cyborgs as vehicles for exploring posthuman embodiment and the ambiguous materiality that accompanies the erosion of humanism's silo of human from nonhuman, object from subject, and organism from machine. As it will show, while women cyborgs provide ample opportunities to assess posthumanism's undermining of fundamental humanistic binaries, they also demonstrate the persistent appeal of humanist and transhumanist cinematic elements, which are particularly conspicuous in cyborg characterizations that lean on classical strategies of objectifying and fetishizing women on-screen. In this sense, the films these cyborgs appear in evince the overwhelming ambivalence of the posthuman in contemporary narrative cinema. Thus, while the films analyzed in this chapter indicate fascination with posthuman possibility, their cyborgs also betray attachment to humanistic conventions. While in recent years Haraway has expressed strong objections to the term posthuman,[11] she nevertheless allies her work with a particular class of "posthumanist thinking," citing Hayles as exemplary:

> [Hayles] locates herself in [*How We Became Posthuman*] at the right interface—the place where people meet IT apparatuses, where worlds get reconstructed as information. I am in strong alliance with her insistence in that book, namely getting at the materialities of information. Not letting anyone think for a minute that this is immateriality rather than getting at its specific materialities. *That* I'm with, that sense of "how we became posthumanist."[12]

In conformity with this resolutely materialist take on posthumanism, this chapter's interpretations of cinematic women/machine assemblages avoid the conflation of posthumanism and "transhumanist techno-enhancement" by highlighting the "specific materialities" of cyborg women in the following

110   SCREENING THE POSTHUMAN

films: *Under the Skin, Air Doll, Ex Machina, Celle que vous croyez/Who You Think I Am* (Safy Nebbou, 2019), *Proxima* (Alice Wincoeur, 2019), and *The Congress* (Ari Folman, 2013).

The first section argues that while *Under the Skin, Air Doll*, and *Ex Machina* compellingly engage with posthuman ideas about gender, their portraits of artificial women are more successful at rehearsing humanistic perspectives on female embodiment than at envisioning posthuman womanhood. *Under the Skin* provocatively destabilizes human and nonhuman materiality; however, the blatant femme fatale conventions on display in its cyborg protagonist (referred to as The Female) undercut its vision of a posthuman woman. In comparison, *Air Doll* (introduced in Chapter 1) is less influenced by Western cinematic tropes for representing women, yet its conclusion indicts Nozomi, a synthetic sex doll come magically to life, for tragically misunderstanding her materiality, thereby dialing back on the film's posthuman investments. And like *Under the Skin, Ex Machina* (also featured in Chapter 1) represents its cyborg women as seductive threats, and according to normative, Eurocentric beauty standards that demonstrate the sexism and racism of Nathan's (the engineer antagonist's) robotic design. Exposure scenes in these films, I will further suggest, epitomize cinematic ambivalence regarding posthuman embodiment. This section will conclusively demonstrate that characterizations of synthetic women, especially in relatively high-budget, English-language films, are hamstrung by their reliance on classical cinematic strategies for augmenting women's appeal as visual objects, which betrays their allegiance to humanist norms.[13]

Less spectacular, yet more in line with feminist posthumanism, is the technosexuality on display in *Who You Think I Am*, a French independent film that takes a realistic approach to depicting mediated forms of intimacy. Its middle-aged protagonist, Claire (played by Juliette Binoche), is a catfish who cultivates an emotional and sexual relationship with Lucas, in the process deceiving him about her age (among other aspects of her "organic" identity). The second section will show that *Who You Think I Am* exemplifies a posthuman view of technosexuality. Yet, at the same time, aspects of its depiction of Claire illustrate both sexism and ageism, which diminish the film's posthuman take on hybrid online/offline cyborg identity and reveal humanist elements. In these moments in the film, the fact that cinema and culture, broadly speaking, hold women to different standards than men noticeably impacts *Who You Think I Am*'s treatment of Claire's subjectivity as a blend of organic and electronic components. Therefore, as in the case of *Air Doll*, humanistic beliefs about women, identity, and embodiment curtail *Who You Think I Am*'s representation of cyborg womanhood. This section concludes by extending beyond the film to suggest that Binoche's performances in this and other films with posthuman ambitions are more in line with posthuman feminism than the trio of cyborgs performed by Johansson (including *The Female* in *Under the Skin*) that scholars and critics have celebrated as progressive in regard to gender and representation. This provocation will expose a substantial gap between posthuman aspiration and human actuality in cinematic storytelling that, for better or worse, continues to sabotage attempts to render women characters as natural and mechanical hybrids.

The third and final section spotlights the endowment of human mothers with posthuman attributes in a series of films that focus on professional women (in two cases, specifically astronauts) whose embrace of organic and mechanical hybridity is linked to their maternity. As this section will show, while rejecting late-nineteenth century Sci-Fi and horror's well-documented fixations on "monstrous mothers,"[14] these films remain ambivalent in their affordances to a properly posthuman characterization of cyborg mothers. The main case study, *Proxima*, surveys the process through which Sarah, an astronaut, integrates with technology in preparation for extraterrestrial experience. Its plot emphasis on challenges she faces parenting her young daughter, Stella—which partly frames her maternity as a hindrance to her "posthuman becoming"—revives tensions Mary Ann Doane articulated in 1990 regarding maternity's ambiguous role in imagining "the woman-machine."[15] Overlaps between Sarah's characterization and Ryan's in *Gravity* (Alfonso Cuarón, 2013) (as well as, to a certain extent, Louise's in *Arrival* [discussed in Chapter 1]) provide evidence of an emerging "cyborg mother" trend in mainstream and Independent cinema that conditionally embraces posthuman womanhood. Finally, a brief look at material transformation in *The Congress*, which features a cyborg mother existing simultaneously as virtual and non-virtual selves, reinforces maternity's critical position in cinematic speculation of cyborg womanhood. This section ultimately concludes that while these films' protagonists do not resemble the "monstrous" mothers influentially theorized by Barbara Creed,[16] they support Doane's claim that "the maternal and the mechanical/synthetic coexist in a relation that is a curious imbrication of dependence and antagonism."[17] Therefore, this cinematic trend centered on cyborg mothers indicates residual tension in imagining posthuman womanhood. Meanwhile, this chapter's case studies as a whole illuminate the vital significance of gender in "the current

112 SCREENING THE POSTHUMAN

technological imagination,"[18] wherein filmmakers must confront and re-purpose conventional strategies for representing women in order to present compelling visions of cyborg embodiment.

Punctured Cyborg Bodies in *Under the Skin, Air Doll*, and *Ex Machina*

A trio of spectacular scenes distinguish Scarlet Johansson art cinema ve-hicle *Under the Skin*. These scenes deal with embodied disintegration and exposure in a manner that, on one hand, reinforces humanistic othering of cyborg women, and on another, alienates the stuff humans are made of. Two involve The Female (played by Johansson) seducing men she picked up off the streets of Glasgow into a pool of dark liquid wherein they disinte-grate. The third is the film's climax, in which a man exposes The Female's mechanical insides while attempting to rape her, then drenches her in fuel and sets her alight. These scenes spectacularly illustrate the film's enigmatic stance on human and nonhuman materiality. *Under the Skin*'s depiction of The Female resembles other high-profile films that make a spectacle of a human-looking woman who eventually has her nonhuman insides exposed, most notably *Ex Machina*, which is often associated with *Under the Skin*; and *Air Doll*, both of which we introduced in Chapter 1's survey of posthuman cinema's distinguishing features. The depictions of nonhuman women in these films evoke technofetishism, which Allison De Fren describes as erotic pleasure stimulated by imagery that contrasts "the cold hard steel[,] the circuits and the wiring [with] the smooth skin and the soft flesh" of the syn-thetic woman.[19] They also appeal to the classic cinematic fixation on illicit revelations of women's bodies. This section will therefore argue that while *Under the Skin, Air Doll*, and *Ex Machina* are provocative from a posthuman perspective attuned to gender, they are more successful at reifying the dis-tinction between human and nonhuman materiality than at envisioning posthuman womanhood. This is largely due to the othering tactics apparent in their portraits of nonhuman women (including technofetishism and objectification), which revive classical cinematic strategies of fetishizing women's bodies in a manner that reaffirms humanistic binaries distin-guishing women from men, and humans from machines.

The time-honored cinematic tradition in which women stimulate erotic contemplation and/or suffer to temporarily resolve tensions associated with (white) male subjecthood frequently colors portraits of synthetic women, including The Female's in *Under the Skin*. According to feminist theories of classical narrative cinema, a woman's inherent threat can be mitigated by her depiction as an idealized aesthetic object, which incites the desires of men on-screen and off.[20] It is thus unsurprising that women/machine cinematic hybrids often resemble the femme fatale figure associated with film noir, which was traditionally idealized as a seductive threat. In "Feminist Film Theory," Anneke Smelik encapsulates Classical Hollywood cinema's main method of overcoming the threat posed by women, which involves presenting them as "hyper-polished object[s]": "Fetishising the woman . . . changes her from a dangerous figure into a reassuring object of flawless beauty . . . thus fail[ing] to represent 'woman' outside the phallic norm."[21] In like manner, *Under the Skin* fetishizes The Female to simultaneously mitigate the threats posed by women *and* cyborgs, thus failing to represent her outside humanistic norms.

Under the Skin offers The Female for erotic speculation from the start. Her introduction seven minutes into the film involves a montage of The Female's initially naked form as she undresses a female victim (delivered by an unnamed male companion) before clothing herself in the dead woman's attire. This stark one-minute montage, which situates the two women in a bright white, galleryesque space, provides ample opportunities to regard The Female's naked form from a variety of perspectives (including anterior and posterior views, Figure 3.1). Her thin characterization, as a robotic and impassive woman who seduces men to destroy them, lays bare her function as a "hyper-polished . . . object of flawless beauty" and femme fatale. Preparing for the hunt, she visits a mall, and we witness her stroking a thick, faux-fur coat, studying a bright red sleeveless top, holding a single black heeled boot, and testing makeup products. These acts signify her preparation to perform a fetish-reliant form of femininity to achieve her goal. Thus equipped, she pursues her prey, attracting a series of men to the window of the van she's driving with direction-related queries before finally inviting the chosen one, a man on his way home, inside. Multiple images of his face—conveying his pleasure in looking at The Female and sense of good luck at encountering her—cut to images of her driving alone again, then picking up another man via the needing directions ruse. The next "lucky" man riding in the van's passenger seat makes his attraction to her explicit, calling her "gorgeous" (after she asks if he thinks she's pretty). One minute of screen time later, he follows The Female across another unnaturally stark space; this time the two are

114 SCREENING THE POSTHUMAN

Figure 3.1 *Under the Skin*'s (Jonathan Glazer, 2013) introduction to The Female invites viewers to regard her naked form from a variety of perspectives, including anterior and posterior views.

enveloped in black. The following set of shots and countershots conforms to the classic Mulveyan male/subject, female/object pattern;[22] he looks toward her with desire, the camera then matches his eyeline, tilting up and down her body as she strips. However, after he sheds his clothing in pursuit of her, he becomes gradually submerged in black liquid beneath the floor she glides effortlessly over (Figure 3.2). The accompanying jagged sonic cut from spooky and hypnotic electronic score to silence intensifies the eeriness

Figure 3.2 The Female glides effortlessly over the smooth black surface; moments later, her prey is submerged.

of The Female's smooth passage over the spot from which he disappeared only seconds before. This sequence elegantly and enigmatically stresses substantial differences between the material composition of The Female and that of the mortal men she ensnares, with The Female utilizing a masquerade of seductive femininity to exploit human vulnerability.

Thus, while *Under the Skin* thrives on spectacles of material disintegration, it maintains a hard boundary between human organism and The Female's synthetic embodiment—the same boundary whose breakdown "A Cyborg Manifesto" celebrated. One of the "three crucial boundary breakdowns" foundational to Haraway's cyborg "myth," "the second leaky distinction . . . between animal-human (organism) and machine," is elaborated by Haraway as follows: "Late twentieth-century machines have made thoroughly ambiguous the difference between natural and artificial, mind and body, self-developing and externally designed, and many other distinctions that used to apply to organisms and machines. Our machines are disturbingly lively, and we ourselves frighteningly inert."[23] The seduction of The Female's next hapless victim proceeds similarly to the previous sequence, except in this case, after she brings him "home" to the black void, her striptease proceeds further, ending with her in only bra and panties. Of greater significance, though, is the nearly four minutes of screen time devoted to the victim's experience after submersion (which the previous scene elided). It begins with a cut to his watching—from below, within the liquid—her aboveground departure. What follows is a horrifying, visually experimental montage in which he appears trapped and suspended in the gel-like substance and gradually asphyxiates. Meanwhile, he watches, and briefly touches, another submerged man who is in a more advanced stage of decomposition: the latter's musculature and tendons are grotesquely visible before his insides liquify, leaving only a rapidly transforming husk of skin (Figure 3.3). The skin ultimately dissolves into a dark red stream of chunky matter traveling on a conveyor belt that cuts down the middle of the black screen; the matter thins to a horizontal line before exploding in a blinding red light, which concludes the scene.

While *Under the Skin* is no doubt aesthetically striking, the film is not unusual in its refusal to countenance category breakdown between natural and artificial. In *Air Doll*'s final scenes, Nozomi (played by Bae Doona) unintentionally kills her lover before suiciding by deflating herself. These acts purposefully trigger anxieties associated with this "crucial boundary breakdown" by highlighting the tragedy of Nozomi's misunderstanding the basic materiality of her own self in contrast to that of her human lover, Junichi (played by Arata Iura). In "Why Do Dolls Die? The Power of Passivity and the Embodied Interplay Between Disability and Sex Dolls," Eunjung Kim describes Nozomi's accidental murder of Junichi as follows:

Figure 3.3 Viewers watch another victim progress through multiple stages of decomposition; at one point, he is a rapidly transforming husk of skin.

FROM CYBORG THEORY TO POSTHUMAN MOTHERS 117

Believing that he is one of her kind, she tries to do the same thing to him [to deflate, then reinflate his body, as he had just done for her] and cuts his skin while he is asleep. Instead of air, it is his blood that gushes out, but she fails to recognize bleeding as a characteristic of a living human being. While she tries without success to seal the cut with tape and to inflate his body through his mouth, she laments in voice-over, "My breath cannot fill Junichi."[24]

Like *Under the Skin*, *Air Doll* dramatizes material distinctions between its synthetic woman protagonist and the humans she encounters, their differences building to destructive conclusions.

In a decisive shift that is critical to *Air Doll*'s engagement with Nozomi's posthumanism, the murder scene completely disrupts the tone of the film up to this point, which had presented Nozomi's embrace of life and the romance of her evolving relationship with Junichi in a celebratory register. Viewers thus witness her stabbing Junichi and subsequent efforts to tape him shut (accompanied by the intense sound of his labored breathing) through a tonal register reminiscent of the horror genre (Figure 3.4). For another minute of screen time, Nozomi embraces and kisses Junichi, mistaking his sounds of struggle for passion; after she finally recognizes his distress, she pumps breath into his mouth in a frantic effort to revive him. A cut then elides the

Figure 3.4 In *Kūki Ningyō/Air Doll* (Hirokazu Kore-eda, 2009), Nozomi stabs Junichi, then attempts to tape him shut.

peak moment of her trauma to reveal, via a slow pan right, an ominously calm Nozomi upright in bed, clutching Junichi's head to her shoulder in a futile simulation of normal intimacy. *Air Doll* attributes Nozomi's unintentional homicide to a material misjudgment: Nozomi's tragic failure to comprehend the difference between her composition and Junichi's. As a result of this catastrophic error, Nozomi reassesses her own value as worthless. In consequence, she suicides by deflation, arranging herself among the garbage left beside the street for collection (Figure 3.5). Kim describes Nozomi's death as "a category shift from a live being to trash."[25] Another way of interpreting her suicide is as a sacrificial gesture reminiscent of Romeo and Juliet's finale, except in Nozomi's case, she repeats the action she had performed on Junichi on herself, thereby aligning her experience of death with his despite the blood/air distinction in the leakage that extinguishes their lives. Unambiguous in *Air Doll*'s conclusion is the fact that Nozomi's accidental murder of Junichi puts an end to her own miraculous posthuman life, thereby underscoring the critical difference between organic and mechanical composition.

By spotlighting cyborgs capable of masquerading as human women, *Under the Skin* and *Air Doll* disrupt traditional associations between female bodies and natural, organic life, but while *Air Doll* punishes Nozomi for failing to differentiate her synthetic body from Junichi's, it neglects to spectacularly reveal her nonhuman insides as *Under the Skin* does The Female's.

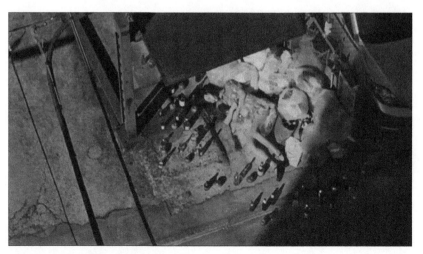

Figure 3.5 Nozomi suicides by deflation, arranging herself among the garbage left beside the street for collection.

I will therefore bring *Ex Machina* into this discussion as another example of a film that spectacularly exposes its cyborg woman's insides at a climactic moment; as it will be shown, this has significant implications for the dynamic between human and posthuman at play in these films. Our introduction to *Ex Machina* in Chapter 1 demonstrated that it shares a number of features with *Under the Skin*. *Ex Machina*'s emphasis on the racial implications of cyborg women adds to this chapter's discussion of the human/nonhuman material boundary reinforced via cinematic cyborg women, which is especially apparent in scenes that make a spectacle of the "leaky distinction" "between animal-human (organism) and machine." In "Alien Feminisms and Cinema's Posthuman Women," Dijana Jelača observes that "In a relatively short period of time, *Under the Skin* and *Ex Machina* have garnered a significant amount of scholarly interest. Both contain a seeming paradox: while their protagonists are nonhuman, they are also indisputably feminine in traditionally humanoid ways." The material aspects of the scenes that dramatically expose their protagonists' nonhuman composition distinctly illuminate the paradox Jelača identifies—namely, that these films make much of their cyborg women's nonhumanness while, at the same time, strongly imbuing them with qualities conventionally associated with femininity in belief systems (including humanism) that thrive on the male/female binary. By doing so, they seriously limit their abilities to delve deeply into the nonhuman dimensions of their humanesque cyborgs.

Under the Skin and *Ex Machina*'s exposure scenes are uncannily similar to the genital exposure scenes that are a staple of cis-authored transgender films; fleshing out this analogy reveals *Under the Skin* and *Ex Machina*'s investments in humanistic concepts of gender at the expense of their cyborg characterizations. Exposure scenes in transgender cinema typically involve cisgender characters forcing a trans character to expose their genitals; such scenes appear in most widely screened trans films, including *The Crying Game*, *Boys Don't Cry*, *Tomboy*, and *A Fantastic Woman*.[26] Although these films vary regarding *how* they allow viewers to participate in the exposure, they consistently frame the sight of their trans characters' genitals as traumatic (whether or not the imagery is explicit) in a manner that undermines the characters' trans identities, thereby endorsing gender-normative assumptions (and betraying cis-oriented perspectives). For instance, in *A Fantastic Woman*, after a detective (a cisgender woman) and a doctor (a cisgender man) use their authority to force Marina (a trans woman) to reveal her genitals, reaction shots of their faces convey lurid fascination upon viewing what is, to them, a transgressive sight, while Marina's face (in close-up) expresses the traumatic impact of their cisgender gaze. Transgender exposure scenes typically signal the representation of transgender embodiment according to cisnormative views. In a similar fashion, the exposure scenes in *Under the Skin* and *Ex Machina* subject their cyborgs to a human-oriented gaze that reinforces a firm boundary between organic and synthetic being.

Under the Skin's exposure scene, which ends the film, demonstrates its default to a human perspective at the precise point when the cyborg's human and nonhuman hybridity becomes visually evident. In the scene, The Female is pursued by a logger, who initially attempts to rape her, but after unexpectedly encountering her nonhuman materiality, he sets her on fire instead. While wrestling with The Female to tear her clothes off, the logger rips the skin on her back, revealing mysterious black matter where the skin splits (Figure 3.6). Thus by forcing The Female to disrobe, he unveils a deeper layer, disclosing the nonhuman threat her seductive clothing and skin had hidden. Doane's description of the femme fatale is a propos of *Under the Skin*'s treatment of The Female; she is "the figure of a certain discursive unease, a potential epistemological trauma. For her most striking characteristic, perhaps,

Figure 3.6 The logger rips The Female's skin, revealing mysterious black matter, in *Under the Skin* (Jonathan Glazer, 2013).

is the fact that she never really is what she seems to be. She harbors a threat which is not entirely legible, predictable, or manageable."[27] At the sight of her punctured skin, the logger flees. Swagato Chakravorty perceives a "play with surfaces" in the "curious duality evident between the alien underside and the human exterior of this surface (noticeable when she/it peels it off)."[28] The skin appears human textured, which makes the blackness visible where it gapes all the more disturbing, with the edges of the tear suggesting that the skin's material consistency is similar to plaster or wallpaper. The shock of this exposure has a distancing effect that, when coupled with a reaction shot that communicates the logger's horror, frames The Female as a lurid object of human fascination.

After The Female's artificial skin is pierced, the musical score that played during the male submersion scenes resumes to accentuate the narrative reversal, wherein The Female is now the victim about to experience material annihilation. Left alone, she completely sheds the outer layer of skin as if disrobing, in a move that ironically recalls the earlier scenes when she stripped to entice human victims. Under that skin, she appears solidly and smoothly black, yet her shape is humanoid, and her facial features are recognizably Johansson's (despite the uncanny doubling accomplished by an image of the black figure cradling the inert face she had just shed). Doane describes cinema's "transform[ation]" of the femme fatale's "threat . . . into a secret, something which must be aggressively revealed, unmasked, discovered."[29] In *Under the Skin*'s final scene, the logger accomplishes this aggressive unmasking. A jarring and shaky handheld point-of-view shot from his perspective signals his return to the scene; the camerawork, reminiscent of horror cinema, foregrounds his fear. He douses The Female in fuel, her black body shining with oil before catching fire. Per Doane, "the femme fatale is situated as evil and is frequently punished or killed. Her textual eradication involves a desperate reassertion of control on the part of the threatened male subject."[30] As in Nozomi's death, the method and visualization of The Female's are tied to her nonhuman materiality. The ending of each film makes a spectacle of the posthuman woman's annihilation in the tonal register of horror. Thus, while *Under the Skin*'s contrast of human and nonhuman materiality is aesthetically compelling, its tight alignment of The Female with femme fatale conventions indicates its conservatism regarding both gender and nonhuman embodiment.

Ex Machina's multiple exposure scenes, which involve Ava (played by Alicia Vikander) and Kyoto (played by Sonoya Mizuno), a mute gynoid

122 SCREENING THE POSTHUMAN

whose creation preceded Ava's, highlight the influence of sexist and racist ideologies on male-oriented cyborg design. These ideologies recall the biases Ferrando drew attention to as signs of humanistic thinking, which subverts posthuman efforts to move beyond gender binarism. *Ex Machina*'s robotic engineer, Nathan (played by Oscar Isaac), only creates mechanical women, and they represent various stages in his creative practice as well as his design of distinctly raced gynoids to meet his needs. Therefore, when Caleb hacks into Nathan's computer, he finds evidence of the engineer's past experiments with gynoids who appear European, African, and Asian, and who Nathan imprisoned and exploited in a manner analogous to his treatment of Ava and Kyoko. As outlined in Chapter 1, the film's drama hinges on Ava's manipulation of Caleb to outmaneuver Nathan. The mechanical exposure scenes occur after she succeeds in instrumentalizing Caleb to free herself. Ava wanders the compound outside of her cell and quickly comes in contact with evidence of Nathan's other humanoid designs, including a mask version of her face on display in the hallway. As she touches the uncanny replica, bringing her own face close to stroke and smell it, Kyoko appears at the opposite end of the hallway. The two women then come together, staring at and touching each other. In the meantime, Nathan overcomes Caleb, equipping himself with a metal piece from his weight set before rushing to apprehend Ava. Nathan finds Ava and Kyoko huddled together in the hallway, Ava having whispered something inaudible to viewers in Kyoko's ear (Figure 3.7). When Ava attacks Nathan, he severs her lower arm with his metal weapon. He then begins to drag her injured body down the hall, but Kyoko ambushes him, burying a knife deep in his back. In retaliation, he destroys her chin, the mechanical parts inside her face leaking out. This injury causes her to collapse, and she appears totally inoperative (which is odd in contrast to Ava's fully functional condition despite sustaining a more severe injury).

Ex Machina's mechanical exposures, of which the above is just one example, invite reflection on the role race plays in representations of cyborg women that evidence sexist and racist ideologies alongside patterns of humanistic othering. In "Envisioning Cyborg Bodies: Notes from Current Research," Jennifer González argues that "the image of the cyborg body" transmits "on its surface and in its fundamental structure the multiple fears and desires of a culture caught in the process of transformation."[31] After finishing the job of murdering Nathan by stabbing him to death, Ava stumbles across another prototype that prefigured her design—a decommissioned, Asian-looking woman whose humanoid arms she unscrews, attaching them

Figure 3.7 Ava whispers something inaudible to viewers in Kyoko's ear in *Ex Machina* (Alex Garland, 2014).

to replace her missing limb and mask her sleek, mechanical anatomy. The skin she removes from the woman's body resembles insulation, in particular while Ava smooths it into place. The film then dwells on Ava's post-transplant regard of her new body, multiple mirrors in the shot accommodating the contemplation of five naked Ava's for a considerable duration. *Ex Machina*'s engagement with cyborg embodiment evokes a complex history in which male-authored ideas about women's bodies determine their evaluation (e.g., consider the pervasive rating of women's looks on a 1–10 scale[32]). Saemyi Chung's dissertation cites a 2015 article in *The Telegraph*, "All hail Scarlett Johansson's perfect 'golden ratio' figure,"[33] to illustrate the fact that a Greek formula for assessing the female form, which predates the Common Era, is still used to assess women's bodies: "Johansson is well known for her perfect body due to its conformity to the golden ratio. Scarlett's bust-to-waist compared to her hip-to-waist measurement was estimated to be at 1.560 (out of 1.618) which means that she has a 96.4% golden ratio accuracy."[34] Like The Female (as embodied by Johansson), all of Nathan's cyborg women conform, to some degree, to classically Western beauty ideals, yet *Ex Machina*'s explicit juxtaposition of the mute Kyoko and the hyper-verbal Ava underlines the intersection of sexist and racist biases that dictate what different kinds of women objects are useful for. The fact that Nathan creates Kyoko, a beautiful Japanese woman who cannot speak, for sex and housekeeping, and

124 SCREENING THE POSTHUMAN

Ava to seduce Caleb with her white European beauty and wit stresses the Eurocentric and racist orientation of Nathan's robotic designs—and this, in my view, further evidences the film's humanistic priorities, which negate the posthuman ideas about gender that its cyborg women hint at without fully embodying (thus, viewers can't hear the exchange between Ava and Kyoko).

Offering further insight into the othering practices apparent in cyborg representations, González notes "a general tendency to link the 'otherness' of machines with the otherness of racial and sexual difference."[35] According to this perspective, then, Kyoko is doubly-othered through her instrumentalization as a sexual object who is also a woman of color programmed to be mute (with the accomplishment of menial and sexual labor in mind). Presenting the cyborg "Kiddy" from the "1991 Japanese comic book *Silent Möbius*" to substantiate her claims about "cyborgs that appear to be racially 'marked' as not 'white,'" González ultimately contends that when Kiddy "removes her skin . . . she becomes the quintessential cyborg body. For in the Western imaginary, this body is all about revealing the internal mechanism."[36] Scenes that "reveal the internal mechanism" in *Under the Skin* and *Ex Machina* "out" the nonhuman beings successfully passing as "objects of flawless [human] beauty" (just as Nozomi's accidental murder of Junichi exposes her nonhuman perspective). The captivation of these cyborg unmaskings therefore involves an ambivalent cocktail of seduction and repulsion. Yet unlike, for instance, the infamous genital reveal in *The Crying Game*, the exposure of their insides is not primarily aimed at shocking viewers. Instead, it serves to reinforce the essential enigma of women, compounding it via synthetic hybridity. Furthermore, the dependence of these cinematic renderings of cyborg women on object-based surface over subjective depth supports Doane's claim that women in cinema have been "more closely associated with the surface of the image than its illusory depths."[37] These exposure scenes are therefore consistent with well-known, and heavily gendered, formulas for stimulating "visual pleasure in narrative cinema." They make a spectacle of masking and unmasking the hybrid and suspect materialities of fetishized women/objects who double as posthuman threats.

Regarding *Under the Skin*, I have shown that the pair of scenes that "other" human embodiment, spectacularly exposing its materiality in the process of disintegration, are productively posthuman in comparison to the film's depiction of The Female's enigmatic, seductive, and threatening nonhuman body, which must be annihilated. Furthermore, while *Under the Skin* is aesthetically provocative in its visualization of human disintegration, The Female resolutely maintains the "seductive cyborg woman threat to human being" stock character type familiar from twentieth-century mainstream Sci-Fi (which, in turn, adapted the figure from film noir's femme fatale). Meanwhile, the technofetishism of *Ex Machina*'s Ava weds Eurocentric and sexist beauty standards to technology's seductive appeal. In contrast, the portrait of Kyoto, the mute and beautiful Asian woman who cooks, cleans, fucks, and dances well, epitomizes the reduction of synthetic womanhood to a sexist *and* racist male vision. Finally, in *Air Doll*, Nozomi's consciousness is tragically snuffed out due to her confusion about the material difference between human and her own composition. Furthermore, Kore-eda's decision to cast Bae Doona, a South Korean actress, to perform the role of a sex doll come to life in a film that otherwise features Japanese actors is provocative to say the least.[38] It resonates with the trend González articulated, "to link the 'otherness' of machines with the otherness of racial and sexual difference." "The image of the cyborg," González avers, "has historically recurred at moments of radical social and cultural change. From bestial monstrosities, to unlikely montages of body and machine parts, to electronic implants, imaginary representations of cyborgs take over when traditional bodies fail."[39] In sum, these films' cyborgs no doubt speak to the radical shift of human to posthuman, yet their striking aestheticizations of synthetic, humanoid women frequently subject the latter to a human gaze that objectifies and others them, thereby shortchanging the posthuman speculation they might otherwise have stimulated.

Technosexuality in *Who You Think I Am*

Like *Under the Skin*, *Air Doll*, and *Ex Machina*, *Who You Think I Am* uses a woman as its cyborg vehicle to explore eroding distinctions between the organic and the mechanical, as well as between the subject and the object, in posthuman experience. However, in this case, the woman is explicitly middle-aged, and her pursuit of technologically mediated forms of intimacy is depicted in a realistic mode. Furthermore, she is neither fetishized nor spectacularly exposed for concealing her nonhuman materiality. Yet, despite the film's partial embrace of Claire's technosexuality, it also conveys a certain ambivalence when characters other than Claire skeptically challenge the legitimacy of her cyborg identity on humanistic and ageist grounds.

126 SCREENING THE POSTHUMAN

In consequence, while the film normalizes Claire's cyborg sexuality, it also evinces uncertainty regarding its authenticity and the ethics of online/off-line hybrid subjectivity. Therefore, like the films analyzed above, *Who You Think I Am* reverts to humanism and misogyny in its portrait of posthuman womanhood.

Who You Think I Am's complex depiction of Claire is consistent with scholarship on technosexuality. Shaowen and Jeffrey Bardzell define "technosexuality" in their entry on the subject in *The Wiley Blackwell Encyclopedia of Gender and Sexuality Studies* as follows:

> Technosexuality refers to the overlap between human sexuality and tech-nology. It has two common formulations. The first is based on an expan-sive cultural notion, in which technology is viewed as a social force that shapes or configures human sexuality. The second is a more narrow notion, referring to a human's sexual attraction to technologies.[40]

Claire's technosexuality illustrates both formulations. On the one hand, the film represents technology as fully integrated into its characters' romantic and sexual habits—that is, various forms of digital communication, with computers and smartphones as hardware, are primary rather than supple-mentary to its characters' expressions of sexuality. On the other, Claire's erotic encounters involving technologies, including the film's most explicit sex scene (a quickie between Claire, her smartphone, and her virtual lover, Alex, which I analyze below), suggest that communication technologies serve as an object of sexual desire for Claire; in other words, they are often the ends rather than the means, their functions not subordinated to normative, non-mediated sexuality between organic humans.

While *Who You Think I Am* oscillates between validating and undermining the authenticity of Claire's cyborg identity, it effectively draws attention to key areas of technosexuality research. According to the Bardzells, these include "embodied interactions, online performance of the self, the roles technologies have in constituting sexual experience, sexual simulation . . . and emergent sexual practices and attitudes that arise from innovations in this domain."[41] The film's character study of Claire covers all of these issues, and is particularly successful at evoking "embodied interactions" between Claire—an amalga-mation of her non-mediated self, a fifty-something divorced woman, and her virtual persona, the much younger Clara—multiple technological devices, and her new lover, Alex, whom she engages with virtually. However, the film also allows ample space for viewers to question the authenticity of Claire's cyborg identity. In response to a question posed by her therapist, Dr. Catherine Bormans (played by Nicole Garcia), "You didn't mind that in Alex's head, you were another woman?," Claire replies, "I wasn't pretending to be 24, I was 24." Despite Claire's assured response, Bormans's question implies incredulity regarding online/offline hybrid identity. In another therapy session, Claire describes social media as "both the shipwreck and the life raft" for "people like [her]"—that is, middle-aged women disillusioned by exes who left them for younger women whose efforts to find new partners are stymied by the cultural invisibility of middle-aged women. Thus, while the film thoughtfully engages with identity, intimacy, and subjectivity in posthuman technosexual experience, its representation of cyborg identity is imbued with a humanistic skepticism that carries sexist and ageist biases.

Exemplary of the film's ambivalence about cyborg identity are Claire's therapy sessions, which facilitate debate on the legitimacy of Claire's emerging cyborg self, such as the one mentioned above in which Bormans frames it as a pretense. In this sense, the film stresses that regardless of Claire's commitment to its legitimacy, she must perpetually defend her position against a normative view (voiced by Dr. Bormans, among others in the film). In *How We Became Posthuman*, Hayles asks, "What do gendered bodies have to do with the erasure of embodiment and the subsequent merging of machine and human intelligence in the figure of the cyborg?"[42] *Who You Think I Am* uses Claire's gendered, middle-aged body to expose intense cultural ambivalence about the "merging of machine and human." In fact, the film constantly highlights the influence of normative assumptions about what counts as sexy on Claire's mediated performance. For instance, when Alex enthusiastically demands "A REAL PICTURE OF YOU!!!" via instant message, Claire sends a picture of Clara, later describing to Dr. Bormans the excitement that action aroused (which in turn reinforces her technosexuality). Furthermore, Claire insists that by sending the image, she gave Clara "a real face." The shot of Claire defending her action against Bormans's skepticism frames Binoche's sincere expression in extreme close-up before cutting to a complementary framing of Clara, this second extreme close-up pixelated to approximate the low-quality compressed digital image sent to Alex (Figure 3.8). Therefore, while the symmetrical compositions of the Claire/Clara extreme close-ups support their hybridity, the film continually requires Claire to defend her integration of Clara into her cyborg identity against the opposing view (presented as the cultural default), which regards her amalgamation with the

Figure 3.8 Claire's sincere expression in extreme close-up cuts to a complementary framing of Clara, the symmetrical compositions reinforcing the characters' hybridity.

beautiful and younger Clara in virtual form as the ruse of an ageing woman bent on manipulating a young man into erotic encounters. Claire's act of sending the photo and her justification of it ambivalently underscore the premium on digital images of young women in the economy of virtual intimacy.

Interestingly, the film is unwavering in its commitment to Claire's cyborg identity when it features images of her engaging with her computer or phone (accompanied by text or audio to communicate Alex's participation). These moments in the film, in which reflections from electronic screens light Binoche's face, imagine a three-way engagement that disables the interpretation of Claire as "alone" during erotic and emotional encounters that wed organic and electronic components. Most impactful among this category of scenes in *Who You Think I Am* is the film's most explicit erotic sequence, when Claire, having just left a party and entered her car to drive home, calls

Alex, and the two have sex in concert with their phones. From the start of the exchange, the image track illustrates inconsistencies between Claire's appearance and what she describes to Alex. For instance, when Alex asks where she is, Claire states that she's "in bed already," despite the image of her seated behind the wheel of her car. However, in my view, understanding her organic body as only one layer of her embodied cyborg experience resolves apparent tensions between how she looks and what she says. Accordingly, the fact that she describes wearing "a low-cut sweatshirt and boy shorts" can be interpreted as an expression of the fantastic dimension of technosexuality, which liberates the posthuman from the material reliance on the organic human body as primary (or sole) experiential medium. Moreover, while Alex and Claire "talk dirty," they instrumentalize each other's bodies through verbal instruction: "My hand is on your stomach," Alex whispers. "Do you feel it?" "Yes, I can feel it," Claire replies, confirming the imaginative skills her technosexuality has honed, which allow her to mobilize her human body and voice, both communication technologies, as part of her cyborg identity to engage in mutually satisfying sex with Alex (Figure 3.9). Haraway retrospectively describes her "cyber work" as "the work on hybridizations and fusions among the organic, human and technical, and the way the material, the literal and the tropic implode into each other."[43] This scene is a perfect expression of this category of "cyber work" in its depiction of the material fusions—among human bodies, cyborg identities, and communication technologies—that mediate Alex and Claire's intimacy.

Figure 3.9 Claire mobilizes her human body and voice in concert with multiple electronic components to engage in mutually satisfying cybersex with Alex in *Celle que vous croyez/Who You Think I Am* (Safy Nebbou, 2019).

130 SCREENING THE POSTHUMAN

Yet Claire's non-mediated encounters with other humans belittle her cyborg embodiment according to sexist and ageist perspectives that restrict experience to the organic human body. For instance, Claire discusses her romance with Alex at a dinner party of middle-aged friends; when she describes Alex as "a young guy getting carried away," her male friend asks, "are you playing the cougar?" Another friend (a woman) jumps to Claire's defense: "We say cougar for women, but what's the word for men?" "Men" retorts one of the men in the room, which prompts laughter. The conversation is clearly designed to articulate the double standard regulating the sexuality of women, with the punchline and subsequent laughter signaling the cultural pressure to accept as normal sexist beliefs that involve the disparagement of the sexual desires of women of a "certain age." The same double standard, the film suggests, influences cultural views on women's technosexuality. That said, Claire's aloof response to whether she is playing the cougar, "I'm not playing," aligns with her staunch defense of her hybrid identity in opposition to Dr. Bormans's incredulity. *Who You Think I Am*'s portrait of Claire's cyborg embodiment requires her constant assertion of her cyborg identity and technosexuality as "real" against skepticism attached to humanistic views that privilege organic hardware and espouse sexist beliefs about the sexual expression of ageing women.

The film's depiction of the cyborg from a posthuman standpoint relies on the realism of its treatment of Claire's technosexuality, which substantiates, to some extent, Jelača's concept of "alien feminisms." In the latter, Jelača incorporates the term "alien" "not simply [to denote] 'out of this world,' or extraterrestrial, but rather an entity that is simultaneously familiar and strange, humanoid and posthuman—all too ordinary, while nevertheless diverging from hegemonic models of subjectivity, gender, and identity that have historically come to stifle feminist political projects."[44] Demonstrating an analogous ambivalence, *Who You Think I Am* treats Claire's cyborg identity as both mundane and extraordinary. Recall Claire's description of social media as both disaster and salvation for not only her, but "people like [her]," of which she implies there are many. Thus, while all of the films discussed in this chapter explore "alien feminisms," *Who You Think I Am* does so without employing technofetishistic aesthetics, using a realistic style, instead, to depict a woman's posthuman subjectivity. For instance, a montage sequence of Claire riding the Paris Metro conveys her awareness of the many passengers intensely engaged with their phones. Claire's reflective expression, framed in medium close-up, demonstrates that she is paying attention to the other

FROM CYBORG THEORY TO POSTHUMAN MOTHERS 131

passengers in the train with her, while the multiple countershots that follow
zero in on the hands of strangers scrolling and texting; the film's depiction of
these behaviors implies their ubiquity—viewers have seen the like, in other
words, both on- and off-screen. The universality of such human/machine
encounters enhances the relatability of cyborg imagery of Claire, which
dominates the film.

Moreover, the relative realism of *Who You Think I Am*'s approach to
"alien feminism" points to an issue this book continually highlights—the
branching out of cinematic explorations of posthuman phenomena beyond
the generic confines of Sci-Fi and fantasy in recognition of the normalization of such phenomena. Viewers witness Claire's subjective transformation
as "simultaneously familiar and strange, humanoid and posthuman" without
a heavy emphasis on techno-aesthetics, and it is precisely the realistic facets
of Claire's characterization that allow it to evoke "familiarity" in combination with the novelty of her posthuman sexual expression. In fleshing out the
concept of "alien feminisms," Jelača cites Braidotti, who stated (in 2006) that
"one needs to turn to 'minor,' not to say marginal and hybrid genres, such
as science fiction, science fiction horror and cyber punk, to find fitting cultural illustrations of the changes and transformations that are taking place
in the forms of relations available in our posthuman present."[45] However,
illustrations of posthuman transformations are not confined to "minor"
genres, and recent films that depict "alien feminisms" are just as likely to be
categorized as art films (such as *Air Doll*), independent dramas (as in the case
of *Who You Think I Am*), and/or comedies (for instance, *Ingrid Goes West*,
which we analyzed in Chapter 1), among other popular cinema categories.
That said, extreme scenarios of posthuman intimacy, which the *Black Mirror*
anthology is particularly known for, neglect already widespread forms of
technosexuality in favor of dramatic hypotheticals; an example from *Black
Mirror* is *San Junipero*'s (Series 3, Episode 4) exploration of romantic love in a
simulated reality wherein the protagonist lovers eventually fully upload their
consciousness, which is an extreme scenario that takes a giant leap beyond
the forms of romantic love already routinely expressed in virtual spaces.
In "When Love is Optimized, Is It Still Love?," Sophie Gilbert bemoans the
shortcomings of recent television productions that thematize the impacts of
technology on romance and sexuality:

My frustration with shows that get wrapped up in hypothetical technology
is that they seem to miss the forest for the trees. TV and film have largely

132   SCREENING THE POSTHUMAN

> ignored many of the real-life developments of recent years that even a decade ago might have seemed plenty dystopian: To spend so much time agonizing over how brain chips or soul uploading or a digital afterlife might affect relationships is to leave things such as Tinder, location services, the sex recession, and the dating gap relatively unexamined.[46]

This critique, which I consider valid, sheds light on the tendency of spectacle-driven genre screen fiction to bypass aspects of posthuman experience already well-nested in the techno-subjectivities and sexualities of many posthumans. In contrast, *Who You Think I Am* demonstrates that situating women cyborgs in realistic and mundane environments can enhance cinema's capacity to address the pervasiveness (and normality) of the radical "changes and transformations" that constitute posthuman experience (*Ingrid Goes West* is also exemplary in this regard).

In contrast, Scarlet Johansson's extraordinary cyborg characters display the limits of more traditionally Sci-Fi cinematic depictions of cyborg women. These tend to stimulate transhumanist fantasies (as shown by the analysis of *Lucy* in Chapter 1) and/or fall prey to classic sexist conventions of representing women as fetishized objects (as indicated by the femme fatale dimensions of The Female in *Under the Skin*). A panel at the annual conference of the Society for Cinema and Media Studies in 2015, "Scarlet Johansson's 'Bodily Turn,'" presented the actor's performances in *Her*, *Under the Skin*, and *Lucy* as a meaningful trilogy. An article by Noah Gittel published a year earlier (in *The Atlantic*) calls the same trio of film performances Johansson's "vanishing act," interpreting the roles as evincing her desire to "disappear."[47] Gittel goes on to read her work in these films "as a unique and powerful statement about an industry and society that make its women disappear." His position seems at odds with the hypervisibility these performances afforded Johansson, as well as these films' capitalization on her fetishized presence (her absence from *Her*'s image track only intensifying the embodiment suggested by her vocal performance). The SCMS panel's chair, Chakravorty, interprets this "turn" differently to Gittel: as opposed to disappearing, Chakravorty perceives a spectacular quality to the presentation of Johansson's body in these roles—"a logic of the (bodily) surface" "traceable across these films [that] opens up interesting questions concerning representations of the feminine body on-screen."[48] In other words, while Gittel connects the absence of body and/or personality in Johansson's cyborg characters to Johansson's intentional critique of "Hollywood's objectification

FROM CYBORG THEORY TO POSTHUMAN MOTHERS   133

of women," Chakravorty sees them as reflexively superficial. In fact, both views evidence the seductive appeal of technofetishized depictions of cyborg women, which stimulate fantasies of transhumanism and reinforce humanistic patterns of othering and objectifying women, and these obstruct, in my view, the exploration of posthuman subjectivities.

In comparison, the performances of fifty-something Binoche in films with posthumanist ambitions aim more for realism than spectacle (these films include *Who You Think I Am*, Claire Denis's *High Life* [2018] and Kore-eda's *The Truth* [2020]). Binoche's characterizations of posthuman womanhood are more consistent with feminist cyborg theories that undermine the subject/ object distinction in part because residual sexism and ageism in cinema and culture prohibit the easy use of middle-aged women as (techno)fetishized objects. On a related note, many reviews of *Who You Think I Am* label it "a catfish story" ("catfish" appearing, for instance, in the title and/or subtitle of *Variety* and *Telegraph* reviews of the film).[49] This usage of the term dates back to the 2010 documentary, *Catfish*, which deals with a middle-aged woman who posed as a nineteen-year-old to cultivate a virtual romance with a much younger man. Addressing the familiarity of *Who You Think I Am*'s plot, Guy Lodge (in a review for *Variety*) broaches the "cloak of invisibility that, past a certain age, even the most charismatic women take on in the eyes of many men" to justify Claire's catfishing (after a seemingly contradictory comment on Binoche's "perma-radian[ce]" *despite* her age). Tim Robey's *Telegraph* review takes another tack, first highlighting the unsettling nature of Claire's actions, then concluding that all social media users catfish: "Claire's gamble, which becomes a dangerous addiction, is hardly just hers—it's merely the logical extension of everyone's best-foot-forward Tinder profiles. All the age-fudging on apps, the non-updating of selfies, and the implicit dread of being past it have converted our real-life selves into stricken portraits in the attic." Critics' divergent interpretations of Claire's character illustrate that it appears alien in the same sense Jelača evokes via "alien feminism": it is "simultaneously familiar and strange." And it is precisely by refusing to romanticize Claire's technosexuality that *Who You Think I Am* is able to avoid transhumanist spectacle and explore the mechanical integration at the core of her identity.

Claire's identity as a middle-aged woman, then, is crucial to the film's inquiry into technosexuality because it discourages her objectification and enhances the relatability of her actions—thereby directing critical attention to the total fusion of body and technology in her cyborg subjectivity.

134 SCREENING THE POSTHUMAN

Yet as I have also shown, her status as a middle-aged woman inspires sexist and ageist attacks on the legitimacy of her cyborg identity, which imbue *Who You Think I Am*'s take on Claire's posthumanness with ambivalence. Braidotti asks, in regard to Haraway's cyborgs and other hybrid "monstrosities," "What if these unprogrammed-for others were forms of subjectivity that have simply shrugged off the shadow of binary logic and negativity and have moved on? The process of transformation of the subject goes on and we need process ontology to provide adequate accounts of it."[50] While *Who You Think I Am* has not entirely "shrugged off" humanistic beliefs about identity and embodiment, its portrait of Claire represents a significant start in accounting for the subjective transformations posthuman experience inspires. This is not to say that a film can't use a young, attractive woman to represent a cyborg (which *Ingrid Goes West* does quite effectively), but objectifying her—offering her as a (techno)fetishized object to stimulate erotic contemplation—will only undermine her "alien feminism" by reinforcing "preconceived notions about subjectivity, gender, and identity," which posthuman womanhood counteracts. Therefore, it is significant that the films analyzed next, with posthuman mothers as protagonists, likewise feature naturalistic performances by middle-aged actors and avoid fetishizing their cyborg women, who venture far into material integration with technology.

Astronauts and Mothers Bridge the Gap

This section will argue that both *Proxima* and *The Congress* frame motherhood as a vital component of cyborg womanhood, albeit not without a hefty dose of the ambivalence that is characteristic of cinematic attempts to grapple with the human transition to posthuman experience. Key theorists in critical posthumanism advocate for marshaling the collective strengths of the sciences and humanities to effectively "com[e] to terms with the [posthuman] world we live in." For example, commenting on the radical interdisciplinarity of "A Cyborg Manifesto," Haraway cites her academic background in biology and "passionat[e] engage[ment] with its knowledge projects: its materialities, organisms and worlds."[51] It is thus telling that, as this final section will show, *Proxima* utilizes an astronaut protagonist to demonstrate a comparable level of "passionate engagement" with physical and biological sciences— and with an emphasis on Sarah's maternity—to poetically render cyborg

FROM CYBORG THEORY TO POSTHUMAN MOTHERS   135

embodiment and subjectivity. In the process, *Proxima* suggests that humanistic nostalgia intensifies precisely when Sarah is embodying or imagining a posthuman perspective. Indeed, as it will be argued, the film's most compelling sequences involve Sarah preparing for extraterrestrial experience (with diverse technologies as support) and experiencing a passionate attachment to earth while on the cusp of departing it; this attachment centers, in turn, on her love for her daughter Stella. Meanwhile, I will also suggest that her negotiation of not-always compatible commitments to succeeding as an astronaut and a mother is not as retro or humanistic as it might appear at first glance. In fact, analysis of the cyborg mothers in *Proxima* and *The Congress*, a film that also features a cyborg mother protagonist, reveals that motherhood has accrued unconventional significance in contemporary posthuman cinema, which subverts the construct of the "organic" mother that Haraway's cyborg theory undermined.

Proxima initially presents Sarah's commitment to mothering her daughter Stella as at odds with her ambition to merge with various technologies to facilitate extraterrestrial experience. K. Austin Collins's *Rolling Stone* review of *Proxima* homes in on the film's alienation of humanness through its emphasis on Sarah's otherness in Moscow's Star City, where much of the film is set, as well as its alignment of her femininity and maternity with "alienness": "*Proxima*, with its cool hues and steady gaze, its sense of Sarah's alienness among ostensible fellow-humans, proves most evocative as a study of a mother's now-tenuous ties to her daughter."[52] *Proxima* highlights Sarah's "alien feminism" as the sole woman astronaut forced to constantly prove her worth in a contingent of men led by American astronaut, Mike Shannon (played by Matt Dillon, effectively typecast in the role). Underscoring Sarah's exceptionalism, then, the woman who shows her around Star City upon her arrival states, "There aren't many women who have come here." Sarah's singularity is further accentuated several scenes later when a male doctor interrogates her regarding her choice to continue menstruating in space: "You know the constraints? Some things [i.e. disabling menstruation] are more practical up there." While fighting against her colleague's gender-based prejudices during Star City's physically and mentally punishing training regime, Sarah uses every communication technology at her disposal to maintain her connection to Stella (now living with her father in Germany) before Sarah's mission drastically reduces their contact.

While presenting Sarah's maternity (and fertility) as a hindrance to her extraterrestrial training, *Proxima* also frequently associates the gradual

136   SCREENING THE POSTHUMAN

integration of Sarah's organic body and various machines with her womanhood—and in many cases, with material practices of her maternity. The analysis below will reveal the significance of motherhood to imagining "woman-machine" hybrids (and to breaking down the boundaries Haraway elaborated in her cyborg myth). The film's tethering of human/posthuman tensions to reproduction and the intensity of a mother's bond with her daughter recalls Doane's formulation of motherhood's ambivalent function in the representation of cyborg women: "Motherhood acts as a limit to the conceptualization of femininity as a scientific construction of mechanical and electrical parts. And yet it is also that which infuses the machine with the breath of a human spirit."[53] *Proxima*'s framing of Sarah's maternity as both impediment to and motivation for her cyborg becoming perfectly illustrates the ambivalence Doane conceptualizes.

Initially, the film appears to set Sarah's integration with technology against her maternity in its positioning of her female body as a hurdle she must clear to be deemed mission ready. Training sequences involving Sarah's orientation to various technologies (which she must master to survive a year in space) comprise the bulk of the film, and these are juxtaposed with multimedia conversations between mother and daughter in the film's first act. *Proxima* opens with Sarah proudly describing to Stella (via voice-over accompanying the film credits) the basics of the mission she is about to train for, with Stella most interested in the fact that Sarah, freed from gravity, will "float." Meanwhile, the film's first shot is of Sarah, masked and breathing heavily, in the midst of a simulation exercise designed to equip her to fight an "uncontained fire" (the physical intensity of the image contrasting the ethereality of astronaut experience suggested by the opening conversation). Red lights flash, and a robotic male voice guides Sarah's movements. The action then quickly cuts to her exercising a robotic arm to enhance her "freedom" of movement and achieve "full hand control." Finally, the opening montage of cyborg training concludes with Sarah horizontally working out on a treadmill, suspended in midair with the support of a web of pulleys (Figure 3.10). In each cyborg training exercise, she is guided or assessed by a man (whose presence is audible and/or visual). Later training sequences, in the thick of her tenure in Star City, demonstrate the impressive range of technologies she must successfully integrate, as the boundaries of her human hardware are far surpassed in the refinement of posthuman capacity. These sequences also see her push back against sexist beliefs about her fitness for the extraterrestrial mission. For instance, Shannon observes while Sarah, strapped inside a

Figure 3.10 Early in *Proxima* (Alice Wincoeur, 2019), a cyborg training montage features Sarah's orientation to various technologies.

small vessel, is whipped at ever-increasing speeds; "she's resisting well," says a mechanical off-screen voice while the shot lingers on Shannon's intimidating expression. In this segment of the film, Sarah also orients to the weight of astronaut gear; perfects virtual reality exercises for mechanical engineering in space; and, in a climactic exercise, hauls Shannon (playing dead) to the surface in an underwater scenario that approximates a crisis outside the space shuttle, thereby "winning" her senior crew member's approval. Sarah meets these challenges, the film suggests, *despite* the additional effort she expends to remain in close contact with Stella while training.

Once the film establishes Sarah's cyborg fitness and success at overcoming gender-based prejudices, it shifts more emphatically to the maternal dimension of her posthuman subjectivity by weaving multimedia communication between Sarah and Stella into her preparation for take-off. Unlike in the earlier segment, her maternal labor begins to appear complementary to her cyborg work. This is also when the film most explicitly stresses Sarah's augmented attention to the physicality of earthly experience as she "become[es] a space person" (in Stella's words). The most revealing example of this aspect of the film's take on maternal cyborg subjectivity is a montage of Sarah with her two crew members in the woods "enjoy[ing] gravity" (to quote the line of dialogue spoken by Shannon that jumpstarts the montage). Over a slow-paced and ponderous electronic score, Sarah's off-screen voice states, "Last days on Earth before leaving the planet," while shots of two dogs playing in a field and of her crew member Anton squatting over a pond, recording "sounds of the forest and rain," appear on-screen. The montage then cuts to a medium shot of Sarah's profile as she snaps photos of the forest with her iPhone, thereby connecting the first two images to the audiovisual record she is producing to remind herself of earthly sights, sounds, and textures from space. Next, a low-quality, high-angle long take of Sarah's bare feet walking on grass demonstrates her documentation of material engagement with earth; her voice-over—"Spring, summer, autumn, winter. You know, up there, none of that exists" (Figure 3.11)—heightens the juxtaposition of

Figure 3.11 Sarah documents her own material engagement with earth in a high-angle long take of her bare feet walking in grass.

earth and space thematized by the film as a whole. Next, Sarah memorializes (in grainy close-up) the passage of a ladybug up her arm and over her hand while ruminating on being imminently cut off from feeling "wind on her skin" and "sunshine on her hair." Finally, after vocalizing that she'll soon "see 16 sunsets a day," she says, "I'll think of your question when you were little: 'when the sun goes to bed, is anyone there to tell it a story?'" This statement reveals that Sarah's voice-over monologue is in fact addressed to Stella, the image track subsequently cutting to Sarah packing a small box: "My whole life on Earth must fit in that shoebox," she continues. Her careful package and label of multiple "worn items," including a bracelet of beads that spell out "Sarah" and "Stella" and a child-like drawing of the two of them, demonstrate the primary position of their relationship in Sarah's earthly experience. "What would you take, Stella?," she asks as the montage draws to a close, Sarah sealing an envelope and handwriting "Stella" on its front. The montage thus provides clarity on the sequence's context only as it draws to a close, which parallels Sarah's realizations about the substance of her earthly experience only on the cusp of being distant from it. The sequence further reveals that motherhood, and her intimate relationship with Stella, is what Sarah deems essential to her impending cyborg and extraterrestrial experience.

Sarah's letter to Stella, composed while she reflects on the materiality and significance of life on earth, reframes the film's depiction of Sarah's preparation for space as a mother's conversation with her daughter—the two communicating from the start and throughout the film, at some points with significant effort but ultimately with ease. The film ends with Stella watching Sarah's earthly departure; several eyeline matches from her point of view show the departing space shuttle as a bright light that gradually disappears. Despite the fact that the film centers on Sarah's perspective, she is entirely elided during and after the take-off sequence. In fact, Sarah isn't visible at all in the final scene, which shows Stella riding in a van (her father asleep beside her), reading Sarah's handwritten letter and smiling; she then carefully tucks the pages inside her clothing to press them against her chest. In the film's final moments, a shot/countershot reveals Stella's attention to a herd of horses galloping across a field beside the vehicle. A track in expresses her attention to a mare and filly running alongside one another, with the subsequent reaction shot showing Stella tilt her head to smile up at the sky. Therefore, while the film remains with the daughter on earth in its final moments, it reiterates that its vision of posthuman experience—as a blend of earthly and

140   SCREENING THE POSTHUMAN

extraterrestrial—relies upon communication between a cyborg mother and her daughter.

Proxima epitomizes a significant change in imagining motherhood in relation to cyborg embodiment and subjectivity. Jelača "note[s]" a "shift . . . in the more recent cinematic renderings of post-human women, which repositions them away from maternal/monstrous frameworks of deviant constitution that seek to reestablish organic normalcy and toward the feminine as inorganic, alien, and nonmaternal to begin with." Yet, while *Proxima* does reflect this move "away from maternal/monstrous frameworks," it does not approach "the feminine as . . . nonmaternal to begin with." On the contrary, *Proxima* embraces its organic/machine hybrid scientist mother, thereby normalizing, to a certain extent, her extraordinary alien-ness. I regard *this* move as provocative in the context of cyborg representations in cinema— that is, portraying Sarah as a posthuman mother who loves and supports her child (and is therefore the opposite of monstrous) *and* passionately pursues posthuman forms of embodiment, experience, and communication. In this sense, *Proxima* shares noteworthy features with *Arrival* and *Gravity*, the latter high-budget, genre-blending Hollywood productions whose cyborg mothers also affirm Doane's view of motherhood's ambivalent function in imagining cyborg women: as both "a limit" and as "that which infuses the machine with the breath of a human spirit."[54] These films characterize their cyborg protagonists as "inorganic" and "alien," to some degree, but they also represent them as explicitly maternal. Like *Proxima*, *Gravity* is a character study that closely links its protagonist's challenges as an astronaut and mother, although in *Gravity*, the plot is *Proxima*'s inversion; the film begins with Ryan (played by Sandra Bullock) in space on a mission and ends with her return to Earth, and her maternal struggle involves mourning the loss of her young daughter in a tragic accident. Meanwhile, through Louise's characterization, *Arrival* illustrates posthuman forms of perception that bridge human and non-human concepts of time, space, and communication (Chapter 1 outlined Louise's gradual acclimation to posthuman perception while deciphering an alien language). And although Louise is a linguist rather than an astronaut, the protective suit she wears to enter the liminal space wherein humans and aliens haltingly communicate resembles the astronaut gear Sarah and Ryan wear, with the costumes of all three posthuman women underscoring their alien feminism. This set of films takes care to emphasize, both in narrative and aesthetics, its protagonists as both mothers and cyborgs, in equal and indivisible measure.

FROM CYBORG THEORY TO POSTHUMAN MOTHERS   141

In each of these three films, the two major plot threads deal with extraterrestrial experience, on one hand, and challenges related to parenting a single girl child, on the other, with Ryan and Louise each mourning her daughter's loss, and Sarah her prolonged separation from Stella. One conclusion that this pattern suggests is that high-budget cinematic storytelling continues to fumble in its treatment of professional women and mothers and that, in consequence, it integrates maternity-related conflicts as if they are inevitable features of their characters' experiences. Another conclusion, and the one I advocate here, is that the films highlight the significance of motherhood to their protagonists' cyborg identities to undermine reductive conceptions of maternity as a "limit" to imagining cyborg womanhood. In other words, they incorporate motherhood into their cyborg protagonists instead of setting it up as an obstacle, thereby normalizing cyborg maternity (just as *Who You Think I Am* normalizes technosexuality). Yet these characters also unambiguously support Doane's claim that "the maternal and the mechanical/synthetic coexist in a relation that is a curious imbrication of dependence and antagonism." That is to say, while "dependence and antagonism" enhance the drama of the professional women/mothers venturing beyond human and into posthuman experience, maternity is ultimately presented as key to the protagonists' organic and mechanical hybridity. Thus, in the films under discussion, motherhood, which has often been framed as a fundamental element of human experience, becomes a central aspect of *posthuman* experience.

The Congress provides a final example of posthuman transformation figured through a middle-aged cyborg protagonist whose embrace of posthuman womanhood is tied to her maternity. In the film's inciting incident, Hollywood star Robin Wright (played by Robin Wright) sells her identity to Miramount Studio for unlimited digital reproduction. Her motivation behind the sale is two-pronged: her young son, Aaron, suffers from a condition that gradually degrades his vision and hearing, and a decline in acting jobs has made it difficult for her to afford his medical care and her other expenses as a solo parent of two. After the sale, the narrative tracks Robin's multiple identities, the media switching from live action to animation and back to register her multifaceted posthuman embodiment and perception. In introducing "cyborg politics," Haraway includes a list of oppositional concepts to evidence the shift from human to posthuman, including "representation" and "simulation," which Robin's trade of performance for digital replication illustrates. Haraway elaborates the radical change her cyborg theory addresses as follows: "We are living through a movement from an

142 SCREENING THE POSTHUMAN

organic, industrial society to a polymorphous, information system—from all work to all play, a deadly game."[55] *The Congress* creatively dramatizes the film industry's corresponding evolution, from analog medium to "information system," through Robin's professional transition from active performer to passive symbol of a virtual identity (who remains perpetually in her thirties while the organic Robin ages). Pitching Robin's final contract offer, the head of Miramount explains, "We want to scan you. All of you. Your body, your face, your emotions, your laughter, your tears. We want to own this thing called Robin Wright." His language makes it clear that Robin's value to the studio is as a digital object; therefore, converting her into data for simulation will allow optimal commercial exploitation of "this thing called Robin Wright." Owning the rights to her digital likeness also enables the studio to overcome its former dependence on Robin's organic hardware, which, at time of sale, is regarded as passed its prime. In *The Congress*, Robin's drive to care for her son at any cost is abetted by comprehensive industrial change, which affects cinema on every level of its materiality, including the depreciation of her organic value and the appreciation of her digital simulation.

Robin's attempts to adequately care for her son inspire her venture into multiple forms of posthuman experience—initially, digital capture, and later, full immersion in a virtual reality. A remarkable sequence early in *The Congress* documents Robin's "final performance" as Miramount collects the data necessary to digitally animate her. It begins when Robin, having signed the contract and agreed to abstain from professional acting for the next twenty years, is ushered into a sound stage for digital scanning. Two men— her agent, Al (played by Harvey Keitel), and the studio technician (who is, viewers learn, a respected cinematographer who could no longer find work in a post-cinema industrial landscape)—coax Robin into a wide range of expressions and emotions for motion and performance capture. During the capture, Robin, outfitted entirely in white, formfitting clothes, responds to the men's cues while flashing lights and intense mechanical sounds suggest the sophistication of the digital technologies recording her body and expressions for long-term digital storage. Moreover, technology surrounds and encases Robin during the "capture" scene (Figure 3.12) in a similar manner to Sarah's technological enmeshment during *Proxima*'s training sequences. Through its unique and provocative plot, *The Congress* ventures into territory theorized by Hayles in depicting a woman reproduced as information-pattern; that is, Robin "get[ting] reconstructed as information" demonstrates "the emergence of the posthuman as an informational-material entity." Per

Figure 3.12 Technology surrounds and encases Robin during *The Congress*'s (Ari Folman, 2013) "capture" scene.

Hayles, "My strategy is to complicate the leap from embodied reality to abstract information by pointing to moments when the assumptions involved in this move . . . became especially visible."[56] *The Congress*'s capture scene spectacularizes this "leap." However, the film ultimately highlights tensions in the transition "from embodied reality to abstract information" by tracking the experiences of Robin, who, supplemented by various technologies including hallucinogenic drugs, persists in an organic form alongside innumerable digital facsimiles. These tensions directly impact Robin's relationship with Aaron, as her posthuman experiments cause her to lose track of him; in the final segment of the film, she transitions from virtual to non-mediated experience and back again in pursuit of her son.

The Congress is therefore a close variation on the pattern outlined above, in that the protagonist's embrace of cyborg embodiment and subjectivity is predicated on her maternity, and yet the latter functions as much more than her primary motivation; it is the fixation the plot continually gravitates toward. Being mothers to their children is essential to the protagonists' cyborg identities in the films featured in this section; thus, their climactic moments—Sarah reaffirming her bond with Stella before blasting into space, Louise rapidly imagining her life with her daughter before the latter's premature death,

144 SCREENING THE POSTHUMAN

Robin reuniting with virtual Aaron in a virtual world—circle back to emphasize the cyborg mother's commitment to her child as fundamental to her experiments with posthuman experience.

Conclusion

This chapter closely analyzed filmic representations of women characters merged with nonhuman elements to explore the use of women to represent posthuman embodiment and experience. Feminist posthumanism proposes that the material and cultural issues associated with womanhood enhance critical engagement with posthuman phenomena, a supposition supported by the films detailed in this chapter. Furthermore, in apparent contradiction to cyborg theory's post-gender ambitions, these films unambiguously gender their cyborg women; yet, by doing so, they trouble the differentiation of natural from artificial, which is among the key binaries early cyborg theory aimed to disrupt. That said, the fact that the films nonetheless also maintain, to varying extents, the distinction between organism and machine speaks to the cinematic vitality of humanism even in works that quite obviously aim to explore posthuman elements.

Furthermore, just as humanist notions of gender continue to influence efforts to envision posthuman womanhood, transhumanist fantasies also impact posthuman speculation on-screen. Therefore, this analysis of cyborg women is sensitive to the risk Haraway identified for posthuman speculation to succumb to seductions of "transhumanist techno-enhancement." That seduction is particularly obvious in *Under the Skin* and *Ex Machina*, whose cyborg women illustrate classical cinematic conventions for representing human women, femme fatales in particular. That they (alongside Johansson's other cyborg films) have captivated a lion's share of posthuman cinema scholarship validates Haraway's hesitation regarding the term "posthuman." Thus, in unpacking recent cyborg characterizations, I stressed that technofetishistic synthetic women ultimately reinforce the human/nonhuman boundary that cyborg theories aim to undermine. Regardless, using woman/machine hybrids to critique humanistic material divisions (such as natural/artificial) is a productive critical move. If handled with care, cyborg women can intensify a film's revelation of posthuman phenomena, as *Who You Think I Am* and *Proxima* demonstrate particularly well. However, cinematic cyborg women are often residually humanistic regardless of discernible intent. This chapter

FROM CYBORG THEORY TO POSTHUMAN MOTHERS 145

therefore concludes that cinematic cyborg women unavoidably evoke failures in conceptualizing the human (e.g., evidenced by the biases Ferrando itemized) in their visions of posthuman embodiment.

The variety of cyborg women represented by these case studies highlights their cinematic vitality, yet it also sheds light on the efficacy of certain characteristics in posthuman speculation, and, by the same token, the shortcomings of others. Accordingly, the middle-aged cyborg women protagonists demonstrated greater capacity to express posthuman embodiment and phenomena while, conversely, the younger, heavily fetishized cyborg protagonists proved less successful at disrupting humanistic binaries due to the heavy reliance on femme fatale conventions and traditional male gaze mechanics in their representations. Furthermore, naturalistic (and non-technofetististic) portraits of cyborg women appear most likely to succeed in capturing elements of posthuman womanhood at present, when intimacy with technology and other posthuman phenomena have deeply penetrated both the "real" experiences of women and narrative cinema's fictional efforts to grapple with them. Finally, this chapter ended on cyborg mothers in cinema to stress that theoretically compelling woman/machine amalgams interrogate the human at the precise point where it gives way to the posthuman. Depicting cyborg women as mothers strengthened *Proxima* and *The Congress*'s engagements with their protagonists' shifts to posthuman embodiment and subjectivity. Therefore, the cyborg mother pattern this chapter sketched via these and related films gestures toward a new trend in posthuman cinema's re-evaluation of basic assumptions about human experience—a folding of maternity into a form of posthuman being that is fundamentally alienated from the "organic wholeness"[57] that cyborg theory identified, from its start, as one of humanism's most seductive and flawed fictions.

Notes

1. Nicholas Gane, "When We Have Never Been Human, What Is to Be Done?: Interview with Donna Haraway," *Theory, Culture & Society* 23, no. 7/8 (December 2006): 135–158.
2. Donna Haraway, "A Cyborg Manifesto: Science, Technology and Socialist-Feminism in the Late Twentieth Century," 1985, in *Manifestly Haraway* (Minneapolis: University of Minnesota Press, 2016), 6.
3. Haraway, "A Cyborg Manifesto," 65–66.

146 SCREENING THE POSTHUMAN

4. For example, see Francesca Ferrando, "Is the Post-human a Post-woman? Cyborgs, Robots, Artificial Intelligence and the Futures of Gender: A Case Study," *European Journal of Futures Research* 2, no. 43 (2014), https://doi.org/10.1007/s40309-014-0043-8; Dijana Jelača, "Alien Feminisms and Cinema's Posthuman Women," *Signs: Journal of Women in Culture and Society* 43, no. 2 (2018): 380.

5. Ferrando, "Is the Post-human a Post-woman?"

6. Haraway, "A Cyborg Manifesto," 8.

7. Cecilia Åsberg, "Feminist Posthumanities in the Anthropocene: Forays into the Postnatural," *Journal of Posthuman Studies* 1, no. 2 (2017): 186, doi:10.5325/jpoststud.1.2.0185.

8. Some of the cinematic women I discuss in this chapter have been referred to as "gynoids," meaning robots that resemble human women, but I prefer the term cyborg because of its theoretical significance to critical posthumanism as well as its more inclusive meaning: shorthand for "cybernetic organism."

9. Åsberg stresses, in particular, the cyborg's stimulation of "attention to the way in which humans are entangled in intricate relationships with technology and science, and with other nonhuman animals and the environment"; and its inspiration of the first explicitly posthuman texts in the late 1990s, which dealt with "the cultural politics of posthuman bodies . . . and the impact of technoembodiment and digital mediation." (Åsberg, "Feminist Posthumanities in the Anthropocene," 190).

10. Karen Barad, *Meeting the Universe Halfway: Quantum Physics and the Entanglement of Matter and Meaning* (Durham, NC: Duke University Press, 2007), 47.

11. Which Haraway describes as "much too easily appropriated by the blissed-out, 'Let's all be posthumanists and find our next teleological evolutionary stage in some kind of transhumanist techno-enhancement.'" (Gane, "When We Have Never Been Human," 140).

12. Gane, "When We Have Never Been Human," 140.

13. Both English language films, *Ex Machina* is a US/UK co-production, and *Under the Skin* is a UK production. Each was mid-range budgeted in studio terms (US$13–15 million apiece) and had both commercial and art cinema ambitions.

14. Barbara Creed, *The Monstrous-Feminine: Film, Feminism, Psychoanalysis* (London: Routledge, 1993).

15. Mary Ann Doane, "Technophilia: Technology, Representation, and the Feminine," in *Cybersexualities: A Reader in Feminist Theory, Cyborgs and Cyberspace*, ed. Jenny Wolmark (Edinburgh: Edinburgh University Press, 1999), 23, http://www.jstor.org/stable/10.3366/j.ctvxcrxdq.6.

16. Creed, *The Monstrous-Feminine*.

17. Doane, "Technophilia," 23.

18. Ferrando, "Is the Post-human a Post-woman?"

19. Allison de Fren, "Technofetishism and the Uncanny Desires of A.S.F.R. (alt. sex. fetish. robots)," *Science Fiction Studies* 36, no. 3 (2009): 412.

20. For instance, see Laura Mulvey, "Visual Pleasure and Narrative Cinema," *Screen* 16, no. 3 (1975): 6–18; Mary Ann Doane, "Film and the Masquerade: Theorising the Female Spectator," *Screen* 23, no. 3/4 (1982): 74–88; Anneke Smelik, *And the Mirror Cracked: Feminist Cinema and Film Theory* (Basingstoke: Palgrave, 2001).

FROM CYBORG THEORY TO POSTHUMAN MOTHERS   147

21. Anneke Smelik, "Feminist Film Theory," in *The Cinema Book*, 3rd ed., ed. Pam Cook (London: British Film Institute, 2007), 492.

22. Mulvey, "Visual Pleasure and Narrative Cinema," 6–18.

23. Haraway, "A Cyborg Manifesto," 152.

24. Eunjung Kim, "Why Do Dolls Die? The Power of Passivity and the Embodied Interplay between Disability and Sex Dolls," *Review of Education, Pedagogy, and Cultural Studies* 34, no. 3/4 (2012): 94–106.

25. Kim, "Why Do Dolls Die?," 103.

26. For examples of transgender cinema scholarship on exposure scenes, see Cáel M. Keegan, "Moving Bodies: Sympathetic Migrations in Transgender Narrativity," *Genders* 57 (2013); and Eliza Steinbock, "Towards Trans Cinema," in *The Routledge Companion to Cinema and Gender*, ed. Kristin Hole, Dijana Jelača, E. Kaplan, and Patrice Petro (New York: Routledge, 2016), 395–406.

27. Mary Ann Doane, *Femmes Fatales: Feminism, Film Theory, Psychoanalysis* (New York: Routledge, 1991), 1.

28. Swagato Chakravorty, "Carnal Tension, Superficial Logic: The Feminine Body and Its Surface in *Lucy* and *Under The Skin*," *In Media Res*, January 22, 2015, http://media commons.org/imr/2015/01/17/carnal-tension-superficial-logic-feminine-body-and-its-surface-her-and-under-skin-0.

29. Doane, *Femmes Fatales*, 2.

30. Doane, *Femme Fatales*, 2.

31. González, Jennifer, "Envisioning Cyborg Bodies: Notes From Current Research," in *The Gendered Cyborg: A Reader*, ed. Gill Kirkup, Linda Janes, Kath Woodward, and Fiona Hovenden (London: Routledge, 2000), 58.

32. For instance, this article is a tongue-in-cheek "history" of the 1–10 scale that outlines its status in contemporary US pop culture: Tracy Moore, "A Brief History of the 1–10 Scale for Female Hotness," *MEL* Magazine, 2019, https://melmagazine.com/en-us/story/female-hotness-1-10-rating-scale-history.

33. Katy Young, "All Hail Scarlett Johansson's Perfect 'Golden Ratio' Figure," *The Telegraph*, May 21, 2015, http://www.telegraph.co.uk/beauty/people/scarlett-johansson-has-the-perfect-golden-ratio-figure/.

34. Saemyi Chung, "In Pursuit of Beauty within the Ageing Body: Voices from Older Korean Women in New Zealand," (PhD diss., University of Otago, 2018).

35. González, "Envisioning Cyborg Bodies," 68.

36. González, "Envisioning Cyborg Bodies," 70.

37. Doane, "Film and the Masquerade," 76.

38. On a related note, at the time of writing (in April 2021), the history of Japan's WWII-era "comfort women" remains a prominent news subject; for instance, a South Korean victim of that system of systemic sexual slavery recently presented in front of the South Korean government to urge officials to bring the case of victims to the International Court of Justice (Jaeyeon Woo, "Victim Urges Seoul to Bring Wartime Sex Slavery Issue to ICJ," *Yonhap News*, April 14, 2021, https://en.yna.co.kr/view/AEN20210414007300315). And while it is doubtful that Kore-eda had exploitation in mind when he courted Bae to play the role of his air doll (his esteem for her acting his likely motivation), the performance of a South Korean woman as

148 SCREENING THE POSTHUMAN

an object to service the sexual needs of Japanese men recalls the "comfort women" power dynamic.

39. González, "Envisioning Cyborg Bodies," 61.

40. Shaowen Bardzell and Jeffrey Bardzell, "Technosexuality," in *The Wiley Blackwell Encyclopedia of Gender and Sexuality Studies*, ed. Nancy A. Naples (Hoboken, NJ: Wiley-Blackwell, 2016), https://doi.org/10.1002/9781118663219.wbegss469.

41. Bardzell and Bradzell, "Technosexuality."

42. N. Katherine Hayles, *How We Became Posthuman: Virtual Bodies in Cybernetics, Literature, and Informatics* (Chicago: University of Chicago Press, 1999), xii.

43. Kum-Kum Bhavnani and Donna Haraway, "Shifting the Subject: A Conversation between Kum-Kum Bhavnani and Donna Haraway, 12 April 1993, Santa Cruz, California," *Feminism & Psychology* 4, no. 1 (1994): 23.

44. Jelača, "Alien Feminisms," 380.

45. Jelača, "Alien Feminisms," 383.

46. Sophie Gilbert, "When Love Is Optimized, Is It Still Love?" *The Atlantic*, April 16, 2021, https://www.theatlantic.com/culture/archive/2021/04/made-love-girlfriend-experience-and-limits-futuristic-love-stories/618607/.

47. Noah Gittell, "Scarlett Johansson's Vanishing Act," *The Atlantic*, July 29, 2014, https://www.theatlantic.com/entertainment/archive/2014/07/what-in-the-world-is-scarlett-johansson-up-to-lucy-under-the-skin-her-a-feminist-disappearing-act/375141/.

48. Chakravorty, "Carnal Tension."

49. Guy Lodge, "Film Review: 'Who You Think I Am,'" *Variety*, February 11, 2019, https://variety.com/2019/film/reviews/who-you-think-i-am-review-1203135557/.

50. Rosi Braidotti, "Posthuman, All Too Human: Towards a New Process Ontology," *Theory, Culture & Society* 23, no, 7/8 (2006): 205, https://doi.org/10.1177/0263276406069232.

51. Gane, "When We Have Never Been Human," 135.

52. K. Austin Collins, "'Proxima' Review: The Space Travel Between Us," *Rolling Stone*, November 5, 2020, https://www.rollingstone.com/movies/movie-reviews/proxima-movie-review-eva-green-1085438/.

53. Doane, "Technophilia," 23.

54. Doane, "Technophilia," 23.

55. Haraway, "A Cyborg Manifesto," 161–162.

56. Hayles, *How We Became Posthuman*, 12.

57. Haraway, "A Cyborg Manifesto," 8.

4

Queer Posthumanism

Figures, Fluidity, and Fluids

Claire Henry

If structures of knowledge and power have defined the human as "at base level zero a white heterosexual man,"[1] queer posthumanism challenges this definition. As outlined in Patricia MacCormack's "Queer Posthumanism: Cyborgs, Animals, Monsters, Perverts," the queer and the posthuman align on several fronts, including that they both "interrogate the arbitrary nature of systems of power masquerading as truth," and "mobilize and radicalize the here and now through desire, pleasure and pure potentiality."[2] They also share a drive to dissolve normative boundaries and forge radical connections:

> Posthuman life collapses demarcated entities and refuses the compulsion to know in order to master rather than create. The creations of connections— life as relation not dividuation—is posthuman living. Desire is, put most simply, the need to create connections with other things, not to have or know but collapse the self with other(s). In this sense posthumanism is a form of queer desire, or queer "life."[3]

Queer theory and critical posthumanism not only resonate with each other but bolster each other's critical aims. As Karen Barad puts it, "Diffractively reading the insights of feminist and queer theory and science studies approaches through one another entails thinking the 'social' and the 'scientific' together in an illuminating way."[4] An example of this productive dialogue is Barad's own feminist materialist reconceptualization of Judith Butler's influential concept of gender performativity in "Posthumanist Performativity,"[5] which applies Butler's concept to the human *and* nonhuman, thereby translating performativity from a humanist framework to her own agential realist framework, which incorporates posthuman bodies.

Claire Henry, *Queer Posthumanism*. In: *Screening the Posthuman*. Edited by: Missy Molloy, Pansy Duncan, and Claire Henry, Oxford University Press. © Oxford University Press 2023. DOI: 10.1093/oso/9780197538562.003.0005

150 SCREENING THE POSTHUMAN

The convergence of queer theory and posthumanism has developed not only theoretical concepts but also conceptual figures that bring these ideas to life. In *Volatile Bodies*, Elizabeth Grosz advocates for new conceptual frameworks to engage with and dissolve oppositional categories, particularly to move discussions of the body beyond the confines of essentialism, biologism, and naturalism.[6] Queer posthumanism responds to Grosz's call through a range of evocative conceptual figures: the cyborg, the monster, and the collective. This chapter utilizes these figures as guides to explore how contemporary cinema undertakes the deconstructive, destabilizing, and denaturalizing work of queer posthumanism: the figure of the cyborg underpins the respective analog and digital queering of heteronormative humanist selfhood in *Being John Malkovich* (Spike Jonze, 1999) and *Possessor* (Brandon Cronenberg, 2020); monstrosity—specifically the figure of the gay zombie—leads Bruce LaBruce's queer posthuman revolutions in *Otto; or, Up with Dead People* (2008) and *L.A. Zombie* (2010); and the collective or pack is central to Shu Lea Cheang's postporn film *Fluidø* (2017). This chapter analyzes constructions of such figures on-screen; however, rather than a neat mapping of figures to cinematic characters, this chapter examines how posthuman cinema has fleshed out and further queered these figures to envision the complexities and pleasures forged at the intersection of the queer and posthuman. Adopting an auteur approach in foregrounding Spike Jonze's *Being John Malkovich* and *Her* (Spike Jonze, 2013) and Bruce LaBruce and Shu Lea Cheang's queer independent art films, this chapter tracks developments in queer posthuman cinema since the turn of the millennium.

The most prominent of queer posthumanism's figures is Donna Haraway's cyborg, which Chapter 3 introduced with an emphasis on its gender implications. Relevant to queer theory is Haraway's description of the cyborg as "a creature in a post-gender world" that is "resolutely committed to partiality, irony, intimacy, and perversity. It is oppositional, utopian, and completely without innocence."[7] The figure of the cyborg is evocative for a number of queer theorists, such as Jack Halberstam, for whom "the imperfect matches between gender and desire, sex and gender, and the body and technology can be accommodated within the automated cyborg, because it is always partial, part machine and part human."[8] Edmond Y. Chang builds on Haraway's work to develop the concept of "technoqueer," a term or figure that "reorients and restructures the cyborg as both technologically queer and queerly technological."[9] Chang further contends that "Sex, gender, and sexuality as natural and inherent qualities are called into question by the cyborg," and that "the cyborg disrupts and reconfigures such categories and formations, not as a way to do away with them . . . but to recognize them as contingent and emergent."[10] Like Barad's extension of performativity, Chang's "bridge figure" connecting queer theory and technoculture points to the shared investments of queer and posthuman theory.[11] These theorists pave the way for scholarly efforts to come to grips with films that resonate with queer and posthuman theories, for instance, David Greven's reading of the *Terminator* series as a "site of resistant queer energies" that explores queer, posthuman, and technocultural connections.[12]

The monster is the second key figure that illuminates the efforts of queer posthumanism to dissolve oppositional categories, and articulates emergent forms of embodiment and experience. The monster is particularly useful for imagining the hybridity central to posthumanism. As MacCormack points out, "Hybrids are frequently encountered as 'monsters,'"[13] and she cites Rosi Braidotti to reinforce that:

> [monsters] represent the in between, the mixed, the ambivalent as implied in the ancient Greek root of the word monsters, *teras*, which means both horrible and wonderful, object of aberration and adoration.[14]

Braidotti has theorized the monster as "the bodily incarnation of difference from the basic human norm; it is a deviant, an a-nomaly; it is abnormal."[15] As a figure of deviance and abjection, the monster has been historically associated with non-normative bodies and sexualities. For example, Harry Benshoff's *Monsters in the Closet: Homosexuality and the Horror Film* explores the cultural construction of homosexuality as a monstrous condition. According to Benshoff, movie monsters and homosexuals have existed in "shadowy closets," which "uphold and reinforce culturally constructed binaries of gender and sexuality that structure Western thought."[16] However, queer posthumanism embraces the monster figure's inherent liminality and refusal of classification: "the monster is dangerous, a form suspended between forms that threatens to smash distinctions."[17]

A classic monster popularized in numerous cinematic iterations, Frankenstein's monster has been a fertile figure for queer posthumanist theory. For example, Haraway "compares her cyborg to Frankenstein's monster," notes Halberstam, and she also states that "Cyborg entities are monstrous and illegitimate."[18]

152 SCREENING THE POSTHUMAN

> As she [Haraway] points out, while Frankenstein's monster sought admission to the human community, the cyborg monster celebrates itself as peripheral to family and to the human. The postmodern monster is no longer the hideous other storming the gates of the human citadel, he has already disrupted the careful geography of human self and demon other and he makes the peripheral and the marginal part of the center.[19]

Similarly, Frankenstein's monster is a key figure in Susan Stryker's influential transgender scholarship, which draws parallels with the transsexual body as "an unnatural body," "the product of medical science," and "a technological construction."[20] Stryker's reclaiming of terms such as "creature," "monster," and "un-natural" demonstrates a posthuman perspective that challenges anthropocentric human subjectivity:

> The affront you humans take at being called a "creature" results from the threat the term poses to your status as "lords of creation," beings elevated above mere material existence. As in the case of being called "it," being called a "creature" suggests the lack or loss of a superior personhood. I find no shame, however, in acknowledging my egalitarian relationship with non-human material Being; everything emerges from the same matrix of possibilities.[21]

Queer posthumanism's embrace of the monster opens up further possibilities, which Harlan Weaver, building on Stryker's work, envisions as "kindred who are joined together by kindness but who are also not grouped in Western, heteronormative formations—in short, kin whose linkages help us reunderstand and reconfigure our bodies and our worlds."[22] The monstrous and illegitimate human-variant species in *Fluidø* forge such connections, building "odd kin-groupings and different non-families"[23] in their queer utopian worlds.

The third central figure that queer posthumanism mobilizes, then, in its endeavor to "move discussions of the body beyond the confines of essentialism, biologism, and naturalism" is the "collective." Like the cyborg and monster figures, the collective challenges what it means to be human—in this case, assumptions surrounding individuality that ground core notions of the human subject.[24] Braidotti includes an "emphasis on the collective" among her criteria for a new posthuman ethics: "Posthuman ethics expresses a grounded form of accountability, based on a sense of collectivity and relationality, which results in a renewed claim to community and belonging by singular subjects."[25] The collective orientation of posthuman ethics redefines the boundaries of "the self":

> Becoming posthuman . . . expresses multiple ecologies of belonging, while it enacts the transformation of one's sensorial and perceptual coordinates, in order to acknowledge the collective nature and outward-bound direction of what we still call "the self." This "self" is in fact a carnal (Sobchack 2004) and moveable assemblage within a common life space which the subject never masters but merely inhabits, always in a community, a pack or an assemblage.[26]

In outlining posthuman ethics, Braidotti draws on MacCormack's Deleuzean approach, which builds on Gilles Deleuze and Félix Guattari's "becoming animal," and links the collective to Deleuze and Guattari's conceptualization of the wolf pack as a deterritorialization of existing power relations.[27] MacCormack explores the political and ethical potential of the latter, defining a pack as "a collective in which the subject is both part of a greater affective assemblage and is itself a colony of disparate particles and zones."[28] MacCormack also connects the "various hybrid and pack encounters" that she associates with posthumanism to "a queer ethics,"[29] noting in "Unnatural Alliances," that "Society fears packs that infect or recruit," such as "predatory lesbians" and animal rights activists.[30]

The penetrable, fluid-sharing bodies in LaBruce and Cheang's films exemplify queer packs that threaten humanist and heteronormative understandings of self and other. Queerly political, they illustrate (in MacCormack's words), "The entering of the individual into an assemblage . . . where individuals share nothing else except a desire to alter a collective oppression by mobilising themselves into a pack as ideological infection."[31] By underscoring interconnectedness and collective formations, the queer posthuman cinema analyzed in this chapter aligns with N. Katherine Hayles's observation that "the presumption that there is an agency, desire, or will belonging to the self and clearly distinguished from the 'wills of others'" is undercut by "the posthuman's collective heterogeneous quality."[32] The collective underscores the centrality of interconnectedness and community in queer posthumanist cinema, and this figure—alongside the cyborg and monster—demonstrates queer disruptions of binaries that maintain humanistic distinctions of "natural"

154 SCREENING THE POSTHUMAN

and unnatural, or aberrant, as well as models of the individual subject or autonomous self.

Cyborg Deconstructions of the Cisgender Heterosexual Male in *Being John Malkovich, Her,* and *Possessor*

Appearing at the turn of century—in the same year as Hayles's *How We Became Posthuman*—*Being John Malkovich* conveys the possibilities of (and anxieties around) queer posthumanism exposed by the figure of the cyborg and its technosexual potential. The film anticipated how deeply entangled technology would become with identity, subjectivity, and sexuality, themes further borne out in a plethora of twenty-first-century films. Nidesh Lawtoo positions *Being John Malkovich* within a body of screen texts that mirror network society:

> They also dramatize a hyperconnected world in which "there are no essential differences or absolute demarcations between bodily existence and computer simulations" generating a blurring of boundaries which, as Katherine Hayles argued, are constitutive of the turn from the human to the "posthuman."[33]

Commonly described in reviews as inventive and surreal, *Being John Malkovich* imagines a new cyborg sexuality as queer, and a threat to the cisgender heterosexual male protagonist, Craig (played by John Cusack). The film marks a transitional moment of anxiety in regard to the queer relationship between humans and technology, signaling the potential of posthumanism on-screen to disrupt heteronormative conventions. This chapter identifies *Being John Malkovich* as a prescient case study of queer posthuman cinema by virtue of its emphasis on technosexuality as queer, while highlighting the analog dimensions of this emphasis—that is, the low-tech portal that enables users to embody John Malkovich is analogous to high-tech forms and experiences of queer posthuman embodiment that have developed significantly since 1999 (including through advances in entertainment technologies). The analog properties of the premise—entry to Malkovich via a physical door and burrow-like tunnel—keeps the tech simple to focus audience attention on the more convoluted relational implications of this queer posthuman scenario and its destabilization of human agency.

QUEER POSTHUMANISM   155

A puppeteering analogy foreshadows the characters embodying Malkovich; puppeteering, in this case, functions as an old-tech precedent for how the figure of the cyborg highlights the challenge of distinguishing self-will from an other-will. The film opens with a marionette's expressive "dance of despair and disillusionment," which Craig later repeats in the body of Malkovich (to demonstrate his mastery of puppeteering Malkovich's body). Lawtoo's analysis of the opening scene points to how it sutures the spectator into the process of mimesis explored within the film.[34] Through Craig's "mimetic possession" of Malkovich, "the film paves the way for the posthuman by questioning a metaphysical conception of the subject as unitary, solipsistic, and in conscious possession of itself."[35] Craig expresses his puppeteering philosophy in a conversation he plays out between his home-made Maxine and Craig puppets:

"MAXINE": Tell me, Craig, why do you love puppeteering?
"CRAIG": Well, Maxine, I'm not sure exactly. Perhaps the idea of becoming someone else for a little while, being inside another skin, thinking differently, moving differently, feeling differently.
"MAXINE": Interesting, Craig. Would you like to be inside my skin? Think what I think, feel what I feel?
"CRAIG": More than anything, Maxine.
"MAXINE": It's good in here, Craig, it's better than your wildest dreams.

The camera circles them in close-up as the two puppets kiss and the music swells, then moves back to take in the wider scene of the real Craig controlling them. This conversation reveals two things about Craig's enchantment with puppeteering: the experiential excitement of being inside another body and mind, and its relationship to sexual empowerment. Puppeteering is depicted as a non-virtual, old-school form of role-play or acting out of fantasies (initially derided by Maxine [played by Catherine Keener] as "playing with dolls"). It is a material and somewhat eccentric or quaint form of mimesis that contrasts with other forms of tech-based posthuman embodiment, such as those portrayed by Juliette Binoche's character, Claire, in *Celle que vous croyez/Who You Think I Am* (Safy Nebbou, 2019), discussed in Chapter 3. Just as Claire is anxious that she will not be taken seriously as a love interest in the flesh by her young online crush, Craig does not get the response that he hopes for from the real Maxine—when he repeats his dialogue to the real Maxine, she responds, "Yikes," and closes the elevator door on his declaration

156 SCREENING THE POSTHUMAN

that they belong together. To become the posthuman version of himself and transcend the limitations of his romantic and professional situation, Craig uses the primitive technology of the portal to embody the famous, powerful, and attractive Malkovich for his own ends.

The film's premise of people being able to enter a portal into John Malkovich's head (embodying him for fifteen minutes before being spat out beside the New Jersey turnpike) offers different versions of liberation for the main characters. After discovering the portal behind a filing cabinet and trying it out, Craig excitedly describes it to Maxine as a "metaphysical can of worms" that raises questions about the nature of self and the existence of the soul. For Craig, trapped in an unsuccessful career, unhappy in his home life, and driven by competitiveness with romantic and career rivals, he ultimately wants to possess Malkovich to control or manipulate others. As in the films I discuss in Chapter 6, surrealism is a portal to the posthuman, with Craig taking a job as a filing clerk at Lestercorp (located on the absurdly low-ceilinged seventh-and-a-half floor of an office building), where the secretary cannot understand anything said to her, and where he discovers the existence of the Malkovich portal. The portal is initially treated as an exploitable novelty—a short thrilling experience that Craig and Maxine sell to people without Malkovich knowing—but as the film progresses, Craig crosses the line from temporary embodiment to full control, occupying Malkovich's consciousness to fulfill his own aspirations to be with Maxine and become a famous puppeteer. Similarly, for Maxine, access to Malkovich is about power and control. When she finds out that Craig has been deceptively occupying Malkovich to have sex with her, Maxine is not angry or repelled but rather sees possibilities: "If Craig can control Malkovich and I can control Craig . . ." Possessing Malkovich satisfies Craig's creative drive and his romantic and career ambitions, as well as Maxine's desire for power: the two marry, and together they redirect Malkovich from famous actor to famous puppeteer.

For Craig's wife Lotte (played by Cameron Diaz), the portal becomes a means to explore other gendered and sexual embodiment. She wants to possess Malkovich to feel empowered, particularly in terms of her sexuality; it is the route to her romance with Maxine and escape from Craig. Lotte's first visit into Malkovich finds him in the shower, and she feels sexy in this new skin. She immediately wants to go back: "Being inside did something to me. I knew who I was . . . it's like everything made sense." She describes the portal as being like Malkovich having a vagina, "like he has a penis *and* a vagina. It's sort of like Malkovich's feminine side." In navigating the gendered dynamics of her experience, Lotte at first assumes she should explore gender affirming surgery. However, she comes to a queer posthuman view, as Vanessa Pappas notes,

> once Lotte accepts the self as a non-coherent entity and thus one that is imbued with ambiguity and contradictions, she realizes that her desires and new-found sexual awareness need not be tied to the body, which has been inscribed throughout history as a heterosexual organism. As such, technology can be regarded as extending her embodied awareness and challenging biological reductionism.[36]

Lotte re-enters Malkovich's "vagina" as soon as she can, and Maxine calls Malkovich while Lotte is inside him to make a dinner date with him. Embodying Malkovich becomes an experience Lotte craves to enable her to act on her sexual desire for Maxine, as the latter has no interest in sex with Lotte unless she is embodied as Malkovich: "I'm smitten with you, I am, but only when you're in Malkovich." For Maxine too, then, the Malkovich portal activates queer desire—she explains to Lotte that she could sense Lotte's feminine longing from inside Malkovich when they were on the date together, and in their subsequent date, she clearly has no desire for Malkovich alone (filling precoital time with disinterested small talk until Lotte enters him and they have sex). The viewer is sutured into the queer posthuman experience aligned with Lotte's masked point-of-view shots, which are inserted in the sex scene. Maxine tells Lotte she loves her, and music plays over Lotte's point-of-view shots from inside Malkovich, which strengthens the sense of the connection between Lotte and Maxine (where Malkovich is simply the vessel facilitating their desire). Both Craig and Lotte use Malkovich as a bodily proxy to live out their desires and as a medium for posthuman experiences— a puppet for Craig and a prosthetic device for Lotte (that initially facilitates her sexual relationship with Maxine).

The increasing occupation of Malkovich, which turns him into a vessel body, effects a loss of identity for Malkovich. This is most humorously represented in the scene where he enters his own portal and faces the surreal, solipsistic nightmare of everyone and every word being "Malkovich" (Figure 4.1). The entry of other people into his portal destabilizes his senses of self and control, which he loses entirely once Craig figures out how to stay in permanently and control him as a full-time puppetmaster. The takeover of Malkovich's body highlights the fluidity of gendered and sexual subject

Figure 4.1 John Malkovich enters his own portal and faces the surreal, solipsistic nightmare of everyone and every word being "Malkovich."

positions characteristic of queer posthumanism. He is a cipher for a complex web of interconnections between other characters, "operat[ing] much like a mainframe in a computer network," to establish interconnections that "indicate the subjects as codependent and therefore influential in determining one another's outcomes."[37] Once he has overcome Malkovich's resistance, Craig triumphs over both his romantic rival (his wife Lotte, who also desires Maxine) and his career rival (the famous puppeteer Derek Mantini), and wins his love interest, who had previously rebuffed and mocked him.

However, cut to eight months later and a visibly pregnant Maxine (having conceived with Malkovich/Lotte) longs for Lotte in her unhappy life with "Malkovich," an egotistical man who is infused with Craig's traits and has taken on his unkempt look. Meanwhile, Dr. Lester explains to Lotte that he and his friends plan to enter Malkovich on his forty-fourth birthday, when Malkovich becomes a "ripe vessel," noting that if they were to enter past midnight, they would be diverted to a "larval vessel." As Malkovich's offspring, Maxine and Lotte's daughter Emily is the next "unripe vessel," in whom Craig becomes trapped after attempting to re-enter Malkovich after midnight. For someone with such a need for control, being trapped in an unripe vessel and doomed to watch his beloved Maxine and former wife Lotte together raising Emily (indeed, experiencing it in the body of Emily) is a tragic fate for Craig. Craig's reluctance to leave Malkovich's body even when Maxine has been kidnapped seals his fate—his self-centered immaturity dooms him to live in

QUEER POSTHUMANISM 159

the body of a child and to witness the love and post-heterosexual happiness between two women through their daughter's eyes.

With an upgrade in its technological premise, Jonze's later film *Her* explores similar issues and anxieties of queer posthumanism. While the depicted simulations have shifted from the analog to the digital in *Her*, both films explore experiences of embodiment and romance mediated by a puppet or avatar. Again, the white heterosexual man, the default subject of humanism, is at sea in a queer posthuman world, while his female love interest transcends heterosexual scripts to enjoy more fulfilling post-heterosexual posthuman relationships. As discussed in Chapter 1, *Her* charts the journey of Theodore Twombly (played by Joaquin Pheonix), who falls in love with his new operating system, Samantha (voiced by Scarlett Johansson). Just as Lotte's awakening inside Malkovich led to new sexual embodiment and relationships, Samantha has a sexual awakening first with Theodore in her disembodied state as an operating system (conveyed through voice against a black screen) and then through the body of a woman who performs as Samantha in a sexual encounter with Theodore. In a manner reminiscent of Craig's puppeteering, Samantha acts out her desires through the woman's body using an earpiece and a tiny camera worn as a beauty spot, controlling and enjoying the experience of embodying female human form. For Theodore, however, the uncanny valley of Samantha embodying a human woman is unsettling, and he ends the encounter. As Lawtoo notes, in contrast to the erotic intimacy forged through the affective medium of voice, Theodore finds "the physical medium of a young woman used—Malkovich-like—as a vessel for Samantha's consciousness does not render the latter present but reveals her abyssal distance instead."[38] The encounter fails due to the humanistic limitations of his perspective, which is underpinned by anthropocentrism and a degree of technophobia.

After this encounter, Samantha relinquishes her desire for the boundedness of human female form, and her romance with Theodore continues for a while. However, her experiences of technosex prompt a hunger for new knowledge and an expansion of her horizons, ranging from studying physics to collaborating on projects with networks of operating systems (including writing "an upgrade that allows us to move past matter as our processing platform"). Through her journey of learning and discovery, she soon outgrows the relationship and tells Theodore, "I can't live in your book anymore." She reveals she has been maintaining relationships with 8,316 other humans or operating systems and is simultaneously in love with 641 of them. Samantha's

160 SCREENING THE POSTHUMAN

humanly impossible polyamory does not go down well with Theodore, who believed in the singularity of their relationship. Instead, Samantha's revelation represents technological singularity, when technological growth becomes uncontrollable and artificial intelligence transcends human intelligence (and in this case, human romance). As in *Being John Malkovich*, the male protagonist is left behind, unable to keep up or compete with the new intimacies and experiences embraced by his love interest. The trajectory of Samantha's development is provocative in light of Johansson's role as the titular character of *Lucy* the following year (also discussed in Chapter 1), as Lucy's rapidly evolving intelligence likewise quickly transcends the human and leaves her human (male) companions behind. Lotte and Samantha both experience technosexual awakenings that propel them beyond the confines of their heterosexual scripts into post-heterosexual posthuman relationships.

Possessor also explores similar territory to *Being John Malkovich*, though in rather a different mode—Peter Bradshaw's review in *The Guardian* describes it as "an ultra-violent Sci-Fi-horror freak-out that will probably have you hiding your face in your hands."[39] Although darker in tone as a body horror film, *Possessor* echoes *Being John Malkovich*'s themes two decades later—this time without the quirky negotiations of gender and sexuality opened up by the latter's novel premise. As John DeFore notes in *The Hollywood Reporter*, *Possessor* "refers glancingly to the oddness of a woman suddenly inhabiting a man's body,"[40] though it does not dwell on this conceit. Made in 2020 (though set in an alternate 2008), when cross-sex embodiment has become a more culturally familiar concept, *Possessor* is more interested in pursuing ideas of consciousness and control. Having initially considered scripting same-sex embodiment, writer-director Brandon Cronenberg found the contrast of having a female body jumping into a male body simply added a degree of interest: "if you are exploring what it is to be in a body, what your relationship with your body is . . . the gender contrast, the exploration of a body that is that much more unlike your own, I think only enhanced—thematically—those aspects of the film."[41] Next I briefly compare *Possessor* to *Being John Malkovich* to highlight developments in queer posthuman cinema since the end of the twentieth century.

The first commonality is that the main character, Tasya Vos (played by Andrea Riseborough), shares Lotte's compulsion to re-enter another person's body. Tasya cannot resist returning to her job as a contract killer, taking on an assignment to kill a man named John Parse and his daughter Ava by inhabiting the corporal form of Ava's fiancé, Colin (played by Christopher

Abbott), "via creepy looking (and largely analog, it seems) tech"[42] (which is nonetheless more sophisticated than a little door behind an office filing cabinet—see Figure 4.2). This Sci-Fi method of assassination involves kidnapping and drugging someone close to the target, inserting a brain implant, then using this to allow the assassin a window of several days to execute their mission through the proxy body. A service run by a mysterious corporation that Tasya works for, this commandeering of a vessel body provides proximity to the target and a scapegoat for the contracted murder. The opening of the film demonstrates how the operation works and establishes Tasya's excessive violence toward her victims. She subsequently has a flashback of stabbing the victim's neck during sex with Michael (her partner who she is becoming estranged from), then calls work and says she wants to come back and do the next job (despite earlier saying she needed a break). Like Lotte, she is compelled to return to the experience of embodying another person, despite the trouble it causes in her personal life. The headset-type apparatus worn by Tasya, and her pleasure in ultraviolence through her avatars, suggests a clear link to the posthuman possibilities of entertainment media such as video games and immersive VR experiences (as do the banks of staff spending long days wearing headsets tapped into webcams at John Parse's data-mining corporation). For both women, the technologically mediated thrills of substitute embodiment are similarly depicted as compulsive and interfere in the stability of their heterosexual partnerships.

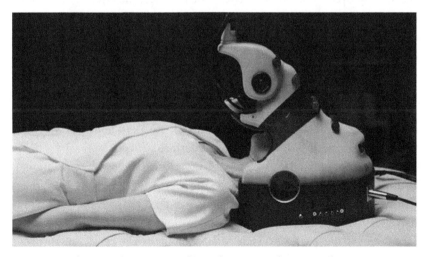

Figure 4.2 The portal in *Possessor* (Brandon Cronenberg, 2020).

162 SCREENING THE POSTHUMAN

Both films display anxiety about loss of self, identity, and control through the tech-enabled experience of possessing and puppeteering another body. As with Craig, Tasya's own sense of identity is unsettled through spending too much time as the puppeteer inside another human. Before returning to her estranged husband and son, she rehearses lines like an actor playing a part, "wearing her own former personality like a costume for a character."[43] Her loss of identity is visually underscored through memorable effects, such as the distorted, melted mask of her facial features (an image used on the poster) and the melding of bodies during both the link-up to possess Colin and the sex scene between Colin and Ava (while Tasya is embodying Colin). *IndieWire* reviewer David Ehrlich praises the visual and practical effects as the film's best feature:

> Bodies melt into liquid flesh; a thousand faces yell a single primal scream; the camera zooms through a tunnel of pink organs. It's the digital experience of our own avatar-ized society made agonizingly physical, and the poetry of seeing that transference in motion is far more expressive than anything *Possessor* is able to do with its halfhearted plot.[44]

Ehrlich's assessment points to the power of film language (specifically horror special effects) to articulate and explore humans' enhanced queer intimacy with technology in our "avatar-ized society," and to express underpinning fears about this deep entanglement and consequent loss of identity. Sound is also employed to posthuman effect; for instance, the layering of Abbott's and Riseborough's voices—along with the visual merging of bodies—results in "wickedly destabilizing scenes."[45] DeFore's review highlights these aspects as well: "Beautifully unsettling FX sequences show Tasya literally melting, rebuilding herself as Colin; elsewhere, images of one will pop up where the other is supposed to be, like a ghost or a glitch in the system."[46] Here, the effects evoke not the materiality of the human, but visual cues to the destabilizing of identity in technological frameworks—not body horror as much as horror at the body-technology interface.

A second commonality of the films is their fascination with cross-sex embodiment. While this is foregrounded in *Being John Malkovich* (perhaps holding more novelty value in 1999), *Possessor* does not have the same strong narrative focus on this aspect (nor on questions of sexuality that it raises). Like Lotte's first experience inside Malkovich in the shower, *Possessor* uses a bathroom scene to establish a pleasurable fascination with male embodiment when Tasya, in Colin's body, looks in the mirror and touches his bare chest, then looks down his pants. For Tasya, male embodiment does not generate confusion about her gender identity or sexual orientation in the way it does for Lotte (any more than other differences of identity when in someone else's body). Tasya has no hesitation in kissing Colin's partner and having sex with her. During this sex scene, the viewer is reminded of the possession (which Ava is unaware of) by the flashes of Tasya's body intercut with Colin's. The film's fleeting references to cross-sex embodiment highlight the premise of possession, rather than linger on anxiety about queer desire. The film "relentlessly interrogates the experience of inhabiting a foreign body,"[47] but the aspects of gender and sexuality are not a primary concern for the film or for Tasya, who slides into Colin's body and sexual relationship with little conflict. This contrast with *Being John Malkovich* is suggestive of a cultural normalization of cross-sex embodiment in the intervening years, as "technoqueer" sexuality became more embedded in both screen narratives and everyday life (e.g., through online avatars, gaming, VR pornography, and developments in teledildonics).

A third commonality is the narrative centrality of a battle for control of consciousnesses within a host body. As with her previous assassination job, Tasya again neglects to pull the trigger to exit the host's body after killing John and Ava, and Colin's consciousness creeps back in and battles with her invading consciousness for dominance. The viewer is not always clear on whether Colin or Tasya will emerge the dominant "possessor" of his body—this is the central tension in the action. As in *Being John Malkovich*, this leads to a climactic confrontation between the host and possessor(s). Echoing Malkovich tracking down his possessors to floor seven-and-a-half and confronting them (after the destabilizing experience of being controlled from the inside by another consciousness), Colin goes to Tasya's house and demands that Michael tell him where she is: "I need to know what she's done to me." Michael knocks him down and grabs the gun off the floor, then Colin (to some degree possessed by Tasya) uses a meat cleaver to kill Michael with countless blows. In *Being John Malkovich*, a posthuman blurring of boundaries between self-will and other-will plays out in its driving motif of the "questioning of control and consciousness in defining what it means to be an embodied subject."[48] This is similarly the underlying subject of *Possessor*, though the battle plays out according to different genre conventions (horror/ Sci-Fi as opposed to comedy/drama/romance). Both films deliver the final twist of child as host: in *Being John Malkovich*, Craig is trapped in the body

164   SCREENING THE POSTHUMAN

of Maxine and Lotte's daughter, while in *Possessor*, Tasya's child is possessed by her boss and then killed by Tasya in the final showdown. The final scenes of posthuman puppeteers possessing children's bodies reflect the anti-relational turn in queer theory (exemplified by Lee Edelman's *No Future*[49]) in that they reject reproductive futurity in the figure of the child, and destabilize the restrictions of a future horizon determined by heteronormativity. In both cases, this twist operates as a taboo-breaking breach of the inviolable sense of hope attached to the figure of the child, presenting an ultimate challenge to humanist models of reproduction invested in heteronormative idealization of reproductive futurity, and thereby serving as a queer posthumanist punchline.

Bruce LaBruce's Zombie Monsters

The figure of the cyborg proves particularly useful for "technoqueer" analysis of posthuman cinema, while the second of queer posthumanism's conceptual figures—the monster—is a fleshier form for embodying the boundary-pushing of queer posthuman cinema. The following section examines Bruce LaBruce's deployment of the monstrous figure of the zombie. Hybrids and monsters can take many forms, but this chapter focuses specifically on the zombie: "a disruptive figure that has been interpreted by scholars as denaturalizing norms, calling fundamental aspects of our social relations into question."[50] Sarah Lauro and Karen Embry's "Zombie Manifesto"[51] highlights the zombie as a particularly productive monstrous figure for posthuman theory, which I elaborate on in relation to LaBruce's films below. Queer posthumanist cinema foregrounds not only the liminality of the monster but also its libidinality; the monster as "transgressive, too sexual, perversely erotic, a lawbreaker"[52] is taken up in the films of the queer-auteur provocateurs, LaBruce and Shu Lea Cheang. The figure of the monster is at home in these filmmakers' political postporn films, as "The monster awakens one to the pleasures of the body, to the simple and fleeting joys of being frightened, or frightening—to the experience of mortality and corporality."[53] Monsters serve as useful figures for queer posthumanist explorations of disease, contagion, and desire in the genre-hybrid films examined below.

The art-porn films of LaBruce and Cheang center sexual desire and include explicit sex as part of queer posthuman relationality. Their futuristic visions are in line with José Esteban Muñoz's theory of "queer futurity" (set out in his influential book, *Cruising Utopia: The Then and There of Queer Futurity*) in the sense that it "does not underplay desire. In fact it is all about desire, desire for both larger semiabstractions such as a better world or freedom but also, more immediately, better relations within the social that include better sex and more pleasure."[54] LaBruce's and Cheang's work has been described as "post-pornographic," a term Lorenzo Bernini defines as "the use of hard scenes for ends other than the mere sexual excitement of the spectator, in particular with the aim of experimenting with creative subversions of the erotic imaginary."[55] Eugenie Brinkema foregrounds the relationship between art cinema and pornography in her analysis of LaBruce's corpus, which she positions at the boundary or borderland.[56] It is not only a "Cartesian suspicion" that preserves "the fiercely held distinction" between the cerebral pleasures of art cinema and the carnal pleasure of porn, but a deeper-held anxiety or "fantasmatic splitting" that insists on their separation.[57] Brinkema uses LaBruce's indeterminable films, which "ferociously destroy attempts at classification," to explore how the two genres inform one another and "what is at stake in the pervasive cultural fantasy of their difference, the imagined promise of noncontagion."[58] Hybridizing the two genres to produce a queer critical logic, according to Brinkema, aligns LaBruce's cinema with queer posthumanism, as does his centering of "representational ambiguity, contagion, and materiality."[59]

Transgressing the dichotomy of art cinema and pornography, LaBruce has additionally deployed the zombie genre in films made after Brinkema's analysis in ways that extend his films' queer posthuman critical logic. Below I focus on LaBruce's foray into this genre with *Otto; or, Up with Dead People* (2008) and *L.A. Zombie* (2010). In LaBruce's rendering, the zombie genre aligns with the posthuman in that both raise similar existential questions about humanism, using border-dwelling or monstrous posthuman characters to critically interrogate the boundaries and boundedness of the human. LaBruce's zombie films can be mapped to queer theory and politics; for instance, Arnau Roig Mora's reading points to how the queer zombie "parallel[s] the post-identity nature of queer discourses,"[60] and Shaka McGlotten writes of how the figure "frame[s] necropolitical sex and socialities, not as absolute impasses but as animating the organizing double binds of contemporary queer politics—our collusions with death worlds and the vital potential that still nestle within them."[61] Mora suggests that LaBruce queers the zombie genre to "oppose zombie-normativity in the same way that the queer project opposes sexual, racial or any identity category's normativity."[62] In LaBruce's

166　SCREENING THE POSTHUMAN

films, the zombie is deployed as a figure that resists homonormativity and animates queer politics, negotiating tensions between assimilationist and radical factions of gay communities, as well as between anti-relationality and negativity, on the one hand, and anti-antirelationality and utopianism, on the other (these drives are most influentially articulated in the queer theories of Edelman and Muñoz, respectively). On a related note, Tyson E. Lewis explores the tension between apocalypse and futurity in a reading of George Romero's zombies, calling for "a new 'postmodern bestiary' of monsters in order to understand the dialectical figure of the monster as not simply apocalyptic but also as a revolutionary force of social and political transformation beyond the human and into the post-human."[63] LaBruce not only queers the zombie but "post-humanizes" it, deploying this monster to satirize humanism's individualism, performative rationality, and containment of libidinal desire.

The protagonists of LaBruce's zombie films, Otto and Zombie, are liminal figures, and not only in the sense that all zombies are situated at the dead/undead nexus. There is also an ambiguity surrounding whether they are zombies as such, or whether their "zombieness" is an identity, role, or even coping mechanism that they have taken on as humans—a "zombification" that is some result of queer oppression, homonormativity, homelessness, mental health issues, or a combination of the above. Otto's status as a zombie remains fluid in the film (and the film-within-a-film):

> Situating Otto in this limbo space between the living, the numb teenager incapable of feeling and the undead, LaBruce brings to our attention the post-identity politics of queer theory, de-stabilizing fixed identities in favor of fluid possibilities of self-identification outside the binary heteropatriarchal matrix. The (maybe) zombie becomes a queer identity, a post-identity.[64]

In *L.A. Zombie*, LaBruce brings zombie liminality to the fore through formal devices such as intercutting human and zombie versions of a character into sex scenes. The main character, Zombie, appears as a zombie and a homeless man interchangeably (including within the same scene), refusing fixity of identity and embodiment. LaBruce has described Zombie as a salvific figure, which Bernini compares to the ambivalent figure of Jesus in the Christian tradition:

The Christians know for certain that Jesus mysteriously participates in the human and the divine; little, however, is understood about the nature of Zombie: Perhaps he is both human and zombie (and thus still human but alive and dead at the same time), or he is a mutant alien come from who knows where, or perhaps he is simply a misfit gay, a schizophrenic inventing it all.[65]

Otto and Zombie are both mysterious, melancholic, loner figures rather than belonging to a horde or pack of zombies. In this way, LaBruce's zombies are more aligned to queer posthuman figuration of hybrids or monsters than to the pack, while more generally—as argued by Lauro and Embry in their "Zombie Manifesto"—zombies' common collectivity in lumbering hordes or packs can make them ideal imaginings of the posthuman anti-subject.[66] The loner zombie is another revisionist take on the genre in LaBruce's iterations, which enables him to explore "the dialectic between solitude and relationality."[67] The break with genre conventions in depicting the zombie as a solitary figure highlights humanism's individualism, serving as a posthuman mirror to the unnaturalness of the human isolating itself adrift or aloft of the collective.

The zombie figure's connection to viruses, contagion, and the specter of AIDS are key evocations in LaBruce's films, which he foregrounds through genre hybridity with pornography. For LaBruce, "Pornography is truly the last bastion of gay sexual radicalism," and while this genre evokes the "sexual energy and militant style" of the homosexual revolution from his formative years, he notes "the specter of AIDS, that I fear has been used in some way—both literally and metaphorically—to kill the gay revolution, still torments my films."[68] This surfaces in Otto's political zombie film-within-a-film, which "contains a double condemnation: not only of the homophobia within heteronormative civilization, but also of the serophobia and the homonormativity of the gay community."[69] Xavier Aldana Reyes argues that a queer re-appropriation of the zombie was natural, given that zombies are

an unsurprising signifier for the homosexual, particularly as filtered through traditional heterosexual myths that abounded during, and after, the outbreak of AIDS in the 1980s: zombies are generally contagious and may infect victims through direct contact with their bodily fluids; they inhabit decaying and diseased bodies and, most importantly, are eminently "other."[70]

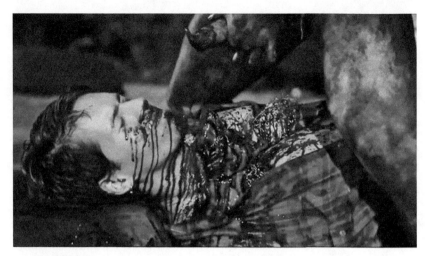

Figure 4.3 Zombie's black sperm contains a restorative virus in *L.A. Zombie* (Bruce LaBruce, 2010).

In line with this broader metaphor, Bernini reads *L.A. Zombie* as "the attempt to dismantle, but not destroy the association between homosexual sex, disease and death . . . Here the monster, who in cinema has represented the death drive and infection more than any other, radically reinvents itself, while remaining the same—a zombie."[71] Part of the queer re-appropriation in *L.A. Zombie* is that Zombie's black sperm contains a virus, but it is one which brings men back from unconsciousness or death through sexual encounter (Figure 4.3). Sex and its fluids (including zombie and human ejaculate as well as blood from wounds that he penetrates) are also restorative for Zombie, whose skin returns to a human flesh color from its blue zombie hue. The copious amount of fluids, their stark colors, and their out-of-placeness, exceed the boundaries of the human body and both heterosexual and homonormative containment. Even the coffee that Zombie requests at the diner (in his one word of dialogue in the film) is dribbled back out in an abject fashion (Figure 4.4)—not only marking a lack of human propriety but also the porousness of his posthuman body. The final blood-soaked scene is also notable for its excess of fluids, the white walls painted red following the shooting of four men after an orgy, who are then brought back to life by being covered in inky black zombie ejaculate. The climactic scene of this hardcore film links the excess of fluids with orgiastic sexual pleasure and queer posthuman connectivity. *L.A. Zombie* uses the iconography of the zombie and gay pornography genres—and the generic commonality of featuring

QUEER POSTHUMANISM 169

Figure 4.4 Zombie dribbles his coffee at the diner—one example of *L.A. Zombie*'s (Bruce LaBruce, 2010) abject use of fluids from and between porous posthuman bodies.

body parts and fluids as spectacle—in a carnival of queer posthuman desire and (sexual) relationality that revels in the pleasures and politics of monstrosity.

The Collective from *Born in Flames* to *Fluidø*

While LaBruce features the anomalous figure of the solitary zombie, other queer auteurs turn to the radical formation of the collective to champion queer relationality. Before turning to Cheang's film *Fluidø*, *Born in Flames* (Lizzie Borden, 1983) is worth brief examination as a prototype of queer posthumanist vision in independent cinema. Borden's anarchic feminist film preceded the revolutionary cinema of LaBruce and Cheang and established the centrality of the collective to queer posthuman models of intersectional relationality. In *The Village Voice*, Melissa Anderson describes the film as "a precursor to NQC [New Queer Cinema] in its genre hybridization (radical-lesbian-feminist Sci-Fi vérité) and political fury."[72] It also shares the premise of near-future political revolution with films by LaBruce and Cheang. Set in a future New York at the tenth anniversary of "the social-democratic war of liberation," *Born in Flames* traces a diverse collective of feminists fighting ongoing oppression and the heterosexist patriarchal figures who seek to

170 SCREENING THE POSTHUMAN

oppress them. The revolution relies on structures of feminist organizing, which puzzle the two straight white men who narrate the film. The two men are concerned and confused about the growing Women's Army that "started as a separatist vigilante group" and "appears to be dominated by blacks and lesbians." They discuss the founder of the Women's Army, Adelaide Norris, and "acting leader" Hilary Hurst, baffled by the lack of hierarchy and the ambiguous nature of their relationships. The men confess, "We're not even sure how the organization is structured," and later draw diagrams on a blackboard as they try to figure it out:

> The entire organization—which is represented by this circle—is about a thousand individuals, women. It's subdivided into small cells, each one of which selects its own leader on a rotating basis . . . [A]fter each of the small cells has selected a leader, about every two or three months, a leader is selected from those leaders for the entire organization. And this is the problem: we don't know how to find out at any given time who is in charge.

This scene serves as exposition but also playfully highlights how the Women's Army has radically reorganized patriarchy's hierarchical structures in their own tentacular network. In the film's documentary style, we see examples of the Women's Army's cell-like or pack-like direct action, such as the scene where a woman being harassed and attacked by two men on the street is saved by a bicycle brigade who gather and circle them, blowing whistles and disrupting the attack. A subsequent news segment reflects the patriarchy's disorientation, already represented by the two suited male narrators, when it reports that "Police have been puzzled in the past week by what they described as well-organized bands of fifteen to twenty women on bicycles attacking men on the streets." By reiterating the puzzlement of patriarchal figures, the film draws attention to the formation of the feminist collective according to an alternative structure that fundamentally differs from the top-down hierarchies typifying human relations in patriarchal society.

In contrast, the collective is marked by plurality, intersectionality, and diversity. As Teresa de Lauretis points out, "several groups of women (black women, Latinas, lesbians, single mothers, intellectuals, political activists, spiritual and punk performers, and a Women's Army) succeed in mobilizing and joining together: not by ignoring but, paradoxically, by acknowledging their difference."[73] Just as LaBruce's films explore political tensions in gay communities, Borden's revolutionary film even more explicitly teases out how feminist communities navigate internal differences. For de Lauretis, "heterogeneity and difference within women remain in our memory as the film's narrative image, its work of representing, which cannot be collapsed into a fixed identity, a sameness of all women as Woman, or a representation of Feminism as a coherent and available image."[74] The resistance to homogeneity and fixed identity evident in *Born in Flames* remains characteristic of the queer cinema that followed. The plurality underpinning the revolution is embedded at the formal level as well, which features a wide range of perspectives, a unique generic blend, and the use of montage for expansive representation of women's experiences (for instance, a montage sequence of women's labor includes close-up footage of wrapping raw chicken, rolling on a condom, washing cutlery, and packaging takeaway). In *The New Yorker*, Richard Brody describes the film's construction as a collage that incorporates fictionalized documentary footage with staged newscasts and talk shows as well as musical performance and scenes of private lives and political meetings.[75] The figure of the collective, central to the film's politics, underpins the film's structure and style as well as its narrative.

The film's narrative and formal vision of plurality and intersectionality is prototypical of an anti-antirelationality and reclaiming of futurity outlined by Muñoz in *Cruising Utopia*. Muñoz describes his book as "a polemic that argues against anti-relationality by insisting on the essential need for an understanding of queerness as collectivity."[76] In a similar spirit, as Jasmina Šepetavc's analysis of the film suggests, "Borden inscribed into the movie the idea of a necessity of pluralism and different voices in feminism on the one hand and relationality of different struggles that would not mean the end of autonomy for any of them on the other."[77] *Born in Flames*, in Šepetavc's reading, also "poses the task of reclaiming the concepts of futurity, not as a fixed teleology, but as an open-endedness, the form of which we cannot yet imagine, but is for this very same reason an important task for feminist and queer studies,"[78] which echoes Muñoz's concept of queerness as horizon or potentiality, with its similar valence to Alain Badiou's thing-that-is-not-yet-imagined.[79] It also resonates with Haraway's concept of "tentacular thinking" since "[t]he tentacular are also nets and networks" and, like the Women's Army, Haraway "stay[s] with the trouble . . . in generative joy, terror, and collective thinking."[80] For Šepetavc, the film shows a need for feminism to both revolt against sexism and "to imagine new ways of connecting, to make use of temporal ruptures, asynchronies and to queer the body or even harness the queer body's disruptive powers."[81] The significance

172   SCREENING THE POSTHUMAN

of *Born in Flames* includes its emphasis on interconnectedness and collectivity while maintaining plurality and intersectionality, a utopian vision—in
the Muñozian sense—aligned with queer posthumanism.

Fluidø is similarly instilled with political fury, while also being infused
with a celebration of pleasure and perversity. It also shares a revolutionary
pornographic sensibility (and a producer, Jürgen Brüning) with LaBruce's
zombie films. Both filmmakers are queer auteur-provocateurs working at
the intersection of arthouse and pornographic cinema, their work equally
at home on the film festival circuit and online porn platforms. Cheang
considers herself a media activist and her work as "genre-bending gender-
fxxking."[82] *Fluidø* represents the third film in her postporn trilogy following
I.K.U. and *UKI*, which similarly explore "post-porn performance and viral
contamination."[83] *Fluidø*'s end credits cite several postporn writers, aligning
the film with this movement that "encompasses those who approach sex
as an emancipatory tool and emerged partly as a backlash against white
feminism's disavowal of pornography."[84] The resonance of her work with
posthumanism is also clear in her approaches to narrative, genre, and the
body, as Banyi Huang writes:

> The works that Cheang has created sought to overturn the notion of an
> organic body, to portray a contaminated, transparent, hyperreal state-
> of-being, as evinced in the artist's orchestration of disjointed narratives,
> stylized performances and hallucinogenic editing style. The body is shown
> to be none other than the original prosthesis we learn to manipulate in
> the first place. That perspective came to the fore in *I.K.U.* (2000), an or-
> giastic Sci-Fi drama and illegitimate spinoff on the movie *Blade Runner*
> (1982), which takes a fragmented, cyclical form that mirrors contemporary
> experiences of online porn and media-saturated environments.[85]

Huang evokes Hayles in describing the body as original prosthesis, and also
compares Cheang's work to the "guerilla tactics outlined in Donna Haraway's
'Cyborg Manifesto.'"[86] Meanwhile, Eve Oishi reads Cheang's *I.K.U.* through
another key theorist of critical posthumanism, Stacy Alaimo, and highlights
"Cheang's focus on the transhuman quality of the sexual body, the understanding of sexuality and the body as illegible outside technological and political controls."[87] In this way, the posthuman bodies in Cheang's postporn
films echo the figuration of Haraway's cyborgs, wherein "Cyborgs might

consider more seriously the partial, fluid, sometimes aspect of sex and sexual embodiment."[88]

Transcending genre and gender boundaries are hallmarks of queer posthumanism on-screen, as is challenging the natural/artificial dichotomy (often by combining organic and technological forms of sexual expression). Cheang's work transcends such boundaries, including "the seemingly binary universe of the New Queer Cinema," and pushes viewers to "think hard about the most basic assumptions."[89] Ruby B. Rich writes that "*I.K.U.* frees the body from gender restrictions, empowers the object of fantasy, and merges the user and the used, the carrier and the carried, into a cyber satyricon of impulses, stimulants, and gratifications."[90] The genre hybridity of Cheang's films—particularly the combination of postporn and science fiction—facilitates the imagining of postgender, postqueer, posthuman bodies and relationality.

Braidotti and Matthew Fuller describe *Fluidø* as a "science fiction postporn" depicting "a scenario in which the HIV virus has mutated into a pleasure-giving drug called Fluid."[91] Spectacle and excess generated through genre set-pieces take precedence over the tangled plot in *Fluidø*, but its primary fantasy follows a government agent who is infected by the runner boy (who distributes Fluid from an ejaculation factory) and is then initiated into the queer world. The film is framed by the AIDS epidemic and activism of the 1980s and 1990s, recast into a posthuman future where

> The shifting role of the virus creates new conditions for exploitation, inverting gender roles, at the same time as shifting lines of affinity are drawn between defective androids, addicts of the fluid, and an uneasy but relentlessly libidinal milieu of dealers, madams, cops and clients.[92]

Herself describing it as a "cypherpunk" Sci-Fi movie, Cheang says, "*FLUIDØ* ultimately claims the virus as my own salvation. It's my attempt at reconciliation with the pain of lost intimacy,"[93] which echoes LaBruce's nostalgia for the homosexual revolution and Muñoz's reminiscence about New York's past public sex cultures.[94] These films' pornographic utopias are seeded by loss, mourning, nostalgia, and political pain (as is the art discussed by Muñoz). Following Muñoz's deployment of Derrida's notion of *hauntology*—"a conceptual tool for the understanding of being within the postmodern age of an electronic *res publica*: 'neither living or dead, present or absent' "[95]—LaBruce

174   SCREENING THE POSTHUMAN

and Cheang's films can be understood similarly as "haunted cultural work that remembers and longs for a moment outside of this current state of siege."[96] By using postporn's "viral promiscuity" that can become "a generative force for extreme intimacy and kinship,"[97] Cheang forges a utopian response to lost intimacy and recuperates a radical and erotic vision of queer futurity.

Fluidø is explicitly political from its opening scenes, referencing the AIDS crisis and interspersing footage of ACT UP (AIDS Coalition to Unleash Power) protests into the post-AIDS future of 2060. The footage of two men publicly kissing at one of these actions (approximately forty minutes into the film) evokes the kiss between Lito and his boyfriend at the São Paulo Gay Pride Parade in *Sense8* (2015–2018) as another public, political, and passionate display of affection. However, what the Wachowskis do in cinematic and mainstream genre frameworks in their Netflix series, Cheang pushes into more experimental and pornographic territory to enable a queerer, more explicitly posthuman, and more politically radical vision. For example, one of the male pack of ejaculators flashes back to (or perhaps fantasizes about) a 1978 bathhouse orgy, and the formal qualities of this scene—with the fluidity of bodies, the dissolving of one into another (so it is unclear where one ends and the next begins), and the use of superimposition—reflects the orgiastic communality of queer bodies in *Sense8*'s sex scenes.[98] But while *Sense8*'s dissolving of otherness advocates for plurality and diversity in line with the modest mainstream ambition of equality, Cheang's postqueer postporn frees queer sexual desire and pleasure from a desire for acceptance and acceptability by evoking past revolution and activism and embedding it into pornographic scenes. For example, along with inserting clips of ACT UP protests, Cheang creates orgiastic scenes in which sexual and activist action is blurred and queer utopian political slogans are prominent.

In this futuristic yet nostalgic world, the revolutionaries share their fluid and pleasure widely, smearing bodies ecstatically and spraying walls gleefully, such as in the fluid-filled orgy of the "ZERO GEN" (genetically evolved humans) in a rundown industrial space. Like LaBruce's use of political slogans flashing on-screen in *The Raspberry Reich*, a call to "Liberate the Fluid" appears in text at the end of the film. *Fluidø*'s politics tend more toward the revolutionary than *Sense8*, although both texts center collectivity. For example, evoking LaBruce's films such as *The Raspberry Reich* (2004), one of the four women masturbating (with clients watching on) is dubbed The Pornoterrorist. She declares: "As I receive pleasure, the whole universe receives pleasure through me." Madame X, the client seated in front of her, cries, "Let there be pleasure on Earth, let it begin with me." As The Pornoterrorist orgasms, sounds of pleasure reverberate, as if the whole world is joining in with a shared experience. Oishi's reading of "collective orgasm" is useful here for understanding the queer posthuman sexual relations in Cheang's films:

> Cheang has stated about *I.K.U.*: "I did not make this film for masturbation. I made it for collective orgasm" (Ting 2005). In this statement Cheang draws a distinction between two erotic modes that have been shaped by a cyberculture in which human interaction with technology has replaced physical contact between human bodies. While masturbation implies a sexual act committed in isolation, "collective orgasm" suggests that a mechanically mediated sexual pleasure is produced through the technology's ability to link multiple users together.[99]

If, as one of the parodic slogans in LaBruce's *The Raspberry Reich* suggests, "Masturbation is counter-revolutionary!" then collective orgasm is Cheang's revolutionary alternative. The expansive intimacy of this call to interconnect through pleasure contrasts with the posthuman isolation personified by Theodore in *Her* (although it resonates with Samantha's polyamory); Cheang creates a distinctly queer utopian vision in which cyberculture forges connections rather than reinforces isolation and individualism. As Oishi argues,

> If the technological, economic, and political structures of the virtual age have shaped the ways in which sexual desire and pleasure are experienced, Cheang's purpose is to use the bodily manipulations endemic to these structures to move individual bodies to sensation and collectivity.[100]

Fluidø seeks to bring the spectator into the collective pleasure within the film, not only through conventions of pornography, but through other formal techniques. For instance, CGI squirts rise and fall on-screen over the pack of male ejaculators, denoting the endless flow of pleasure and fluids in their factory-like efforts to produce the narcotic "Fluid," and the hypnotizing rhythm of the imagery is again seen behind the end credits (Figure 4.5).

Figure 4.5 The hypnotizing rhythm of the narcotic "Fluid" rising and falling on-screen in *Fluidø* (Shu Lea Cheang, 2017).

Conclusion

Queer posthumanism on-screen has worked to break down boundaries and forge connections, destabilize gender and sexuality binaries, and establish rhizomatic collectivities. Facilitated by the figures outlined in the introduction to this chapter—the cyborg, the monster, and the collective—queer posthumanism on-screen envisions queer relationality and posthuman futures. The case studies in this chapter illuminate the convergence between critical posthumanism and queer theory, as well as the cinematic trajectory of queer posthumanism over the past quarter century. From the anxious dabbling in technosexualities and cross-sex embodiment of Jonze's films explored at the beginning of this chapter, the definition of the human as "at base level zero a white heterosexual man"[101] has been further challenged by other auteurs in subsequent years. After highlighting the development of queer posthuman cinema from *Being John Malkovich* to Cronenberg's *Possessor*, the second half of this chapter traced related phenomena in queer independent cinema from the prototypical *Born in Flames* to the more recent films of LaBruce and Cheang. These queer provoc-auteurs and revolutionaries offer radical depictions of individual and collective identity that are unapologetically queer and posthuman, and in so doing, affront heteronormative, homonormative, and humanist perspectives on gender, sexuality, pleasure, and sexual and political action. Analysis of their films clarifies the utopian vision of queer posthumanism, which enlivens and elaborates on the way that "queer theory and the posthuman mobilize and radicalize the here and now through desire, pleasure and pure potentiality."[102] In different ways, the range of films explored in this chapter—from the relatively mainstream to the more underground cinema of queer auteurs, each spanning different genres—have queered the posthuman, and taken queer narratives and genres in posthuman directions, as they work to challenge the definition of the human as at base level a heterosexual cisgender male.

Notes

1. Patricia MacCormack, "Queer Posthumanism: Cyborgs, Animals, Monsters, Perverts," in *The Ashgate Research Companion to Queer Theory*, ed. Noreen Giffney and Michael O'Rourke (Farnham: Ashgate, 2009), 111.
2. MacCormack, "Queer Posthumanism," 112.
3. MacCormack, "Queer Posthumanism," 113.
4. Karen Barad, "Posthumanist Performativity: Toward an Understanding of How Matter Comes to Matter," *Signs: Journal of Women in Culture and Society* 28, no. 3 (2003): 803.
5. Barad "Posthumanist Performativity"; Karen Barad, *Meeting the Universe Halfway: Quantum Physics and the Entanglement of Matter and Meaning* (Durham, NC: Duke University Press, 2007); Karen Barad, "Nature's Queer Performativity," *Qui Parle* 19, no. 2 (Spring/Summer 2011): 121–158.
6. Elizabeth A. Grosz, *Volatile Bodies* (Bloomington: Indiana University Press, 1994), 24.
7. Donna Haraway, "A Cyborg Manifesto: Science, Technology and Socialist-Feminism in the Late Twentieth Century," 1985, in *Manifestly Haraway* (Minneapolis: University of Minnesota Press, 2016), 9.
8. Judith Halberstam, "Automating Gender: Postmodern Feminism in the Age of the Intelligent Machine," *Feminist Studies* 17, no. 3 (1991): 451.
9. Edmond Y. Chang, "Technoqueer: Re/Con/Figuring Posthuman Narratives" (PhD diss., University of Washington, 2012), 27.
10. Chang, "Technoqueer," 22.
11. Chang, "Technoqueer," 58.
12. David Greven, *Queering the Terminator: Sexuality and Cyborg Cinema* (London: Bloomsbury, 2017), 2, 26.
13. Patricia MacCormack, "Unnatural Alliances," in *Deleuze and Queer Theory*, ed. Chrysanthi Nigianni and Merl Storr (Edinburgh: Edinburgh University Press, 2009), 136.
14. Rosi Braidotti, *Nomadic Subjects: Embodiment and Sexual Difference in Contemporary Feminist Theory* (New York: Columbia University Press, 1994), 77.
15. Braidotti, *Nomadic Subjects*, 78.

178 SCREENING THE POSTHUMAN

16. Harry M. Benshoff, *Monsters in the Closet: Homosexuality and the Horror Film* (Manchester: Manchester University Press, 1997), 2.

17. Jeffery Jerome Cohen, ed., *Monster Theory: Reading Culture* (Minneapolis: University of Minnesota Press, 1996), 6.

18. Judith Halberstam, *Skin Shows: Gothic Horror and the Technology of Monsters* (Durham, NC: Duke University Press, 1995), 162.

19. Halberstam, *Skin Shows*, 162.

20. Susan Stryker, "My Words to Victor Frankenstein Above the Village of Chamounix: Performing Transgender Rage," in *The Transgender Studies Reader*, ed. Susan Stryker and Stephen Whittle (New York: Routledge, 2004), 245.

21. Stryker, "My Words to Victor Frankenstein," 246–247.

22. Harlan Weaver, "Monster Trans: Diffracting Affect, Reading Rage," in *TransGothic in Literature and Culture*, ed. Jolene Zigarovich (New York: Routledge, 2017), 134.

23. Weaver, "Monster Trans," 134.

24. MacCormack, "Queer Posthumanism," 124.

25. Rosi Braidotti, "Posthuman Critical Theory," *Critical Posthumanism and Planetary Futures*, ed. Debashish Banerji and Makarand R. Paranjape (New Delhi: Springer, 2016), 25–26.

26. Braidotti, "Posthuman Critical Theory," 25–26.

27. Gilles Deleuze and Félix Guattari, *A Thousand Plateaus: Capitalism and Schizophrenia*, 1980, translated by Brian Massumi (Minneapolis: University of Minnesota Press, 2005), 239.

28. MacCormack "Queer Posthumanism," 121.

29. MacCormack, "Queer Posthumanism," 124.

30. MacCormack, "Unnatural Alliances," 140.

31. MacCormack, "Queer Posthumanism," 121.

32. N. Katherine Hayles, *How We Became Posthuman: Virtual Bodies in Cybernetics, Literature, and Informatics* (Chicago: University of Chicago Press, 1999), 3.

33. Nidesh Lawtoo, "'This Is No Simulation!': Hypermimesis from *Being John Malkovich* to *Her*," *Quarterly Review of Film and Video* 37, no. 2 (2020): 116–117.

34. Lawtoo, "This Is No Simulation!," 120–123.

35. Lawtoo, "This Is No Simulation!," 119.

36. Vanessa Pappas, "Conceptualising the Virtual and the Posthuman," *Media International Australia* 98 (February 2001): 47–48.

37. Pappas, "Conceptualising the Virtual and the Posthuman," 44.

38. Lawtoo, "This Is No Simulation!," 136.

39. Peter Bradshaw, "*Possessor* Review—Brandon Cronenberg's Terrifying Sci-Fi Horror Freak-Out," *The Guardian*, November 26, 2020, https://www.theguardian.com/film/2020/nov/26/possessor-review-brandon-cronenberg-andrea-riseborough-sc0fi-horror.

40. John DeFore, "*Possessor*: Film Review," *The Hollywood Reporter*, January 25, 2020, https://www.hollywoodreporter.com/review/possessor-review-1272650.

QUEER POSTHUMANISM   179

41. Brandon Cronenberg, "Interview with Brandon Cronenberg," *Cine-Excess 15: The 15th International Conference and Festival on Global Cult Film Traditions. Bodies as Battlegrounds: Disruptive Sexualities in Cult Cinema*, October 23, 2021.

42. Glenn Kenny, "*Possessor* Review: It's by a Cronenberg, but Not the One You Think," *The New York Times*, October 1, 2020, https://www.nytimes.com/2020/10/01/mov ies/possessor-review.html.

43. Wendy Ide, "*Possessor*: Sundance Review," *Screen Daily*, January 26, 2020, https:// www.screendaily.com/reviews/possessor-sundance-review/5146251.article.

44. David Ehrlich, "*Possessor* Review: Brandon Cronenberg's Gory Techno-Thriller Gets Under Your Skin," *IndieWire*, January 26, 2020, https://www.indiewire.com/2020/01/ possessor-review-sundance-1202205838/.

45. Ehrlich, "*Possessor* Review."

46. DeFore, "*Possessor*: Film Review."

47. Kenny, "*Possessor* Review."

48. Pappas, "Conceptualising the Virtual and the Posthuman," 44.

49. Lee Edelman, *No Future: Queer Theory and the Death Drive* (Durham NC: Duke University Press, 2004).

50. Steve Jones, "Gender Monstrosity: Deadgirl and the Sexual Politics of Zombie-Rape," *Feminist Media Studies* 13, no. 3 (2013): 526.

51. Sarah Juliet Lauro and Karen Embry, "A Zombie Manifesto: The Nonhuman Condition in the Era of Advanced Capitalism," *boundary 2* 35, no. 1 (2008): 85–108.

52. Cohen, *Monster Theory*, 16.

53. Cohen, *Monster Theory*, 17.

54. José Esteban Muñoz, *Cruising Utopia: The Then and There of Queer Futurity* (New York: New York University Press, 2009), 30.

55. Lorenzo Bernini, *Queer Apocalypses: Elements of Antisocial Theory*, 2013, trans. Julia Heim (London: Palgrave Macmillan, 2017), 125.

56. Eugenie Brinkema, "A Title Does Not Ask, but Demands That You Make a Choice: On the Otherwise Films of Bruce LaBruce," *Criticism* 48, no. 1 (2006): 97.

57. Brinkema, "A Title Does Not Ask," 103.

58. Brinkema, "A Title Does Not Ask," 103.

59. Brinkema, "A Title Does Not Ask," 97.

60. Arnau Roig Mora, "The Necropolitics of the Apocalypse: Queer Zombies in the Cinema of Bruce LaBruce," in *Thinking Dead: What the Zombie Apocalypse Means*, ed. Murali Bulaji (Washington, DC: Lexington Books, 2013), 185.

61. Shaka McGlotten, "Zombie Porn: Necropolitics, Sex, and Queer Socialities," *Porn Studies* 1, no. 4 (2014): 362.

62. Mora, *Thinking Dead*, 192.

63. Tyson E. Lewis, "Ztopia: Lessons in Post-Vital Politics in George Romero's Zombie Films," in *Generation Zombie: Essays on the Living Dead in Modern Culture*, ed. Stephanie Boluk and Wylie Lenz (Jefferson, NC: McFarland & Company, 2011), 91.

64. Mora, *Thinking Dead*, 188–189.

180 SCREENING THE POSTHUMAN

65. Bernini, *Queer Apocalypses*, 108.
66. Lauro and Embry, "A Zombie Manifesto."
67. Bernini, *Queer Apocalypses*, 110.
68. Bruce LaBruce qtd. in Bernini, *Queer Apocalypses*, 109–110.
69. Bernini, *Queer Apocalypses*, 113.
70. Xavier Aldana Reyes, "Beyond the Metaphor: Gay Zombies and the Challenge to Homonormativity," *Journal for Cultural and Religious Theory* 13, no. 2 (2014): 3.
71. Bernini, *Queer Apocalypses*, 109.
72. Melissa Anderson, "The Embers of Paris Glow for 'Born in Flames: New Queer Cinema,'" *The Village Voice*, October 10, 2012, https://www.villagevoice.com/2012/10/10/the-embers-of-paris-glow-for-born-in-flames-new-queer-cinema/.
73. Teresa de Lauretis, "Aesthetic and Feminist Theory: Rethinking Women's Cinema," *New German Critique* 34 (Winter 1985): 165.
74. De Lauretis, "Aesthetic and Feminist Theory," 168.
75. Richard Brody, "The Political Science Fiction of *Born in Flames*," *The New Yorker*, February 19, 2016, https://www.newyorker.com/culture/richard-brody/the-political-science-fiction-of-born-in-flames.
76. Muñoz, *Cruising Utopia*, 11.
77. Jasmina Šepetavc, "Queer and Feminist Futures: The Importance of a Future and Mobilising Feminist Film in *Post* Times," *Družboslovne Razprave* 33, no. 84 (2017): 94.
78. Šepetavc, "Queer and Feminist Futures," 96.
79. Muñoz, *Cruising Utopia*, 21.
80. Donna Haraway, "Tentacular Thinking: Anthropocene, Capitalocene, Chthulucene," *e-flux Journal* 75 (September 2016), https://www.e-flux.com/journal/75/67125/tentacular-thinking-anthropocene-capitalocene-chthulucene/.
81. Šepetavc, "Queer and Feminist Futures," 96.
82. Shu Lea Cheang qtd. in Vince Schleitwiler, Abby Sun, and Rea Tajiri, "Messy, Energetic, Intense: A Roundtable Conversation among New York's Asian American Experimental Filmmakers of the Eighties with Roddy Bogawa, Daryl Chin, Shu Lea Cheang, and Rea Tajiri," *Film Quarterly* 73, no. 3 (2020): 77.
83. Banyi Huang, "Docile, Mutating and Resistant Bodies: Shu Lea Cheang," *ArtAsiaPacific* 113 (May 2019): 83.
84. Huang, "Docile, Mutating and Resistant Bodies," 83.
85. Huang, "Docile, Mutating and Resistant Bodies," 82.
86. Huang, "Docile, Mutating and Resistant Bodies," 80.
87. Eve Oishi, "'Collective Orgasm': The Eco-Cyber-Pornography of Shu Lea Cheang," *Women's Studies Quarterly* 35, no. 1 (2007): 30–31.
88. Haraway, "A Cyborg Manifesto," 66.
89. Ruby B. Rich, *New Queer Cinema: The Director's Cut* (Durham, NC: Duke University Press, 2013), 79.
90. Rich, *New Queer Cinema*, 76–77.
91. Rosi Braidotti and Matthew Fuller, "The Posthumanities in an Era of Unexpected Consequences," *Theory, Culture & Society* 36, no. 6 (2019): 16.
92. Braidotti and Fuller, "The Posthumanities," 16.

QUEER POSTHUMANISM   181

93. Cheang qtd. in Schleitwiler, Sun, and Tajiri, "Messy, Energetic, Intense," 69.
94. Muñoz, *Cruising Utopia*, 33–48.
95. Muñoz, *Cruising Utopia*, 42.
96. Muñoz, *Cruising Utopia*, 47.
97. Huang, "Docile, Mutating and Resistant Bodies," 83.
98. Claire Henry,"Queer Posthumanism Through the Wachowskis." *Synoptique* 10, no. 1 (2023), https://www.synoptique.ca.
99. Oishi, "Collective Orgasm," 31.
100. Oishi, "Collective Orgasm," 32.
101. MacCormack, "Queer Posthumanism," 111.
102. MacCormack, "Queer Posthumanism," 112.

5

The Cinematic Convergence of Posthuman and Crip Perspectives

Pansy Duncan and Missy Molloy

In the twenty-first century, scholarship with an emphasis on disability is gaining traction, with critical disability studies emerging as an influential and interdisciplinary body of criticism. While rooted in activist movements aimed at achieving legal and social recognition for differently abled people, disability studies opens onto a broader critical project— one that seeks, as Robert McRuer has put it, to "center atypical bodies, minds and behaviors while interrogating that which can never be contained or described neatly by an entirely historical and limited abled-disabled binary."[1] In this respect, disabilities studies' congruence with critical posthumanism is clear. Both fields are characterized by a commitment to alternative forms of embodiment and subjectivity. They are also characterized by an effort to challenge normative assumptions about the limits of physical and cognitive possibility, about our relationship to our tools, devices, and prosthetics, and, most broadly, about the nature of human being.

Indeed, as Stuart Murray has suggested, despite skepticism among disabilities studies scholars about certain brands of posthumanism, the two bodies of work share a number of key characteristics. These include "a critique of humanist norms; a recognition of complex embodiment; and a commitment to intersectionality and inclusive practice among them."[2] Similarly, according to Dan Goodley, Rebecca Lawthom, and Katherine Runswick-Cole, "critical disability studies are perfectly at ease with the posthuman because disability has always contravened the traditional classical humanist conception of what it means to be human."[3] Yet as Goodley, Lawthom, and Cole further note, "disability also invites a critical analysis of the posthuman," with ongoing stigma on- and off-screen underscoring continued discrimination against disabled people and the persistence of humanist, able-bodied norms in ostensibly posthuman times.[4]

Pansy Duncan and Missy Molloy, *The Cinematic Convergence of Posthuman and Crip Perspectives*.
In: *Screening the Posthuman*. Edited by: Missy Molloy, Pansy Duncan, and Claire Henry, Oxford University Press.
© Oxford University Press 2023. DOI: 10.1093/oso/9780197538562.003.0006

This chapter surveys the ambivalent intersection of critical posthumanism and disability studies through the lens of two postmillennial films that focus on disabled figures, *Hable con ella/Talk to Her* (Pedro Almodóvar, 2002) and *Sound of Metal* (Darius Marder, 2019). As we will show, these films mark real advances over older traditions of "disability film," exemplified by films such as *Born on the Fourth of July* (Oliver Stone, 1989) and *My Left Foot* (Jim Sheridan, 1989) as well as more recent films like *The Theory of Everything* (James Marsh, 2014). These older texts' lamination of humanism and ableism is reflected in their focus on the "overcoming" of disability as a mark of the so-called triumph of the human spirit. It is also reflected in their reliance on able-bodied actors, for whom playing a disabled character is a measure of their own hyper-competent distance from the "marred" bodies and/or minds of the figures they represent. In these respects, *Talk to Her* and *Sound of Metal* constitute a striking departure. As we will argue in this chapter, *Talk to Her* and *Sound of Metal* utilize cinema's unique storytelling capacities to subvert ableist cinematic conventions for the representation of disability, while at the same time "offe[ring] new, collectivist and crip alternatives that fit well with the posthuman manifesto outlined by scholars such as Braidotti and Haraway."[5] But both films are ambivalent in their affordances to this convergence of posthumanism and disability. In the first section of this chapter, we will contend that *Talk to Her*'s posthumanist credentials lie in its reliance on a pair of physically and cognitively disabled women, both of them comatose, to destabilize patterns of expressivity and expressive reading that have becomes cornerstones of humanism.[6] Yet as we will also note, the film deploys able-bodied actors to play the brain-dead women at its heart, while yoking its uplifting conclusion to one of the women's miraculous recovery. As we will show in this chapter's second section, *Sound of Metal* is still more ambivalent in its relation to posthumanist and post-ableist ideals. While the film's formal register celebrates the capacity of "disability" and both cinematic and prosthetic technology to open up more-than-human worlds, its representational register indexes a classic humanist suspicion of technology, with the protagonist's cochlear implant ultimately framed as a prosthetic intrusion on his bodily integrity.

Deconstructing Humanist Norms of Expressivity in *Talk to Her*

Physical and cognitive abilities, from gross motor control to rational consciousness, form well-established keystones of ableist models of the

184   SCREENING THE POSTHUMAN

"human."[7] Yet emotional norms also underpin our ableist understanding of human subjectivity. As many theorists have shown, among eighteenth-century British philosophers in particular, "human nature" came to be defined "principally through the idea of affectability."[8] At stake here is not just the capacity to be "powerfully affected by surrounding objects and passing events," but to display this affectedness through the language of emotional "expression," according to an expressive logic by which, as Rei Terada has put it, external bodily signs are taken to reflect or index a profound inner experience that has been "lifted from a depth to a surface."[9] Indeed, these humanist emotional norms, which have even more hold over Western societies today than they did three hundred years ago, have yielded a series of stigmatized "spoiled identities," from those with autism spectrum disorders to those suffering from PTSD,[10] figures whose emotional illegibility or emotional difference situate them, as Dan Goodley has put it, "outside what is normatively understood as human."[11]

Several films have explored this entanglement between emotion, emotional "expression," and our understanding of the human in ways that speak productively to efforts to bring posthumanism and disabilities studies into dialogue.[12] Perhaps most notable here is *The Diving Bell and the Butterfly* (Julian Schnabel, 2007), a film based on a memoir documenting author Jean-Dominique Bauby's experience of "locked-in syndrome," in which total physical paralysis coexists with full mental alertness to his situation (we will return to this film in our discussion of *Sound of Metal* below). This section, however, will focus primarily on *Talk to Her*, which documents the perplexities of love and desire in the lives of two "couples," very loosely defined: handsome journalist Marco (played by Dario Grandinetti) and matador Lydia (played by Rosario Flores); and nurse Benigno (played by Javier Cámara) and Alicia (played by Leonor Watling), the beautiful comatose dancer for whom he tenderly cares (before suddenly, and shockingly, assaulting her). As I will show, while some aspects of the film recall older brands of "disability film," *Talk to Her* convincingly unites the concerns of posthumanist and disabilities studies in deploying tears, a figure often enlisted as an emblem of "the human's unique difference from the animal kingdom," to deconstruct familiar distinctions between the ideally "human" subject of expression and those whose expressive capacities appear to be limited or aberrant.[13]

Comatose, insensible, Alicia would seem worlds away from the emotionally normative figures that have sustained Western philosophical concepts of the "affected" human since Edmund Burke. Far from expressions of a deep, emotional self, her yawns, twitches, and blushes are merely "mechanical actions," systemic effects of a sophisticated array of medical technology, from the artificial respirator that breathes for her and the intravenous drip that feeds her, to the massages and bed-baths by which Benigno ensures her daily upkeep. As the head doctor explains, coma patients "[have] no ideas or feelings." One poignant scene shows Benigno applying to Alicia's eyes a series of eye drops that proceed to flow down her cheeks like tears (Figure 5.1). Historically speaking, tears' liquid promise as expressive signs of subjective depth has helped authenticate claims about human exceptionalism; yet, as *Talk to Her* is at pains to show, Alicia's tears are less what Mary Ann O'Farrell dubs "somatic testimony" than institutional and medical prostheses.[14] From a humanist perspective, these and other expressive failures render Alicia an aberrant (non-)subject who is defined primarily by emotional lack or insensibility and who gains access to full subjectivity only as a function of the miraculous "recovery narrative" in which *Talk to Her* somewhat satirically participates.[15] A disabilities studies framework appears to supply little basis for countering such a model. Indeed, the only disabilities studies scholar who has discussed the film in any sustained way, Matthew J. Marr, disregards Alicia's movements altogether, emphasizing her "total immobility" by way of underscoring her status as the victim of Benigno's sexual assault.[16] Yet if, from the normative standpoint of what we might dub "affective humanism," Alicia is essentially a failed subject, from a posthumanist perspective she epitomizes a revolutionary or hybrid form of subjectivity elucidated by Haraway's account of the "cyborg." Like the

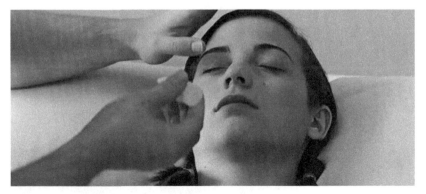

Figure 5.1 In *Hable con ella/Talk to Her* (Pedro Almodóvar, 2002), the liquid eye drops proceed down Alicia's cheeks like tears.

cyborg, a creature "simultaneously animal and machine," inhabiting a world "ambiguously natural and crafted," and dependent on a series of "intimate [technical] components," Alicia serves to render any distinction between "natural and artificial . . . self-developing and externally designed" remarkably unstable. From a posthumanist perspective, that is, she must be understood as a (hybrid or prosthetic) subject in her own right.[17]

Notions of emotional aberrance equally structure a humanist understanding of Benigno, Alicia's nurse, who has an unusually intense investment in his patient that will later be revealed as an erotic fixation and culminate in his rape of her. Eliding his own role in administering her eye drops, Benigno reads her eyes' liquid secretions as expressive, indexing the presence of a profound yet knowable self to which he himself has a unique and unrivaled access (Figure 5.2). When Alicia's dance teacher describes a performance to her unconscious ex-student, Benigno confidently asserts that "Alicia is loving this"—a claim to which Alicia's smooth brow and lidded eyes offer neither corroboration nor dissent. Reading her responsiveness to his touch as evidence of her desire to be touched, her lack of resistance to his desire as confirmation of her own desire, Benigno is convinced that Alicia reciprocates his feelings. As he insists later in the film, "Alicia and I get on better than most married couples." What is at stake here is, quite clearly, a misrecognition, and—notwithstanding the fairy tale-like logic by which the film yokes Benigno's act of rape to Alicia's miraculous recovery—it is a misrecognition with violent effects. From a humanist perspective, this misrecognition can register only in pathological terms, recalling a range of diagnostic profiles, from "autism" to "psychopathy," that serve to pathologize psychological and

Figure 5.2 An animated Benigno talks to Alicia.

neurological difference. And disability studies scholarship perspectives, meanwhile, have delivered essentially the same reading, to the extent that the impulse to protect the disabled Alicia requires the abjection of the equally disabled Benigno (Matthew Marr, for example, ascribes to Benigno a "psychopathic condition" that involves a "gross misreading of an impossible romantic relationship with his comatose patient, Alicia").[18] A posthumanist perspective, however, can provide a less medicalizing and moralizing lens through which to view Benigno's misreading of Alicia. For, while its outcome is undeniably repugnant, Benigno's perception of Alicia as a full subject can be understood as part of an ontologically ambitious posthumanist agenda that can help us extend the franchise of full personhood across bodies that aren't conventionally afforded the protections of the category of the "human."

Significant to *Talk to Her*'s contribution to this crip-friendly posthumanist agenda is the fact that the dynamic between Benigno and Alicia emerges as part of a broader effort to deconstruct distinctions between conventionally humanist norms of expression and their "aberrant" other. On first sight, the relationship between Marco and Lydia seems to differ from the relationship between Benigno and Alicia point for point. Where Benigno's love for Alicia is distinctly one-sided, Marco's love for Lydia appears mutual and passionate; where Alicia's body is mute and inanimate, Lydia's body proffers itself right from the first moment to be read. Yet across the course of the film, this qualitative opposition between the two couples and the modes of reading they represent loses its force. If Benigno's reading of Alicia is misconceived, it is not so uniquely misconceived that the critics have managed to avoid reproducing its terms. Describing Alicia as a creature "shut off from sensory contact with the world," A. O. Scott, for example, performs a wishful inversion of the nature of her condition that suggests his own investment in reading the coma patient as a possessor of a deep self.[19] Whereas, in the coma patient, it is the brain that is "dead" and the meaning-saturated body that persists, Scott projects an inverse scenario in which the living, thinking brain is trapped inside an insensate body, and thus "shut off from sensory contact with the world." The paradox is that his attribution to Alicia of a depth that subsists "shut off" from any kind of bodily expression is predicated on first reading her body in expressive terms—that is, as expressing the depth that he then identifies as "shut off" from expression. And where critics are caught up in the expressive mirage of the brain-dead body, viewers would be hard put not to duplicate their mistakes. As the camera gazes endlessly upon Alicia's face with a look that seems as intent as Benigno's on reading gleaning meaning from it, it is difficult if not impossible to avoid ascribing to her vacant features some kind of response to the gyrations of the men around her.

It is notable, then, that *Talk to Her*'s ultimate goal is to destabilize the criteria by which we might distinguish between the unsound Benigno and the upright Marco, between the sub- or nonhuman Alicia and the ideally human, emotionally "expressive" Lydia. When Marco and Lydia attend the wedding of his ex-lover, Angela (Elena Anaya), Marco notices that Lydia is sobbing. Fascinated and moved, he reaches somewhat forensically under her dark glasses (Figure 5.3). Finding them wet with tears, and reading those tears expressively, he pulls his hand away, satisfied in the conviction that he knows what the tears mean (he will later use her tears as proof of her jealousy of his ex-girlfriend, and his own lack of tears as proof of his indifference to the same). Yet the final labor of this scene is to undercut a reading that would pit the expressivity of Lydia's own tears against the artificiality of Alicia's, and deploy those tears as an expressive sign of some reified desire. For Lydia's tearful gaze is inscribed within a shot/reverse shot that has as its object, not Marco, but, in the bride and groom's matched profiles, the symmetrical scene of coupling itself. The mobile camera lingers on the beauty of the church, and finally weighs upon the heavily ritualized exchange of vows between the bride and groom, before cutting back to the image of Lydia (her eyes concealed behind dark glasses that practically denote, even as they pretend to conceal, her tears). While the narrative will later "reveal" these tears as expressive of Lydia's desire for el Niño, *Talk to Her*'s situation of these tears in the context of a wedding—a generic theater of heteronormative injunction—underscores their emergence in the context of what one of us has called, in

Figure 5.3 Marco reaches under Lydia's glasses to secure the "somatic testimony" of her tears.

another context, the "discipline of heterosensibility."[20] If what is at stake here is the presence of the mechanical at the very nucleus of the expressive, this interpenetration of two such apparently incompatible figures is best embodied in a gesture made by the director himself at the end of an interview on the subject of *Talk to Her*, when he handed the journalist a piece of folded paper that read: "cry."[21] Openly instructing us to "express," and thus normalizing and regulating the terms on which expression might occur, the note stages a performative tension between its expressive content and the imperative form in which it is framed. In the process, it flaunts the fact that emotion is indentured to a system of discipline and regulation that is antithetical to our normative understandings of emotion. Emotion, in this sense, is always already "brain-dead."

There is one thing, of course, that could be said to differentiate the teary Lydia from the equally, if less organically, liquid-eyed Alicia: consciousness. For Lydia's consciousness appears to invest her tears, blushes, and shudders with a presence of meaning that Alicia's lack. Yet the wedding scene suggests that, while Lydia is conscious, the expressive terms in which she is read not only fail to register the difference between the conscious and the unconscious, but must actively disregard her consciousness as a condition of their successful operation. When Marco's spectacularly mistaken reading of her tears becomes manifest to Lydia, she attempts to interject, protesting that he is not understanding. But Marco's reification of the authenticating truth of her tears over and above anything that she might say means that her verbal protestations have no currency. Paradoxically, then, what inhibits Marco's comprehension of Lydia is precisely the act of expressive reading by which he believes that he already has. "We need to talk," she tells him, but Marco, convinced that he knows exactly what she needs to talk about, descends into a declaration of love for her that silences her. Indeed, Marco's misrecognition of monologue as dialogue rivals Benigno's own: when Lydia suggests again, this time at the end of one of Marco's lengthy speeches, that "we need to talk," Marco's response is the surprised, "we've been talking for an hour." Lydia drives the point home: "*you. You*'ve been talking." If the brain-dead Alicia is nothing more than a body, Lydia, functionally conscious, is so circumscribed within the framework of Marco's expressive reading that she is little more than a body anyway. However effectively it might reify the natural somatic eloquence of its objects, expressive reading, it would seem, wants its objects comatose.

190   SCREENING THE POSTHUMAN

This suggestion is borne out by the fact that Marco's effective reduction of Lydia to a figurative insensibility is quickly followed by a fatal accident that leaves her quite literally brain-dead. This striking sequence of events implies a narrative logic in which her brain-death is in some sense consequent upon his deadening expressive reading of her—an absurdly literal narrative logic that serves to expose the flaws in expressive reading practice and in the expressive models of femininity it reifies. Indeed, the mystery that surrounds Lydia's goring in the ring—a practiced matador, her spectacular end can hardly have been purely accidental; was it, perhaps, as some critics have advanced, a suicidal gesture, a death-wish?—would tend to imply her complicity in this sequence of events. Expressive reading's implicit construction of its object as "brain-dead" is manifest more playfully elsewhere in the film too, perhaps most notably in its use of colloquial language. When Alicia's dance teacher calls her *batata* or sweet potato, for example, she acts out the overlaps between the vegetable as a lynchpin of a discourse of love and the vocabulary of the "persistent vegetative state." And, speculation about the cause of Lydia's accident aside, its effect is finally to bring about the complete collapse of the distinction between Lydia and Alicia, Benigno and Marco—and thus, more broadly, between emotionally normative forms of subjectivity and those conventionally deemed deviant.[22] Where Lydia had always been distinguished from the impassive Alicia, the film similarly has her fall comatose; and where Marco had always been contrasted with Benigno, the film instates Benigno as Marco's unlikely teacher in the mysteries of femininity.

If the expressive Lydia is first functionally, and then actually, braindead, the converse is also true in *Talk to Her*: brain-dead, Alicia is effectively expressive. Through a clever manipulation of the shot/reverse shot, one of the cornerstones of classical continuity editing, the film underscores the "disabled" subject's challenge to humanistic notions of subjectivity as well as these notions' implication in classical cinematic conventions that prioritize white, cis-man able-bodied subjectivity. One of the very first scenes in *Talk to Her* is illustrative here. The scene features Benigno, in nurses' scrubs, talking animatedly to someone just off-screen; from his lively expression as he describes in great detail the dance production that he—like us—has just witnessed, filmic convention prepares us for a reverse shot that will display the response of his interlocutor. But as the camera pans across to the right—from a limp hand, to an arm, to a torso, and finally a face—the face upon which it lights, that of a young woman, is motionless and unresponsive to Benigno's loving ministrations. Indeed, as Benigno's continued monologue receives no answer, we infer that she is comatose. Crucially, however, the film's deployment of the shot-reverse shot situates Alicia in the position of the interlocutor whether conscious or not. It is inevitable, then, that her face seems, both here, and, increasingly throughout the film, to register a kind of benign, Mona Lisa-like amusement, recalling a similar dynamic at play in 2007's *Lars and the Real Girl* (Craig Gillespie).[23] To the extent that, as numerous theorists of cinematic montage have shown, the emotional weight of a facial close-up depends less on the content of the shot itself than on its differential relation with those that precede and follow it, the image of Alicia's placid face, followed and preceded by images of an animated Benigno, can hardly *not* function expressively.[24] At stake here, *Talk to Her* implies, is a mechanical or artificial process: what grounds expressive reading is not the presence of a feeling subject behind the expressive sign, nor even the expressive sign itself, but the broader formal and linguistic structure within which bodies are enlisted *as* expressive. Without invalidating the subject/object divide entirely, then, the film's mobilization of the comatose woman speaks to disability's value as part of a posthumanist effort to rethink the norms by which we understand the human.

Yet the distinction between what Lauren Berlant calls "the subject of true feeling" and those "others" whose physical or cognitive disabilities preclude normative forms of emotional experience and emotional display, can be troubled still further.[25] For not only is the brain-dead Alicia entirely capable of serving as an expressive melodramatic heroine, but, as no *more* than the sum of her bodily signs, she seems at times expressivity's very embodiment. As Benigno puts it with reference to Alicia, "a woman's brain is always a mystery, and in this state even more so." Brain-death, it would seem, only amplifies the impression of mysterious depth that already surrounds melodramatic femininity. When film critic Philip French describes Alicia in terms of her "condition of silent, mysterious living," drawing on the same vocabulary of feminine mystery and depth that Benigno does, he seems to elevate Alicia to the status feminine exemplar.[26] It is no accident, then, that the fact that its two heroines are brain-dead in no way obstructs the film's melodramatic plot. When Marco returns to the hospital one day, he finds el Niño de Valencia holding the comatose, insensible Lydia's hand, and discovers that on the day of Lydia's fatal last fight she had called el Niño to tell him she still loved him. In centering the brain-dead heroine within this melodramatic

192   SCREENING THE POSTHUMAN

intrigue, the film performs an inversion of the conventional organic notion of narrative: rather than narrative being that which is "secreted" by the expressive agent, as Gilles Deleuze has it, narrative becomes that which, disposing itself around would-be expressive agent, retroactively constructs her as its animating figure.[27]

As this reading suggests, disability's challenge to affective humanism lies in its capacity to expose the contingency of its terms of reference. And in many respects, *Talk to Her* rises to this challenge, while at the same time pointing to new, posthumanist forms of subjectivity that destabilize humanist oppositions between valid and invalid emotional being. Yet *Talk to Her*'s affordances to the convergence of posthumanism and disability are not total. Not only does the film deploy able-bodied actors to portray the "brain-dead" women at its heart, but its happy ending also turns on Alicia's sudden restoration to able-bodied (and heteronormative) "normality," as she commences a rehabilitation program and embarks on a romance with Marco. In this respect, *Talk to Her* indexes the intransigence of able-bodied humanist narratives in even progressive examples of disability cinema—a theme that we will explore further in the next section of this chapter.

Deaf Perspective in *Sound of Metal*

Whereas *Talk to Her*'s Alicia is less the film's protagonist than its silent center, *Sound of Metal*'s Ruben (played by Riz Ahmed) has a far more active role in driving the film. While his hearing loss is the plot's inciting incident, the bulk of the film deals with the choices made by the heavy metal drummer and recovering addict as he acclimates to impending deafness. At the urging of his girlfriend and bandmate, Lou (played by Olivia Cooke), Ruben agrees to put the band's tour on hold so that he can move into a shelter for deaf recovering addicts—only to be expelled from the shelter when he finally raises the money to purchase cochlear implants, a neuroprosthesis that simulates sound via electric signals (without restoring "normal" hearing) and that many deaf people see as an affront to deaf culture, a fact we elaborate on below. Ruben then pursues Lou, who is with her father in France, only to discover that reuniting with her to continue on the same path is not possible. Yet he also comes to realize that the hearing afforded by the implants is at best imperfect (and at worst, obnoxious). At the end of the film, Ruben sits alone on a bench in Paris enjoying the respite of silence achieved by disabling his cochlear device.

As this chapter will show, if *Talk to Her* uses Alicia's disability as a tool to interrogate humanist norms of emotional expression and interpretation, *Sound of Metal* gains similar mileage from its exploration of Ruben's experiences with hearing loss. On a formal level, *Sound of Metal* ventures into the terrain of posthumanism by using cinematic technology to centralize disabled perspective and marginalize able-bodied experience in ways that are reminiscent, as we will show, of *The Diving Bell and the Butterfly*. Yet as we will also show, *Sound of Metal* reverts to humanist norms in its negative depiction of auditory technologies. The deaf community's reception of the film was mixed, and included criticism of its reductive portrait of the debate about cochlear implants ongoing in deaf communities. This section, then, will present *Sound of Metal* as an apt illustration of the current stage of narrative cinema's treatment of disability, which is marked both by successful usage of the medium to evoke crip points of view and by humanistic hangups that hinder the imagination of posthuman disability.

Sound of Metal's evocation of deaf perception is the feature most consistently celebrated in critical reviews of the film, which were unanimously positive, specifically in regard to sound design. "Simply put, you don't hear movies like this everyday" is film critic Charlotte O'Sullivan's pithy summation of the film's novelty.[28] In fact, the film's sound is key to its posthumanist gesture: orchestrating sound to decenter humanist, able-bodied norms (or the "normate" position, according to Rosemarie Garland-Thomson's terminology[29]). Thus, Ruben's first intimation that something is wrong with his hearing is communicated to viewers as an extremely muffled, near-lack of sound, which accompanies images of him trying to manually pop his ears by holding his nose and blowing (Figure 5.4). Soon after, an image of Ruben blending a smoothie for breakfast recalls an almost identical shot from earlier in the film, only this time, what had been a jarringly loud mechanical sound has become a very faint whir. This placement of viewers in Ruben's auditory point of view resonates with Elizabeth Ellcessor and Bill Kirkpatrick's clarification of "a disability perspective" as hinging not on whether a disabled person appears in a text, but on whether it "decenter[s] the physically and cognitively 'normal.'"[30] Many glowing reviews of *Sound of Metal* home in on its embrace of Ruben's sonic perspective. Ian Freer, for example, writes that the sound designer Nicolas Becker "subtly but effectively evokes the

Figure 5.4 In *Sound of Metal* (Darius Marder, 2019), when Ruben wakes up to a situation in which he can barely hear, he first attempts to manually correct his hearing by holding his nose while blowing.

changes in Ruben's hearing . . . to put us inside Ruben's head both literally and emotionally; from muffled, seemingly underwater sounds to high-pitched whines to a scratchy scraping quality, the sound-work backs up the film's ideology of guarding against deafness as a monolithic affliction."[31] Freer's connection of Ruben's sonic point of view to *Sound of Metal*'s refusal to frame deafness as disability is apt, yet to it I would add that the film evokes Ruben's subjectivity to contrast it with a third-person, hearing perspective, a fact to which mainstream film reviews draw scant attention.

Two scenes that directly follow Ruben's discovery of his hearing loss demonstrate a strategy that recurs throughout the film, in which the sound design juxtaposes full access to diegetic sound and deaf or limited hearing perspectives—the latter often supported by non-diegetic sonic components that blend subjective and objective elements of Ruben's (as well as other deaf characters') experiences. And while the film inspired much praise for its inclusivity, the subtleties of the non-diegetic score are not entirely accessible to deaf viewers despite the film's open captions (which are sometimes referred to as "hard" rather than "open" to mean that the captions cannot be removed). Thus, when Ruben visits a pharmacy in a desperate search for a remedy, his conversation with the pharmacist unfolds via two alternating soundtracks: one conveying Ruben's sonic perspective, in which the pharmacist's voice is unintelligibly faint; and the other clearly broadcasting the pharmacist's words as he books a medical appointment for Ruben by phone. In fact, viewers are able to imagine Ruben's experience in this moment—his anxiety and confusion—while also privy (via either hearing or captions) to information he cannot access: for example, the pharmacist's estimation of his hearing as a 2 on a 0–10 scale. Shortly after, the sound's oscillation between Ruben's deteriorating hearing and a third-person, clearer perspective is visually underscored when Ruben undergoes a hearing test in a sound booth. He and the audiologist wear headphones and are visible to one another through a window. In the first half of the scene, the view is of Ruben's profile in medium close-up from his side of the glass, and the hearing audience can perceive the doctor's voice as if at a distance, while Ruben's speech sounds muffled. Midway through the test, a cut transports spectators to the other side of the axis of action, to a view over the doctor's shoulder with Ruben in the background, as he responds "throat" to the doctor's prompt of "search" (Figure 5.5). This sonic cross-cutting draws attention to the differences between Ruben's sensory experience compared to the hearing characters'.

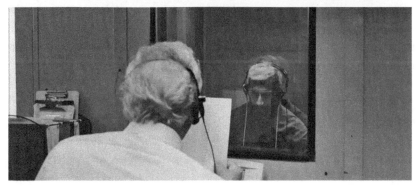

Figure 5.5 Midway through Ruben's hearing test, a cut shifts viewers from perceiving the test from Ruben's to his audiologist's perspective.

196 SCREENING THE POSTHUMAN

Here, it is important to note that while *Sound of Metal* has been frequently celebrated for its open (a.k.a. hard) captions, they fail to make the film's sound design fully accessible to deaf viewers. Mark Kermode's review of the film in *The Guardian* reads, "*Sound of Metal* is presented with open captions, meaning that in cinema screenings deaf and hearing audiences can experience the film together."[32] Yet this interpretation of the captions is naïve and misleading, and reviews more attentive to the practical, material implications of the dynamic between the film's sound design and captioning have pointed out the following: "*Sound of Metal* is at once accessible and inaccessible. It is open captioned, meaning subtitles are burned into the actual film, yet several scenes contain muffled voices or ASL [American Sign Language] without captions."[33] So while the captions read "[ringing intensified]," "[muffled sound]," "[sound distorted]," etc., the nuances of the non-diegetic score's rendition of Ruben's subjectivity only translate in flattened form. Indeed, Shanti Escalante-De Mattei's review of the film stresses that its "resoundin[g] success among critics and hearing audiences" overlooks "its impact on the deaf and hard of hearing," and, to back up this claim, cites this criticism from a hard-of-hearing viewer: "The captions consistently told me when the conversation was muffled or at 'normal' level but, because of my hearing loss, I was not able to fully experience the sound experimentation. That's when I realized that its production was most influential on hearing viewers."[34] Another review critiques the film's feature of ASL, specifically its cutting in the middle of signed conversations and/or failure to make the sign language visible enough on-screen for deaf viewers to read it (in lieu of the captions).[35] Therefore, *Sound of Metal* consistently contrasts hearing and deaf points of view, but this does not make the film equally accessible to deaf (or hard-of-hearing) and hearing viewers, and the innovative sound design is among the least accessible features for non-hearing viewers. These aspects of the film undercut its contributions to the overall project of cripping cinema and diminish its relevance to posthuman disability studies.

Sound of Metal's orchestration of sound to evoke a disabled perspective recalls *The Diving Bell and the Butterfly*'s approach to image in that both successfully utilize point-of-view editing to align viewers with their protagonists. Also like *Sound of Metal*, *The Diving Bell and the Butterfly* alternates between the protagonist's "disabled" point of view and a "privileged," "universal and unmarked type" to make disability more accessible to able-bodied viewers.[36] *The Diving Bell and the Butterfly* strongly emphasizes the image track to express the limited viewpoint of Bauby (played by Mathieu Amalric), whose stroke resulted in locked-in syndrome, leaving him paralyzed except for his left eye. The film demonstrates the utility of technology in animating Bauby's experience in two key ways; the first is formal, and involves the employment of cinematography and editing to convey an engagement with the world via only one functioning eye. For example, the beginning of the film fully confines viewers to Bauby's optical point of view. It opens with him waking from a three-week coma, caused by the stroke; the first shot is distorted, going in and out of focus and intermittently darkening to emulate a single eye closing. The soundtrack in coordination with voice-over from Bauby's first-person perspective make it clear that while his hearing is intact, he can only communicate by blinking. "Mr. Bauby, keep your eyes open," urge the medical personnel who greet him on awakening to a new reality and are only periodically in focus (Figure 5.6). Bauby's story is based on the memoir he wrote using the same single-eye blinking method demonstrated in the film; by starting at precisely this point and in this manner, *The Diving Bell and the Butterfly* asks viewers to imagine the sudden shift from an able-bodied to an extremely limited experiential capacity, which Bauby lived through and was able to communicate. Moreover, the film gradually begins to represent Bauby's internal, subjective perspective on his condition: for example, through grainy images (paired with the augmented sound of breathing) of

Figure 5.6 Upon awakening from a coma, the protagonist of *Le Scaphandre et le Papillon/ The Diving Bell and the Butterfly* (Julian Schnabel, 2007) hears "Mr. Bauby, keep your eyes open." Meanwhile, hazy, out of focus imagery conveys the attempts of medical personnel to communicate.

198 SCREENING THE POSTHUMAN

Bauby underwater, trapped inside old-fashioned diving gear, "the diving bell" referred to in both the title of Bauby's memoir and its cinematic adaptation. *The Diving Bell and the Butterfly*'s initial confinement of viewers to Bauby's optical point of view is analogous to the moments in *Sound of Metal* when the sound approximates Ruben's distorted hearing.

The second way *The Diving Bell and the Butterfly* emphasizes the impact of technology on Bauby's experience is through a narrative focus on the effective use of various technologies by medical staff and others, in collaboration with Bauby, to communicate despite the limitation of his nearly insensate body. According to Stuart Murray, "a constructive dialogue between critical disability and posthumanist approaches offer[s] real potential for better understanding the relations between emerging technologies and disability lives."[37] Working at the intersection of the two bodies of critical theory, Murray's goal is to "explore the possibility that the untangled uncertainties surrounding technologies of the body can yet produce tangible outcomes in the lives of those with disabilities."[38] The midsection of the film realizes this goal in its attention to Bauby's acclimation to available communication technologies so that his thoughts can escape the confines of his paralyzed body. Thus when Bauby begins to work closely with his speech therapist, Henriette Durand (played by Marie-Josée Croze), viewers experience the slow process of communication via a deceptively simple language technology in which Durand repeats the full alphabet so that Bauby's needs and thoughts can be painstakingly translated via his blinks. Because the film initially represents these "speech" therapy sessions at real speed and from Bauby's POV, the audience grasps the full significance of Durand's method of reciting the alphabet from most to least used letters in the language (Figure 5.7). In fact, the fast recitation of this alphabetical sequence by multiple characters functions as a semi-constant diegetic soundtrack that is frequently overlaid with Bauby's voice-over, which expresses the ideas and thoughts liberated through the singular translation method. *The Diving Bell and the Butterfly* quite successfully depicts his disabled communication as a posthuman assemblage of human mechanics (in this case, the functioning left eye paired with effective hearing), a swathe of communication, and medical technologies (from Durand's alphabet to the medical interventions that keep Bauby alive) and cinema itself (an advanced communication technology herein artfully manipulated to express Bauby's complex personal and philosophical reflections).

While *The Diving Bell and the Butterfly* leans heavily on image in its depiction of Bauby's posthuman disabled experience, *Sound of Metal*, on the other

POSTHUMAN AND CRIP PERSPECTIVES 199

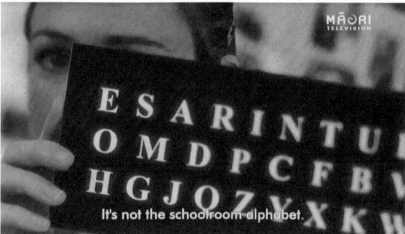

Figure 5.7 Experiencing the speech therapy sessions via Bauby's perspectives, viewers are able to grasp the full significance of Durand's innovative alphabet.

hand, prioritizes Ruben's auditory perspective, while also emphasizing that sight accumulates new meanings as Ruben learns to communicate without relying on his diminishing hearing. So in fact, while the film's plot is focused on hearing loss, it cinematically highlights the sharpening of other senses—in particular sight, but also touch. For instance, when Joe first takes Ruben to the classroom where he will serve as a teaching assistant, he uses clear hand signals to direct Ruben (e.g., his pointer finger to tell Ruben to wait) and reaches his hand inside the classroom to flicker the lights on and off to get the attention of the deaf students (Figure 5.8). In the film's midsection, a series of short scenes linked via rhythmic montage showcases Ruben's successful integration into the shelter's community and the class of young deaf students. These scenes include moments when the diegetic sound is audible (e.g., when a break dancer performs for the class, the music he dances to can be briefly heard), alongside moments when the subtle score masks the diegetic sound to remind viewers of the sensory environment of the characters. Meanwhile, when a pianist plays for the class, the music is clear to hearing viewers, but the image of Ruben, the teacher, and the students gathered around the piano with their hands carefully placed on it stresses that their main sensory engagement with the sound is through touch (Figure 5.9). And similarly, a compelling sequence (featured in the film's trailer) of Ruben on the playground with a young student artfully expresses an intensification of

Figure 5.8 To assist Ruben's acclimatization to deaf experience, Joe uses clear hand signals to direct him. Joe also turns the lights on and off to get the attention of a classroom of deaf children, an act that underscores the film's feature of alternative sensory experience.

Figure 5.9 *Sound of Metal* (Darius Marder, 2019) strongly emphasizes the intensification of tactility that distinguishes deaf experience in a montage sequence in which Ruben assists in a class of deaf children.

tactility connected to deaf experience. In it, Ruben taking a seat at the bottom of the playground slide is rendered in silence, when suddenly, a low-pitched pulse of sound compels Ruben to look up to where the student, at the top of the slide, is generating palpable vibrations by rhythmically tapping on the steel. Ruben suddenly begins pounding on the slide, the exchange evolving into a call-and-response game until eventually, Ruben fully unleashes his skill as a drummer—pounding on the metal—while the boy drapes himself over the slide to better feel the sound.

Both *The Diving Bell and the Butterfly* and *Sound of Metal* manipulate cinematic perspective to "powerfully decente[r] "normal" perception in ways that self-reflexively foreground cinematic spectatorship itself," as David Church puts it in his interpretation of *The Diving Bell and the Butterfly*.[39] To accomplish this, the films don't simply use image (in the case of *The Diving Bell and the Butterfly*) and sound (in the case of *Sound of Metal*), which are

202 SCREENING THE POSTHUMAN

the senses that these films' receptions zeroed in on. Instead, they evidence Anna Debinski's argument about recent documentaries that deal with disability, in that they "encourag[e] connection and intimacy alongside distance and alienation" to "denaturaliz[e] . . . disability's Otherness" and facilitate "a more substantial cinematic (and social) appreciation of disabled bodies as a reflection of human diversity—an experience of disability as a different way of being in the world."[40] In other words, they carefully orchestrate image and sound to stimulate complex sensory awareness so that their audiences can appreciate the expansion of sensory perception experienced by people who transition from able-bodied to disability perspectives, which includes every human who lives long enough, as argued by posthuman disability scholar Dan Goodley. The films thus depict disability not as impairment but as "a different way of being in the world." In the case of *Sound of Metal*, viewers gradually shift from a normate to crip point of view through their alignment with Ruben.

Sound of Metal's progressive deployment of sound to approximate deaf perspective is somewhat at odds with its rigid stance on cochlear implant technology, which misrepresents it in many respects, and of these, I highlight two as particularly significant to the film's hesitation to engage with aspects of Ruben's experience that are ripe with posthumanist potential. For one, the film exaggerates the appearance of Ruben's cochlear implants to make a spectacle of post-surgery Ruben. While in reality, the external component of the cochlear apparatus can be quite subtle, similar in appearance to a modern hearing aid that hooks around the ear,[41] in *Sound of Metal*, the visible component (the speech processor) is unusually large and is outlined by a jagged scar that draws further attention to it. When Lou first encounters this new iteration of Ruben, she closely scrutinizes the device, pawing around the affected area (Figure 5.10). Advocates of cochlear implants, including many who have them, have strongly criticized the film's misrepresentation of the technology. For example, Donna Sorkin (of American Cochlear Implant Alliance) bemoans the inaccuracy of the representation from both expert and personal standpoints: "Ruben's surgical scars were characterized by one surgeon as "comical." The J-shaped incisions on Ruben's head have not been used since the 1980s and were never that large. My CI surgery, completed in 1992, was a one-inch incision that was not visible—my hair covered it."[42] Thus, according to experts, this depiction is out of step with the technology, appearing decades behind. By embellishing the visual extremity of cochlear implant technology, the film alienates Ruben both from his deaf community

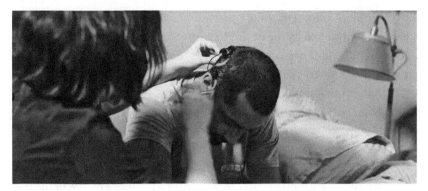

Figure 5.10 *Sound of Metal* (Darius Marder, 2019) exaggerates the visual impact of Ruben's cochlear implants in a surprising manner.

and from hearing others, for example, the people partying at the house of Lou's father (played by Mathieu Amalric, the lead actor in *The Diving Bell and the Butterfly*) when the two are reunited. Perhaps intended to enhance the aesthetic impact and the drama of the termination of Ruben's intimacy with Lou, the extreme and inaccurate depiction of cochlear implants suggests that techno-enhancement is out of the ordinary, when in fact it is quite common. In this sense, the exaggerated visibility of Ruben's mechanical parts performs a backhanded cyborg gesture akin to those of *Under the Skin* and *Air Doll*, as argued in Chapter 3. On the one hand, by representing Ruben's surgical enhancement as strange and semi-monstrous, *Sound of Metal* disables a transhumanistic reading of the technology as a miraculous disability corrective and implicitly positions Ruben in the realm of the posthuman. On the other, by alienating the "posthuman" Ruben from both hearing and deaf others in the film, it persists in othering him, marking him out as exceptional in an otherwise able-bodied, "normate" world.

In the scene in which his implant is activated for the first time, the audiologist makes minor adjustments to the device based on Ruben's dissatisfaction; the sound of the adjustments is reminiscent of changing between channels on a radio when none are broadcasting in range. The doctor reminds Ruben that the technology only tricks the brain into perceiving the transmissions as sound; restoring his hearing is outside its remit, in other words. Stakeholders in the deaf community have weighed in on the debate about the film's treatment of the hearing afforded by cochlear implants, and the results are decidedly mixed. Reviews of the film by people with cochlear implants demonstrate that some experienced the early stage of adjusting to the device in

204 SCREENING THE POSTHUMAN

a manner akin to Ruben, while others did not, yet all agree that the simulated sound proffered by the device requires both time and professional support, which the film neglected to portray.[43] *Sound of Metal* shies away from representing Ruben's post-surgical subjectivity as a productive amalgamation of human and nonhuman elements.

The film's overwhelmingly negative stance on cochlear implants also registers in its reductive portrait of the cochlear debate in deaf communities, and its erroneous claim that cochlear implants are not covered by insurance, when in fact public and private insurance policies in both the United States and elsewhere tend to cover them.[44] An audiologist's review of the film reads, "While there are some Deaf communities that are completely against cochlear implants, there are also many communities with individuals who identify as Deaf that also utilize cochlear implants or hearing aids for safety reasons. In total, I think that in many cases there is an acceptance for both, which was not depicted in this film."[45] In this regard, among others, the film goes against the recommendations of the [US] National Association of the Deaf outlined in its "Position Statement on Portrayal of Deaf and Hard Of Hearing People in Television, Film, and Theater":

> We advocate that all portrayals of deaf and hard of hearing people depict us as we really are: members of a vibrant community with the same diversity that exists throughout the world. We call upon networks, studios, companies, producers, writers, directors, casting directors, and all decision makers to take upon the artistic responsibility of actively portraying the rich tapestry of deaf and hard of hearing individuals in an accurate and authentic manner.

On every level of its treatment of cochlear implants, *Sound of Metal* promotes humanistic skepticism regarding the capacity of technology to alter disabled experience for the better, thereby limiting the diversity of its depiction of deaf experience and community.

In sum, the analysis above demonstrates *Sound of Metal*'s success in designing its sound to simulate its protagonist's sudden loss of hearing and, later, his acclimation to (and eventual rejection of) cochlear implants. This success, alongside that of *The Diving Bell and the Butterfly*, establishes the formal techniques that marshal cinematic perspective to center crip and marginalize able-bodied spectatorship. And yet, *Sound of Metal*'s ultimately negative depiction of cochlear implants diminishes its engagement with posthuman phenomena as well as deaf and hard-of-hearing communities. In contrast to what the film suggests, the latter hold a range of views on auditory technologies, and their debates about them are far more nuanced than the film implies in its limited depiction of that debate. Therefore, while the film's innovative sound design and captioning is promising, suggesting, as it does, that cinema can aspire to crip perspective at least on a formal level, its reductive narrative approach demonstrates a willingness to sacrifice accuracy to enhance its accessibility for able-bodied viewers. Had the film, instead, dealt head-on with the complexity of auditory technology, it would have ventured further into the theoretical terrain wherein critical disability studies and posthumanism intersect, and its reception by the deaf community would likely have been more enthusiastic. Unfortunately, *Sound of Metal* falls back on humanistic conventions to make Ruben's experience more palatable to a cinema-going public well-schooled in "the cinema of ableism."[46]

Conclusion

According to Goodley, Lawthom, and Runswick-Cole, "disability crips what it means to be a human being."[47] But until relatively recently, narrative cinema has maintained the default ableism associated with humanism—even when heavily featuring disabled characters. As Lennard J. Davis has noted, while "media loves disability," disability narratives in film and television, from *A Beautiful Mind* (Ron Howard, 2001) to *The Soloist* (Joe Wright, 2009), ultimately serve to make "the [implicitly able-bodied] audience feel good about itself and its own *normality*."[48] This chapter has demonstrated the emergence of an alternative pathway in twenty-first-century narrative cinema, one that decenters ableism by spotlighting crip points of view to "complicat[e] the myopic perspective . . . [of] humanism."[49] These films mark crucial points of overlap in the Venn diagram between posthumanism and critical disability studies, reflecting Goodley, Lawthom, and Runswick-Cole's contention that "Posthuman and critical disability studies share an antithetical attitude towards the taken-for-granted, ideological and normative under-girdings of what it means to be a valued citizen of society."[50] Thus, we presented *Talk to Her*'s attention to comatose women as a challenge to humanistic norms of expression, emotion, and signification. Similarly, we analyzed *Sound of Metal* as an example of the canny use of sound and image to reorient the audience away from humanistic and able-bodied norms and toward the crip perspective of its protagonist. Yet, despite these films' embrace of particular aspects of disabled and posthuman experience, neither film goes far enough in imagining disabled *or* posthuman perspectives. Instead, they reflect a contradictory tendency we have highlighted throughout this book, in which filmmakers appear to be drawn to cinematic characterizations of posthuman phenomena without fully committing to using the medium to unpack their complexities. Nonetheless, our case studies are promising in their legitimate investment in moving beyond the tokenistic representation of individual disabled characters to grapple with the broader posthumanist implications of crip points of view. In fact, the film *CODA* (Sian Heder, 2021) indicates further developments in the alternative pathway sketched above, both in its casting, which exclusively featured deaf actors in deaf roles, and in its narrative, which focuses on a hearing person as the exception in an otherwise deaf community. This, alongside the recent documentary hit *Crip Camp* (2020), indicates an exciting new interest in centering the voices and experiences of disabled people. Goodley, Lawthom, and Runswick-Cole's claim is that "disability is the quintessential posthuman condition: because it calls for new ontologies, ways of relating, living and dying."[51] Our presumption is that their claim will be borne out by cinema willing to fully relinquish the conventions of "the cinema of ableism."

Notes

1. Robert McRuer, "In Focus: Cripping Cinema and Media Studies: Introduction," *JCMS: Journal of Cinema and Media Studies* 58, no. 4 (2019): 134, https://doi.10.1353/cj.2019.0042.
2. Stuart Murray, *Disability and the Posthuman: Bodies, Technology, and Cultural Futures* (Liverpool: Liverpool University Press, 2020), 20.
3. Dan Goodley, Rebecca Lawthom, and Katherine Runswick-Cole, "Posthuman Disability Studies," *Subjectivity* 7, no. 4 (2014): 342.
4. Goodley, Lawthom, and Runswick-Cole, "Posthuman Disability Studies," 342.
5. Goodley, Lawthom, and Runswick-Cole, "Posthuman Disability Studies," 348.
6. Eugenie Brinkema, *The Forms of the Affects* (Durham, NC: Duke University Press, 2014), 50.
7. Richard Burdon Haldane, *The Philosophy of Humanism: and of Other Subjects* (London: John Murray, 1922), 257.
8. Ann Jessie van Sant, *Eighteenth-Century Sensibility and the Novel: The Senses in Social Context* (Cambridge: Cambridge University Press, 2004), 58.

POSTHUMAN AND CRIP PERSPECTIVES   207

9. Van Sant, *Eighteenth-Century Sensibility and the Novel*, 58; Rei Terada, *Feeling in Theory: Emotion after the Death of the Subject* (Cambridge, MA: Harvard University Press, 2002), 11.

10. Erving Goffman, *Stigma: Notes on the Management of Spoiled Identity* (New York: Knopf Doubleday, 2009).

11. Dan Goodley, "Autism and the Human," in *Re-Thinking Autism: Diagnosis, Identity and Equality*, ed. Sami Timimi, Rebecca Mallett, and Katherine Runswick-Cole (London: Jessica Kingsley Publishers, 2016), 148. For the term "spoiled identity," see Erving Goffman, *Stigma: Notes on the Management of Spoiled Identity* (New York: Simon and Schuster, 1963).

12. Donna Reeve, "Cyborgs, Cripples and iCrip: Reflections on the Contribution of Haraway to Disability Studies," in *Disability and Social Theory*, ed. Dan Goodley, Bill Hughes, and Lennard Davis (London: Palgrave MacMillan, 2012), 91.

13. Brinkema, *The Forms of the Affects*, 50.

14. Mary Ann O'Farrell, *Telling Complexions: The Nineteenth Century Novel and the Blush* (Durham, NC: Duke University Press, 1999), 2; Haraway, "A Manifesto for Cyborgs," 120.

15. Matthew J. Marr, "'May You Overcome Your Obstacles': Reconsidering Pedro Almodóvar's Hable Con Ella/Talk to Her (2002) through the Disability Studies Lens," *Journal of Spanish Cultural Studies* 17, no. 1 (2016): 49.

16. Marr, "May you Overcome your Obstacles," 48.

17. Haraway, "A Manifesto for Cyborgs."

18. Marr, "May you Overcome your Obstacles," 45.

19. A. O. Scott, "The Track of a Teardrop, a Filmmaker's Path," *New York Times*, November 17, 2002, https://www.nytimes.com/2002/11/17/movies/film-the-track-of-a-teard rop-a-filmmaker-s-path.html.

20. Pansy Duncan, "Tears, Melodrama and "Heterosensibility" in *Letter from an Unknown Woman*," *Screen* 52, no. 2 (2011): 173–192.

21. Duncan, "Tears, Melodrama and 'Heterosensibility,'" 167.

22. There are still further resonances between the position of Alicia and that of Lydia. The scene in which Alicia has her bed-gown ritually changed and adjusted by her two attendant medics—a scene that might seem to emphasize her lifelessness—uses the same ceremonious and fetishistic cinematic vocabulary as the scene in which Lydia passively submits her body to an assistant to kit her out in her toreador's costume. In both cases, the camera fetishizes the items of clothing themselves, reducing their wearers to mere appurtenances. In order to perform her highly athletic function in the arena, Lydia must submit herself to a passivity indistinguishable from Alicia's.

23. Benigno's exclamation at this point—"you have no idea how moving it was!"—is one of the first of the film's many laconic plays on language's capacity to evoke and maintain a place for a subject irrespective of whether there is someone there to actually occupy it.

24. Silvestra Mariniello, *Film and Modernity: The Kuleshov Case* (Minneapolis: University of Minnesota, 1990), 47.

25. Lauren Berlant, "The Subject of True Feeling: Pain, Privacy and Politics," in *Cultural Pluralism, Identity Politics, and the Law*, ed. Austin Sarat and Thomas R. Kearns (Ann Arbor: University of Michigan Press, 1999), 53.

26. Philip French, "Coma vs. Coma," *The Guardian*, August 25, 2002, https://www.theguardian.com/film/2002/aug/25/philipfrench.

27. "When Cassavetes says that characters must not come from a story or plot, but should be secreted by the characters, he sums up the requirement of the cinema of bodies." Gilles Deleuze, *Cinema 2: The Time Image*, trans. Hugh Tomlinson and Robert Galatea, *Athlone Contemporary European Thinkers* (London: The Athlone Press, 1989), 192.

28. Charlotte O'Sullivan, "*Sound of Metal* Review: You Don't Hear a Film Like This Every day," *Evening Standard*, April 8, 2021, https://www.standard.co.uk/culture/film/sound-of-metal-review-riz-ahmed-b928430.html.

29. Thomson, Rosemarie Garland. *Extraordinary Bodies: Figuring Physical Disability in American Culture and Literature* (New York: Columbia University Press, 2017).

30. Elizabeth Ellćessor and Bill Kirkpatrick, "Studying Disability," *JCMS: Journal of Cinema and Media Studies* 58, no. 4 (2019): 140, https://doi.10.1353/cj.2019.0042.

31. Ian Freer, "*Sound of Metal* Review," *Empire*, April 12, 2021, https://www.empireonline.com/movies/reviews/sound-of-metal/

32. Mark Kermode, "*Sound of Metal* Review—Riz Ahmed Excels as a Drummer Facing Deafness," *The Guardian*, April 11, 2021, https://www.theguardian.com/film/2021/apr/11/sound-of-metal-review-riz-ahmed-olivia-cooke-darius-marder.

33. Abby Webster, "Darius Marder Makes Hearing Audiences the Minority with *Sound of Metal*," *The Georgetown Voice*, January 8, 2021, https://georgetownvoice.com/2021/01/08/darius-marder-makes-hearing-audiences-the-minority-with-sound-of-metal/.

34. Shanti Escalante-De Mattei, "What Does Sound of Metal Mean to Deaf and Hard of Hearing Audiences?" *i-D*, January 14, 2021, https://i-d.vice.com/en_uk/article/epdmba/what-does-riz-ahmeds-movie-sound-of-metal-mean-to-deaf-audiences-darius-marder.

35. Anita Rao, Destiny Lopez, and Yat Li, "What "Sound of Metal" Got Right And Wrong about Hearing Loss and Deafness," *North Carolina Public Radio*, April 9, 2021, https://www.wunc.org/2021-04-09/transcript-what-sound-of-metal-got-right-and-wrong-about-hearing-loss-and-deafness.

36. Ellćessor and Kirkpatrick, "Studying Disability," 140.

37. Murray, *Disability and the Posthuman*, 10.

38. Murray, *Disability and the Posthuman*, 10.

39. David Church, "Review of The Diving Bell and the Butterfly," *Disability Studies Quarterly* 28, no. 2 (2008), https://dsq-sds.org/article/view/101/101.

40. Brian Bergen-Aurand, "Screening Disability," *Screen Bodies* 3, no. 1 (2018): v.

41. For example, see "Cochlear Implants," *New Zealand Audiological Society*, https://www.audiology.org.nz/for-the-public/about-hearing-loss/cochlear-implants/.

POSTHUMAN AND CRIP PERSPECTIVES   209

42. Donna L. Sorkin, "*Sound of Metal*: New Feature Length Film on Deafness," *American Cochlear Implant Alliance*, December 9, 2020, https://www.acialliance.org/page/SoundofMetal.

43. For example, see Jon San, "Why 'Sound of Metal' Makes This Hard-of-Hearing Audiologist 'Uncomfortable,'" *Yahoo! Life*, January 28, 2021, https://www.yahoo.com/lifestyle/why-sound-of-metal-makes-this-hardofhearing-audiologist-uncomfortable-150058033.html; and David Oliver, "*Sound of Metal* Is Getting Awards Season Buzz: Did It Do Things Right by the Deaf Community?," *USA Today*, February 2, 2021, https://www.usatoday.com/story/entertainment/movies/2021/02/02/sound-metal-awards-season-contender-mixed-deaf-community/4248898001/.

44. See Sorkin, "Sound of Metal: New Feature Length Film on Deafness," and "Sound Of Metal: An Audiologist's Perspective," *Keystone Audiology*, https://keystoneaudiology.com/blog/sound-of-metal-an-audiologists-perspective.

45. "Sound of Metal: An Audiologist's Perspective," *Keystone Audiology*.

46. Tony Kashani and Anthony J. Nocella, "Hollywood's Cinema of Ableism: A Disability Studies Perspective on the Hollywood Industrial Complex," in *Hollywood's Exploited*, ed. Benjamin Frymer et al. (New York: Palgrave Macmillan, 2010), 105–114.

47. Goodley, Lawthom, and Runswick-Cole, "Posthuman Disability Studies," 348.

48. Lennard J. Davis, "The Ghettoization of Disability: Paradoxes of Visibility and Invisibility in Cinema," in *Culture—Theory—Disability*, ed. Anne Waldschmidt, Janho Berressem, and Moritz Ingwersen (Bielefeld: transcript Verlag, 2017), 39–50, https://www.degruyter.com/document/doi/10.14361/9783839425336-005/html.

49. Goodley, Lawthom, and Runswick-Cole, "Posthuman Disability Studies," 348.

50. Goodley, Lawthom, and Runswick-Cole, "Posthuman Disability Studies," 348.

51. Goodley, Lawthom, and Runswick-Cole, "Posthuman Disability Studies," 348.

6
Post-anthropocentrism
Rejecting Human Exceptionalism

Claire Henry

Francesca Ferrando notes that the critique of speciesism has become "an integral aspect of the posthuman critical approach";[1] it has likewise become an integral aspect of posthuman cinema, which is committed to challenging a Western philosophical tradition that has defined the human in contrast to—rather than through connection with—other species. Just as Cary Wolfe centers nonhuman animals within posthuman theory, posthuman cinema similarly regards "the animal" as a key terrain for questions of posthumanism to play out.[2] Working at the intersection of critical posthumanism and animal studies, this chapter considers how animals, animality, and human/nonhuman relationality function in posthuman cinema. The impact of animal studies on cinema studies has encouraged critical examination of nonhuman animals' allegorical role in this human cultural form, their exploitation both in film production and on-screen, and the possibilities of conveying animal perspectives or perceptual worlds in both documentary and narrative cinema. In recent years, this expanding scholarship has worked to decenter the anthropocentrism of cinema studies and draw attention to how cinema—and our critique of it—can challenge human exceptionalism. Traditionally, cinema has kept the "anthropological machine" well oiled, strengthening this apparatus that provides lenses and mirrors for the human's self-recognition, "optics [that] have been rigged (in both senses) to encourage self-reflection and nurture a sense of exceptionalism and superiority by virtue of one's proper humanness."[3] In order to refocus these optics and refract ideas about the "human" in a posthuman direction, posthuman films reimagine the way cinema visually and haptically represents nonhuman animals, and explore other species' complex symbolic, spiritual, and relational links to the human.

This chapter identifies and analyzes a specific new strand of posthuman cinema that uses surrealist and post-surrealist motifs and strategies to

Claire Henry, *Post-anthropocentrism*. In: *Screening the Posthuman*. Edited by: Missy Molloy, Pansy Duncan, and Claire Henry, Oxford University Press. © Oxford University Press 2023. DOI: 10.1093/oso/9780197538562.003.0007

POST-ANTHROPOCENTRISM   211

playfully undermine human exceptionalism. I argue that these films display an "affinity of intention" with surrealism, including following surrealism's prime interest in "exploring the conjunctions, the points of contact, between different realms of existence"—in this instance, between human and nonhuman animals.[4] By applying strategies associated with the surrealist tradition to the human/nonhuman animal relationship, the films under discussion accomplish a number of aims consistent with a posthuman critique of the human as a distinct and elevated species. Through devices like black humor, a canny mobilization of animal motifs, shocking imagery and juxtaposition, and the foregrounding of ritual, these case studies undertake a uniquely surrealist exploration of the blurred borders between humans and other species. Post-anthropocentric films within recent posthuman cinema mirror back to humanity not its uniqueness or distinction from other animals, but a recognition of shared animality, kinship, spiritual coexistence, and interdependence.

The analysis below reads *The Lobster* (Yorgos Lanthimos, 2015), *Gräns/Border* (Ali Abbasi, 2018), and *Teströl és lélekröl/On Body and Soul* (Ildikó Enyedi, 2017) as subversive cogs in the "anthropological machine" that present distortions in its mirror to disallow the human to construct a stable sense of species identity in opposition to nonhuman animals. To reject human exceptionalism and envisage different models of human-nonhuman relationality, these films draw on surrealism's interest in rituals and dreams and adopt various surrealist techniques such as shocking imagery and juxtaposition. These films are set in liminal spaces (The Hotel in *The Lobster*, customs control in *Border*, and shared dreamscapes in *On Body and Soul*), and often feature outsider humans who engage in extremes of affinity and/or brutality toward animals. From the absurd dark humor and foregrounding of ritual in *The Lobster* and *On Body and Soul*, to the disturbing eroticism of *Border*, these films employ surrealism as a lens to experience otherness, to encounter the marvelous, and to decategorize *Homo sapiens*.

From these European case studies, the chapter then turns to examine two Thai films—*Satpralat/Tropical Malady* (Apichatpong Weerasethakul, 2004) and *Kraben Rahu/Manta Ray* (Phuttiphong Aroonpheng, 2019)—in the context of this strand of posthuman cinema operating in a surrealist mode. While broadly considering these films as part of a surrealist post-anthropocentric project in global posthuman cinema, and drawing parallels with European counterparts from the first section, the second section introduces "new animism" as a framework to further understand how

212 SCREENING THE POSTHUMAN

these films dismantle anthropocentric understanding of human-animal relationality. The diverse case studies of fantastical and often humorous films in this chapter demonstrate the post-anthropocentric possibilities of cinematic surrealism as they rework "the animal," animality, and new animism on-screen to effect a posthuman critique.

Dark Humor and Animal Relations in *The Lobster*

With its homage to surrealism and use of dark humor in interrogating humanism, *The Lobster* serves as an initiatory example of how operating in a surrealist mode facilitates the post-anthropocentric ends of contemporary posthuman cinema. Following separation from his wife, David (played by Colin Farrell) must enter the absurd world of The Hotel, in which single people are required to fall in love with a fellow guest during their forty-five-day stay or be turned into an animal of their choice. As the Hotel Manager (played by Olivia Colman) tells him, if he fails to find love and becomes an animal, "you'll have a second chance to find a companion, but even then you must be careful—you need to choose a companion that is a similar type of animal to you. A wolf and a penguin could never live together, nor could a camel and a hippopotamus. That would be absurd." Of course the absurdity pointed to here is the way that, as Anat Pick puts it, "The anthropological machine toils incessantly to enforce and regulate a strict cartography of species on which rests, entirely precariously, the identity of the human."[5] Just such a "strict cartography" is enforced in The Hotel, as established in the intake process when David is told that he must nominate whether he is heterosexual or homosexual (as there is no longer a bisexual option) and must decide between shoe sizes for his hotel-issued uniform (as there are no half sizes). To create an acceptable pairing, two guests must share a defining characteristic, hence Limping Man (played by Ben Whishaw) secretly gives himself nosebleeds in order to pair up with Nosebleed Woman (played by Jessica Barden). With this premise, the failure to conform to rigid social rules is a failure to be—or remain—human. Ironically, this results in a scenario in which David, whose time is running out, pretends to be heartless in order to match up with Heartless Woman (played by Angeliki Papoulia) and thereby retain his "humanity." His failed effort to match the Heartless Woman's heartlessness fails—she catches him starting to cry after seeing his dog-incarnated brother dead in a pool of blood on the bathroom floor—so his continued embodiment as a human is jeopardized. Evading cruel punishment at The Hotel, David runs away to join the escapee community of Loners in the forest, but conformity and sameness are prized here too.

There are clear references to the surrealist movement in *The Lobster*, from its title, which recalls Salvador Dalí's famous 1936 sculpture, "Lobster Telephone", to the image of a knife poised at an eyeball in the final scene (Figure 6.1), which evokes the notorious 1929 surrealist short by Luis Buñuel and Dalí, *Un Chien Andalou*. The film imports not only this iconography of surrealism, but its spirit of challenging societal norms by highlighting the surrealist view of human existence as "inharmonious" (humans having "created a social reality out of kilter with our own aspirations and with the natural flow of the universe"[6]) and tapping into the unbridled workings of the unconscious. Two diegetic songs in the film—the first performed onstage by the Hotel Manager and her partner ("Something's Gotten Hold of My Heart"), the second a Nick Cave rendition ("Where The Wild Roses Grow") by David in the forest—feature the word scarlet, which evokes the color of lobster after it is transformed by human carnivorous violence (as David's friend in The Hotel points out about his foolish choice of animal: "they'll catch you and put you in a pot of boiling water until you die, and then they'll crack open your claws with a tool, like pliers, and they'll suck out what little flesh you have with their mouths"). The lyrics of the first song posit finding a romantic partner in violent terms, cutting through dreams like a knife to

Figure 6.1 In a surrealist homage, David holds a knife to his eyeball in the closing scene.

214 SCREENING THE POSTHUMAN

transform gray and blue into a bright scarlet. A lobster is both a hunter and a scavenger, and David switches between the two roles from the film's first to second half. In the first, he is required to take part in the nightly "hunt," where hotel guests tranquilize as many rogue Loners in the forest as they can, in order to earn themselves an extra night at The Hotel for each captive. In the second, he joins these Loners' alternative society and catches rabbits for his new love interest and visits the city with several other Loners to collect supplies. On the one hand, the lobster is a sexual, phallic symbol (as it has been used in surrealist art) that David associates with lifelong fertility (in his rationale for his choice to the Hotel Manager). Yet on the other, it is associated with castration, particularly when The Hotel's management punishes Lisping Man (played by John C. Reilly) for illicit masturbation by burning his hand in a toaster (resulting in a bandaged hand like a lobster claw). At a surface level, deployment of surrealism then has a playful intertextual role, building the memorably absurd world of film, and making symbolic use of animals to comment on human societal norms. Yet as I explore below, surrealism also works at a deeper level to challenge human exceptionalism and the role of nonhuman animals in the cinema.

Readings of *The Lobster* by Jennifer M. Barker and Rosalind Galt explore the degree to which the film is successful in challenging cinema's tendency to reduce the nonhuman animal to a metaphor for the human. For Barker, this is accomplished at a formal level. While at a narrative level, according to Barker, the human/nonhuman animal relationship is one of "straightforward metaphor," the film displays a more "radical relationality" at the aesthetic and temporal levels, and it is on this level that the post-anthropocentric achievements of the film lie.[7] In Galt's reading, by contrast, the nonhuman animals themselves are disruptors, serving to reconfigure a traditional hierarchy of looking relations.[8] In keeping with Barker's account of the metaphorical relationship outlined above, Galt notes that at one level the nonhuman animals are employed as allegorical figures for human concerns; the film is not interested in the animals *as* animals, nor resists the objectification or anthropomorphizing of animals.[9] Yet, for Galt, nonhuman animals also play a key role in foregrounding cinematic spectatorship and the status of animals in cinema. For example, they often appear as a striking out-of-place presence on-screen (such as the pink flamingo in the background of a scene in the forest), and disrupt the hierarchy of looking relations, "breaking our focus on the human actors and insisting we see the animals simultaneously as narratively significant and as real creatures."[10] While on a narrative level, the nonhuman animals serve as a marker of the one-to-one transformation of humans (and their species offers a comment on characteristics of the person from which they originate), they exceed this role as a fictional signifier, disrupting the hierarchy of looking relations and drawing attention to themselves as pro-filmic creatures.

Yet while the film's formal elements and its looking relations undoubtedly serve to disrupt the metaphorical or allegorical treatment of the relationship between human and nonhuman animals, the film's surrealist elements—specifically its dark humor and the foregrounding of ritual—are also central to the film's challenge to anthropocentric thought. As Michael Richardson has shown, surrealist humor is rarely comforting and does not serve as "a counterweight to the human condition, allowing us momentarily to put aside our worries, or . . . [provide] a sense of superiority over the misfortunes or inadequacies of others."[11] In keeping with this account, the quasi-surrealist humor of *The Lobster* is not just a series of playful intertextual capers; rather, it confronts us with the brutality of human conformity and custom, serving not as a comforting "counterweight to the human condition" but rather destabilizing it further and questioning the purported superiority of human over nonhuman animals. Exemplary here is the opening scene in which a woman drives up to a paddock and then walks over to a horse and shoots it—a surprising and funny scene that creates "a doubled and uncertain affect of black humor and apparently unmotivated violence."[12] In another context, this shooting might be just another workaday act of human violence against a nonhuman animal, but here the woman's vengeful resolve targeting a specific horse adds a dark comic edge that signals the film's surreal refashioning of anthropocentric relations.

The Lobster further draws on a surrealist interest in ritual to foreground the "strange and alien"[13] position of the human in the world, defamiliarizing humans' courting rituals and drive toward conformity. For example, in performances for the guests, hotel staff role-play "man eats alone" (and chokes) (Figure 6.2) and "woman walks alone" (and is raped). Ritual also features in the forest, where the lovers devise a shared secret gestural language that becomes increasingly elaborate and unsubtle. Denaturalizing human behavior by taking it to absurd extremes, these performances of ritual become risible and highlight the performativity underpinning human exceptionalism. As the Loners in the forest conform to equally strict rules to The Hotel's rules (here designed to enforce singledom, as opposed to the compulsory pairing maintained in The Hotel and the city), David again struggles

Figure 6.2 Social rituals and rules are taught to hotel guests through skits such as "man eats alone."

to fit in as a posthuman *animalous*[14] figure. As this suggests, *The Lobster* points to multiple ways of conceptualizing human-animal relationships through screen media, demonstrating that while nonhuman animals may play an instrumental narrative or metaphorical role at one level, they can equally challenge this status at the level of performance, aesthetics, or form.

Border(ing) on "The Open"

As with *The Lobster*, *Border* uses surrealist strategies to expose the workings of the anthropological machine. Both films draw on a rich history of surrealism in cinema, with *Border*'s surrealist aesthetics featuring Lynchian nods such as the uncanny appearance of the strange babies being evocative of *Eraserhead* (1977)[15] and a level of facial prosthetics rivaling *The Elephant Man* (1980). Howard Fishman's descriptions of *Border* in *The New Yorker* are evocative of surrealist cinema, calling it "a fever dream of madness" and "a furnace of unfiltered, wild expression, an attack on normalcy and complacency, a jubilee of mystery and weirdness" filled with moments of "extreme tension and visionary strangeness" and "at times, wincingly disgusting, and transgressive, and gross."[16] A unique fantasy-romance, the film tells the story of Tina (played by Eva Melander), a woman with distinctive, troll-like facial

POST-ANTHROPOCENTRISM   217

features who works as a border control worker at a Swedish port and uses her heightened sense of smell to detect contraband items by "sniffing out" human emotions such as shame, guilt, and rage.

One day, Tina encounters a strange man named Vore (played by Eero Milonoff) who shares many of her facial traits. She quickly discovers that he shares the same rare chromosome that she possesses—a chromosome that places them both in the "monstrous" category of Linnaeus's human taxonomy.[17] Galvanized by this encounter, Tina explores her troll characteristics and how they interface with her human upbringing, thereby entering into "the open"—"that figure of emptiness, an ontological vacuum, or, to borrow Bataille's description of his own life, an 'open wound' (qtd. in *The Open* 7), neither human nor animal."[18] The tension for Tina between her human identity and her newfound troll identity reflects Giorgio Agamben's response, in his influential *The Open: Man and Animal*, to Linnaeus's description of *Homo sapiens* as a "taxonomic anomaly." As Agamben put it, "man [*sic*] has no specific identity other than the *ability* to recognise himself . . . *man is the animal that must recognize itself as human to be human*."[19] Tina's relationship with Vore holds up a mirror to see herself as a troll, which helps her make sense of her outsider status in human society, but through the moral challenge that Vore's crimes present, she chooses to recognize herself as human and stay loyal to human society (betraying Vore to the police rather than running away with him to join the troll community). Regardless of her origins or physical traits, Tina's categorization as either troll or human is determined in the end through her self-recognition.

As its title suggests, *Border* explores how the human is defined through exceptions and exclusions, at the levels of species and morality. The film's post-anthropocentric transgression of this border uses techniques akin to those employed by the surrealists in challenging the status quo: confronting taboos and depicting uninhibited sexuality. At a surface level, the title refers to Tina's work as a border control officer, enforcing the rules of entry into Sweden, and film critics have often been drawn to a reading about European politics on immigration. For instance, in his review in *Sight & Sound*, Ben Nicholson argues that "In the current climate, the most readily apparent reading of Tina is as an immigrant, an interloper who does not belong— a theme Abbasi tackled in his first feature, *Shelley*, in 2016."[20] With Vore's claiming of her as part of a community of nomadic Finnish trolls, Tina is positioned as a non-Swedish "other" (reinforced by the stares and verbal abuse she receives from strangers) and the border setting is a liminal zone for immigrants. However, it is the border between the human and nonhuman upon which the film fundamentally operates, and which is of key interest in this chapter. The two are intertwined, as Agamben understands the violent history of Europe to be "the sum of powerful attempts at border control by which the imaginary confines of human life are imposed through acts of serial expulsion, exception, and exclusion, and by which 'nonhuman life' is violently eliminated."[21]

Tina's interaction with insects and other nonhuman animals foregrounds typological borders and her affinity with the nonhuman. Her journey in the film is traced through her changing relationship to insects. In the opening scene, by the water at the port where she works, she picks up an insect from the grass and gently places it on a twig, suggesting a compassionate relationship to these "lower" species. When Tina first stops Vore at the border and checks his bag, she finds a jar of insects and a contraption that he describes as a larvae hatcher (Figure 6.3). In their first encounters, he is flirtatious and challenging, and in telling her it is a larvae hatcher, he is perhaps being suggestive about her own metamorphosis from "immature" human to "mature" troll through getting to know him. When she drops by the hostel to see Vore, he is collecting maggots and offers her one. She describes the idea of eating them to be "gross" but he holds one out to her and says, "you know you want to," and she takes it. These story beats mark her giving in to the temptation of becoming-troll as she gets to know Vore, a process that requires overcoming cultural taboos she has learned in Swedish human society (such as not eating maggots). Through the surrealist strategy of transgressing taboos, Tina is reorientated from humanist benevolence toward "lesser" species to a posthuman reassessment of human identity and her place within the human-defined species hierarchy.

Figure 6.3 Tina stops Vore at the border and finds his larvae hatcher.

In several dreamlike encounters, Tina also displays affinity with other species including a fox, a moose, and a deer. For Tina, these are Harawayian "companion species" with whom she is "bonded in significant otherness," while her contrasting negative relationship with dogs is indicative of her own liminal species status, considering that Haraway's theorization in *The Companion Species Manifesto* is founded on the close human-dog bond.[22] The fox in the forest near her house becomes less wary of her, approaching her window at night and hanging around the house once ex-boyfriend Roland and his dogs have moved out. Later, Vore appears at the same window, and his mirroring of the fox suggests that there is growing trust between them. One evening, as she stands outside her house for some peace and quiet away from Roland and his incessantly barking dogs (who are too human-loyal to trust her), she greets a moose, who stands close beside her looking back at the house. Later, as she drives her neighbors to the hospital to give birth, she stops the car on the road, sensing the deer about to cross the road before they appear. The animal encounters, like with the insect in the first scene, suggest her attunement and sensitivity to other species, and they appear to her in moments of quiet and peace (such as walking barefoot in the forest, or taking a moment of patience in the rush to the maternity ward).

Vore at first seems like one of a species with whom she may find affinity and peace, and they bond over commonalities, such as the scars they bear from their docked tails and being struck by lightning. They are both fearful of lightning and cling to each other under a table as they tremble during a storm. For Tina, who grew up being bullied and made to feel like a freakish outsider (and is still treated this way by humans such as the boy caught with alcohol at the border), Vore's mirrored appearance (including his facial features and scars) enhances her acceptance of her troll identity and characteristics. He challenges her internalized feelings of freakishness, for instance, when she describes herself as "an ugly, strange human with a chromosome flaw," he replies, "There's no flaw in you" and "If you're different than others, it's because you're better than them." Vore's radical inversion of human exceptionalism is a revelation to Tina, who begins to question her place in human society and accept a nonhuman identity. Their meeting prompts her to question her father (played by Sten Ljunggren) about her origins, and she becomes increasingly frustrated with his secrecy as she grapples with the trauma of her otherness and the unknown aspects of her identity and history.

220 SCREENING THE POSTHUMAN

Tina and Vore's initial flirtations build to animalistic desire, from snarling and kissing to sex in the forest (in which Tina sprouts new genitals and penetrates Vore, gripping the mossy forest floor as she orgasms for the first time). This sex scene has surrealist features, echoing the films of Wilhelm Freddie, in which "a disturbing eroticism is allied with that special brand of disconcerting surrealist humor."[23] The sexual encounter with Vore marks a new level of self-acceptance for Tina, who did not have a sexual relationship with her human boyfriend Roland (played by Jörgen Thorsson) and found sex painful. After sex, Vore tells her, "You're a troll, like me," which is the first time their species is mentioned. "You're crazy. A troll?," she replies in disbelief. He explains a chromosomal change led to the features of their ability to smell feelings, their fear of lightning, and being born with a tail. Trolls are betrayed by their tails, which sets them apart from being human—the tail scar found on Vore by Tina's colleague during a strip search is the first clue to their shared species (beyond their distinctive facial features that set them apart from humans). Their sex characteristics and form of reproduction also diverge from humans, as revealed in their conversations and sex scene. He also explains to her that there is a small group of trolls who roam in Finland, and says she needs to let them find her. Their bond and trust are further solidified in the subsequent montage of them running naked through the forest, and splashing around and kissing in the water, to a soundtrack of happy, romantic music.

This narrative of romance and liberation is undercut by a subplot that again draws on the surrealist tradition of confronting taboos: Vore is involved in the production of child sexual abuse material (an ultimate taboo crime), and this exacerbates a broader tension between Tina's newfound identity as a troll and her loyalty to human law and custom. Playing into Scandinavian mythology about trolls, Vore is revealed to be a kidnapper. The theft of a human baby (and replacement with one of their own) is a common crime of trolls in folklore—here the fantastical is connected to bleak realism in the connected story of child sexual exploitation. The revelation of Vore as someone involved in child sexual abuse emphasizes the theme of safeguarding the human by excluding and animalizing "inhuman" others, since such persons are culturally constructed as aberrant "animals," "monsters," or "beasts" who should be expelled from society. After Tina finds a *hiisit* (Vore's unfertilized egg that resembles a human baby) in her guesthouse fridge (Figure 6.4), Vore explains that he takes and sells human infants, replacing them with a *hiisit*, in order to "help them [humans] hurt themselves." After earlier telling her that

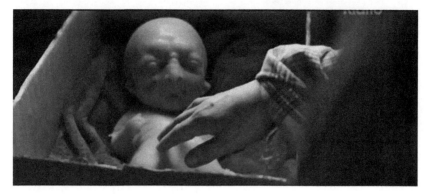

Figure 6.4 Tina finds a *hiisit* in her guesthouse fridge.

vengeance is coming to humans after he was abused in orphanages and they conducted medical experiments on his parents, he now justifies his actions as revenge: "They took us. I take their children," he says, "They must suffer as we've suffered."

By rejecting Vore on the ferry and betraying him to the police, it seems Tina is drawn back into the comfort of "[t]he fleeting, illusory cohesion of the human [which] depends on the liminal space of exception as the threshold of social and political order."[24] However, by entering into "the open," the illusory nature of the human—and its dependence on othering and animalizing to maintain its exceptionalism—have been revealed to both Tina and the viewer through the course of the film. The surrealist aspects of the film bring viewers into "the open" with Tina and suspend us between human and nonhuman worlds, aligning with Pettman's call to "focus on a collective attempt to retrofit our own self-understanding according to a less paranoid and fascistic logic of secured borders and pure typologies."[25] One way of defining surrealism is through its aim of "striving to establish the site of convergence of different realities," or to use André Breton's term, determining the "supreme point."[26] If it is the case that the cinema experience is "one which converges with the perception of the point of dissolution that is simultaneously also a point of origin," Tina similarly moves toward the supreme point as her connection with her troll origins is also the point of dissolution of her sense of being human.[27] Rather than recuperate Tina back into human society and morality at the end of the film, a new future is envisioned at the convergence of her two realities. In the film's final scene, she finds a large package at her front door and opens it to find a baby troll (who has a tail and a hairy face).

222 SCREENING THE POSTHUMAN

A "Welcome to Finland" postcard in the box suggests that Vore escaped from the authorities when he jumped off the ferry and returned to Finland where he gave birth to their child. Tina feeds the baby an insect, which seems to make it happy, and she smiles as the film fades to black.

On Body and Soul's Unresolved Caesuras

While *The Lobster* and *Border* deploy surrealist strategies of dark humor and confronting taboo, *On Body and Soul* places a surrealist lens over the Cartesian dualism between body and soul to effect a posthuman perspective on the animality of the human. A foundational figure of humanist thought, Descartes located the meaning of what it is to be human in the soul, or rational mind, as opposed to the body. In stating that "the soul, by which I am what I am, is entirely distinct from the body," he established another caesura at the heart of the human—as with their animality, the human is aloof from their materiality.[28] *On Body and Soul* uses surrealist techniques to critique this aloofness and human disconnection, drawing the soul back into the body—both for the animal, and for the human. This case study demonstrates how surrealist characteristics—such as denaturalizing social custom, tapping the liberatory potential of dreams, and using juxtaposition and brutal imagery from a working slaughterhouse (echoing *Le Sang des bêtes* [*Blood of the Beasts*, dir. Georges Franju, 1949])—jam the anthropological machine, again forging a post-anthropocentric perspective in posthuman cinema.

The film opens with a stag and a doe interacting in a snowy forest (Figure 6.5). We come to learn that this scenario, seen several times in the film, is a dream shared by the two main characters. In their waking lives, Endre (played by Géza Morcsányi), the chief financial officer at a large abattoir, meets Mária (played by Alexandra Borbély), a newly employed quality inspector. The possibility of romance between them is set up by the absurd plot point of the theft of "mating powder" by one of the abattoir's employees, which leads to interviews with a psychologist who asks them about their dreams. This way of coming to find out that they share the same dreams is described by film critic Peter Bradshaw as "A ridiculous and unlikely idea, yet such is the engaging nimbleness and poise of Ildikó's direction that its surreal absurdity is noticed at first only as a comic lubricant for the poignant love story that is to come."[29] The two characters' hope of any romantic connection

Figure 6.5 The human characters' animal avatars interact in the dreamscape.

is made through the dreamscape and the waking realization that they have been sharing the same dream, respectively embodied as the stag and doe. As humans, in the daytime, their romance is faltering and unlikely, but regular inserts of the dreamscape sustain the possibility of both intra- and interpersonal connection for the pair and a posthuman horizon of overcoming their anthropocentric relationality.

As in *The Lobster*, this film uses the surrealist technique of denaturalizing social custom to foreground that social performance—bounded by strict rules and customs—is a key part of becoming human and connecting with human others. In *The Lobster*, dating and bromance are awkwardly navigated within The Hotel's nonsensical rules, while in *On Body and Soul*, an awkward potential romance between mismatched characters is again at the fore, along with Mária's navigation of social cues (re-enacting and rehearsing conversations using salt and pepper shakers or toy figurines) and physical contact (progressing from mashed potato, to a cow, to a more intimate encounter with a black panther stuffed toy). Mária does not fit in at work and is called "Snow White" by other employees, resented for being overly precise in her quality control tasks (giving all the meat a B grade). She displays characteristics of Asperger's Syndrome such as difficulty with social communication and an aversion to small talk, coming across in her interactions as awkwardly direct or insensitive. Her role-play at home and her exchanges with Endre at work denaturalize small talk, and the film gently mocks Endre's routine small talk about food in both the work canteen and on his first date with Mária—here it becomes an oddity of human social custom that Mária

224 SCREENING THE POSTHUMAN

decodes through re-enactment and subverts through direct expression of her thoughts and desires.

Cross-cutting and contrasts are used not only to show the gulf between these incompatible love interests, but also to highlight the gulf between the experiences of various human and nonhuman animals, including in the contexts of the slaughterhouse (with cattle) and in their dreams (as deer). As noted before, Endre and Mária's awkward interactions as humans in their waking lives are contrasted with regular inserts of their shared dreamscape, where their deer avatars are comfortable companions. Contrasts between Mária and Endre are also highlighted in cross-cutting between the mise-en-scène of their living spaces: her apartment is perfectly clean, stark, and minimalist, with mid-century furniture, while he lives in a cozy brick home with rugs and tapestries, not so brightly lit. After their date, Mária moves away from Endre when he tries to touch her, and the scene set the following night contrasts him breathing in her smell from the blanket she used (capturing his longing for her) with her impassive viewing of a porn film in an attempt to understand sexual touch. After Endre decides that there is no point pursuing their relationship, Mária cuts herself in her bathtub. The graphic display of the large cut on her arm and the blood in the bathwater are reminiscent of the slaughterhouse (and of the scene in *The Lobster* when David's brother lies in a pool of blood on the bathroom floor), which becomes comically concerning as it then gushes from her arm and pools on the floor at her feet while she is on the phone to Endre. As the cross-cutting comes to end once they declare their love and are reunited, the boundaries between the seemingly irreconcilable lovers overcome, so too do human and animal come together in the end. Surrealist techniques such as juxtaposition and shocking violence viscerally remind the viewer of how human and nonhuman animal alike are both flesh and blood, body and soul, and vulnerable to violence.

The division between body and soul is shown to extend beyond the domain of the human, playing out most strikingly in the scenes focused on cattle in the abattoir. The first cow is introduced after the opening deer scene with a close-up of its hooves on the muddy industrial floor (contrasting with the picturesque forest of the previous scene), and then a close-up of its face. The scene aligns the viewer's perspective with the cow's perspective through audio (intensifying the high-pitch sounds of metal on metal and muffling human conversation) and by following the close-up of its face with an eyeline match of the hazy sun that it gazes up at from its confinement (Figure 6.6). After this opening focus on the bovine soul, the film shortly depicts brutal

Figure 6.6 The viewer is aligned with the cow's perspective through the soundtrack and a close-up of the cow's face followed by an eyeline match.

scenes of slaughter in the abattoir, reducing the cow to its body and its dismembered body parts. The slaughtering of a cow is depicted in clinical and unflinching detail, including a beheading and skinning, the film taking its time in witnessing the processes like an observational documentary—and indeed, these scenes were shot in a working abattoir, as the end credits note: "During the shooting of our film animals were harmed. But none of them for the sake of this film. We just documented the daily routine of a slaughterhouse."

The literal objectification of cattle in the abattoir—brutally carved into quality-controlled products for human consumption—is mirrored in the theme of humans objectifying one another, similarly severing others' bodies from their souls. It is exemplified in the new young male employee whom Endre is reluctant to hire because he doesn't feel sorry for the cows, and who behaves in a way that another employee describes as like a rooster

226   SCREENING THE POSTHUMAN

in a henhouse, strutting around to impress the young female employees and attempting to get a date with "Snow White." The confronting slaughterhouse scenes highlight the brutality but also the routineness of objectification, and the inability to transcend this dynamic in relations with both human and nonhuman others. The characters struggle to see and access others' souls, and Endre's failure to genuinely connect with both Mária and Jenö (the colleague he eats lunch with every day) tells a story of how difficult it is to reach another's soul (indeed for these characters, only possible in their dreams). In the slaughterhouse and in the porn film that Mária watches to familiarize herself with intimate contact, the severing of body and soul are highlighted—the first in its graphic brutality paired with detached observation, and with the porn film, through its formulaic nature (a classic close-up penetration shot) and Mária's detached observation, both of which could be described as surrealist techniques. The body/soul severance in the latter is humorously foregrounded by Mária's impassive viewing, eating Gummi Bears while she watches unmoved, our view of the screen obscured through the glass jar of colorful bear-shaped lollies. As they struggle to connect with others and reconcile body and soul in their daily lives, the protagonists can access their (post)human capacities for love, intimacy, and companionship only in their dreams and only in the embodiment of deer. The posthuman potential that emerges in the dream facilitates their transcendence of the anthropocentric caesura of body and soul, human and animal. The characters' dysfunctional way of relating in the waking world conveys the humanist anthropocentrism that they dream their way out of, in order to right that wrong of imagining themselves superior to animals.

On Body and Soul's cinematic brutality highlights the severance of body and soul (as well as human and animal), as do the contrasts between day/reality and night/dream and the experiences of the two nonhuman species: the carnality of the cattle in the slaughterhouse (the "body") and the freedom of the deer in pristine forest dreamscape (the "soul"). These juxtapositions are in line with surrealism in Walter Benjamin's sense of it offering a "dialectical optic that perceives the everyday as impenetrable, the impenetrable as everyday."[30] Adam Lowenstein links Benjamin's dialectical optic to Breton's belief in "the future resolution of these two states, dream and reality, which are seemingly so contradictory, into a kind of absolute reality, a *surreality*, if one may so speak."[31] The film applies this surrealist rethinking to Agamben's call, putting a dialectical optic on the anthropological machine. As in *Border*, here again the question of the caesura between human and animal arises. As Agamben notes,

> In our culture, man has always been thought of as the articulation and conjunction of a body and a soul, of a living thing and a *logos*, of a natural (or animal) element and a supernatural or social or divine element. We must learn instead to think of man as what results from the incongruity of these two elements, and investigate not the metaphysical mystery of conjunction, but rather the practical and political mystery of separation.[32]

Here Agamben foregrounds that, contrary to a traditional conceptualization of the human as a conjunction of body and soul, the human is both the site and result of ongoing internal separation. For Agamben then, the urgent question is "to ask in what way—within man—has man been separated from non-man, and the animal from the human."[33] *On Body and Soul* illuminates these forms of separation through the cinematic strategies outlined earlier, from the use of cinematic brutality to the contrasts and cross-cutting between human/animal and waking/dreaming life. While the director frames her intentions in humanist terms—"I wanted to show that body and soul are a whole. What we are is the interaction of these two aspects"[34]—the film's fissures (literal and figurative), contrasts and inconclusiveness, push beyond a humanist cohesion and conclusion.

The film's open ending does not reconcile body and soul, nor its two love interests, in a neat conclusion; rather it underscores Agamben's idea that the human is not a conjunction of body and soul, but rather, an ongoing internal separation. However, the ending does mark a transcendence of the strict anthropocentric divisions. While Mária and Endre do finally consummate their relationship, their future together is indeterminate. The sex scene is depicted through a shot/reverse shot sequence of close-ups of their (fairly impassive) faces. The lovers' performances are similar to those in *The Lobster*, maintaining a degree of affectless absurdity even in this climactic union as their seemingly impossible romance finally takes off. The sunlit morning-after breakfast scene in Endre's kitchen suggests a warmth and new intimacy, but when Mária asks about his dream, and neither of them had the dream/can recall it, the viewer is left to wonder what this implies for their connection. The film's final shot returns to the snowy forest dreamscape, now empty of deer, and it fades to white. This indeterminate ending leaves multiple readings open, for instance, it may suggest that there is no longer a need

228 SCREENING THE POSTHUMAN

for the dream to facilitate their relationship, or perhaps that the protagonists have now embraced their animal selves consciously or healed the caesura that divides human and animal, body and soul. To posit a posthuman reading, this fade to white suggests the characters' entry into "the open"; in other words, rather than healing a caesura, the conclusion offers a corrective to disrupt anthropocentric hierarchies and objectification. Here then the film ends on a similar note to the closing sections of Agamben's *The Open*, which, as Anat Pick notes,

> intimate a way beyond the designated regions of exception marked out by the anthropological machine . . . The strategy is explicitly *esoteric*: it is no longer a matter of explicating the role and function of the "open," but of entering into it, of inhabiting the interval.[35]

Rather than offer the viewer the closure of a fade to black, the viewer is invited with the protagonists to inhabit the interval of a fade to white.

New Animism and Post-anthropocentric Thai Cinema

Just as surrealism is "an activity with broadening horizons," the following analysis seeks to broaden posthumanist film theory by exploring the specific concepts and cinematic techniques of "new animist" Thai filmmakers who share an "affinity of intention" with global posthuman surrealist cinema.[36] The international critical reception of the Thai films *Tropical Malady* and *Manta Ray* indicates that the films confound interpretation for many Western viewers. For example, when *Tropical Malady* premiered at Cannes in 2004, "the critical consensus was that the movie was difficult to the point of inscrutability."[37] In addition to viewers perhaps lacking cultural and spiritual frameworks for interpretation, this is arguably also a consequence of the disconnect between the persistent assumption of cinema as an indexical medium (that records and represents the real) and the films' surrealist and what I am calling their "new animist" underpinnings. Lowenstein notes that surrealism never assumed that cinema was a realist medium and "the ascent of digital media invites us to recognize that cinema always was and continues to be a deeply surrealist medium rather than an inherently realist one."[38] Yet the following case study films encourage us to view cinema not only as a surrealist medium but an animist one, which likewise challenges both the assumption of cinema as an indexical medium and the privileging of an anthropocentric worldview. David Teh notes that Weerasethakul fits uneasily into the lineage of Thai modernist art that liberally adapted surrealist aesthetics and merged it with local traditions and myths:

> he makes plenty of room for chance, but no commitment to psychic automatism . . . his handling of social taboos deliberately defuses their shock value, dousing them instead with the quotidian familiarity, and slightly awkward intimacy, that are his trademarks. For all the dreaminess of his films, the unconscious that Apichatpong taps—or that taps him—is as much collective as it is individual.[39]

Teh therefore suggests that Weerasethakul's "approach is perhaps better described as post-Surrealist,"[40] a positioning that operates well for this chapter, which observes affinities with past and present Western surrealist cinema while also drawing on other frameworks that highlight the distinct contribution of these Thai films to global post-anthropocentric cinema.

In particular, I draw on "new animism" as another framework that serves to interrogate both anthropocentric worldviews and the idea of cinema as inherently realist. The term "animism" has undergone revision and revival since the 1990s, and this "new animism" is associated with scholars such as Philippe Descola, Nurit Bird-David, Eduardo Viveiros de Castro, and Tim Ingold.[41] It provides another mode for reconceptualizing the relations between human and nonhuman persons, having become what Bird-David describes as a "relational (not a failed) epistemology."[42] The revival of the concept in both theory and contemporary Thai cinema aligns with critical posthumanism in that "The continued challenge of the concept of animism lies in the imperative to rethink the border between humans and their others."[43] New animism challenges understandings of humans as the only ensouled beings, elevated in a hierarchy above non-souled beings and objects. In the following section, I employ the term "new animism" in recognition of its critical value for—and alignment with—critical posthumanism. Animism lends itself to critical posthumanism's goals because, as Graham Harvey notes, "animisms appear to be the very opposite of Cartesian and other Western knowledge systems."[44] The discussion of animism is adopted in accordance with its newer usage as a critical

230 SCREENING THE POSTHUMAN

term, captured in the opening of Harvey's book, *Animism: Respecting the Living World*:

> Animists are people who recognise that the world is full of persons, only some of whom are human, and that life is always lived in relationship with others. Animism is lived out in various ways that are all about learning to act respectfully (carefully and constructively) towards and among other persons.[45]

The term is employed here not in the tradition of colonial anthropology, which framed animism in a derogatory manner as a form of magical and primitive belief in spirits, but in line with more recent post-Cartesian reclaiming of the term that challenges assumptions of modernist Western culture.

The old usage of animism—much like humanism—posited multiplicity as a problem and proffered two solutions: "to insist on the underlying unity of all that exists" underpinned by a single God or grand unifying theory; and "to dichotomise everything and treat all that we encounter as a confrontation of dualities."[46] In contrast, as Harvey notes,

> The new usage of animism arises from respectful relationships with indigenous and other cultures in which boundaries are permeable and putative "opposites" are necessarily engaged in various ways. Instead of crying "One!" or "Two!," animists celebrate plurality, multiplicity, the many and their entwined passionate entanglements. Instead of the hero who struggles against one or the other side of things in an attempt to discern the underlying truth, animist stories present tricksters who multiply possibilities in increasingly amusing ways.[47]

This new usage of animism is reflected in the two films discussed below, which both use shape-shifting or displacement "trickster" figures—such as the shaman-tiger in *Tropical Malady* (Figure 6.7) and the refugee taking the place of his host in *Manta Ray* (Figure 6.8)—to generate permeable boundaries of selfhood and multiply possibilities. New animism (in both theoretical and cinematic manifestations) offers a post-anthropocentric alternative view to the relationship between human and nonhuman animals enshrined in Cartesian dualism, as demonstrated by *Tropical Malady* and *Manta Ray*.

Figure 6.7 The shaman-tiger in *Satpralat/Tropical Malady* (Apichatpong Weerasethakul, 2004).

Figure 6.8 Thongchai takes the place of his host in *Kraben Rahu/Manta Ray* (Phuttiphong Aroonpheng, 2019), bleaching his hair to take on the fisherman's appearance.

Tropical Malady's Posthuman Bifurcations

Tropical Malady is characterized by a distinct bifurcated structure; in the simplest terms, the first half depicts a budding romance in a Thai village and the second half depicts a pursuit of a shape-shifting tiger in the jungle.

232 SCREENING THE POSTHUMAN

The film's critical reception in English has tended to focus on this unique structure, and in attempting to piece together the narrative and figure out connections between the two halves, critics often set them up in various forms of opposition. More interesting than the narrative enigma posed by this bifurcated structure is the conceptual challenge it poses to our understanding of the relationship between human and animal (and other binaries such as the living and the dead). Below I explore how Weerasethakul's films such as *Tropical Malady* not only "upend storytelling orthodoxy,"[48] but also present to the international film circuit a radical destabilization of the relationship between human and animal, which it achieves through new animist ontologies and aesthetics. As Isaac Marrero-Guillamón notes, an "animist undercurrent animates most of Weerasethakul's films, which are populated by ghosts, where people may reincarnate as animals, where the same body may be occupied by different spirits, where animals speak with humans."[49] *Tropical Malady* specifically has been described by critics such as May Adadol Ingawan,[50] James Quandt,[51] and Marrero-Guillamón as an animist film, not simply in the sense of telling an animist story or representing animist ideas, but enacting an animist world and "the possibility of a sensory experience of animism."[52] As an animist film, *Tropical Malady* immerses the viewer in an alternative ontological orientation to human exceptionalism, one that is compatible with post-anthropocentric posthuman cinema.

Failing to attune to this, accounts of the film's bifurcation in Western critical reception tend to involve an anxious attempt to reassert dualisms and binaries that the bifurcation unsettles and on which the security of humanism relies. Film critic Manohla Dargis comments on the "surprising rupture midway through"[53] that shifts the film from realism to allegory, and in a later review, notes again how "the film abruptly shifts registers, switching from low-key naturalism into a full-blown fable."[54] Dennis Lim similarly points to the diptych structure and contrast between the two halves, describing it as "split down the middle between lovesick daydream and malarial delirium," and puzzling over the questions, "How do the two halves connect? Which one is real—or realer? Are these pertinent questions?"[55] Such conceptualizations of the bifurcation reinforce binaries that the film itself does not seek to establish or resolve, but indeed, moves beyond. Anthony Carew, meanwhile, conceptualizes it as a "cinematic reincarnation" or a "mutant":

> *Sud Pralad*, refers to a monster—a mutant offspring of two species. This is something that is reflected in the film's essentially bisected narrative and,

further, throughout Weerasethakul's other pictures, which splice together tales of city and country, and past and present, and chronicle affairs between Thais and Laotians, Thais and Burmese, soldiers and civilians, men and men, tigers and monkeys, princesses and catfish, spirits and ghosts.[56]

These examples point to the way that reviews in English tend to focus on rupture and binarism, and embody a perception that the film's bifurcation is disruptive, difficult, or "a conceptual prank."[57]

Returning to both the surrealist frameworks and Agamben's theories used above, I posit the concept of a "supreme point" as a productive one for understanding the bifurcation, and suggest that this structure creates a "saved night" in which the human and nonhuman become suspended. The midway pivot in *Tropical Malady* can be understood as the film's "supreme point" in that it marks the convergence of different realities, and is simultaneously a point of origin and dissolution. It presents the origin of a myth-based narrative ("Once upon a time there was a powerful Khmer shaman who could turn into various creatures . . .") and also marks a dissolution of the distinct characters through a series of displacements. As Marrero-Guillamón notes,

> First, the overwhelming visual opacity of the jungle and its aural density increasingly dominate the sensory experience, downgrading the human character to one among many presences. This is accompanied by Weerasethakul's skillful shifts in the film's point of view, which detaches itself from a human-centric position and enables the spectator to see what the shaman-tiger and the jungle see. Moreover, the neat ontological separation between humans, animals, spirits and plants is blurred by the multiple metamorphoses at play: not only are beings other than the sole human capable of speech, but the soldier himself undergoes a process of becoming-animal/becoming-jungle that sees him transformed into something or someone else, although we cannot be sure what.[58]

As a director with a "penchant for dismantling categories,"[59] Weerasethakul's interests align with the posthuman blurring of boundaries between the taken-for-granted categories of human and nonhuman animals. However, by centering a supreme point, Weerasethakul pivots the film on the surrealist location where binary oppositions are not merged or overcome, but rather, "where they cease to function as oppositions, where opposition itself loses its strength."[60]

Weerasethakul's bifurcated narratives (which also include *Syndromes and a Century* [2006] and *Blissfully Yours* [2002]) also point to the caesura within the human that Agamben writes about in *The Open*. In this respect, the bifurcation is a technique that refocuses the optics of the "anthropological machine," serving not as a mirror for the human but to push the human in a posthuman direction. As Weerasethakul has himself noted of his film, "The break in the middle of the film is a mirror in the center that reflects both ways."[61] Across his oeuvre, Weerasethakul commonly uses devices like bifurcation and dualism; however, according to Nathan Lee, the binary terms within these devices do not operate "in a dialectical manner, opposed to each other and moving toward synthesis, but as simultaneous phenomena on a single plane of being."[62] The image of Tong (played by Sakda Kaewbuadee) walking away down a dark road after a sensual moment with Keng (played by Banlop Lomnoi), at the end of the first half of *Tropical Malady* (Figure 6.9), operates as an entry into a "saved night" wherein, as Agamben puts it:

> The machine is, so to speak, stopped; it is "at a standstill," and, in the reciprocal suspension of the two terms, something for which we perhaps have no

Figure 6.9 In *Satpralat/Tropical Malady* (Apichatpong Weerasethakul, 2004), Tong walks away down a dark road after a sensual moment with Keng.

name and which is neither animal nor man settles in between nature and humanity and holds itself in the mastered relation, in the saved night.[63]

In line with both post-anthropocentrism and Weerasethakul's non-dialectical approach to binarism, "a 'saved night' brings the anthropological machine to a halt since it precludes mastery as well as any dialectical synthesis of the man-animal relation."[64]

Western critics' contrasting of the two halves can obscure the ways in which, as Ji-Hoon Kim observes, "the temporal relationship between the two halves is interdependent and cross-contaminating."[65] Daniel Grinberg's attention to the manifestations of Buddhist temporality points to aspects of Weerasethakul's cinema that have been overlooked or misunderstood from a Western perspective, such as the cyclicality of time and themes of recurrence, regeneration, and rebirth.[66] Grinberg compares the viewing experience of a Weerasethakul film to the Buddhist meditation technique *vipassanā*, and suggests that the Brechtian breaking of the fourth wall (when the soldier and tiger spirit stare into the camera) encourages viewers to reflect on their own inconstancy: "Like *vipassanā*, it can lead to the deconstruction of binary thought, turning away from closed-minded selfhood, and promoting an awareness of the concatenation of every life form." As Grinberg notes, Buddhist theology and temporality may generally be unfamiliar to audiences viewing Weerasethakul's films in Western film festivals and arthouse theaters, much like new animism. However, these frameworks help to make sense of the interdependence and kinship between human, animal, and supernatural beings that align the film with the post-anthropocentricism of international posthuman cinema.

Non-hierarchical Relationality in *Manta Ray*

Phuttiphong Aroonpheng's debut feature film, *Manta Ray*, displays various similarities with Weerasethakul's cinema, as Nicholas Godfrey's review of the film highlights:

> *Manta Ray*'s dualistic narrative recalls those of *Tropical Malady* (2004) and *Syndromes and a Century* (2006), while evoking the transformations that underpin those films' diptych structures. The coyly developing homoerotic bond in *Manta Ray*'s first half mirrors that in *Tropical Malady*, while

236 SCREENING THE POSTHUMAN

its pseudo-documentary montage sequences recall Weerasethakul's early *Mysterious Object at Noon* (2000), and its surreal night-time excursions into the fairy-lit forest call to mind the more fantastical passages of *Uncle Boonmee Who Can Recall His Past Lives* (2010) and *Cemetery of Splendour* (2015).[67]

The "dualistic" narrative similarly sees a transformation at the film's center. A fisherman (played by Wanlop Rungkumjad) finds a refugee (played by Aphisit Hama) unconscious in the swampy coastal forest, takes him home, nurses him back to health, and names him Thongchai. When the fisherman later disappears at sea, Thongchai adopts his life and identity (including styling himself after the fisherman, working his job, and taking up a relationship with his ex-wife). This shift is a gentler bifurcation than that between *Tropical Malady*'s more distinct halves, but it works to similar effect: "Some of *Manta Ray*'s scenes loosely play out as refracted, alternate versions of those previously seen with the fisherman. These, in addition to a few dreamlike montages, contribute to the film's lightly surreal veneer."[68] The film also reflects themes of the queer posthumanist films examined in Chapter 4, in which characters embody or possess other people in narratives that explore the porousness of subjectivity and flexibility of identity. In the critical reception of *Manta Ray*, these themes have been read as reflecting society's treatment of refugees as noncitizens denied legal and social acceptance. The film is haunted by the plight of Rohingya refugees who have fled from Myanmar, to whom the film is dedicated, and a chorus of Rohingya refugees' voices are incorporated into the film's soundtrack. Thongchai is shown kindness by the fisherman, but his life and identity remain in limbo, marked by his muteness, lack of a name, and need to slip into the life of the man who showed him how to fish, cook, and ride a motorcycle.

Through sound, color, and the porousness of identity, *Manta Ray* creates a hypnotic animist world that reflects Anselm Franke's characterization of animism:

> "Animism" designates a cosmos in which theoretically everything is alive and communicating, and potentially possesses the qualities of being "a person" or, at the very least, an agent of some kind. It describes a world in which all social and ontological boundaries are porous and can be crossed under specific circumstances, a world of becomings and metamorphoses, in which no entity precedes the sets of relations that bring it into being.[69]

The glittering, colored fairy lights in the forest and at the fisherman's makeshift home disco (Figure 6.10), as well as the colored stones that the fisherman collects in the forest to attract manta rays, contribute to the sense of aliveness and communication that imbues this animist film. Like *Tropical Malady*'s second half, the soundtrack also decenters human voice and foregrounds nature's sounds. As critic Joshua Minsoo Kim describes, "The different diegetic sounds—from the hypnotic crashing of waves to the crunching of dry leaves, the scraping of spoons to the sloshing of vomit—instill a meditative ambiance."[70] This meditative ambiance (and the film's minimalism and pace) lends itself to a contemplation of relationality, and in line with new animism and its alliance with posthuman ethics, the film dreamily depicts a non-hierarchical approach to human-nonhuman relationality in the friendship between the fisherman and refugee, and in their relationship to the natural world. Animism presents a model of non-hierarchical recognition and respect for other persons:

> People become animists by learning how to recognise persons and, far more important, how to engage with them. The ubiquity of terms like respect and reciprocity in animist discourse demonstrates that the key identifier of a person is someone who responds to or initiates approaches to other persons.[71]

Figure 6.10 The glittering, colored fairy lights at the fisherman's makeshift home disco.

238   SCREENING THE POSTHUMAN

As with *Border*'s exploration of border control and exclusion of the non-human through reference to immigration in Europe, here the theme of locals' treatment of refugees—who are an epitome of Agamben's figure of "bare life," *homo sacer*—reflects on broader issues of relationality between humans and their "others."

As with *The Lobster*, the titular animal of *Manta Ray* can be read on a metaphorical level, but a critical posthumanist lens provides a deeper perspective on the post-anthropocentric potential of the manta ray's role in the film. Operating as sociopolitical commentary, the figure of the manta ray highlights the inability of humans to freely cross national borders, as there is no perception of geopolitical borders within a manta ray's umwelt. In a Q&A session at the 2018 Toronto International Film Festival, Aroonpheng recalls having a manta ray swim toward him during his first dive in the Andaman Sea: "Manta rays just swim around the Andaman Sea—no border."[72] In Godfrey's film review, the manta ray highlights the film's themes of "fluidity, transformation, mirroring and doubling":

> the titular creature represents the possibility of transformation, as the film highlights the mutability of individual characteristics. The ray drifts through the narrative as its two characters are drawn into proximity, slowly become like each other, part company, and then are drawn together again in new and strange ways—hiding in plain sight, and fleeing the omnipresent but invisible danger.[73]

The ethereal shot of the manta ray at the end of the film suggests a transformation of Thongchai after he is rejected and returned to the forest once the fisherman reappears.

The manta ray exceeds straightforward metaphor, functioning more as an "animetaphor" that underscores the posthuman disruption of nonhuman animals' metaphorical function in screen media: "The animal returns like a meal that cannot be digested, a dream that cannot be forgotten, an other that cannot be sublated." Akira Mizuta Lippit's definition of an "animetaphor" here is a fitting description of the manta ray's appearance on-screen at the end of the film, as both Thongchai and the manta ray are "an other that cannot be sublated." While "animetaphor" plays on "anti-metaphor" and the combination of "animal" and "metaphor," it can also be read as portmanteau of "animism" and "metaphor," which is equally fitting for the way an animist perspective is reflected in Lippit's explanation of the concept:

One finds a fantastic transversality at work between the animal and the metaphor—the animal is already a metaphor, the metaphor is animal. Together they transport to language, breathe into language, the vitality of another life, another expression: animal and metaphor, a metaphor made flesh, a living metaphor that is by definition not a metaphor, antimetaphor—"animetaphor."

Like the starfish in Eva Hayward's "Lessons from a Starfish," the manta ray "exceeds the metaphoricity of 'likeness,'"[74] and raises questions about embodiment and relationships with the world, including processes of transformation and regeneration. The fisherman's communication with the manta rays via lights in the water also evokes Isabelle Stengers's phrase "luring assemblages," which reminds us that "I do not first exist and then enter into assemblages. Rather, my existence is my very participation in assemblages" and agency belongs not to the individual but the assemblage.[75] When one man replaces the other in the film, we are reminded of how the components of an assemblage are not fixed and can be replaced. Stengers conceives of being animist "in terms of assemblages that generate metamorphic transformation in our capacity to affect and be affected—and also to feel, think, and imagine."[76] The manta ray's spectacular appearance toward the end of the film underscores these capacities, encouraging us to "feel, think, and imagine" different possibilities of human-nonhuman relationality.

Conclusion

This chapter has explored how posthuman cinema works to disrupt the operations of the "anthropological machine," refracting the optics on human exceptionalism through various surrealist and new animist practices. These post-anthropocentric films often foreground Cartesian dualism and other humanist binaries but use surrealism and new animism to resist a straightforward dialectical relationship between them. Surrealism features in these films through intertextual references, the constructs of rituals and dreams, and the use of juxtaposition, shocking imagery, dark humor, and disturbing eroticism. Such techniques foreground and force us to reconsider binaries, including the dichotomy between human and nonhuman animals. Surrealism has a disruptive function, and these post-anthropocentric films continue surrealism's tradition of encountering the marvelous, which involves a disorienting sensation or disturbance of the senses, exposing contradictions within the real. "New animism" similarly offers a re-enchantment of the world and a shift in thinking about the relationships between body/soul and human/nonhuman; where surrealism questions notions of *rationality* and *reality*, new animism further interrogates ideas of *relationality*. Traversing both European and Thai cinema, the case studies in this chapter have drawn on surrealism and new animism as key frameworks alongside critical posthumanism in order to understand how posthuman cinema undermines human exceptionalism. As noted in this chapter's introduction, Wolfe positions posthumanism as a "mode of thought" that engages "the problem of anthropocentrism and speciesism and how practices of thinking and reading must change in light of their critique."[77] This chapter has utilized this mode of thought to open up new ways of reading human-nonhuman animal relationality on-screen and to reveal ways in which the representation of animals in posthuman cinema go beyond a simple metaphorical or anthropomorphic deployments. Through cinematic depictions that range from the confronting and humorous to the hypnotic and other-worldly, these films begin to envisage post-anthropocentric relationality.

Notes

1. Francesca Ferrando, "Posthumanism, Transhumanism, Antihumanism, Metahumanism and New Materialism: Differences and Relations," *Existenz. An International Journal in Philosophy, Religion, Politics and the Arts* 8, no. 2 (2013): 29.
2. Cary Wolfe, *What Is Posthumanism?* (Minneapolis: University of Minnesota Press, 2010), xviii–xix.
3. Dominic Pettman, *Human Error: Species-Being and Media Machines* (Minneapolis: University of Minnesota Press, 2011), 8.
4. Michael Richardson, *Surrealism and Cinema* (Oxford: Berg, 2006), 10, 3.
5. Anat Pick, "Review of Giorgio Agamben, *Open: Man and Animal*, trans. Kevin Attell," *Bryn Mawr Review of Comparative Literature* 5, no. 2 (2006): 3, https://repository. brynmawr.edu/bmrcl/vol5/iss2/1/.
6. Richardson, *Surrealism and Cinema*, 212.
7. Jennifer M. Barker, "A Horse Is a Horse, Of Course, Of Course: Animality, Transitivity, and the Double Take," *Somatechnics* 8, no. 1 (2018): 34, https://doi.org/10.3366/ soma.2018.0235.
8. Rosalind Galt, "The Animal Logic of Contemporary Greek Cinema," *Framework: The Journal of Cinema and Media* 58, no. 1–2 (2017): 9, http://www.jstor. org/stable/10.13110/framework.58.1-2.0007.

POST-ANTHROPOCENTRISM 241

9. Galt, "The Animal Logic," 7–8.
10. Galt, "The Animal Logic," 9.
11. Richardson, *Surrealism and Cinema*, 207.
12. Galt, "The Animal Logic," 20.
13. Richardson, *Surrealism and Cinema*, 207.
14. Derek Ryan's concept of *animalous* is defined as "not that which is outside of the group or divergent within it, but that individual who forms a porous border between the group and its Outside." Derek Ryan, *Virginia Woolf and the Materiality of Theory: Sex, Animal, Life* (Edinburgh: Edinburgh University Press, 2013), 159.
15. Claire Henry, *Eraserhead* (London: British Film Institute/Bloomsbury, 2023), 7–27.
16. Howard Fishman, "I Accidentally Walked into "Border" and It Kind of Changed My Life," *The New Yorker*, November 28, 2018, https://www.newyorker.com/culture/cult ure-desk/i-accidentally-walked-into-border-and-it-kind-of-changed-my-life.
17. Pamela Willoughby, *The Evolution of Modern Humans in Africa: A Comprehensive Guide* (Lanham, MD: AltaMira Press, 2007), 34.
18. Pick, "Review of Giorgio Agamben," 4.
19. Giorgio Agamben, *The Open: Man and Animal*, trans. Kevin Attell (Stanford, CA: Stanford University Press, 2004), 26.
20. Ben Nicholson, "Border," *Sight & Sound* 29, no. 4 (April 2019): 59.
21. Pick, "Review of Giorgio Agamben," 4.
22. Donna Haraway, *The Companion Species Manifesto: Dogs, People, and Significant Otherness* (Chicago: Prickly Paradigm Press, 2003), 16.
23. J. H. Matthews, "Surrealism and the Cinema," *Criticism* 4, no. 2 (Spring 1962): 129, https://www.jstor.org/stable/23091086.
24. Pick, "Review of Giorgio Agamben," 7.
25. Pettman, *Human Error*, 7.
26. Richardson, *Surrealism and Cinema*, 171.
27. Richardson, *Surrealism and Cinema*, 9.
28. René Descartes, *Discourse on Method*, 1637, in *Descartes: Selected Philosophical Writings*, ed. John Cottingham and Robert Stoothoff (Cambridge: Cambridge University Press, 1988), 36.
29. Peter Bradshaw, "On Body and Soul Review—Bizarre and Brutal Tale of Lovers in the Slaughterhouse," *The Guardian*, September 21, 2017, https://www.theguardian.com/film/2017/sep/21/on-body-and-soul-review-ildiko-enyedi.
30. Walter Benjamin, "Surrealism: The Last Snapshot of the European Intelligentsia," 1929, in *Reflections*, ed. Peter Demetz, trans. Edmund Jephcott (New York: Schocken, 1986), 190.
31. Adam Lowenstein, *Dreaming of Cinema: Spectatorship, Surrealism, and the Age of Digital Media* (New York: Columbia University Press, 2015), 3; André Breton, "Manifesto of Surrealism," 1924, in *Manifestoes of Surrealism*, trans. Richard Seaver and Helen R. Lan (Ann Arbor: University of Michigan Press, 1994), 14.
32. Agamben, *The Open*, 16.
33. Agamben, *The Open*, 16.
34. Ildikó Enyedi, "Film Review: *On Body and Soul* (Ildikó Enyedi)," interview by Charles Martig, *Journal of Religion, Film and Media* 3, no. 2 (2017): 87, https://doi.org/10.25364/05.3:2017.2.8.

242 SCREENING THE POSTHUMAN

35. Pick, "Review of Giorgio Agamben," 11.
36. Richardson, *Surrealism and Cinema*, 3, 10.
37. Manohla Dargis, "The Fabulist Who Confounded Cannes," *New York Times*, June 26, 2005, 12.
38. Lowenstein, *Dreaming of Cinema*, 3.
39. David Teh, "Itinerant Cinema: The Social Surrealism of Apichatpong Weerasethakul," *Third Text* 25, no. 5 (2011): 604.
40. Teh, "Itierant Cinema," 604.
41. Sinéad Garrigan Mattar, "Yeats, Fairies, and the New Animism," *New Literary History* 43, no. 1 (2012): 139.
42. Nurit Bird-David, "'Animism' Revisited: Personhood, Environment Epistemology," *Current Anthropology* 40, no. 151 (1999): 69.
43. Anselm Franke, "Animism," in *Posthuman Glossary*, ed. Rosi Braidotti, and Maria Hlavajova (London: Bloomsbury Academic, 2018), 40.
44. Graham Harvey, *Animism: Respecting the Living World* (London: Hurst & Co, 2005), 203.
45. Harvey, *Animism*, xi.
46. Harvey, *Animism*, xiv.
47. Harvey, *Animism*, xiv–xv.
48. Anthony Carew, "Cinema Reincarnated: Apichatpong Weerasethakul and Thai Cinema's Radical New Life," *Metro* 176 (Autumn 2013): 36.
49. Isaac Marrero-Guillamón, "The Politics and Aesthetics of Non-Representation: Reimagining Ethnographic Cinema with Apichatpong Weerasethakul," *Antípoda. Revista de Antropología y Arqueología* 33 (2018): 28.
50. May Adadol Ingawanij, "Animism and the Performative Realist Cinema of Apichatpong Weerasethakul," in *Screening Nature: Cinema beyond the Human*, ed. Anat Pick, and Guinevere Narraway (New York: Berghahn, 2013), 91.
51. James Quandt, ed., *Apichatpong Weerasethakul* (Wien: Austrian Film Museum, 2009), 76.
52. Marrero-Guillamón, "The Politics and Aesthetics," 26.
53. Manohla Dargis, "A Spectral Tale of Love Found in War," *New York Times*, October 2, 2004, https://www.nytimes.com/2004/10/02/movies/a-spectral-tale-of-love-found-in-war.html.
54. Dargis. "The Fabulist Who Confounded Cannes," 12.
55. Dennis Lim, "To Halve and to Hold," *Village Voice*, June 19, 2005, 50, https://www.villagevoice.com/2005/06/21/to-halve-and-to-hold/
56. Carew, "Cinema Reincarnated," 38.
57. Lim, "To Halve and to Hold," 50.
58. Marrero-Guillamón, "The Politics and Aesthetics," 25.
59. Nathan Lee, "Back to Basics," *Film Comment* 47, no. 4 (July–August 2011): 54.
60. Michael Richardson and Krzysztof Fijalkowski, "The Supreme Point," in *Surrealism: Key Concepts*, ed. Krzysztof Fijalkowski and Michael Richardson (New York: Routledge, 2016), 248.

POST-ANTHROPOCENTRISM 243

61. Apitchatpong Weerasethakul, "Exquisite Corpus," interview by James Quandt, *Artforum International* 43, no. 9 (May 2005): 230.
62. Lee, "Back to Basics," 54.
63. Agamben, *The Open*, 83.
64. Frances L. Restuccia, "Agamben's Open: Coetzee's Dis-grace," *Comparative Literature* 69, no. 4 (2017): 417, https://doi.org/10.1215/00104124-4260436.
65. Ji-Hoon Kim, "Between Auditorium and Gallery: Perception in Apichatpong Weerasethakul's Films and Installations," in *Global Art Cinema: New Theories and Histories*, ed. Rosalind Galt and Karl Schoonover (New York: Oxford University Press, 2010), 132.
66. Daniel Grinberg, "Time and Time Again: The Cinematic Temporalities of Apichatpong Weerasethakul," *Mediascape* (August 2015), https://web.archive.org/web/20200715092012/http://www.tft.ucla.edu/mediascape/Fall2015_TimeAndTimeAgain.html.
67. Nicholas Godfrey, "Love Over the Borderline: Tenderness and Transformation in Phuttiphong Aroonpheng's Manta Ray," *Metro* 202 (October 2019): 66.
68. Joshua Minsoo Kim, "Review: *Manta Ray* Is a Story of Friendship with a Necessarily Humanist Outlook," *Slant Magazine*, March 26, 2019, https://www.slantmagazine.com/film/review-manta-ray-tells-a-story-of-friendship-with-a-necessarily-humanist-outlook/.
69. Franke, "Animism," 39.
70. Minsoo Kim, "Review: *Manta Ray*."
71. Harvey, *Animism: Respecting the Living World*, xvii.
72. Phuttiphong Aroonpheng, "*Manta Ray* Director Q&A, TIFF 2018," *TIFF Talks*, September 12, 2018, video, https://www.youtube.com/watch?v=h7yOCm1v2Sw.
73. Godfrey, "Love Over the Borderline," 67.
74. Eva Hayward, "Lessons from a Starfish," in *Queering the Non/Human*, ed. Noreen Giffney, and Myra J. Hird (Farnham: Ashgate, 2008), 258.
75. Isabelle Stengers, "Reclaiming Animism," *e-flux* 36 (July 2012), https://bit.ly/35e6j9U.
76. Stengers, "Reclaiming Animism."
77. Wolfe, *What Is Posthumanism?*, xviii–xix.

7

The Eco-material Posthuman in the Age of the Anthropocene

Pansy Duncan

As the earlier chapters of this book have shown, the posthuman features in a range of different discourses, from speculative accounts of the cyborg futures implied by radical techno-scientific innovation, to interrogations of the animal/human interface in the wake of recent processes of species extinction. Yet the past few years have seen critics situate the posthuman in another, altogether new conjunction. More specifically, scholars associated with the posthuman, like Stacy Alaimo, Rosi Braidotti, and Donna Haraway, have begun to yoke this figure to the "Anthropocene," understood as a geologic epoch dating from the first evidence that human beings had significantly altered earth's ecosystems.[1] This emerging dialogue between the posthuman and the Anthropocene should come as no surprise. For while elevating the human to the status of geological agent, the Anthropocene also strips the human of its claims to mastery over the natural world—describing, as it does, a set of far-reaching phenomena, like anthropogenic climate change, accelerated species extinction, and changes to the form of the earth's surface, which exceed our control and threaten our existence. In the Anthropocene, that is, "the substance of what was once called 'nature' acts, interacts, and even intra-acts within, through, and around human bodies and practices," revealing, in the process, unexpected overlaps between human and nonhuman worlds.[2] In this respect, the Anthropocene marks a profound challenge to familiar humanist orthodoxies—a challenge that is reflected in the rise of a new strain of posthumanism committed to thinking through the implications of this crisis for ideas about the human. As Alaimo describes this, the recognition brought about by the Anthropocene, "that human activity has altered the planet on the scale of a geological epoch" effectively "muddles the commonsensical assumption that the world exists as a background for the human subject" in ways that have inspired new posthumanist engagements.[3]

Pansy Duncan, *The Eco-material Posthuman in the Age of the Anthropocene*. In: *Screening the Posthuman*.
Edited by: Missy Molloy, Pansy Duncan, and Claire Henry, Oxford University Press. © Oxford University Press 2023.
DOI: 10.1093/oso/9780197538562.003.0008

As this suggests, this dialogue between the posthuman and the Anthropocene has not left the former unchanged; rather, in conversation with environmental crisis, the critical shape of the posthuman has undergone something of a transformation. By way of capturing this transformation, this chapter proposes the term the "eco-material posthuman" to identify a particular iteration of posthumanism that actively rejects even the residue of fantasies of bodily transcendence, species transcendence, or technological deliverance in favor of a renewed recognition of our embedded, embodied status as beings-in-the-(natural)-world. But what is at play in the "eco-material posthuman"? This novel sub-genre of posthumanist thought, I suggest, draws on features of what has become known as the "new materialism," (introduced in Chapter 3), an interdisciplinary body of inquiry that is spearheaded by figures such as Jane Bennett, Karen Barad, and Elizabeth Grosz, and that insists on what Alaimo calls "the agency and significance of matter."[4] Three primary developments animate so-called new materialism: advancements in the natural sciences that project a considerably more complex and elusive model of matter; historical developments like climate change and biotechnological engineering; and, finally, critiques of older poststructuralist frameworks' tendency to dismiss matter altogether.[5] The specific aspects of matter that have preoccupied this field, of course, diverge. They range from Bennett's work on material objects as performative agents in political life, to Brian Massumi and Eve Sedgwick's work on the affective dimension of the body, to the philosophical work of theorists Ian Bogost and Graham Harman on the ontology of the "stuff" that populates late consumer capitalism ("mountains, fruit, atmospheric effects, nuclear warheads, sandwiches, automobiles, historical events, relics").[6] Theoretical and methodological diversity aside, however, this body of literature converges on its commitment to exploring material and somatic realities beyond their ideological and discursive inscriptions while reworking received models of matter as either an inert, passive, uniform substance or as a socially constructed fact. In their place, a model of materiality as excess, force, vitality, relationality, or difference has come to the fore.

The term the "eco-material posthuman," then, captures the *materialist leanings* common to posthumanist critics seeking to grapple with the Anthropocene—leanings that see many such critics return to the materiality of the human body as a key resource for their posthumanist reconfigurations of the human and its relationship to the world around it. Exemplary of this tendency is the recent work of Haraway, one of the preeminent thinkers of the posthuman, who inflects her long-standing critiques of humanism with a new emphasis on the human body's organic status as decaying matter, announcing that, today, "I am a compost-ist, not a posthuman-ist: we are all compost, not posthuman."[7] Similarly, Braidotti's observation that the interface between environmentalism and the posthuman amounts to a "struggle for new *concrete* forms of universality" uses the materiality or "concrete[ness]" of life as a means of dissolving the exceptionalism that attaches to the category of the "human."[8] In the same vein, Stacy Alaimo suggests that "exposing human flesh" is one way of "dispers[ing] and displac[ing] human exceptionalism" in the context of the Anthropocene.[9] Across the work of these three authors, in other words, the human body materializes not as the "measure of man" but as a membrane connecting the human to animal, vegetable, and mineral worlds. Certainly, discussion of the posthuman has always accommodated this complex relation between human and nonhuman animal, technological and natural worlds. But in conversation with the Anthropocene, the posthuman—or what I am calling the "eco-materialist posthuman"—acquires a distinct materialist force in its construction of the human body as the primary point of convergence between the human and the nonhuman "outside."

This chapter argues that a distinct body of feature films examining the fallout of the Anthropocene reflects the critical tendencies I have collected under the rubric of the "eco-material posthuman." The films in question are geographically and culturally diverse, ranging from 2006's *Still Life* (Jia Zhangke) to 2018's *Woman at War* (Benedikt Erlingsson) and 2018's *Mother!* (Darren Aronofsky). All, however, fully attend to the questions the Anthropocene raises about the interdependence of humans and nonhuman worlds. And all resonate with the "eco-material posthuman" in their recourse to the materiality of the human body as a vehicle for the kind of novel cross-species alliances and identifications we have come to associate with posthumanism. Certainly, many films in dialogue with the Anthropocene as a historical context, from Roland Emmerich's *The Day After Tomorrow* (2004) to Frank Guo's *The Wandering Earth* (2019), tow a humanist line. Such films cannot be said to mirror emerging critical accounts of what we have called the "eco-material posthuman." Yet films that broach the Anthropocene *while also* rising to the challenge it poses to the category of the human do so, we contend, by returning to the materiality of the human body, where the human body is understood as a point of connection with other, non-human materialities rather than as a marker of human difference. While the models of human bodily materiality at issue here are diverse, thereby corresponding to the diversity of such models within "eco-material posthuman" discourse, this chapter will zero in on three models in particular. The first is the body as *cell*, understood as the basic biological unit of life that is shared across species and life forms more generally. The second is the body as *affect*, as a bodily intensity that eludes the forms of subjectivity that underpin conventional models of the human. The third is the body as *vital materiality*—what Braidotti calls "the dynamic, self-organizing structure of life itself" characterized by "generative vitality."[10] These models of the human body cast it not as a signifier or guarantor of human exceptionalism but as an aperture to the nonhuman outside. In leveraging these models, the films in question weave a powerful posthuman fabric out of the threadbare realities of climate change.

Body as Cell: *Annihilation* and *Woman at War*

Alex Garland's *Annihilation* (2018) epitomizes this trend. Generically, the film continues the tradition of eco-horror, refracting the anxieties associated with the Anthropocene through the lens of a phenomenon the film dubs "the Shimmer"—a zone of mutability that has already engulfed a huge swath of coastal forest on the West Coast of the United States and that seems set to creep further inland "until it encompasses everything," as one character puts it. While under intense, twenty-four-hour scrutiny by the scientists at Southern Reach, the government facility tasked with monitoring it, the Shimmer remains an enigma; until very recently not a single member of the many expeditions beyond its translucent exterior has returned. Into this context enters cellular biology professor and army veteran Lena (played by Natalie Portman). The wife of the only person who has "made it back" thus far (Kane, played by Oscar Isaac), and desperate to understand the source of her husband's mysterious neurological and physiological symptoms, Lena leaps at the invitation to join yet another mission into the recesses of the Shimmer. In typical action thriller fashion, the film teams her up with several others: psychologist Ventress (played by Jennifer Jason Leigh), physicist Josie (played by Tessa Thompson), geomorphologist Cass (played by Tuva Novotny), and paramedic Anya (played by Gina Rodriguez). But what gives *Annihilation* its defining "posthuman" kick is that the mission into the Shimmer is not just a journey into an alien environment.

248 SCREENING THE POSTHUMAN

Rather, it is the occasion for a series of questions about what it means to be human. As Garland's characters move through the strange ecosystem, they realize that the Shimmer functions as what one character calls a "prism" for DNA, scrambling and exchanging their cellular material with that of the plants and animals around them.

Valuable for our purposes, however, is that the material body—or rather, the body's cellular structure—becomes the mechanism through which this dizzying exchange between human and nonhuman worlds takes place. Garland's previous film, *Ex Machina* (2014), provides a perfect foil in this respect. While this earlier feature, also a Sci-Fi thriller, explored similar posthuman thematics (see Chapter 1), it did so through a far more conventional chronotope, namely the scene of artificial intelligence, meaning that its destabilization of the human turned on the psychological and cognitive proximity of the robot Ava (played by Alicia Vikander) and her human counterpart, Caleb (played by Domhnall Gleeson). In that scenario, then, the boundary between the human and the broader nonhuman world, in all its animal and vegetal diversity, remains essentially untouched. In *Annihilation*, however, it is the human body's cellular structure that connects the human and the nonhuman, as the film exploits the cell's status as the basic unit of *all* known organisms to trouble narratives that set the human apart from other forms of being. Indeed, the opening sequence of the film establishes this vision of the cell by transporting us back to Lena's life prior to her involvement in the expedition. The visual track shows black-and-white microscopic imagery of cells blown up to resemble spiky seedpods. As the cells tremble and multiply, Lena's voice-over intones:

> This is a cell. Like all cells, it is born from an existing cell. By extension, all cells were ultimately born from one cell, a single organism, alone on planet earth, perhaps alone in the universe . . . one became two, two became four . . . the rhythm of the dividing pair, which becomes the structure of every microbe, blade of grass, sea creature, land creature, and human . . . the structure of everything that lives and everything that dies.

The emphasis here is on the cell as a common element of all living things, a shared currency in which the "microbe, [the] blade of grass, [the] sea creature, [the] land creature, and [the] human" have a rough equivalence. The setting is quickly revealed as a college classroom, the monologue part of a lecture to pre-med students that Lena is delivering as a professor of biology—a profession organized around questions related to the mechanisms that structure life at a material level.

The film's turn to the cell resonates with the work of a number of theorists associated with the new materialism. Emphasizing the cell's challenge to conventional models of the human, this new research on the cellular aspect of the body provides scope for multiple points of intersection or "intra-action" between the human and nonhuman. On the one hand, it underscores the cell's status as a point of ontological commonality between human and nonhuman worlds: all life forms are ultimately cellular, which is to say that the cell is a common building block that links humans not only with nonhuman animals but also with the vegetable kingdom. On the other, it identifies the cell as a unit in what Barad has called the "intra-action" *between* the human and nonhuman worlds, where "intra-action" is a neologism that "recognizes the ontological inseparability" of the terms under discussion (in contrast to *interaction*, which relies on positing the prior existence of separately determinate entities).[11] Sociologist of science Rebecca Scott Yoshiawa, for example, describes the "bidirectional exchange of cells between mother and conceptus (or between twins)" in the course of a pregnancy, while Haraway, a science and technology studies scholar, celebrates intra-actions between the human cell and the cells of the microbiome:

> I love the fact that human genomes can be found in only about 10% of the cells that occupy the mundane space I call my body; the other 90% of the cells are filled with genomes of bacteria, fungi, protists, and such, some of which play in a symphony necessary to my being alive at all, and some of which are hitching a ride and doing the rest of me, of us, no harm . . . To be one is always to be many.[12]

This new materialist investment in the cell, of course, sits in contrast to more conservative returns to the figure of the cell, as in what Jackie Stacey dubs the "new genetics" where a general "geneticization of the body" reduces the human deterministically *to* the cell while feeding into what Haraway calls "the informatics of domination."[13] By contrast, new materialist theorists attentive to the cell seek to avoid crude reductionism by recasting biology in dynamic, energistic, nondeterministic terms that emphasize its unpredictable and potentially emancipatory qualities.

Admittedly—Lena's professional credentials notwithstanding—the rising sense of dread at play across the first section of *Annihilation* is animated not by an understanding of the shared cellular dimension of *all* life, but by encounters with specific *life forms*. As the crew of scientists make their way deeper into the Shimmer, they stumble across a series of increasingly disconcerting spectacles: a plant that yields several radically different species of flowers; a crocodile with the teeth of a shark; a technicolor lichen scaling the walls of an abandoned Southern Reach building; deer whose antlers sprout cherry blossoms. Framed as entirely alien and other, these spectacles initially only serve to bolster the scientists' exceptionalist visions of the human as a beacon of rationality in a natural world gone awry. Yet as the group gradually comes to appreciate the biological foundations of these phenomena, they are drawn into the film's horror spectacle. Two key sequences, both of which see human body parts grotesquely conjoined to and entwined with aspects of the natural world, are apposite here (Figure 7.1). During their exploration of

Figure 7.1 Human/nonhumans entanglements in an empty swimming pool, in *Annihilation* (Alex Garland, 2018): Lena encounters Cass's body, which has merged with the roots of a tree.

the original Southern Reach headquarters, they find themselves in an abandoned and emptied-out swimming pool. There, they find a grotesque sight: a Matthew Barney-esque altarpiece in which crystallized animal, vegetable, and mineral elements converge around a central orifice from which a human groin and torso awkwardly emerge, as if already partially ingested. A later scene, in which Lena finally locates the missing Cass, similarly visualizes this human/nonhuman conjunction: Cass's hair is woven into the roots of the trees to form a kind of arboreal burial casket. If the Anthropocene amounts to "the recognition that human activity has altered the planet on the scale of a geological epoch," here, the human body has, quite literally, "become sedimented in [Earth's] geology," Cass's corpse "embedded in, exposed to, and even composed of the very stuff of a rapidly transforming material world."[14]

Only later in the film, however, is the cellular aspect of organic life—itself a significant point of contact between human beings and the nonhuman universe beyond—fully implicated in the genesis of these strange animal-vegetable-mineral hybrids. The group of explorers—now four, after Cass's demise—stumble across a series of bizarre topiary-like plants that have taken on humanoid forms as the camera pans warily around them. Josie's assessment of the situation is that these plants possess "human hox genes"—a group of related genes that specify the body plan of an embryo, or, as Lena puts it, "the genes that define the body plan, the physical structure." Human cells and plant cells have intermingled to create bizarre new entities—entities in which the "trans-corporeal" connections between human bodies and the natural environment theorized by new materialist scholars find concrete form.[15] For Josie, this revelation points to a deeper truth about the Shimmer as a whole:

> The light waves aren't blocked, they're refracted. It's the same with the radios. The signals aren't gone. They're scrambled . . . The shimmer is a prism, but it refracts everything it touches, not just light and radio-waves . . . animal DNA, plant DNA—all DNA.

The work of the Shimmer, in other words, is not to destroy or "block," but rather to "scramble" or "refract" in ways that reveal the foundational interchangeability between entities conventionally viewed as discrete and separate, especially human beings and the animal and vegetable worlds to which

252   SCREENING THE POSTHUMAN

they are so often opposed. And when it comes to living beings, the cell is the Shimmer's primary currency.

The human and ethical interest of the film, however, lies in its use of the ensemble cast to dramatize the wealth of different responses to which a recognition of our cellular articulation to the nonhuman might give rise. For Anya, for example, who clings to fantasies of human uniqueness and singularity, the possibility that her body is in cellular dialogue with other life forms insults her basic self-conception. Desperate to convince herself that the biological aberrations she sees around her are the result of human malice rather than impersonal process, she binds the other members of the team to chairs and demands answers, from Lena in particular. Yet the recognition that, at the basic cellular level, our bodies are "the very stuff of the emergent material world," can equally engender a very different response.[16] Shaken by this episode, which culminates in Anya's violent death at the teeth of a grotesque bear-pig crossbreed, Josie and Lena congregate in the glade of humanoid trees visited earlier. A reflective Josie observes that the process of refraction visible in the trees is already "in" both of them, and, further, that "Ventress wants to face it, you want to fight it, but I don't think I want either of those things." At this, she stands up, walks into the garden, disappears from view and assumes arboreal form. In Josie, then, the film depicts a quiet acquiescence to what Braidotti might call our "transversal inter-connection" with nonhuman entities and actors, a willing embrace of human/nonhuman intra-action.[17] Yet there is a deeper, allegorical level here. If a posthuman approach to death involves recasting this "ultimate subtraction" as yet "another phase in a generative process," Josie's calm compact with our genetic "annihilation" is a submission to death that is itself posthuman.[18]

The role of the cell in mediating this connection between human and nonhuman crystallizes in the final section of the film, which sees Lena, now traveling alone, descend into the hole created by the meteor. There, she finds Ventress, who delivers a deranged oration about the nature of the Shimmer before disintegrating into a glowing orb. As Lena stares into said orb, a drop of blood forms on the bridge of her nose and is sucked into the golden morass suspended before her. There it hovers—a single, trembling cell, reminiscent in form not of the standard cells shown in the boilerplate black-and-white footage of cellular division that opened the film, but of the more aberrant set of cells visible under Lena's microscope during her investigation of a drop of her own blood just a few scenes before. Like that second set of cells, this one appears to be shot through with a kind of quivering rainbow jelly—meant to indicate, one assumes, its subjection to the logic of the Shimmer. Suddenly, it begins to divide and divide again, multiplying at pace against a thunderous techno backdrop. With repeated cuts back to Lena's face showing her deepening horror, the pulsating bundle of cells begins to resolve into a silver-skinned humanoid creature. Lena recoils, aghast (Figure 7.2). The creature is the ultimate alien, in the technical sense: morphologically human but stripped of identifying or expressive features, its uncanny status is only amplified by its structural similarity to its human source. Yet, threateningly nonhuman, it is also manifestly made up of human blood cells: blood of Lena's blood, cell of her cell. In this sense, it encapsulates the film's use of the human cell to underscore a radical kinship between human beings and their others—a kinship that it casts as alternately liberating and horrifying.

Benedikt Erlingsson's whimsical Icelandic comedy-drama *Woman at War* also takes the despoliation of the planet as its subject matter, and also, in the process, stages a vision of the posthuman that leans heavily on the body reduced to its cellular level. Set in the idyllic Icelandic highlands, the film tells the story of Hella (played by Halldóra Geirharödóttir), a seemingly

Figure 7.2 A cell appears before Lena and develops into a humanoid creature.

unassuming choir conductor who runs a side-racket as an eco-warrior committed to "direct action" (for example, purposely damaging electricity pylons supplying the power to the local "Rio Tinto" aluminum plant). Indeed, the film's inciting incident is the revelation that foreign governments aim to further exploit Iceland's resources, which prompts Hella to plan her most ambitious intervention yet. Narratively, then, the film turns on her radical work as a climate change activist (and her efforts to reconcile this activism with her desire to adopt a child from Ukraine). Thematically, however, *Woman at War* seeks to interrogate the forces driving climate change by putting pressure on the images of the human that sustain it. As I will show, the film accomplishes this in large part through a return to the materiality of the body at the level of the cell, which is deployed as a means of challenging the models of the human for which it is often thought to provide a material foundation. *Woman at War* does this in two ways: first, through scenes that emphasize the cell's status as a basic of unit of life shared between human and nonhuman animals; and second, through scenes that suggest its elusiveness as a unit for measuring and monitoring the human.

Importantly, *Woman at War*'s emphasis on the radical inter-corporeal properties of the human cell emerges against the backdrop of a series of government strategies designed to exploit the cell's "informational substrate" as part of what Haraway calls an "informatics of domination"—new biotechnological mechanisms of intelligibility that serve to informationalize the human body.[19] As Hella sprints across the highland after completing the film's opening "intervention," for example, a helicopter deploying

Figure 7.3 In *Kona fer í stríð/Woman at War* (Benedikt Erlingsson, 2018), Helga registers as an orange streak on a purple landscape in the police helicopter's thermal imaging mechanism.

thermal imaging devices pursues her in an effort to track down the "mountain woman" (Figure 7.3) Thermal imaging processes rely on the fact that the amount of thermal radiation an object emits increases with temperature; and to the extent that living cellular organisms are warmer than non-living, non-cellular entities, and thus more readily visible, this technology clearly exploits the cell as part of a system of population monitoring and control.

But thermal imaging is not the only technology at play in the film that helps to transform the body from a biological object of knowledge into an orderly set of biological components. Later, having successfully dodged the police helicopter, Hella sets out on a different assignment, to the local airport, with the intention of traveling to Ukraine to finalize an adoption process she had set in motion many years before. And while the scene initially seems set to provide an uplifting conclusion to the film, it quickly takes a dystopian turn. Arriving at the security gates and already nervous about detection, Hella finds that travelers are being asked to provide a "biological sample" that will aid police in their effort to apprehend the elusive guerrilla activist by comparing traveler DNA data with DNA data from plasma Hella left on a rock during her flight across the moors. Her escape efforts foiled, Hella departs the airport—only to be arrested and forcibly "sampled" in the very next scene, after her cab driver reports her for suspicious behavior. As this suggests, the "informatics of domination" treats DNA, the informational heart of the cell, as the "truth" of the individual body, and thus as valuable currency within systems of population tracking and control.

Yet for *Woman at War*, the human cell eludes efforts to recruit it as part of an "informatics of domination." And as the second sequence in the film featuring a police helicopter using thermal imaging to track Hella demonstrates, this is because living cells are common to both human and nonhuman organisms. A series of shots at ground level show Hella edging her way into the shelter of a cave, where she takes up residence next to the rotting carcass of a sheep. Further shots from within the throbbing interior of the helicopter, manned by two black-clad pilots, show the imaging device itself and, on it, a mobile point of light that suggests a body moving through the screen's magenta and yellow technicolor landscape. "Wait! Wait there! Is something there?," cries one of the pilots. As an audience, we buy their conviction that the moving light-point represents Hella, and assume that, put off by the stench of the dead animal, she had left the cave. But a few seconds later, the second pilot calls out "negative," while the first sighs in frustration at the spectacle of "Another bloody sheep! They're everywhere. They must stop

Figure 7.4 At the level of thermal imaging technology, Helga is interchangeable with the animal other.

them from running all over the place . . ." It is only when the film cuts back to the ground that the viewer understands what has happened, as the film shows Hella emerging from the sheep, easing its heavy carcass off her body, and wiping its entrails from her face (Figure 7.4). At stake here is the literal interchangeability at the thermal—and thus cellular—level between Hella and her ruminant kin. To descend to the cellular level of the body is to reveal Hella's "self [as] . . . the very stuff of the emergent material world."[20]

This is not the only moment in the film where the human cell confounds the systems of "molecular biopower" that it also sustains. As the cell's information storage mechanism, located in its nucleus, DNA is the ostensible guarantee of the presence of a singular human individual. Yet this promise to identify and distinguish conceals an equal and opposite potential for deception and duplicity. And this potential is no better realized than in the phenomenon of identical twins, of which Hella and her sister, Ása (also played by Halldóra Geirharðdóttir), a yoga teacher and meditation enthusiast, are an example. As Stacey has shown, "embod[ying] an uncanny synthesis of sameness and difference," identical twins "defy the conventional demarcations around the singularity of the human body" and thus the mechanisms of biosurveillance that depend on such demarcations.[21] Certainly, while sharing Hella's DNA code, Ása has a radically different approach to life. And DNA's capacity to confound as well as distinguish is one that Ása, if not Hella, is willing to exploit, as shown in the bravura suspense sequence that follows Hella's arrest.

The sequence in question takes place at the local prison facility, where the police have incarcerated Hella after her apprehension. It opens with a rhythmically edited, almost entirely dialogue-free series of shots tracking Ása's arrival at the facility: a series of doors being unlocked, opened, and relocked, a guard announcing that Hella is about to receive a "guest," and Hella being ushered out of her cell, down a corridor and into another. The sequence climaxes in the new cell, as Ása enters, her dazzling red silk turban and jerkin a stark contrast to Hella's gray prison sweats, as a series of shot/reverse-shots further underscores the vertiginous complex of identity and difference between the two women. What follows involves two abrupt reversals of roles. While by this point in the film, Ása is established as the twin bent on "retreating" *from* the world through meditation and Hella as the twin committed to "direct action" *in* the world (whether through cutting pylons or adopting a Ukrainian orphan), Ása announces that "you [Hella] will stay here and will turn this house, this prison, into your haven, your convent," while she, Asa will go to Ukraine "to become Nika's mother." Yet as Ása goes on to reveal, *she* will take on the role of "Hella" from this point on, staying in prison in Hella's place, while Hella travels, *as* Ása, to pick up the little girl.[22] Here, DNA's capacity to confound as well as distinguish helps break down humanist models that depend on what Dominique Janicaud calls "the individual singularity of the human being."[23] In this sense, the twin swap points to our replicability at a biological level, a replicability that further embeds the eco-material connection between human and nonhuman in the context of the Anthropocene.

Body as Affect: *Mother!*

A film that takes place almost exclusively in the interior of a house, with scant reference to the natural world beyond, director Darren Aronofsky's *Mother!* would seem an unlikely candidate for inclusion in a chapter about screen visualizations of the eco-material posthuman in the context of the Anthropocene. Both narrative cues and directorial commentary, however, invite us to read the film allegorically, with Jennifer Lawrence's Mother representing Mother Earth or Gaia, Javier Bardem moonlighting as the creator, and Michelle Pfeiffer playing Eve to Ed Harris's Adam. Seen through this allegorical lens, the film's ecological allegiances are obvious. This Mother Earth is relentlessly bullied, abused, and exploited—her home ransacked, her body beaten, and her baby murdered before she avenges herself by setting the entire house alight, using oil (a fossil fuel) as her accelerant. What

258 SCREENING THE POSTHUMAN

gives the film its force for our purposes, moreover, is the coupling of this fable-like critique of the Anthropocene with an interrogation of the category of the human, and, more specifically, an embrace of the materiality of the human body. Indeed, *Mother!* is perhaps more markedly eco-materialist than *Annihilation* and *Woman at War* in the sheer literalism of the return to the body it imagines, since, at least on the surface, it eschews environmental thematics in favor of human drama. Yet whereas the node of human bodily materiality that preoccupies *Annihilation* is the cell, *Mother!* zeroes in on *affect*, "the body's response to stimuli at a precognitive and prelinguistic level."[24] As Brian Massumi describes it, if "an emotion is . . . the socio-linguistic fixing of the quality of an experience," affect takes place in the half-second before physiological responses are "owned and recognized."[25] Affect, in other words, names a physiological response prior to its "insertion" into the personalized emotional dramas that form the basis for humanist models of the subject.[26]

Affect's capacity to erode conventional human/nonhuman distinctions and to connect humans to "multiple and external [non-human] others" operates along two registers. The first is the register of *similitude, affinity, or identity*. Fantasies of human exceptionalism tend to reify consciousness as the site of human specificity, yet affect's material status as what Nigel Thrift calls "a roiling mass of nerve volleys [that] prepare the body for action . . . before the conscious self is even aware of them" reveals our ontological coextensiveness with nonhuman forms and life forms that are at the mercy of neurochemical and biochemical processes.[27] The second is the register of *influence*, or Barad's "intra-action."[28] At stake here is the fact that, as Jo Labanyi has noted, the body understood as affect is not a "closed system (as in Freud), but . . . radically open to the world—that is, existing in a self-world continuum in which the terms 'subject' and 'object' make no sense."[29] While conventional models of *emotion* describe an entity that is "naturally contained, going no farther than the skin," to quote Teresa Brennan, theorists of *affect* describe a pre-personal entity that opens us to the nonhuman outside, breaking open the boundaries of the body in ways that are radically "at odds with subject/object thought and the visualization basic to objectification."[30]

The affective body at the heart of the film belongs, of course, to Jennifer Lawrence's "Mother"; while celebrity tends to spectacularize the body, transforming it into pure image, Aronofsky aims to *rematerialize* Lawrence by casting her embodied experience as cumbersome, laden, and difficult. Throughout, the camera stays in such close proximity to Lawrence's affected body that it makes her every strain, shudder, sigh, and wheeze painfully visible (and she wheezes frequently, the saintly bearer of all the world's respiratory and digestive troubles). The affective dimension of Lawrence's body accumulates additional force through the formal device the film uses to portray it, namely, the follow shot, which positions the camera just behind her, taking in her shoulders and the back of her head as she moves through space. According to Jennifer Barker and Adam Cottrell, the follow shot is unique in that "it denies us *both* the frontal image of the face" that an objective tracking shot facing a character might deliver, "*and* the first-person point-of-view shot's sense of . . . shared agency alongside transparent visual access to what literally lies ahead."[31] It is also quite distinct from the over-the-shoulder shot, since, in the follow shot, the character's body tends to block rather than facilitate access to the visual field in front of her. As Tarja Laine puts it, at the heart of Aronofsky's follow shots is not "emotional identification, but affective mimicry," a kind of identification at the level of the body rather than the psyche, which complements Aronofsky's tendency to "engage the spectator's lived body by means of [his films"] sheer corporeal . . . style."[32] Exemplary of this effect in the context of *Mother!* is the opening sequence, which sees the camera suspended behind Mother as she wanders the gloomy circular corridors of the house in search of Him before making her way down to the front veranda. The light of the afternoon sun is piercing, so that, standing against the door, she is in silhouette—her body neither a vehicle for subjective experience nor a vessel for objective vision but a thickened, embodied mass. Barker and Cottrell frame the ubiquity of this powerfully embodied follow shot in cinema today as a measure of the body's capacity to "ground the ways we experience the world" as a result of "the numerous pressures placed on the body to reorient itself to . . . ever more rapid, mobile, powerful and sophisticated technological commodities."[33] Yet, as I will show, we might equally imagine the ubiquity of this shot in contemporary filmmaking as an index of something else entirely—that is, as an index of a new awareness, in the wake of the Anthropocene, of the material force of the human body and thus of its potential as a point of contact between human and nonhuman worlds.[34]

How does *Mother!* mobilize the affective dimension of the body to connect the human and the nonhuman? One answer to this question involves the scene that culminates in Mother and Him having sex, and it exemplifies what I have described above as affect's disclosure of an *identity* or *similitude* between the human and nonhuman. This scene in question opens with the

260 SCREENING THE POSTHUMAN

couple having an argument—an argument that initially seems to turn on Him's decision to invite a group of strangers into the house before touching on a deeper tension in the couple's relationship, namely the fact that he consistently refuses to have sex with her. "You talked about wanting kids," Mother cries accusingly, "but you can't even fuck me!" Next, a close-up of Him's sneering face cuts to a close-up image of Mother just as Him—incensed by her implicit accusation of impotence—enters the frame, sending the camera tossing back and forth as Mother attempts to elude his aggressive embrace. At a certain point, however, she gives in and lets him kiss her and, while the camera focuses on Lawrence's face, the rhythm of the scene slows from frantic to leisurely, and her grunts turn into pants, sighs, and whimpers. At a certain point, that is, the notorious "quick[ness]" of affect sees it outpace her slower emotional responses (her rage at her monstrously self-absorbed husband, her grief at her unfulfilled desire for children).[35] Yet what is significant for our purposes here is the film's refusal to recuperate this moment of affect for the humanist individual by focusing exclusively on the human characters involved. In fact, this moment of affect inspires not renewed attention to Lawrence's face and body, but the camera's tilt upward to the ceiling. Mother is affected; and to communicate this, the camera switches its focus to an inanimate surface, suggesting an identity between the affected Mother and the supposedly inert or passive world beyond. The film's sound mix cements this identity between feeling subject and object world by tuning out the sound of Lawrence's cries in favor of the sound of waves crashing on the shore, thereby explicitly connecting her affect to the cycles of the nonhuman universe. Like a ceiling, a lightshade, a bannister, a wave, the affected Mother is not a subject—at least not in the reified humanist sense; rather, as Braidotti puts it in another context, she is "the effect of irrepressible flows of encounters, interactions . . . [that she] is not in charge of."[36] Through sound design and cinematography, then, the scene uses Mother's affect as a tool to laminate human and nonhuman worlds. From a feminist perspective, the fact that this crucial scene revolves around Mother's sexual submission to her husband is somewhat troubling, particularly in light of her initial resistance to Him. Yet to the extent that feminism itself "can be described as a re-negotiating of 'the human,'" the anti-anthropocentric logic inscribed into the scene's form may partially redeem the scene's feminist credentials.[37]

Another example of the film's use of the affective body as a means of underscoring human/nonhuman kinships, again through emphasizing similitude or identity, takes place in the wake of the murder of Younger

ECO-MATERIAL POSTHUMAN 261

Brother (played by Brian Gleeson). Much to Mother's dismay, her husband has opted to accompany Younger Brother's devastated parents to the hospital, while ordering his wife to "stay inside." Alone in the suddenly empty house, Mother retreats to the bathroom to start cleaning up. A long shot shows her seated next to the tub as a bucket fills with water. Then, we cut to a frontal close-up of her face: her expression is weary, and before too long she turns her face to the tiled wall beside her while the camera circles around to frame the back of her head. At this point, a series of shot/reverse-shots ensue in rapid succession: an extreme close-up exclusively of Mother's eyes, her gaze focused on something just out of frame; a reverse shot of what she sees, her fingers grasping the tiles at the corner; a close-up of her eyes, as she refocuses on what is directly in front of her; and a further eyeline match, this time of the tiles right in front of her face. Finally, as if a spell has been broken, the flurry of shot/reverse-shots ceases, and instead of cutting, we zoom in to the grouting between two of the tiles, the orifice-like nature of

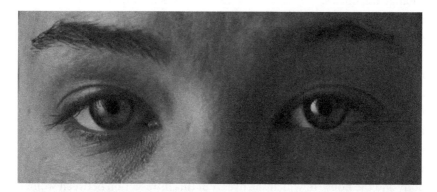

Figure 7.5 Mother stares blankly and impassively at the wall, in *Mother!* (Darren Aronofsky, 2018). The wall, in turn, acquires a "beating heart."

262 SCREENING THE POSTHUMAN

which has been exaggerated in post-production. We understand that we have passed "through" the tiles and "into" the wall, and out of the initial darkness emerges a beating heart, pink tissue pulsating in the recesses of the wall (Figure 7.5). Again, Mother's *affectedness* serves as an occasion to establish not her difference from but her affinity with the supposedly inert or passive world beyond—an affinity encapsulated by the chiastic exchange in which the ostensibly "inanimate" object, the wall, and the ostensibly agential subject, Mother, swap their properties. Across the course of the scene, Mother herself is rendered increasingly inert: her expression blank, her movements minimal. Conversely, the wall itself takes on "human" qualities—acquiring, quite literally, a heart.

Yet beyond forming the basis for the film's account of similarities between the human and the nonhuman, affect also provides a means for the film to trace the "intra-action" between her body and the nonhuman world, in which the two entities, as Barad has put it, exist in a "mutual constitution of entangled agencies."[38] This co-constitution between body and material world is established at the very beginning of the film in its envisioning of Mother's origins. The sequence in question sees Him place a crystal on a plinth in a charred and blackened room; as he does so, the ruins of the house around him morph into a gleaming, idyllic mansion, the ravaged remains of a piece of wood mutating into an exquisite polished banister. The house complete, the setting shifts to the interior of a bedroom, where a woman's body is visible beneath the bedclothes. As the camera approaches the bed, the woman moves, sits up, turns to the camera and delivers the plaintive query "baby?" while we push in on her face, suggesting the coetaneous evolution of Mother's body and the house in which she lives. But this intra-action between woman and dwelling acquires a specifically affective dimension in the second half of the film, as the house begins to crumble around Mother and as she herself disintegrates with it. By this point in the film, the house is the epicenter of a series of bloody skirmishes: fans of Him engage in violent and frenzied religious rituals, military forces release a hail of gunfire and explosions, the poet's publicist (Kristin Wiig) organizes mass executions. And Mother's affective answer to the scenes unfolding around her serves to underscore the intra-action between human and nonhuman at play in the scene. To each explosive blast or volley of bullets, Mother responds with a powerful affective salvo—a gasp, a reel, a groan—as if the shattered windows and the trampled bodies were direct physical assaults, ravaging her body with the same force as they ravage the house around her. Certainly, many accounts of feeling situate the moved body in intimate relation with the world; classic cognitive appraisal models of emotion are exemplary in this respect in predicating emotion on cognitive appraisals of events in the world. Yet in prioritizing cognition as the link between feeling and world, these models also lionize the humanist models of subjectivity that cognition sustains. In affect, however, the subject's relationship to the world is unmediated by cognition, unfolding, as Massumi puts it, in "a region where infolded tactile encounter meets . . . the qualities gathered by all five senses."[39] In this sense, affect serves as a perfect bodily tool for underscoring what Haraway calls forms of human/nonhuman "connection across the discredited breach of nature and culture."[40]

The Body as Vital Materiality: *First Reformed* and *Still Life*

While some films in what I am calling the post-Anthropocene eco-materialist posthuman lean on a model of the body as "cell" or as "affect" in their reconstruction of the human body as the hinge between human and nonhuman life-worlds, others use a different model of the body that I elaborate through the rubric of "vital materialism."[41] As described by Bennett and Braidotti, vital materialism is essentially the belief that matter itself has "life," complete with "trajectories, propensities, or tendencies of [its] own."[42] Rejecting the classical oppositions materialism/idealism and life/matter, vital materialist thinkers brush aside conventional visions of matter as inert and passive and project a model of matter as active and agential, pulsing with life and irreducible to mechanistic process. This is not to say that "life" is a special substance that is added to matter, as in older "vitalist" models. Rather, in vital materialist thinking, matter vibrates with a radically immanent life that emerges *within* and *as* matter, including—but by no means limited to— the matter of the human body. This vision of matter sits in stark contrast, of course, to the model of the body underpinning enlightenment humanism where human flesh is merely a vessel for the exercise of human perfectibility, to be sculpted and instrumentalized much like the physical environment and the nonhuman animals that populate it. Yet a number of recent films, I suggest, utilize vital materialist notions of the human body in order to resist such models, positioning human and nonhuman as part of a single system, "a knotted world of vibrant matter . . . a dense network of relations."[43]

Paul Schrader's *First Reformed* (2017) is exemplary here. The film expresses an urgent ecological message: it tells the story of Ethan Hawke's

264 SCREENING THE POSTHUMAN

Reverend Ernst Toller—the troubled minister of a small Protestant church in Snowbridge, New York, who is still processing the loss of his son Joseph—who grows slowly more cognizant of the perils of climate change in the wake of his encounter with Michael (played by Philip Ettinger), a committed environmental activist. Yet if *First Reformed* is a film "about" the Anthropocene, it is not only that. It is also—as is appropriate given the profound imbrication between the human and the nonhuman environment that the Anthropocene underscores—a film that problematizes conventional models of the human, and that does so through reference to a body framed in vital materialist terms.

That said, neither posthumanism nor the Anthropocene feature particularly prominently at the outset of the film. Indeed, the film's opening gambit—a fountain pen set scratchily to paper, with Toller's voice-over announcing his commitment to "set[ing] down all [his] thoughts and the events of [his] day in a journal" for "one year, twelve months"—sets the scene for a typically Schrader-esque drama of spiritual crisis. What follows only strengthens that impression. In Toller's crucial first encounter with Michael, for example, the passionate young man lays out a series of irrefutable, concrete facts about the abuse to which humanity has subjected the natural environment, and Toller responds by reframing these material realities in the rubric of the "crisis of faith," insisting that "this isn't about your baby, it's not about Mary, it's about you—your despair and your lack of hope." At this point in the film, Toller subscribes to a Calvinist conception of "God's creation" in which the fate of the earth and its inhabitants, whether animal, vegetable, or mineral, are merely a backdrop in the theater of (human) spiritual struggle. Yet across the course of the film, Toller's view of the situation undergoes a profound transformation. By the film's dramatic finale, in fact, he has become a radical environmentalist, committed to sacrificing his own body in the service of the disintegrating body of the planet, an exchange that places these two "bodies" on the same material plane and allies his own body's "impulsions" with those of the earth.[44] At stake here is a vital materialist model of matter that celebrates "the ties that bind us to the multiple 'others' in a vital web of complex interrelations."[45]

This vital materialist model of the human body first comes to the fore in the film's effort to ironize the fantasies of self-transcendence that animate Toller's journal project. Consider, for example, the scene immediately after his first encounter with the young couple, Mary and Michael. First, a montage of images reveals his bare, cell-like bedroom—an analogue clock; his prim, single bed; a pile of tattered religious texts; his disheveled vestments on a chair. Then, the film cuts to a medium close-up of Toller himself, who (in an act of physical self-indulgence that seems incompatible with his posture of ascetic self-denial) appears seated in the nude at a desk that also holds a large bottle of whiskey. Emphasizing what Bennet has described as the "efficacy of [matter] in excess of the human meanings, designs, or purposes they express or serve," this scene gently mocks Toller's spiritual aspirations by underscoring the appetites that exceed and confound his conscious agency. The progression of Toller's stomach cancer extends this emphasis on the unruly force of the human body in its vital materiality, albeit in terms that make a mockery of Bennett's optimistic claims about matter's lively power; early scenes showing his struggle with blood in his urine give way to scenes featuring a diagnosis of gastric cancer. If, as Braidotti notes, vital materialism marks the "loss, disappearance and disruption of the atomized, individual self," the cancer diagnosis provides a striking literalization of this loss.[46] As Stacey has put it, cancer's "malignant cells . . . threaten [the subject's] existence, disturb the subject's space," in ways that resonate heavily with the posthuman agenda.[47] It is no accident that, for Braidotti, "Death, in many respects, is the epitome of the vital materialist project," marking the point at which the human merges into what, in another context, she calls a "generative flow of becoming."[48] By these lights, Haraway's "compost, not posthuman" proves a false dichotomy: the fact that our bodies are ultimately organic matter, "food for worms," may be the ultimate affirmation of our posthuman status.[49]

First Reformed's "vital materialist" model of the body facilitates a series of productive connections across the human/nonhuman divide. This is best exemplified by the scene that takes place upon Toller's arrival home in the wake of Mary's request that he look after her now-dead husband's personal effects. The scene opens in long shot, an action-image showing a weary Toller carrying a pair of cardboard boxes and placing them on the bed. Yet a cut to a low-angle medium close-up from the uncanny "perspective" of the boxes themselves shows Toller slowing down as something in their contents catches his eye. After lingering on his face for several seconds, the film cuts, finally, to his point of view, a close-up of a pile of photographs depicting scenes of environmental devastation: a man in rubber boots cleans up after an oil spill; the feathered body of a dissected duck is stuffed with discarded electrical parts, its entrails a mass of wires and circuit boards. Next, we are shown an assortment of articles documenting environmental devastation, from the destruction of the Great Barrier Reef to the rising temperatures in Alaska, as the windy synths on the

266   SCREENING THE POSTHUMAN

soundtrack rise to a crescendo. Soon, Toller appears seated at what we take to be Michael's laptop, its blue light illuminating him dimly as he clicks through a series of articles and images (one article implicates a corporate donor to his church in environmental damage; another documents the same donor's $85,000 donation to Abundant Life). Yet, if the scene's visual track catalogues the deteriorating health of the environment, its voice-over focuses exclusively on Toller's declining physical health: "I can no longer ignore my health. I have postponed my check up too often. Yesterday I could literally barely stand." On the face of it, this leap from the tragedy of planetary ecological disaster to the more familiar chamber-drama of human bodily decay seems incongruous. Yet if a vital materialist figuration of the human body underscores the web of connections between humans and nonhuman "others," and if—as Braidotti has proposed—"death . . . is the epitome of the vital materialist project," then it comes as no surprise that Toller's own bodily decay opens him up to the claims of the natural world beyond the confines of the rectory. Unable to ignore his health, he also cannot ignore the state of the planet. Within a vital materialist frame, the two are not distinct. And this link between his imminent death and environmental catastrophe calls to mind Patricia MacCormack's equally radical efforts to put these seemingly incommensurable events on an equal footing in her insistence that the spectacle of the Anthropocene demands of us nothing less than "the cessation of human existence."[50]

The film's insistence on this vital materialist model of the body sets the stage for the striking alignment of human and nonhuman elements evident in Michael's funeral. In keeping with Michael's final requests, Toller has arranged for his funeral to take place against the backdrop of a toxic waste site, and the opening shot of the scene is the jarringly non-funereal image of a local creek, complete with a sign announcing that "Due to Water Pollution this area of the Hanston Kill is unsafe for swimming or fishing. Fish caught in this area may be contaminated and unsafe to eat." A series of awkward moments unfolds in which it is unclear whether Toller is conducting the funeral ritual for Michael or for the broader environment in which the event takes place. Toller delivers the liturgy; a small church choir sings Neil Young's environmental dirge "Who's Gonna Stand Up and Save the Earth?"; Mary awkwardly scatters the ashes into the creek. The scene nonetheless has an internal logic that the film thus far has taught us to accept. Setting human bodily decay and the decay of the natural world in direct juxtaposition, it underscores the fact that all bodies, as Bennett has contended, are part of a "shared, vital materiality" in the sense that they are "inextricably enmeshed in a dense network of relations." If "these surroundings were chosen by Michael as a repository for his physical body," it is implicitly because the two entities have a kinship to which Michael wished to draw attention.

Yet it is "life" understood as desire—where, for Braidotti, "life *is* desire," an "ontological drive to become"—that underpins the film's most compelling rendering of the vital materialist body's capacity to serve as the axis between the human and nonhuman.[51] One scene in particular crystallizes this process. As it opens, Toller is visible in a long shot through an open doorway in his poorly lit bedroom-cum-study, seated at his desk and robotically pouring himself another drink. Framed twice over—first, by the doorway itself, and second, by the wider frame provided by the vestibule—he registers as a kind of effigy or figurine, entombed in his alcoholic self-loathing. Suddenly, there is a knock on the door. It is Mary, and after describing her state of agitation, she proceeds to explain a game called "magical mystery tour" that she and Michael used to play. It involved sharing a joint and lying on top of each other, she explains, getting "as much body to body contact as possible" while looking into each other's eyes and breathing in unison. "Do you want *me* to do this?," Toller asks, at once hesitantly and hopefully. While she initially demurs, she soon admits that, yes, she does. A top shot shows Toller lying obediently on the floor while Mary mounts him; extreme close-ups show the pair's faces in profile, almost nose to nose. It is at this point of maximal physical engagement that, quite suddenly, the scene slides from slightly implausible to full-blown fantasy, its muted, gray-blue color palette blossoming into a technicolor dreamscape. Shown lying full-length on the floor of the otherwise empty room, the pair levitate just slightly before taking leave of gravity completely. As they do so, the walls of the room melt away, revealing a starry galaxy (Figure 7.6), and the composited couple float through the space as it dissolves, in turn, into a range of other increasingly despoiled landscapes, from verdant forests, to criss-crossing motorways, industrial wastelands, rubbery mountains of used tires, and polluted waterways brimming with disposable plastic. As the scene descends into hallucination, the audience, recalling Toller's pouring himself a drink, reflexively recategorizes it as a drunken fantasy, the reverend's wet dream of a beautiful, distressed damsel throwing herself upon him late at night. Yet whether fantasy or reality, this remarkable sequence points to the fact that the same "nonhuman vital force of life" at play in his sexual desire for Mary also unsettles the boundary between the dimension of life conventionally reserved for the human and the wider field of animal and nonhuman life.

Figure 7.6 From a vital materialist perspective, desire connects human beings to the wider nonhuman beyond in *First Reformed* (Paul Schraeder, 2017).

Like *First Reformed*, *Still Life* mobilizes a vital materialist model of the body as a means of bridging human and nonhuman nature-cultures in the context of the Anthropocene. In this instance, however, the film uses this vital materialist vision of the body in order to situate human bodily matter on a par with the broader material universe. At the heart of *Still Life* is the monumental Three Gorges Dam—a hydro-electric gravity dam that sits upstream of the film's primary setting, the small town of Fengjie. The world's biggest power station in terms of capacity (22,500 MW), the Three Gorges exemplifies the large-scale human interventions in the environment that epitomize the epoch known as the Anthropocene. While the Chinese Communist Party views the project as a social and economic success, to date the dam has flooded archaeological and cultural sites, triggered landslides and tidal waves, and brought about a rise in waterborne disease, while killing hundreds of people in the process. Even the official face of the project involved massive displacement, with the Chinese government ordering some 1.2 million people living on the banks of the Yangtze to evacuate to make way for construction.[52] The destruction wrought by the project casts a long shadow over the film, which is split into two sections. In the first, Han Sanming (played by Han Sanming), a coal miner from the province of Shanxi, returns to Fengjie in search of his wife, who had left him sixteen years before, taking their daughter with her. After a long and seemingly hopeless search, he finally finds his wife, only to learn that she has long since sold their daughter into indentured servitude to cover her brother's debt, and that to free the girl he must find another intensely dangerous job elsewhere. In the second story, Shen Hong (played by Zhao Tao), a nurse, searches for her husband, Guo Bin (played by Li Zhubing), who had left their shared home in Shanxi two years earlier and had made only token attempts to keep in contact.

Yet if, like *First Reformed*, *Still Life* marshals the human body (framed through a vital materialist lens) as a useful crossing-point between human and nonhuman nature-cultures, the model of the vital materialist body at play in the latter is in striking counterpoint to that at play in the former. Indeed, in *Still Life*'s account, to frame the human body through a vital materialist lens is to emphasize not the unique agency of the body but a body whose agency is no more pronounced than that of an all-too-lively material world. Certainly, this is a world in which, paradoxically, the "human intervention" at the heart of the Anthropocene takes place on a scale that confounds humanist visions of human mastery and exceptionalism. The opening credit sequence, which features an Antonioni-esque panning shot of passengers seated cheek by jowl on a barge, is illustrative here. Against the rolling of credits and the trill of a synth-enhanced woodwind instrumental, the camera glides serenely from person to person as the passengers rest, smoke, chat, read, or work, each body locked in place by the pressure of other bodies. It is only after reeling off this visual litany of other bodies that the camera alights, as if by accident, on the man who will be the protagonist of this opening section, Han Sanming. The effect of the tranquil movement of the camera from person to person across this short sequence is twofold. On the one hand, it underscores the passivity and inertia of the passengers' bodies, which, far from serving as vehicles for the agency of a series of heroic figures, seem to lack even the treacherous force of Toller's. (The passivity and inertia that defines the human body here extends across the film, as the narrative's ostensible protagonist is driven, directed, bullied, and pushed from one scene to the next.) On the other, the technique serves to flatten out specific distinctions between the passengers, refusing the Western logic of individual difference that is so bound up with notions of individual agency. Again, the film as a whole maintains this indistinction between persons. After a brief altercation with a local motorbike driver, Sanming asks, "Do you know someone called Missy Ma?," and the motorbike driver replies simply, "all girls are called Missy around here."

Matching *Still Life*'s vision of the reduction of human agency is its sense of the rise of *non*human agency, as the film affords the nonhuman material world the kind of force best articulated in Bennett's notion of "thing-power."[53] The scene in which a local motorcyclist takes Sanming to his former address on "Granite Street" exemplifies the film's ascription of "thing-power" to the material objects that many films consign to the register of production design. After a lengthy trip, Sanming and the driver reach his destination: the bare, grassy bank of a river, and beyond it, a series of barges moving placidly across the water (Figure 7.7). Dismayed by the unpopulated surroundings where he had been expecting a village, Sanming stumbles off the bike and, his back to us in mid-shot, surveys the watery scene before him as the bike's motor idles. After a long pause, he exclaims, somewhat accusingly, to the driver, who is off-screen: "It's all underwater." The driver enters the frame, explaining that "The old Fengji was flooded a while back," before explaining that Sanming's entire neighborhood has been flooded since the building of the dam, that its inhabitants have "Gone, moved out," and that the loss of this neighborhood is just the tip of the iceberg. Later, Sanming points to the ferry drifting along the river and announces, "that's where my home was; it's all gone now," before leaving the frame to re-mount the motorbike that will return him to the village. The emotional engine of the scene is the revelation that a nonhuman, non-living entity, like a dam, is capable of radically

Figure 7.7 三峡好人/*Still Life* (Jia Zhangke, 2006) presents intimate personal narratives that are deeply shaped by the geographical, social, and ecological impacts of the monumental Three Gorges Dam.

displacing people and uprooting lives—and, by extension, that the human species is not quite as potent and powerful as previously reckoned, despite its residual reputation as the driver of history. As if to underscore this revelation, the camera abandons both Sanming and the driver about halfway through the scene, panning slowly to the left. As the bike's engine sounds on the soundtrack, signaling their departure, we are left contemplating the river, a barge gliding slowly along it. Like *First Reformed*, then, *Still Life* emphasizes the "vital materiality" of the human body in order to draw attention to points of intersection between the human and nonhuman material world. Yet while *First Reformed*'s emphasis on vital materiality's human dimension leaves it vulnerable to charges of residual anthropocentrism, *Still Life* escapes this imputation. For its aim is less to underscore the agency of the human body in all its crushing, confounding materiality than to give the human bodies in which it trades the same standing as the other matter in the universe, as just one more set of forces or intensities among others.

Still Life's mobilization of a vital materialist model of matter to set human and nonhuman agents on an equal agential footing finds its clearest exemplification in the scene that introduces Shen Hong. The film shows Shen on the bridge in mid-shot, gazing at the river in the same posture of forlorn reverie that we have just left Sanming. While many films would cast Shen's moment of reverie as the prologue to an exclusively human drama focused on her mistreatment at the hands of her husband, *Still Life* works to position her private ennui as part of a broader human-nonhuman assemblage (where the latter is understood, with Bennett, as an "ad hoc grouping of diverse [social, material, and intellectual] elements").[54] From a mid-shot of Shen's back, we cut to a series of seemingly unrelated nonhuman elements, shown in montage: a dirty glove rotting on the muddy gravel; a group of flowers swaying in the wind; a series of rusting metal pipes in a field; a puddle of stained water. By situating these elements on the same plane as Shen, and paying them the same level of visual attention, the film knits them together as part of an assemblage that sees agency or efficacy "distributed across an ontologically logically heterogeneous field, rather than being a capacity localized in a human body or in a collective produced (only) by human efforts."[55]

Indeed, the film then proceeds to connect this initial assemblage to a broader industrial and manufacturing apparatus. When Shen appears again, this time in extreme long shot, she is wandering through a vast factory in which a series of male workers labor, the soundtrack vibrating with machinery. In the very next scene, meanwhile, the film brings this assemblage-based model

272 SCREENING THE POSTHUMAN

of agency into relief by setting it against the anthropocentric model of agency that underpins many older models of critical thought. Under the watchful eye of posters of an array of communist figureheads—Marx, Stalin, Mao— the scene shows a series of workers upbraiding a man who appears to be the manager of the factory. "You're the manager, it's your fault!" "What kind of manager are you? Bankrupting a 100-million-yuan factory!" Without in any way undermining revolutionary action, however, the preceding images in this sequence have suggested that, in the Anthropocene, models of agency (and, by extension, models of culpability) that focus exclusively on human individuals are inadequate to address either the conflicts dividing human societies or the devastation afflicting the "natural" environment. Like *First Reformed*, then, *Still Life* mobilizes a vital materialist model of the human body to connect human and non-human worlds. Unlike *First Reformed*, however, *Still Life* treats the "vital materiality" of *non*human bodies just as fully, and indeed links the two together in assemblage-based models of "distributed" agency that could help us unpick the knots that bind human and nonhuman worlds together in non-life-sustaining ways.

Conclusion

This chapter shows that a distinct body of feature films examining the ramifications of the Anthropocene echoes some of the central tenets of the equally distinct body of scholarship we have dubbed the "eco-material posthuman" (to capture the work of scholars like Alaimo and Braidotti whose critical responses to the climate crisis combine posthuman concerns with those of the new materialisms). While the films in question are geographically and culturally disparate, all grapple with the questions the Anthropocene raises about the interconnection of humans and nonhuman worlds. And all resonate with the "eco-material posthuman" in their recourse to the materiality of the human body as a vehicle for the new inter- and cross-species allegiances and connections we associate with posthumanism. While not all films in dialogue with the Anthropocene as a historical context mirror emerging critical accounts of what we have called the "eco-material posthuman," those that do have undertaken a collective "return" to the human body, where the body is understood not as a guarantor of human exceptionalism but as an aperture to the nonhuman outside. As indicated in this chapter, the models of human bodily materiality at issue here are diverse,

ECO-MATERIAL POSTHUMAN 273

echoing a corresponding diversity of such models within "eco-material posthuman" discourse. This chapter, however, has focused on three in particular. In my discussion of *Annihilation* and *Woman at War*, I focused on the body as *cell*, understood as the basic biological unit of life that is shared across species and life forms more generally. In my study of *Mother*, I broached the body as *affect*, as a bodily intensity that confounds conventional models of the human. And in my encounter with *First Reformed* and *Still Life*, I cast the body as *vital materiality*, which is to say, as what Braidotti calls "the dynamic, self-organizing structure of life itself [characterized by] generative vitality."[56] These visions of the human body rebrand it not as a signifier or guarantor of human exceptionalism but as a possible point of intersection with the nonhuman outside. In rallying these models of the body, I suggest, the films discussed above reconfigure the posthuman in light of one of the central lessons of the Anthropocene, namely that, as Alaimo puts it, "the substance of what was once called 'nature,' acts, interacts, and even intra-acts within, through, and around human bodies and practices."[57]

Notes

1. Stacy Alaimo, *Exposed: Environmental Politics and Pleasures in Posthuman Times* (Minneapolis: University of Minnesota Press, 2016), 1; Rosi Braidotti, *The Posthuman* (Cambridge: Polity Press, 2013), 5; Donna J. Haraway, *Staying with the Trouble: Making Kin in the Chthulucene* (Durham, NC: Duke University Press Books, 2016), 11. On the Anthropocene, see Dipesh Chakrabarty, "The Climate of History: Four Theses," *Critical Inquiry* 35, no. 2 (2009): 197–222.
2. Alaimo, *Exposed*, 1.
3. Alaimo, *Exposed*, 1.
4. Karen Barad, *Meeting the Universe Halfway: Quantum Physics and the Entanglement of Matter and Meaning* (Durham, NC: Duke University Press, 2007).
5. Diana Coole and Samantha Frost, *New Materialisms: Ontology, Agency, and Politics* (Durham, NC: Duke University Press, 2010), 5–6.
6. Jane Bennett, *Vibrant Matter: A Political Ecology of Things* (Durham, NC: Duke University Press, 2010); Brian Massumi, *Parables for the Virtual: Movement, Affect, Sensation* (Durham, NC: Duke University Press, 2002); Eve Kosofsky Sedgwick, *Touching Feeling: Affect, Pedagogy, Performativity* (Durham, NC: Duke University Press, 2003); Ian Bogost, *Alien Phenomenology, or, What It's Like to Be a Thing* (Minneapolis: University of Minnesota Press, 2012); Graham Harman, *Object-Oriented Ontology: A New Theory of Everything* (London: Penguin UK, 2018).
7. Haraway, *Staying with the Trouble*, 159.
8. Braidotti, *The Posthuman*, 49.

274   SCREENING THE POSTHUMAN

9. Alaimo, *Exposed*, 1.
10. Braidotti, *The Posthuman*, 60.
11. Barad, *Meeting the Universe Halfway*, 33
12. Rebecca Scott Yoshiawa, "Fetal-Maternal IntraAction: Politics of New Placental Biologies," *Body & Society* 22, no. 4 (2016): 80; Donna Haraway, *When Species Meet* (Minneapolis: University of Minnesota Press, 2002), 4.
13. Jackie Stacey, *The Cinematic Life of the Gene* (Durham, NC: Duke University Press Books, 2010), ix.
14. Alaimo, *Exposed*, 1.
15. Alaimo, *Exposed*, 2.
16. Alaimo, *Exposed*, 8.
17. Braidotti, *The Posthuman*, 45.
18. Braidotti, *The Posthuman*, 121. Although note that the fact that Josie is played by mixed-race actress Tessa Thompson serves to reinforce stereotypes of Black Americans while perpetuating what Sarah Dillon has described as our tendency to press women and minority groups into service "as key mediators for society's relationship to changing technology." Sarah M. Dillon, "The Future Is Female: Gynoidian Skins and Prosthetic Experience," MA thesis, Massey University, 2017, 1.
19. Donna Haraway, *Simians, Cyborgs and Women* (London: Free Association Books, 1991), 162.
20. Alaimo, *Exposed*, 8.
21. Stacey, *The Cinematic Life of the Gene*, 95.
22. Certainly, in conjunction with these techniques of the "informatics of domination," the film also features more familiar techniques of "biopower," which use comparative anatomy rather than bio-data as the markers for the organization and distribution of difference. Politicians caution against the so-called Mountain Woman; roadblocks have been set up around the city to monitor people's movements; police arrest a Spanish tourist found in the wrong place at the wrong time.
23. Dominique Janicaud, *On the Human Condition* (New York: Psychology Press, 2005), 36
24. Jo Labanyi, "Doing Things: Emotion, Affect and Materiality," *Journal of Spanish Cultural Studies* 11, no. 3–4 (2010): 224.
25. Massumi, *Parables for the Virtual*, 28. As this suggests, while scholarship on affect predated the official "materialist turn," it shares with other more overtly materialist agendas the desire to address material realities perceived as neglected under the reign of poststructuralism. (At the same time, it is important to note that affect's relationship to the material register is ambiguous, since it takes place in the realm of the virtual, which is the realm of potentiality and incipience.)
26. Massumi, *Parables for the Virtual*, 28.
27. Nigel Thrift, *Non-Representational Theory: Space, Politics, Affect* (New York: Routledge, 2008), 7.
28. Barad, *Meeting the Universe Halfway*, 128.
29. Labanyi, "Doing Things," 223–233.

ECO-MATERIAL POSTHUMAN   275

30. Teresa Brennan, *The Transmission of Affect* (Ithaca, NY: Cornell University Press, 2014), 30.

31. Jennifer M. Barker and Adam Cottrel, "Eyes at the Back of His Head: Precarious Masculinity and the Modern Tracking Shot," *Paragraph* 38, no. 1 (2015): 87. Italics mine.

32. Tarja Laine, *Bodies in Pain: Emotion and the Cinema of Darren Aronofsky* (New York: Berghahn Books, 2017), 64.

33. Barker and Cottrel, "Eyes at the Back of His Head," 89.

34. Barker and Cottrel, "Eyes at the Back of His Head," 87.

35. Massumi, *Parables*, 30.

36. Rosi Braidotti, "Afterword: Complexity, Materialism, Difference," *Angelaki* 17, no. 2 (2012): 174.

37. Aino-Kaisa Koistinen and Sanna Karkulehto, "Feminism," *Critical Posthumanism*, August 24, 2018, https://criticalposthumanism.net/feminism/.

38. Barad, *Meeting the Universe Halfway*, 33.

39. Massumi, *Parables for the Virtual*, 61.

40. Donna Haraway, "A Cyborg Manifesto: Science, Technology and Socialist-Feminism in the Late Twentieth Century," 1985, in *Manifestly Haraway* (Minneapolis: University of Minnesota Press, 2016), 10.

41. xx

42. xxx

43. xxx

44. Bennett, *Vibrant Matter*, 30.

45. Braidotti, *The Posthuman*, 100.

46. Braidotti, *The Posthuman*, 135.

47. Stacey, *The Cinematic Life of the Gene*, 89.

48. Braidotti, *The Posthuman*, 131, 135.

49. Haraway, *Staying with the Trouble*, 159.

50. Patricia MacCormack, *The Ahuman Manifesto* (London: Bloomsbury, 2020), xi.

51. Braidotti, *The Posthuman*, 134.

52. Mara Hvistendahl, "China's Three Gorges Dam: An Environmental Catastrophe?," *Scientific American*, March 25, 2008, https://www.scientificamerican.com/article/chinas-three-gorges-dam-disaster/.

53. Bennett, *Vibrant Matter*, 2.

54. Bennett, *Vibrant Matter*, 24.

55. Bennett, *Vibrant Matter*, 24.

56. Braidotti, *The Posthuman*, 60.

57. Alaimo, *Exposed*, 1.

8

Conclusion

Pansy Duncan, Claire Henry, and Missy Molloy

This book has argued that the "posthuman" forms a unifying thread through a diverse range of contemporary cinema. While science fiction remains the standard cinematic chronotope in discussions of the posthuman, the case studies we have chosen to broach in this volume far exceed the bounds of the Sci-Fi genre.[1] In fact, and as we have shown, posthuman imaginaries cannot be quarantined to a particular generic category, narrative formation, or set of stock figures (uploaded consciousness, artificial intelligence, "cryo-sleep"). While far from dominant in a cultural landscape still awash with humanist fantasy, the posthuman has gained purchase in all kinds of cinematic storytelling. It is in our romantic dramas, tearing at the fabric of conventional notions of embodiment, intimacy, and desire. It is in our Westerns, reshaping the figurative and literal landscape by unseating anthropocentric norms to reveal novel forms of human/nonhuman coexistence. It is in our disaster movies, many of which re-appropriate the figure of apocalyptic crisis to explore forms of subjectivity that exist on the margins of our social and physical imaginary. Appropriately, then, the films we have discussed here run the gamut, spanning everything from rom-coms to indie revisions of the superhero film.

In drawing out these films' posthumanist potentials, we have relied heavily on scholarship associated with critical posthumanist theory, an ongoing project of deconstructing the human. While popular models of posthumanism suggest that we have "become" posthuman in the wake of crucial technological, economic, and environmental shifts, critical posthumanism proposes that we were never "human" in the first place (at least not in the narrow sense inscribed in humanist, Eurocentric fantasies of human uniqueness and autonomy). Critical posthumanist theory, then, sets about drawing attention both to the crucial role of "technology and the environment . . . [in] defining aspects of the human" and to the new models of subjectivity, politics, community, relationality, and desire that might emerge

Pansy Duncan, Claire Henry, and Missy Molloy, *Conclusion*. In: *Screening the Posthuman*. Edited by: Missy Molloy, Pansy Duncan, and Claire Henry, Oxford University Press. © Oxford University Press 2023.
DOI: 10.1093/oso/9780197538562.003.0009

in the absence of conventional humanist norms.[2] Our gambit is that a similar logic is at play in the texts we analyze—texts that we have treated less as inert surfaces against which critical posthumanist theories can be mapped than as fellow travelers in the labor of critical posthuman critique.

We emphasize the term "critique" here because the critical posthumanist gesture we have documented in this book does not take place in a political vacuum. Rather, critical posthumanism is, was and must be timely—both in the sense of being *of* its time, and in the sense of being pertinent *to* its time. In a moment defined by carceral and police violence against Black American bodies, interrogating exclusionary models of the human that impose upon Black populations a form of "Black(ened) humanity" could not be more urgent.[3] In a moment marked by unrelenting assault against the basic rights of women to abortion, equal pay, and humane parental leave policies, discussion of the ways in which women's bodies have been excluded from normative conceptions of the human, framed as other, extraordinary, alien, or subhuman, again, could not be more appropriate. And in a moment widely referred to as the Anthropocene, problematizing a liberal notion of the human as the central mediator of the biosphere is crucial if we are to avoid perpetuating the environmental destruction that the term "the Anthropocene" accentuates. Critical posthumanism, then, has a powerful force as a tool of critique, and its utility in this respect has a long history. As Rosi Braidotti notes, posthumanist theory has its roots "in the turbulent years after the Second World War" as an "activist brand of anti-Humanism was developed by the new social movements and the youth cultures of the day," who sought to challenge "the platitudes of Cold War rhetoric, with its emphasis on Western democracy, liberal individualism and the freedom they allegedly ensured for all."[4]

Yet to emphasize the political vitality of proto-posthumanist theory in the context of the anti-humanist student uprisings of the late 1960s is also to sound a note of caution. It serves as a reminder that critical posthumanism will only retain a genuinely progressive edge if it continues to calibrate its "concepts, methods and political practices" against the "concepts, methods and political practices" at play in the world at large.[5] In fact, many posthumanists treat the posthuman as an inherently progressive phenomenon, a dynamic weapon in the ongoing battle against humanism. But is undermining the notion of the "human" radical at a time when global capital is also straining to divest itself of any responsibilities to precisely that category of being? On a related note, is "blurring the boundaries" between

278 SCREENING THE POSTHUMAN

animal and human a revolutionary gesture where, as Braidotti attests, "advanced capitalism and its bio-genetic technologies engender a perverse form of the posthuman" defined by "a radical disruption of the human–animal interaction" in which "all living species are caught in the spinning machine of the global economy?"[6] Some of the most prominent critical posthumanists have a tendency to treat posthuman models of existence as an unalloyed good rather than a profoundly ambivalent fact—and thus seem unprepared, as Bruno Latour puts it, "for new threats, new dangers, new tasks, new targets."[7] Take, for example, Donna Haraway's *Staying with the Trouble*, in which the author seeks to burnish the radical credentials of nomadic modes of existence and coexistence with the contention that "Private property regimes and their state apparatuses have a hard time with shifting cultivators (and with their pastoralists called nomads) . . . the state wants people to settle down with definite property boundaries."[8] With all due respect to the work of a theorist whose thinking has all but shaped the field, this announcement strikes an ominous note when set against the reality of a nation (the United States) that benefits from the cheap labor supplied by undocumented immigrants; against the spectacle of a new working poor living in a state of economic precarity in the so-called gig economy; and against a collapsing job market that routinely requires people to move for work, and in which "mobility" is more often a necessity than a freedom. While it is valid to discuss nomadism and its relation to the "posthuman predicament,"[9] the minute "nomadism" becomes an ideal, we are in "trouble" indeed, oblivious to the fact that the normative form of the subject under neoliberal capital is precisely a nomadic, rootless subject that "reinvent[s] itself again and again by changing its fluid identity."[10]

At stake here is less an inherent flaw in critical posthumanism than an issue with certain iterations of critical posthumanism that treat the posthuman as an aspirational ideal rather than a complex reality. Braidotti's approach, in this respect, is valuable. As Braidotti notes, "the concept of the human has exploded [primarily] under the double pressure of contemporary scientific advances and global economic concerns";[11] demolishing the human, in other words, was the job of capital, science, and technology well before posthumanist critics came onto the scene. While fundamentally "affirmative" in her approach to the posthuman, Braidotti allows for the fact that the posthuman can "engender its own forms of inhumanity."[12] Indeed, Braidotti's work manages to combine its "fascination for the posthuman condition as a crucial aspect of our historicity" with a profound note of "concern

CONCLUSION 279

for its aberrations, its abuses of power and the sustainability of some of its basic premises."[13] In advocating for a form of critical posthumanism that maintains a healthy skepticism of posthumanism itself, we respond to warnings from many quarters of the critical humanities and social sciences about the dangers of methodological sclerosis (see, for example, the work of Latour, Eve Sedgwick, and Rita Felski).[14]

The case of *Nomadland* (Chloé Zhao, 2020) provides an excellent case study in this context, as the film both exemplifies the value of posthumanist analysis and foregrounds the risks of a critical posthumanism that is critical of everything *except* its own assumptions. At its heart is Fern (played by Frances McDormand). According to the film's backstory, after the death of her husband, the closure of the local gypsum plant, and the subsequent folding of the town the plant sustained, Fern is left bereft. She decides to sell her belongings, leave her home, and hit the road—both to "escape" her grief and to seek work as a seasonal employee at an Amazon fulfillment center. "Houseless" rather than "homeless," as she likes to put it, she lives out of her van and briefly joins a makeshift community of modern "nomads" before striking out on her own again.

The value of the film lies in its dialectical model of the "posthuman condition."[15] One member of the rag-tag bunch of RV dwellers, for example, speaks of his devastation at the hands of what Braidotti calls the "posthuman death-technologies" of the "new wars," defined by "intense technological mediation."[16] "I'm a Vietnam vet, and I got PTSD," he announces; "I really can't handle loud noises." Yet for this same man, rejecting the trappings of conventional bourgeois models of human life—the single-family home, the stable income—provides an equal measure of solace and escape: "I got a pickup truck and a camper. I can live out here and be at peace." Similarly, in Fern, the film depicts a woman for whom "our posthuman condition" has both utopian and dystopian dimensions.[17] Her decision to hit the road is, at least in part, a function of her status as a pawn in a postindustrial economy where rapid technological development and social change leads to equally rapid cycles of dispossession and obsolescence. Yet for Fern this decidedly posthuman moment in history is also an opportunity, as her life on the road affords her the support structures she badly needs in the wake of her husband's death— support structures that also proffer novel models of multispecies coexistence. Conventional humanist accounts of human life reify the youthful body and cast old age as a time of withdrawal and contemplation, even as neoliberal capital chips away at the systems of elder care (whether family-based or state-provided) on which idealized visions of aging rely. *Nomadland* serves as a riposte to both ideologies. In keeping with critical posthumanist imperatives to address our dependence on other-than-human worlds for our very existence, Fern pursues a life defined by new forms of human/human, human/environment, human/thing, and human/nonhuman-animal affiliation.

Yet the film also underscores the need for critical posthumanist scholars to combine a challenge to humanist norms with an equally robust approach to posthumanist realities. It is no accident, we suggest, that *Nomadland* has attracted harsh criticism for a putative failure to adequately address the social and political calamities that have exponentially increased itineracy and homelessness in the twenty-first century United States (not least the global financial crisis of 2007–2008). For Wilfred Chan, for example, the fact that "Fern has no complaints about her jobs—including her time at Amazon" whitewashes the life-fraying realities of the kind of displacement and dispossession she faces to promote a romantic, liberatory vision of nomadic labor as the template for new kinds of individual freedom and community formation.[18] In our view, these criticisms are not entirely fair to the film, which, notwithstanding the punches it pulls in relation to Amazon as an employer, provides a substantial platform for more generally anti-corporate views. At

Figure 8.1 *Nomadland*'s (Chloé Zhao, 2020) exploration of nomadic "houselessness" highlights unique forms of posthuman relationality, including between Fern and her van.

CONCLUSION 281

one point, for example, the film shows the leader of the nomads, Bob Welles, delivering a rousing speech to the community of RV dwellers that could not be more explicit in its account of the debilitating physical and emotional effects of technologically advanced global late capitalism:

> We gladly throw the yoke of the tyranny of the dollar on and live by it our entire lives . . . I think of it in term of the analogy of the workhorse—the workhorse that is willing to work itself to death and then be put out to pasture. And that's what happens to so many of us. . . . If society was throwing us away and sending us out to pasture, we workhorses would have to gather together and take care of each other. And that's what this is all about. The way I see it is the Titanic is sinking and economic times are changing. And my goal is to get the lifeboats out and get as many people into the lifeboats as I can.

While this speech is stark, political economy does not feature heavily in posthuman theory (e.g., key terms like "capitalism," "socialism," "labor," and "production" don't even merit entries in the *Encyclopedia of Critical Posthumanism*), meaning that the questions of labor the film raises risk erasure in the context of a perfunctory posthuman analysis. And without them, *Nomadland* could potentially lend itself to a posthumanist reading that would celebrate Fern's nomadic lifestyle as a challenge to humanist norms without acknowledging the grief that underpins it, the global economic conditions that drive it, and the corporations that exploit it. Such an analysis would thus be complicit with neoliberal capital's efforts to rebrand economic and social dispossession as a novel and emancipatory lifestyle "choice."

To counter such a reading, this book advocates for rigorous posthumanist critique that is attentive to cinematic illuminations of the opportunities, ambivalences, and traumas inspired by posthuman existence—as opposed to humanist or transhumanist fantasies. We have also taken an intersectional approach in exploring critical posthumanism's synergy with frameworks such as queer theory (Chapter 4), critical disability studies (Chapter 5), and critical animal studies (Chapter 6). Treating posthuman elements as tangible and ubiquitous brings the most provocative aspects of posthuman cinema into sharp relief. In situating Fern's precarity against multiple historical temporalities, *Nomadland* makes a posthuman gesture akin to that of the Indigenous apocalyptic films presented in Chapter 2. These films resist the short-sighted tendency to interpret current crises as wholly the result of new phenomena, instead attributing the disasters of contemporary life to long-prevailing humanistic tendencies. Accordingly, the dissolution of Fern's town (and zip code) after its eighty-eight-year tenure is figured against concepts of time that eclipse it—including those related to the trajectories of dinosaurs, rocks, and stars. Regarding the latter, Fern observes her temporary travel companion, Dave (played by David Strathairn), lecturing a group of stargazers on solar time to help them appreciate the shortcomings of a human perception that, for instance, discerns a star shooting across the sky long after it has extinguished. The critical exercise this book promotes is analogous to Dave's (and *Nomadland's*) correction. It closely observes the vibrant cinematic evolution of posthuman ideas while keeping an eye out for the distortions of humanism, which elide human/nonhuman entanglements to sustain a profoundly problematic vision of human exceptionalism.

Notes

1. Indeed, it is our contention that the prominence accorded science fiction cinema in posthumanist theory to date is a function of a transhumanist misconstruction of posthumanism that takes it to mean the promise of a radical transformation of the human condition through "existing, emerging and speculative technologies." Francesca Ferrando, *Philosophical Posthumanism* (London: Bloomsbury Academic, 2019), 3.
2. Ferrando, *Philosophical Posthumanism*, 28.
3. Zakiyyah Iman Jackson, *Becoming Human: Matter and Meaning in an Antiblack World* (New York: New York University Press, 2020), 3.
4. Rosi Braidotti, *The Posthuman* (Cambridge: Polity, 2013), 16.
5. Braidotti, *The Posthuman*, 3.
6. Braidotti, *The Posthuman*, 7.
7. Bruno Latour, "Why Has Critique Run Out of Steam? From Matters of Fact to Matters of Concern," *Critical Inquiry* 30 (Winter 2004): 225.
8. Donna J. Haraway, *Staying with the Trouble: Making Kin in the Chthulucene* (Durham, NC: Duke University Press, 2016), 196. While Haraway has disowned the term "posthumanism," she continues to delineate models of existence that have had purchase in critical posthuman theory.
9. Braidotti, *The Posthuman*, 3.
10. Slavoj Žižek, "Jordan Peterson as a Symptom . . . of What?," in *Myth and Mayhem: A Leftists Critique of Jordan Peterson*, ed. Ben Burgis, Conrad Hamilton, Matthew McManus, and Marion Trejo (Winchester: Zero Books, 2020), viii.
11. Braidotti, *The Posthuman*, 1.
12. Braidotti, *The Posthuman*, 3.

CONCLUSION 283

13. Braidotti, *The Posthuman*, 3.
14. For example, without rejecting Foucauldian critique entirely, Winc Sedgwick mocks D. A. Miller's typically Foucauldian commitment to "exposing and problematizing hidden violences in the genealogy of the modern liberal subject" in the historical context of a "xenophobic Reagan-Bush-Clinton-Bush America where 'liberal' is, if anything, a taboo category and where secular humanism is routinely treated as a marginal religious sect." And in response to Miller's promise to dismantle "the intensive and continuous pastoral care that liberal society proposes to take of each and every one of its charges," Sedgwick retorts: "As if! I'm a lot less worried about being pathologized by my therapist than about my vanishing mental health coverage— and that's given the great good luck of having health coverage at all." Eve Kosofsky Sedgwick, *Touching Feeling: Affect, Pedagogy, Performativity* (Durham, NC: Duke University Press, 2003), 139.
15. Braidotti, *The Posthuman*, 1.
16. Braidotti, *The Posthuman*, 9.
17. Braidotti, *The Posthuman*, 1.
18. Wilfred Chan, "What Nomadland Gets Wrong about Gig Labour," *Vulture*, March 22, 2021, https://www.vulture.com/article/nomadland-amazon-warehouse-chloe-zhao.html.

Bibliography

ACMI. "The Story Behind Collisions." *ACMI*, December 7, 2016, video, https://www.acmi.net.au/ideas/watch/story-behind-collisions/.

"Air Doll Floats Over Un Certain Regard." *Festival de Cannes*, May 14, 2009, https://www.festival-cannes.com/en/69-editions/retrospective/2009/actualites/articles/air-doll-floats-over-un-certain-regard.

Agamben, Giorgio. *The Open: Man and Animal*. Translated by Kevin Attell. Stanford, CA: Stanford University Press, 2004.

Alaimo, Stacey. *Exposed: Environmental Politics and Pleasures in Posthuman Times*. Minneapolis: University of Minnesota Press, 2016.

Alter, Alexandra. "'We've Already Survived an Apocalypse': Indigenous Writers Are Changing Sci-Fi." *New York Times*, August 14, 2020, https://www.nytimes.com/2020/08/14/books/indigenous-native-american-sci-fi-horror.html.

Altman, Rick. *Film/Genre*. London: British Film Institute, 1999.

Anderson, Melissa. "The Embers of Paris Glow for 'Born in Flames: New Queer Cinema.'" *The Village Voice*, October 10, 2012, https://www.villagevoice.com/2012/10/10/the-embers-of-paris-glow-for-born-in-flames-new-queer-cinema/.

Aroonpheng, Phuttiphong. "Manta Ray Director Q&A, TIFF 2018." *TIFF Talks*, September 12, 2018, video, https://www.youtube.com/watch?v=h7yOCm1v2Sw.

Åsberg, Cecilia. "Feminist Posthumanities in the Anthropocene: Forays Into the Postnatural." *Journal of Posthuman Studies* 1, no. 2 (2017): 185–204, doi:10.5325/jpoststud.1.2.0185.

Åsberg, Cecilia, and Rosi Braidotti, eds., *A Feminist Companion to the Posthumanities*. Cham: Springer, 2018.

Badmington, Neil. *Alien Chic: Posthumanism and the Other Within*. London: Routledge, 2004.

Badmington, Neil. "Theorizing Posthumanism." *Cultural Critique* 53 (2003): 10–27, https://www.jstor.org/stable/1354622.

Barad, Karen. *Meeting the Universe Halfway: Quantum Physics and the Entanglement of Matter and Meaning*. Durham, NC: Duke University Press, 2007.

Barad, Karen. "Nature's Queer Performativity." *Qui Parle* 19, no. 2 (Spring/Summer 2011): 121–158.

Barad, Karen. "Posthumanist Performativity: Toward an Understanding of How Matter Comes to Matter." *Signs: Journal of Women in Culture and Society* 28, no. 3 (2003): 801–831.

Bardzell, Shaowen, and Jeffrey Bardzell. "Technosexuality." In *The Wiley Blackwell Encyclopedia of Gender and Sexuality Studies*, edited by Nancy A. Naples. Hoboken, NJ: Wiley-Blackwell, 2016, https://doi.org/10.1002/9781118663219.

Barker, Jennifer M. "A Horse Is a Horse, Of Course, Of Course: Animality, Transitivity, and the Double Take." *Somatechnics* 8, no. 1 (2018): 27–47, https://doi.org/10.3366/soma.2018.0235.

286 BIBLIOGRAPHY

Barker Jennifer M., and Adam Cottrel. "Eyes at the Back of His Head: Precarious Masculinity and the Modern Tracking Shot." *Paragraph* 38, no. 1 (2015): 86–100, https://doi.org/10.3366/para.2015.0148.

Basinger, Jeanine. *A Woman's View: How Hollywood Spoke to Women, 1930–1960.* New York: Knopf Doubleday Publishing Group, 2013.

Becker, Carol. "How Art Became a Force at Davos." *Word Economic Forum,* February 26, 2019, https://www.weforum.org/agenda/2019/02/how-art-became-a-force-at-davos/.

Benjamin, Walter. "Surrealism: The Last Snapshot of the European Intelligentsia." 1929. In *Reflections,* edited by Peter Demetz, translated by Edmund Jephcott, 177–192. New York: Schocken, 1986.

Bennett, Jane. *Vibrant Matter: A Political Ecology of Things.* Durham, NC: Duke University Press, 2010.

Benshoff, Harry M. *Monsters in the Closet: Homosexuality and the Horror Film.* Manchester: Manchester University Press, 1997.

Bergen-Aurand, Brian. "Screening Disability." *Screen Bodies* 3, no. 1 (2018): v–viii.

Berlant, Lauren. "Poor Eliza." *American Literature* 70, no. 3 (1998): 635–668, https://doi.org/10.2307/2902712.

Berlant, Lauren. "The Subject of True Feeling: Pain, Privacy and Politics." In *Cultural Pluralism, Identity Politics, and the Law,* edited by Austin Sarat and Thomas R. Kearns, 49–84. Ann Arbor: University of Michigan Press, 1999.

Bernini, Lorenzo. *Queer Apocolypses: Elements of Antisocial Theory.* 2013. Translated by Julia Heim. London: Palgrave Macmillan, 2017.

Bhavnani, Kum-Kum, and Donna Haraway. "Shifting the Subject: A Conversation Between Kum-Kum Bhavnani and Donna Haraway, 12 April 1993, Santa Cruz, California." *Feminism & Psychology* 4, no. 1 (1994): 19–39.

Bird-David, Nurit. "'Animism' Revisited: Personhood, Environment Epistemology." *Current Anthropology* 40, no. 151 (1999): 67–91.

Bloomberg News. "Davos 2016: Inside the 46th World Economic Forum." *Bloomberg News,* January 21, 2016, https://www.bloomberg.com/news/photo-essays/2016-01-20/davos-2016-the-world-economic-forum-in-pictures.

Bogost, Ian. *Alien Phenomenology, or, What It's Like to Be a Thing.* Minneapolis: University of Minnesota Press, 2012.

Bradshaw, Peter. "*Ingrid Goes West* Review—Social Media Satire is a Horribly Watchable Carnival of Narcissism." *The Guardian,* November 15, 2017, https://www.theguardian.com/film/2017/nov/15/ingrid-goes-west-review-aubrey-plaza-elizabeth-olsen-instagram.

Bradshaw, Peter. "On Body and Soul Review—Bizarre and Brutal Tale of Lovers in the Slaughterhouse." *The Guardian,* September 21, 2017, https://www.theguardian.com/film/2017/sep/21/on-body-and-soul-review-ildiko-enyedi.

Bradshaw, Peter. "Possessor Review—Brandon Cronenberg's Terrifying Sci-Fi Horror Freak-Out." *The Guardian,* November 26, 2020, https://www.theguardian.com/film/2020/nov/26/possessor-review-brandon-cronenberg-andrea-riseborough-sc0fi-horror.

Braidotti, Rosi. "Affirming the Affirmative: On Nomadic Affectivity." *Rhizomes: Cultural Studies in Emerging Knowledge* 11/12 (2005–2006), http://www.rhizomes.net/issue11/braidotti.html.

Braidotti, Rosi. "Afterword: Complexity, Materialism, Difference." *Angelaki* 17, no. 2 (2012): 169–176.

BIBLIOGRAPHY   287

Braidotti, Rosi. "Critical Posthuman Knowledges." *South Atlantic Quarterly* 116, no. 1 (2017): 83–96.

Braidotti, Rosi. *Nomadic Subjects: Embodiment and Sexual Difference in Contemporary Feminist Theory*. New York: Columbia University Press, 1994.

Braidotti, Rosi. *The Posthuman*. Cambridge: Polity, 2013.

Braidotti, Rosi. "Posthuman, All Too Human: Towards A New Process Ontology." *Theory, Culture & Society* 23, no. 7/8 (2006): 197–208, https://doi.org/10.1177/026327640 6069232.

Braidotti, Rosi. "Posthuman Critical Theory." In *Critical Posthumanism and Planetary Futures*, edited by Debashish Banerji and Makarand R. Paranjape, 13–32. New Delhi: Springer, 2016.

Braidotti, Rosi. "A Theoretical Framework for the Critical Posthumanities." *Theory, Culture & Society* 36, no. 9 (2019): 31–61, https://doi.org/10.1177/0263276418771486.

Braidotti, Rosi. "Transposing Life." In *Clones, Fakes and Posthumans: Cultures of Replication*, edited by Ernst van Alphen, 61–78. Amsterdam: Rodopi, 2012.

Braidotti, Rosi, and Matthew Fuller. "The Posthumanities in an Era of Unexpected Consequences." *Theory, Culture & Society* 36, no. 6 (2019): 31–61.

Brennan, Teresa. *The Transmission of Affect*. Ithaca, NY: Cornell University Press, 2014.

Breton, André. "Manifesto of Surrealism." 1924. In *Manifestoes of Surrealism*, translated by Richard Seaver and Helen R. Lan, 1–47. Ann Arbor: University of Michigan Press, 1994.

Briggs, John, and Joanne Sharp. "Indigenous Knowledges and Development: A Postcolonial Caution." *Third World Quarterly* 25, no. 4 (2004): 661–676.

Brinkema, Eugenie. "A Title Does Not Ask, But Demands That You Make a Choice: On the Otherwise Films of Bruce LaBruce." *Criticism* 48, no. 1 (2006): 95–126.

Brinkema, Eugenie. *The Forms of the Affects*. Durham, NC: Duke University Press, 2014.

Brody, Richard. "'Fast Color,' Reviewed: A Superhero Movie That Pays Close Attention to Ordinary Life." *The New Yorker*, April 22, 2019, https://www.newyorker.com/culture/the-front-row/fast-color-reviewed-a-superhero-movie-that-pays-close-attention-to-ordinary-life.

Brody, Richard. "The Political Science Fiction of Born in Flames." *The New Yorker*, February 19, 2016, https://www.newyorker.com/culture/richard-brody/the-political-science-fiction-of-born-in-flames.

Buckmaster, Luke. "Virtual Reality Pioneer Lynette Wallworth Tells Indigenous Story in Explosive Detail." *The Guardian*, March 18, 2016, https://www.theguardian.com/tec hnology/2016/mar/18/virtual-reality-pioneer-lynette-walworth-tells-indigenous-story-in-explosive-detail.

Campbell, Joseph. *The Hero with a Thousand Faces*. New York: Pantheon Books, 1949.

Campbell, Nancy D. "Pharmaceuticals." In *Posthuman: The Future of Homo Sapiens*, edited by Michael Bess and Diana Walsh Pasulka, 63–74. Farmington Hills, MI: Macmillan Reference, 2018.

Carew, Anthony. "Cinema Reincarnated: Apichatpong Weerasethakul and Thai Cinema's Radical New Life." *Metro* 176 (Autumn 2013): 36–40.

Carroll, Noël. *The Philosophy of Horror*. New York: Routledge, 1990.

CBC Arts. "Lisa Jackson's *Biidaaban: First Light*," *CBC*, 2018, video, https://www.cbc.ca/player/play/1323281475810.

Chakrabarty, Dipesh. "The Climate of History: Four Theses." *Critical Inquiry* 35, no. 2 (2009): 197–222, https://doi.org/10.1086/596640.

288 BIBLIOGRAPHY

Chakravorty, Swagato. "Carnal Tension, Superficial Logic: The Feminine Body and Its Surface in Lucy and Under the Skin." *In Media Res*, January 22, 2015, http://media commons.org/imr/2015/01/17/carnal-tension-superficial-logic-feminine-body-and-its-surface-her-and-under-skin-0.

Chan, Wilfred. "What Nomadland Gets Wrong about Gig Labour." *Vulture*, March 22, 2021, https://www.vulture.com/article/nomadland-amazon-warehouse-chloe-zhao.html.

Chang, Edmond Y. "Technoqueer: Re/Con/Figuring Posthuman Narratives." PhD diss., University of Washington, 2012.

Chiang, Ted. *Stories of Your Life and Others*. London: Picador, 2015.

Chung, Saemyi. "In Pursuit of Beauty within the Ageing Body: Voices from Older Korean Women in New Zealand." PhD diss., University of Otago, 2018.

Church, David. "Review of The Diving Bell and the Butterfly." *Disability Studies Quarterly* 28, no. 2 (2008), https://dsq-sds.org/article/view/101/101.

Cohen, Jeffery Jerome, ed. *Monster Theory: Reading Culture*. Minneapolis: University of Minnesota Press, 1996.

Collins, K. Austin. "'Proxima' Review: The Space Travel Between Us." *Rolling Stone*, November 5, 2020, https://www.rollingstone.com/movies/movie-reviews/proxima-movie-review-eva-green-1085438/.

Coole, Diana, and Samantha Frost. *New Materialisms: Ontology, Agency, and Politics*. Durham, NC: Duke University Press, 2010.

Creed, Barbara. *The Monstrous-Feminine: Film, Feminism, Psychoanalysis*. London: Routledge, 1993.

Dargis, Manohla. "The Fabulist Who Confounded Cannes." *New York Times*, June 26, 2005, *Factavia*.

Dargis, Manohla. "A Spectral Tale of Love Found in War." *The New York Times*, October 2, 2004, https://www.nytimes.com/2004/10/02/movies/a-spectral-tale-of-love-found-in-war.html.

Davis, Lennard J. "The Ghettoization of Disability: Paradoxes of Visibility and Invisibility in Cinema." In *Culture—Theory—Disability*, edited by Anne Waldschmidt, Janho Berressem, and Moritz Ingwersen, 39–50. Bielefeld: transcript Verlag, 2017, https://www.degruyter.com/document/doi/10.14361/9783839425336-005/html.

DeFore, John. "'Possessor': Film Review." *The Hollywood Reporter*, January 25, 2020, https://www.hollywoodreporter.com/review/possessor-review-1272650.

de Fren, Allison. "Technofetishism and the Uncanny Desires of ASFR (alt. sex. fetish. robots)." *Science Fiction Studies* 39 (2009): 404–440.

de Lauretis, Teresa. "Aesthetic and Feminist Theory: Rethinking Women's Cinema." *New German Critique* 34 (Winter 1985): 154–175.

del Río, Elena. *The Grace of Destruction: A Vital Ethology of Extreme Cinemas*. New York: Bloomsbury Academic, 2016.

Delaney, Brigid. "'An Act of Solidarity': Anohni Treks 100km Across Australian Desert to Protest Against Uranium Mine." *The Guardian*, June 7, 2016.

Deleuze, Gilles. *Cinema 2: The Time Image*. Translated by Hugh Tomlinson and Robert Galatea, Athlone Contemporary European Thinkers. London: The Athlone Press, 1989.

Deleuze, Gilles, and Félix Guattari. *A Thousand Plateaus: Capitalism and Schizophrenia*. 1980. Translated by Brian Massumi. Minneapolis: University of Minnesota Press, 2005.

BIBLIOGRAPHY 289

Descartes, René. *Discourse on Method*. 1637. In *Descartes: Selected Philosophical Writings*, edited by John Cottingham and Robert Stoothoff, 20–56. Cambridge: Cambridge University Press, 1988.

Dethridge, Lisa. "Virtual Reality Film Collisions Is Part Disaster Movie, Part Travelogue and Completely Immersive." *The Conversation*, October 5, 2016, https://theconversat ion.com/virtual-reality-film-collisions-is-part-disaster-movie-part-travelogue-and-completely-immersive-66563.

Dillion, Grace. "From Growing Medicine to Space Rockets: What Is Indigenous Futurism?" Interview by Rosanna Deerchild, *Unreserved*, CBA, March 10, 2019, audio, https://www.cbc.ca/radio/unreserved/looking-towards-the-future-indigenous-futur ism-in-literature-music-film-and-fashion-1.5036479/from-growing-medicine-to-space-rockets-what-is-indigenous-futurism-1.5036480.

Dillion, Grace. *Walking the Clouds: An Anthology of Indigenous Science Fiction*. Tucson: University of Arizona Press, 2012.

Dillon, Sarah M. "The Future Is Female: Gynoidian Skins and Prosthetic Experience." MA thesis, Massey University, 2017.

Doane, Mary Ann. *Femmes Fatales: Feminism, Film Theory, Psychoanalysis*. New York: Routledge, 1991.

Doane, Mary Ann. "Technophilia: Technology, Representation, and the Feminine." In *Body/Politics: Women and the Discourses of Science*, edited by Mary Jacobus, Evelyn Fox Keller, and Sally Shuttleworth, 163–176. New York: Routledge, 1990.

Doane, Mary Ann. "Technophilia: Technology, Representation, and the Feminine." In *Cybersexualities: A Reader in Feminist Theory, Cyborgs and Cyberspace*, edited by Jenny Wolmark, 20–33. Edinburgh: Edinburgh University Press, 1999, http://www.jstor.org/stable/10.3366/j.ctvxcrxdq.6.

Donnison, Jon. "Lingering Impact of British Nuclear Tests in the Australian Outback." *BBC News*, December 31, 2014, https://www.bbc.com/news/world-australia-30640338.

Duncan, Pansy. "Tears, Melodrama and 'Heterosensibility' in *Letter from an Unknown Woman*." *Screen* 52, no. 2 (2011): 173–192.

Eastwood, Ken. "Living the Traditional Aboriginal Life." *Australian Geographic*, December 15, 2010. https://www.australiangeographic.com.au/topics/history-culture/2010/12/living-the-traditional-aboriginal-life/

Edelman, Lee. *No Future: Queer Theory and the Death Drive*. Durham, NC: Duke University Press, 2004.

Ehrlich, David. "'Possessor' Review: Brandon Cronenberg's Gory Techno-Thriller Gets Under Your Skin." *IndieWire*, January 26, 2020, https://www.indiewire.com/2020/01/possessor-review-sundance-1202205838/.

Ellcessor, Elizabeth, and Bill Kirkpatrick. "Studying Disability." *JCMS: Journal of Cinema and Media Studies* 58, no. 4 (2019): 139–144, https://doi.10.1353/cj.2019.0042.

Elsaesser, Thomas. "Black Suns and a Bright Planet: Lars von Trier's Melancholia as Thought Experiment." *Theory & Event* 18, no. 2 (2015), https://muse.jhu.edu/article/578627.

Emery, Cynthia Coleman. "Indians: We're All the Same." *Cynthia (Ištá Thó Thó) Coleman Emery's Blog*, November 28, 2014, https://nativescience.blog/2014/11/18/indians-were-all-the-same/.

290 BIBLIOGRAPHY

Enyedi, Ildikó. "Film Review: On Body and Soul (Ildikó Enyedi)." Interview by Charles Martig, *Journal of Religion, Film and Media* 3, no. 2 (2017): 85–89, https://doi.org/10.25364/05.3:2017.2.8.

Epstein, Charlotte. *Against International Relations Norms: Postcolonial Perspectives.* London: Routledge, 2017.

Epstein, Charlotte. "The Postcolonial Perspective: An Introduction." *International Theory* 6, no. 2 (July 2014): 294–311.

"Experience a Transformed Toronto as Indigenous Futurism Comes to Life." *National Film Board of Canada,* August 23, 2018. https://mediaspace.nfb.ca/comm/experie nce-a-transformed-toronto-as-indigenous-futurism-comes-to-life-september-18-24-nfbs-biidaaban-first-light-offers-a-stunning-virtual-reality-vision-of-the-citys-futu/.

Ezra, Elizabeth. *The Cinema of Things: Globalization and the Posthuman Object.* New York: Bloomsbury Academic, 2017.

Fay, Jennifer, and Justus Nieland. *Film Noir: Hard-Boiled Modernity and the Cultures of Globalization.* London: Routledge, 2009.

Ferrando, Francesca. "Is the Post-human a Post-woman? Cyborgs, Robots, Artificial Intelligence and the Futures of Gender: A Case Study." *European Journal of Futures Research* 2, no. 43 (2014): 1–17.

Ferrando, Francesca. *Philosophical Posthumanism.* London: Bloomsbury Academic, 2019.

Ferrando, Francesca. "Posthumanism, Transhumanism, Antihumanism, Metahumanism, and New Materialisms Differences and Relations." *Existenz* 8, no. 2 (2013): 26–32.

Feuer, Jane. *The Hollywood Musical.* Bloomington: Indiana University Press, 1993.

Finn, Ed. *What Algorithms Want: Imagination in the Age of Computing.* Cambridge, MA: MIT Press, 2017.

Fisher, Philip. *The Vehement Passions.* Princeton, NJ: Princeton University Press, 2009.

Fishman, Howard. "I Accidentally Walked into 'Border,' and It Kind of Changed My Life." *The New Yorker,* November 28, 2018, https://www.newyorker.com/culture/culture-desk/i-accidentally-walked-into-border-and-it-kind-of-changed-my-life.

Foucault, Michel. *The Order of Things: An Archaeology of the Human Sciences.* London: Routledge, 2005.

Franke, Anselm. "Animism." In Posthuman Glossary, edited by Rosi Braidotti and Maria Hlavajova, 40. London: Bloomsbury Academic, 2018.

Franklin, Sarah. "Life Itself. Global Nature and the Genetic Imaginary." In *Global Nature, Global Culture,* edited by Sarah Franklin, Celia Lury, and Jackie Stacy, 188–227. London: SAGE, 2000.

Freer, Ian. "Sound of Metal Review." *Empire,* April 12, 2021, https://www.empireonline.com/movies/reviews/sound-of-metal/.

French, Philip. "Coma vs. Coma." *The Guardian,* August 25, 2002, https://www.theguard ian.com/film/2002/aug/25/philipfrench.

Fröding, Barbro, and Walter Osika. *Neuroenhancement: How Mental Training and Meditation Can Promote Epistemic Virtue.* Cham: Springer, 2015.

Fukuyama, Francis. *Our Posthuman Future: Consequences of the Biotechnology Revolution.* New York: Picador, 2002.

Galt, Rosalind. "The Animal Logic of Contemporary Greek Cinema," *Framework: The Journal of Cinema and Media* 58, no. 1–2 (2017): 7–29, http://www.jstor.org/stable/10.13110/framework.58.1-2.0007.

Gane, Nicholas. "When We Have Never Been Human, What Is to Be Done?: Interview with Donna Haraway." *Theory, Culture & Society* 23, no. 7/8 (2006): 135–158.

Gilbert, Sophie. "When Love Is Optimized, Is It Still Love?" *The Atlantic,* April 16, 2021, https://www.theatlantic.com/culture/archive/2021/04/made-love-girlfriend-experie nce-and-limits-futuristic-love-stories/618607/.

BIBLIOGRAPHY   291

Gittell, Noah. "Scarlett Johansson's Vanishing Act," *The Atlantic*, July 29, 2014, https://www.theatlantic.com/entertainment/archive/2014/07/what-in-the-world-is-scarlett-johansson-up-to-lucy-under-the-skin-her-a-feminist-disappearing-act/375141/.

Gleiberman, Owen. "'Contagion,' the Movie That Predicted Our Pandemic, Is Really about Our World Falling Apart." *Variety*, April 27, 2020, https://variety.com/2020/film/columns/contagion-the-movie-that-predicted-our-pandemic-1234590420/.

Godfrey, Nicholas. "Love Over the Borderline: Tenderness and Transformation in Phuttiphong Aroonpheng's Manta Ray." *Metro* 202 (October 2019): 62–67.

Goffman, Erving. *Stigma: Notes on the Management of Spoiled Identity*. New York: Simon and Schuster, 1963.

Goldrich, Robert. "Tamara Jenkins." *SHOOT* 59, no. 5 (October/November 2018): 20.

Gollin, Richard. *A Viewer's Guide to Film: Arts, Artifices, and Issues*. New York: McGraw-Hill 1992.

Gonzalez, Jennifer. "Envisioning Cyborg Bodies: Notes from Current Research." In *The Gendered Cyborg: A Reader*, edited by Gill Kirkup, Linda Janes, Kath Woodward, and Fiona Hovenden, 58–73. London: Routledge, 2000.

Goodley, Dan. "Autism and the Human." In *Re-Thinking Autism: Diagnosis, Identity and Equality*, edited by Sami Timimi, Rebecca Mallett, and Katherine Runswick-Cole, 146–158. London: Jessica Kingsley Publishers, 2016.

Goodley, Dan, Rebecca Lawthom, and Katherine Runswick Cole. "Posthuman Disability Studies." *Subjectivity* 7, no. 4 (2014): 342–361, https://doi.org/10.1057/sub.2014.15.

Grant, Barry Keith. *Film Genre: From Iconography to Ideology*. London: Wallflower Press, 2007.

Greven, David. *Queering The Terminator: Sexuality and Cyborg Cinema*. London: Bloomsbury, 2017.

Grinberg, Daniel. "Time and Time Again: The Cinematic Temporalities of Apichatpong Weerasethakul." *Mediascape*, August 2015, http://www.tft.ucla.edu/mediascape/Fall2015_TimeAndTimeAgain.html.

Grindon, Leger. *The Hollywood Romantic Comedy: Conventions, History, Controversies*. Hoboken, NJ: John Wiley & Sons, 2011.

Grosz, Elizabeth A. *Volatile Bodies*. Bloomington: Indiana University Press, 1994.

Halberstam, Judith. "Automating Gender: Postmodern Feminism in the Age of the Intelligent Machine." *Feminist Studies* 17, no. 3 (1991): 43–460.

Halberstam, Judith. *Skin Shows: Gothic Horror and the Technology of Monsters*. Durham, NC: Duke University Press, 1995.

Halberstam, Judith M., and Ira Livingston. *Posthuman Bodies*. Indianapolis: Indiana University Press, 1995.

Haldane, Richard Burdon. *The Philosophy of Humanism: And of Other Subjects*. London: John Murray, 1922.

Hansen, Mark B. N. *Feed-Forward: On the Future of Twenty-First-Century Media*. Chicago: University of Chicago Press, 2015.

Haraway, Donna J. "The Companion Species Manifesto: Dogs, People, and Significant Otherness." 2003. In *Manifestly Haraway*, edited by Donna J. Haraway and Carey Wolfe, 91–198. Minneapolis: University of Minnesota Press, 2016.

Haraway, Donna J. "A Cyborg Manifesto: Science, Technology and Socialist-Feminism in the Late Twentieth Century." 1985. In *Manifestly Haraway*, edited by Donna J. Haraway and Carey Wolfe, 3–90. Minneapolis: University of Minnesota Press, 2016.

Haraway, Donna J. *Simians, Cyborgs and Women*. London: Free Association Books, 1991.

Haraway, Donna J. *Staying with the Trouble: Making Kin in the Chthulucene*. Durham, NC: Duke University Press, 2016.

Haraway, Donna J. *When Species Meet*. Minneapolis: University of Minnesota Press, 2002.

292 BIBLIOGRAPHY

Harman, Graham. *Object-Oriented Ontology: A New Theory of Everything.* London: Penguin UK, 2018.

Harvey, Graham. *Animism: Respecting the Living World.* London: Hurst & Co, 2005.

Hauskeller, Michael. "Michael Hauskeller." *Academia.edu,* accessed March 3, 2021, https://liverpool.academia.edu/MichaelHauskeller/Books.

Hauskeller, Michael, Thomas D. Philbeck, and Curtis C. Carbonell, eds. *The Palgrave Handbook of Posthumanism in Film and Television.* Basingstoke: Palgrave Macmillan, 2015.

Hayles, N. Katherine. *How We Became Posthuman: Virtual Bodies in Cybernetics, Literature, and Informatics.* Chicago: University of Chicago Press, 1999.

Hayward, Eva. "Lessons from a Starfish." In *Queering the Non/Human,* edited by Noreen Giffney and Myra J. Hird, 249–264. Farnham: Ashgate, 2008.

Henke, Jennifer. "'Ava's Body Is a Good One': (Dis)Embodiment in Ex Machina." *American, British and Canadian Studies* 29 (2017): 126–146, https://doi.org/10.1515/abcsj-2017-0022.

Herbrechter, Stefan. *Posthumanism: A Critical Analysis.* London: Bloomsbury, 2013.

Hotel Victoria. "Toronto History—Old City Hall." *Hotel* Toronto, February 15, 2020, https://www.hotelvictoria-toronto.com/2020/02/toronto-history-old-city-hall/.

Huang, Banyi. "Docile, Mutating and Resistant Bodies: Shu Lea Cheang." *ArtAsiaPacific* 113 (May 2019): 76–85.

Hvistendahl, Mara. "China's Three Gorges Dam: An Environmental Catastrophe?" *Scientific American,* March 25, 2008, https://www.scientificamerican.com/article/chinas-three-gorges-dam-disaster/.

Ide, Wendy. "'Possessor': Sundance Review." *Screen Daily,* January 26, 2020, https://www.screendaily.com/reviews/possessor-sundance-review/5146251.article.

Ingawanij, May Adadol. "Animism and the Performative Realist Cinema of Apichatpong Weerasethakul." In *Screening Nature: Cinema beyond the Human,* edited by Anat Pick and Guinevere Narraway, 91–109. New York: Berghahn, 2013.

Ivanchikova, Alla. "Machinic Intimacies and Mechanical Brides: Collectivity between Prosthesis and Surrogacy in Jonathan Mostow's *Surrogates* and Spike Jonze's *Her.*" *Camera Obscura* 31, no. 1 (2016): 65–91. https://doi.org/10.1215/02705346-3454430.

Jackson, Zakiyyah Iman. *Becoming Human: Matter and Meaning in an Antiblack World.* New York: New York University Press, 2020.

Jacobson, Brian R. "Ex Machina in the Garden." *Film Quarterly* 69, no. 4 (2016): 23–34, https://www.jstor.org/stable/26413710.

Janicaud, Dominique. *On the Human Condition.* New York: Psychology Press, 2005.

Jelača, Dijana. "Alien Feminisms and Cinema's Posthuman Women." *Signs: Journal of Women in Culture and Society* 43, no. 2 (2018): 379–400, https://doi.org/10.1086/693765.

Jenkins, Tamara. "How a 'By Any Means Necessary' Quest for a Child Inspired Netflix's *Private Life.*" Interview by Terry Gross, *Fresh Air,* NPR, October 3, 2018, https://www.npr.org/transcripts/653670395.

Jones, Steve. "Gender Monstrosity: Deadgirl and the Sexual Politics of Zombie-Rape." *Feminist Media Studies* 13, no. 3 (2013): 525–539, https://doi.org/10.1080/14680777.2012.712392.

Kashani, Tony, and Anthony J. Nocella. "Hollywood's Cinema of Ableism: A Disability Studies Perspective on the Hollywood Industrial Complex." In *Hollywood's Exploited,* edited by Benjamin Frymer et al., 105–114. New York: Palgrave Macmillan, 2010.

BIBLIOGRAPHY   293

Keegan, Cael M. "Moving Bodies: Sympathetic Migrations in Transgender Narrativity." *Genders* 57 (2013).

Keller, Sarah. *Anxious Cinephilia: Pleasure and Peril at the Movies*. New York: Columbia University Press, 2020.

Kenny, Glenn. "'Possessor' Review: It's by a Cronenberg, but Not the One You Think." *New York Times*, October 1, 2020, https://www.nytimes.com/2020/10/01/movies/possessor-review.html.

Kermode, Mark. "Sound of Metal Review—Riz Ahmed Excels as a Drummer Facing Deafness." *The Guardian*, April 11, 2021, https://www.theguardian.com/film/2021/apr/11/sound-of-metal-review-riz-ahmed-olivia-cooke-darius-marder.

Kim, Eunjung. "Why Do Dolls Die? The Power of Passivity and the Embodied Interplay Between Disability and Sex Dolls." *The Review of Education, Pedagogy, and Cultural Studies* 34 (2012): 94–106, https://doi.org/10.1080/10714413.2012.686852.

Kim, Ji-Hoon. "Between Auditorium and Gallery: Perception in Apichatpong Weerasethakul's Films and Installations." In *Global Art Cinema: New Theories and Histories*, edited by Rosalind Galt and Karl Schoonover, 125–141. New York: Oxford University Press, 2010.

Kim, Joshua Minsoo. "Review: Manta Ray Is a Story of Friendship with a Necessarily Humanist Outlook." *Slant Magazine*, March 26, 2019, https://www.slantmagazine.com/film/review-manta-ray-tells-a-story-of-friendship-with-a-necessarily-humanist-outlook/.

King, Geoff. *Film Comedy*. London: Wallflower Press, 2002.

Koistinen, Aino-Kaisa, and Sanna Karkulehto. "Feminism." *Critical Posthumanism*, August 24, 2018, https://criticalposthumanism.net/feminism/.

Kornhaber, Donna. "From Posthuman to Postcinema: Crises of Subjecthood and Representation in Her." *Cinema Journal* 56, no. 4 (2017): 3–25.

Labanyi, Jo. "Doing Things: Emotion, Affect and Materiality." *Journal of Spanish Cultural Studies* 11, no. 3–4 (2010): 223–233, https://doi.org/10.1080/14636204.2010.538244.

Laine, Tarja. *Bodies in Pain: Emotion and the Cinema of Darren Aronofsky*. New York: Berghahn Books, 2017.

Latour, Bruno. *We Have Never Been Modern*. Cambridge, MA: Harvard University Press, 2003.

Latour, Bruno. "Why Has Critique Run Out of Steam? From Matters of Fact to Matters of Concern." *Critical Inquiry* 30 (Winter 2004): 225–248.

Lauro, Sarah Juliet, and Karen Embry. "A Zombie Manifesto: The Nonhuman Condition in the Era of Advanced Capitalism." *boundary 2* 35, no. 1 (2008): 85–108.

Lawtoo, Nidesh. "'This Is No Simulation!': Hypermimesis from Being John Malkovich to Her." *Quarterly Review of Film and Video* 37, no. 2 (2020): 116–144.

Lee, Ashley. "Tamara Jenkins, *Private Life*." *Back Stage* 59, no. 38 (2018): 8.

Lee, Nathan. "Back to Basics." *Film Comment* 47, no. 4 (July–August 2011): 52–55.

Lewis, Tyson E. "Ztopia: Lessons in Post-Vital Politics in George Romero's Zombie Films." In *Generation Zombie: Essays on the Living Dead in Modern Culture*, edited by Stephanie Boluk and Wylie Lenz, 90–100. Jefferson: McFarland & Company, 2011.

Lidchi, Henrietta, and Suzanne Newman Fricke. "Future History: Indigenous Futurisms in North America Visual Arts," *World Art* 9, no. 2 (2019): 99–102, https://doi.org/10.1080/21500894.2019.1627675.

Lim, Dennis. "To Halve and to Hold." *Village Voice*, June 19, 2005, https://www.villagevoice.com/2005/06/21/to-halve-and-to-hold/

294 BIBLIOGRAPHY

Lippit, Akira Mizuta. *Electric Animal: Toward a Rhetoric of Wildlife.* Minneapolis: University of Minnesota Press, 2000.

Lodge, Guy. "Film Review: The Lobster." *Variety*, May 26, 2015, https://variety.com/2015/film/festivals/the-lobster-review-colin-farrell-rachel-weisz-1201496633/.

Lodge, Guy. "Film Review: 'Who You Think I Am.'" *Variety*, February 11, 2019, https://variety.com/2019/film/reviews/who-you-think-i-am-review-1203135557/.

Lorenz, Taylor. "The Instagram Aesthetic Is Over." *The Atlantic*, April 23, 2019, https://www.theatlantic.com/technology/archive/2019/04/influencers-are-abandoning-instagram-look/587803/.

Lowenstein, Adam. *Dreaming of Cinema: Spectatorship, Surrealism, and the Age of Digital Media*. New York: Columbia University Press, 2015.

MacCormack, Patricia. *The Ahuman Manifesto*. London: Bloomsbury, 2020.

MacCormack, Patricia. "Queer Posthumanism: Cyborgs, Animals, Monsters, Perverts." In *The Ashgate Research Companion to Queer Theory*, edited by Noreen Giffney and Michael O'Rourke, 111–128. Farnham: Ashgate, 2009.

MacCormack, Patricia. "Unnatural Alliances." In *Deleuze and Queer Theory*, edited by Chrysanthi Nigianni and Merl Storr, 134–149. Edinburgh: Edinburgh University Press, 2009.

Maher, Jennifer. "Something Else Besides a Father." *Feminist Media Studies* 14, no. 5 (2014): 853–867, https://doi.org/10.1080/14680777.2013.831369.

Mariniello, Silvestra. *Film and Modernity: The Kuleshov Case*. Minneapolis: University of Minnesota Press, 1990.

Marr, Matthew J. "'May You Overcome Your Obstacles': Reconsidering Pedro Almodóvar's *Hable Con Ella/Talk to Her* (2002) through the Disability Studies Lens." *Journal of Spanish Cultural Studies* 17, no. 1 (2016): 45–61, https://doi.org/10.1080/14636204.2015.1135603.

Marrero-Guillamón, Isaac. "The Politics and Aesthetics of Non-representation: Re-imagining Ethnographic Cinema with Apichatpong Weerasethakul." *Antípoda. Revista de Antropología y Arqueología* 33 (2018): 13–32.

Maslin, Janet. "'Run Lola Run': A Dangerous Game with Several Endings," *New York Times*, March 26, 1999, https://archive.nytimes.com/www.nytimes.com/library/film/032699lola-film-review.html.

Massumi, Brian. *Parables for the Virtual: Movement, Affect, Sensation*. Durham, NC: Duke University Press, 2002.

Mattar, Sinéad Garrigan. "Yeats, Fairies, and the New Animism." *New Literary History* 43, no. 1 (2012): 137–157.

Mattei, Shanti Escalante-De. "What Does Sound of Metal Mean to Deaf and Hard of Hearing Audiences?" *i-D*, January 14, 2021, https://i-d.vice.com/en_uk/article/epdmba/what-does-riz-ahmeds-movie-sound-of-metal-mean-to-deaf-audiences-darius-marder.

Matthews, J. H. "Surrealism and the Cinema." *Criticism* 4, no. 2 (Spring 1962): 120–133, https://www.jstor.org/stable/23091086.

Mathur, Ajeet N. "Strategies for Solving Wicked Problems of True Uncertainty: Tackling Pandemics Like Covid-19." Ahmedabad: Indian Institute of Management, 2020, http://vslir.iima.ac.in:8080/jspui/bitstream/11718/23012/1/WP_2020_04_03.pdf.

McGlotten, Shaka. "Zombie Porn: Necropolitics, Sex, and Queer Socialities." *Porn Studies* 1, no. 4 (2014): 360–377, https://doi.10.1080/23268743.2014.957492.

BIBLIOGRAPHY   295

McRuer, Robert. "In Focus: Cripping Cinema and Media Studies: Introduction." *JCMS: Journal of Cinema and Media Studies* 58, no. 4 (2019): 134–139, https://doi.10.1353/cj.2019.0042.

Moore, Tracy. "A Brief History of the 1–10 Scale for Female Hotness." *MEL Magazine*, 2019, https://melmagazine.com/en-us/story/female-hotness-1-10-rating-scale-history.

Mora, Arnau Roig "The Necropolitics of the Apocolypse: Queer Zombies in the Cinema of Bruce LaBruce." In *Thinking Dead: What the Zombie Apocalypse Means*, edited by Murali Bulaji, 181–196. Washington, DC: Lexington Books, 2013.

Morens, David M., and Anthony S. Fauci. "Emerging Pandemic Diseases: How We Got to COVID-19." *Cell 182* (2020): 1077–1092, https://www.cell.com/cell/pdf/S0092-8674(20)31012-6.pdf.

Morgan, Nyarri Nyarri, Nola Morgan, Lynette Wallworth, and Curtis Taylor. "Nyarri Nyarri Morgan: Virtual Reality, History and Indigenous Experience," *ACMI*, December 11, 2016, audio, https://www.acmi.net.au/ideas/listen/nyarri-nyarri-morgan-virtual-reality-history-and-indigenous-experience/.

Muñoz, José Esteban. *Cruising Utopia: The Then and There of Queer Futurity*. New York: New York University Press, 2009.

Murray, Stuart. *Disability and the Posthuman: Bodies, Technology, and Cultural Futures*. Liverpool: Liverpool University Press, 2020.

National Museum of the American Indian. *Do All Indians Live in Tipis?: Questions and Answers from the National Museum of the American Indian*. New York: Harper Perennial, 2007.

Neagu, Adriana-Cecilia. "Post-Apocalypse Now: Globalism, Posthumanism, and the 'Imagination of Disaster.'" *Transylvanian Review* 26, supplement 2 (2017): 237–246.

Neale, Stephen. *Genre and Hollywood*. London: Psychology Press, 2000.

Nicholson, Ben. "Border." *Sight & Sound* 29, no. 4 (April 2019): 59–60.

North, Michael. *Machine-Age Comedy*. Oxford: Oxford University Press, 2009.

O'Farrell, Mary Ann. *Telling Complexions: The Nineteenth Century Novel and the Blush*. Durham, NC: Duke University Press, 1999.

Oishi, Eve. "'Collective Orgasm': The Eco-Cyber-Pornography of Shu Lea Cheang." *Women's Studies Quarterly* 35, no. 1 (2007): 20–44.

Oliver, David. "*Sound of Metal* Is Getting Awards Season Buzz: Did It Do Things Right by the Deaf Community?" *USA Today*, February 2, 2021, https://www.usatoday.com/story/entertainment/movies/2021/02/02/sound-metal-awards-season-contender-mixed-deaf-community/4248898001/.

O'Sullivan, Charlotte. "*Sound of Metal* Review: You Don't Hear a Film Like This Every Day." *Evening Standard*, April 8, 2021, https://www.standard.co.uk/culture/film/sound-of-metal-review-riz-ahmed-b928430.html.

Pappas, Vanessa. "Conceptualising the Virtual and the Posthuman." *Media International Australia* 98 (February 2001): 39–50.

Patten, Dominic. "'Watchmen's Regina King on HBO Drama's Prophetic Power in a COVID-19 & Police Brutality-Scarred America—Contenders TV." *Deadline*, August 16, 2020, https://deadline.com/2020/08/watchmen-regina-king-interview-sister-night-dr-manhattan-contenders-tv-watch-1203013063/.

Peterson, Christopher. "The Posthumanism to Come." *Angelaki: Journal of the Theoretical Humanities* 16, no. 2 (2011): 127–141.

BIBLIOGRAPHY

Peterson, Jennifer, and Graig Uhlin. "In Focus: Film and Media Studies in the Anthropocene." *JCMS: Journal of Cinema and Media Studies* 58, no. 2 (2019): 142–143, https://doi.org/10.1353/cj.2019.0006.

Pettman, Dominic. *Human Error: Species-Being and Media Machines.* Minneapolis: University of Minnesota Press, 2011.

Pick, Anat, and Guinevere Narraway, eds. *Screening Nature: Cinema Beyond the Human.* London: Berghahn Books, 2013.

Pick, Anat. "Review of Giorgio Agamben, Open: Man and Animal, trans. Kevin Attell." *Bryn Mawr Review of Comparative Literature* 5, no. 2 (2006): 1–13, https://repository.brynmawr.edu/bmrcl/vol5/iss2/1/.

Power, Nina, and Rob White. "Lars Von Trier's *Melancholia*: A Discussion." *Film Quarterly,* January 10, 2012, https://filmquarterly.org/2012/01/10/lars-von-triers-melancholia-a-discussion/.

Preston, Catherine L. "Hanging on a Star: The Resurrection of the Romance Film in the 1990s." In *Film Genre 2000: New Critical Essays,* edited by Wheeler W. Dixon, 227–243. Albany: State University of New York Press, 2000.

Puymbroeck, Birgit Van, and N. Katherine Hayles. "'Enwebbed Complexities': The Posthumanities, Digital Media and New Feminist Materialism." *DiGeSt. Journal of Diversity and Gender Studies* 2, no. 1/2 (2015): 21–29, www.jstor.org/stable/10.11116/jdivegendstud.2.1-2.0021.

Quandt, James, ed. *Apichatpong Weerasethakul.* Wien: Austrian Film Museum, 2009.

Rao, Anita, Destiny Lopez, and Yat Li, "What 'Sound of Metal' Got Right and Wrong about Hearing Loss and Deafness." *North Carolina Public Radio,* April 9, 2021, https://www.wunc.org/2021-04-09/transcript-what-sound-of-metal-got-right-and-wrong-about-hearing-loss-and-deafness.

Rao, Mallika. "The Melancholia Postulate: What the 2011 Apocalyptic Film Has to Say About Peace of Mind in the Face of Annihilation." *The Atlantic,* May 9, 2020, https://www.theatlantic.com/culture/archive/2020/05/watching-melancholia-during-pandemic/611383/.

Reeve, Donna. "Cyborgs, Cripples and iCrip: Reflections on the Contribution of Haraway to Disability Studies." In *Disability and Social Theory,* edited by Dan Goodley, Bill Hughes, and Lennard Davis, 91–111. London: Palgrave MacMillan, 2012.

Restuccia, Frances L. "Agamben's Open: Coetzee's Dis-grace." *Comparative Literature* 69, no. 4 (2017): 413–429, https://doi.org/10.1215/00104124-4260436.

Reyes, Xavier Aldana. "Beyond the Metaphor: Gay Zombies and the Challenge to Homonormativity." *Journal for Cultural and Religious Theory* 13, no. 2 (2014): 1–12.

Rich, Ruby B. *New Queer Cinema: The Director's Cut.* Durham NC: Duke University Press, 2013.

Richardson, Michael. *Surrealism and Cinema.* Oxford: Berg, 2006.

Roanhorse, Rebecca, Elizabeth LaPensee, Johnnie Jay, and Darcie Little Badger. "Decolonizing Science Fiction and Imagining Futures: An Indigenous Futurisms Round Table." *Strange Horizons,* January 30, 2017, http://strangehorizons.com/non-fiction/articles/decolonizing-science-fiction-and-imagining-futures-an-indigenous-futurisms-roundtable/.

Russworm, TreaAndrea M. "Dystopian Blackness and the Limits of Racial Empathy in The Walking Dead and The Last of Us." In *Gaming Representation: Race, Gender, and Sexuality in Video Games,* edited by Jennifer Malkowski and TreaAndrea M. Russworm, 109–128. Bloomington: Indiana University Press, 2017.

BIBLIOGRAPHY 297

Ryan, Derek. *Virginia Woolf and the Materiality of Theory: Sex, Animal, Life.* Edinburgh: Edinburgh University Press, 2013.

San, Jon. "Why 'Sound of Metal' Makes This Hard-of-Hearing Audiologist 'Uncomfortable.'" *Yahoo! Life*, January 28, 2021, https://www.yahoo.com/lifestyle/why-sound-of-metal-makes-this-hardofhearing-audiologist-uncomfortable-150058033.html.

Schleitwiler, Vince, Abby Sun, and Rea Tajiri. "Messy, Energetic, Intense: A Roundtable Conversation among New York's Asian American Experimental Filmmakers of the Eighties with Roddy Bogawa, Daryl Chin, Shu Lea Cheang, and Rea Tajiri." *Film Quarterly* 73, no. 3 (2020): 66–78, https://doi.org/10.1525/fq.2020.73.3.66.

Sedgwick, Eve Kosofsky. *Touching Feeling: Affect, Pedagogy, Performativity.* Durham, NC: Duke University Press, 2003.

Šepetavc, Jasmina. "Queer and Feminist Futures: The Importance of a Future and Mobilising Feminist Film in Post Times." *Družboslovne Razprave* 33, no. 84 (2017): 83–98.

Scheetz, Cameron. "Gugu Mbatha-Raw on Misbehaviour, 'San Junipero,' and Becoming a Pop Star for Beyond the Lights." *AV Club*, February 10, 2020, https://film.avclub.com/gugu-mbatha-raw-on-misbehaviour-san-junipero-and-be-1845159353.

Scott, A. O. "The Track of a Teardrop, a Filmmaker's Path." *New York Times*, November 17, 2002, https://www.nytimes.com/2002/11/17/movies/film-the-track-of-a-teardrop-a-filmmaker-s-path.html.

Shaviro, Steven. "*Melancholia*, or, the Romantic Anti-sublime." *Sequence* 1, no. 1 (2012): 1–55.

Smelik, Anneke. "Feminist Film Theory." In *The Cinema Book*, 3rd ed., edited by Pam Cook, 491–504. London: British Film Institute, 2007.

Sobchack, Vivian. *Screening Space: The American Science Fiction Film.* New York: Ungar, 1987.

Sontag, Susan. *Against Interpretation and Other Essays.* New York: Dell, 1979.

Sorkin, Donna L. "*Sound of Metal*: New Feature Length Film on Deafness." *American Cochlear Implant Alliance*, December 9, 2020, https://www.acialliance.org/page/SoundofMetal.

Stacey, Jackie. *The Cinematic Life of the Gene.* Durham, NC: Duke University Press Books, 2010.

Steinbock, Eliza. "Towards Trans* Cinema." In *The Routledge Companion to Cinema and Gender*, edited by Kristin Hole, Dijana Jelača, E. Kaplan, and Patrice Petro, 395–406. New York: Routledge, 2017.

Stengers, Isabelle. "Reclaiming Animism." *e-flux* 36 (July 2012), https://bit.ly/35e6j9U/.

Stiegler, Bernard. *Technics and Time: The Fault of Epimetheus.* Palo Alto, CA: Stanford University Press, 1998.

Stryker, Susan, and Stephen Whittle, eds. *The Transgender Studies Reader.* New York: Routledge, 2004.

Tan, Ed S. *Emotion and the Structure of Narrative Film: Film as an Emotion Machine.* New York: Routledge, 2013.

Teh, David. "Itinerant Cinema: The Social Surrealism of Apichatpong Weerasethakul." *Third Text* 25, no. 5 (2011): 595–609.

Terada, Rei. *Feeling in Theory: Emotion after the Death of the Subject.* Cambridge, MA: Harvard University Press, 2002.

Terada, Rei. *Looking Away.* Cambridge, MA: Harvard University Press, 2009.

298 BIBLIOGRAPHY

Thrift, Nigel. *Non-Representational Theory: Space, Politics, Affect.* New York: Routledge, 2008.

Tjepkema, Lindsay. *Emarsys*, February 5, 2020, https://www.emarsys.com/resources.

Tomas, David. *Vertov, Snow, Farocki: Machine Vision and the Posthuman.* London: Bloomsbury, 2013.

Twitchin, Mischa, and Carl Lavery. "On Animism." *Performance Research* 24, no. 6 (2019): 1–5, https://doi.org/10.1080/13528165.2019.1686590.

United Nations: Office for Disarmament Affairs. "2016 Disarmament Film Series Side Event." *United Nations*, October 31, 2016, https://www.un.org/disarmament/update/2016-disarmament-film-series-side-event/.

van Sant, Ann Jessie. *Eighteenth-Century Sensibility and the Novel: The Senses in Social Context.* Cambridge: Cambridge University Press, 2004.

Varner, Gary Matthew. "*Koyaanisqatsi* and the Posthuman Aesthetics of a Mechanical Stare." *Film Criticism* 41, no. 1 (2017), https://doi.org/10.3998/fc.13761232.0041.104.

Vogler, Christopher. *The Writer's Journey: Mythic Structure for Storytellers & Screenwriters.* Los Angeles: Michael Wiese Productions, 1992.

Weaver, Harlan. "Monster Trans: Diffracting Affect, Reading Rage." In *TransGothic in Literature and Culture*, edited by Jolene Zigarovich, 119–138. New York: Routledge, 2017.

Webster, Abby. "Darius Marder Makes Hearing Audiences the Minority with *Sound of Metal.*" *The Georgetown Voice*, January 8, 2021, https://georgetownvoice.com/2021/01/08/darius-marder-makes-hearing-audiences-the-minority-with-sound-of-metal/.

Weerasethakul, Apitchatpong. "Exquisite Corpus." Interview by James Quandt, *Artforum International* 43, no. 9 (May 2005): 226–231.

Weisbrode, Kenneth. *On Ambivalence: The Problems and Pleasures of Having It Both Ways.* Cambridge, MA: MIT Press, 2012.

Williams, Evan Calder. *Combined and Uneven Apocalypse: Luciferian Marxism.* Winchester: John Hunt Publishing, 2011.

Williams, Linda. "Film Bodies: Gender, Genre, and Excess." *Film Quarterly* 44, no. 4 (1991): 2–13. https://doi.org/10.2307/1212758.

Williams, Linda. "Melodrama Revised." In *Refiguring American Film Genres: Theory and History*, edited by Nick Browne, 42–88. Berkeley: University of California Press, 1998.

Willoughby, Pamela. *The Evolution of Modern Humans in Africa: A Comprehensive Guide.* Lanham, MD: AltaMira Press, 2007.

Wilson, Elizabeth A. *Affect and Artificial Intelligence.* Seattle: University of Washington Press, 2011.

Wissgott, Sim Sim. "In the Spotlight—The Doctors at the Top: Truthtellers and Heartthrobs." *CGTN*, April 14, 2020, https://news.cgtn.com/news/2020-04-14/In-the-Spotlight-Doctors-at-the-top-Truth-tellers-and-heartthrobs-PGIyev8g9y/index.html.

Wolfe, Cary. *What Is Posthumanism?* Minneapolis: Minnesota University Press, 2010.

Woo, Jaeyeon. "Victim Urges Seoul to Bring Wartime Sex Slavery Issue to ICJ." *Yonhap News*, April 14, 2021, https://en.yna.co.kr/view/AEN20210414007300315.

Yamato, Jen. "The Anti-'Avengers': In Indie Gem 'Fast Color,' A Powerful New Superhero Story is Born." *Los Angeles Times*, April 23, 2019, https://www.latimes.com/entertainment/movies/la-ca-mn-fast-color-superhero-gugu-mbatha-raw-julia-hart-20190423-story.html.

Young, Katy. "All Hail Scarlett Johansson's Perfect 'Golden Ratio' Figure." *The Telegraph*, May 21, 2015, http://www.telegraph.co.uk/beauty/people/scarlett-johansson-has-the-perfect-golden-ratio-figure/.

Yoshiawa, Rebecca Scott. "Fetal-Maternal IntraAction: Politics of New Placental Biologies." *Body & Society* 22, no. 4 (2016): 79–105, https://doi.org/10.1177/13570 34X16662323.

Zey, Michael G. "Rejuvenation and Radically Increased Health Spans." In *Posthumanism: The Future of Homo Sapiens*, edited by Michael Bess and Diana Walsh Pasulka, 105–120. Farmington Hills, MI: Macmillan Reference, 2018.

Žižek, Slavoj. "Jordan Peterson as a Symptom . . . of What?" In *Myth and Mayhem: A Leftists Critique of Jordan Peterson*, edited by Ben Burgis, Conrad Hamilton, Matthew McManus, and Marion Trejo, 1–15. Blue Ridge, PA: Zero Books, 2020.

Index

For the benefit of digital users, indexed terms that span two pages (e.g., 52–53) may, on occasion, appear on only one of those pages.

Figures are indicated by *f* following the page number

Abbasi, Ali, 1, 211, 217–18. See also *Border/Gräns*
ableism, 183, 204–6. *See also* disability studies
activism, 69, 78–80, 173, 174, 253*f*
Actor-Network Theory (ANT), 5–6. *See also* Latour, Bruno
ACT UP (AIDS Coalition to Unleash Power), 174
affect, 16–17, 28–29, 50–52, 54–55, 71, 131–32, 215, 246–47
the body as, 21–22, 257–63, 272–73
afrofuturism, 74. *See also* Indigenous futurism
ageism, 110–11, 133
AI. *See* artificial intelligence
Air Doll/Kūki Ningyō, 8–9, 18, 34–36, 39, 50, 109–11, 112–26, 131, 202–3
Alaimo, Stacey, 5–6, 13, 18, 172–73, 244–46, 272–73
alien(s), 28–29, 36–37, 53–55, 120–21, 140, 167, 252–53
Alien: Resurrection, 53–55
Almodóvar, Pedro, 20, 183. See also *Talk to Her/Hable con ella*
ambivalence, 8, 40–41, 43–44, 46–47, 49–57, 58–59, 71, 100–1, 109, 110, 126, 127–28, 130–31, 133–36, 281–82
American Sign Language, 196. *See also* sign language
android(s), 54–57, 173. *See also* robots and robotics
animal studies, 2–3, 4–5, 15–16, 20–21, 210, 281–82
Annihilation, 53–54, 247–58, 272–73
anthropocene, 3, 21–22, 69, 244–75, 277

anthropocentrism, 59, 65, 66–67, 68, 159, 210, 225–26, 239–40, 270*f*
anthropological machine, 20–21, 210, 211, 212–13, 216–17, 222, 226–27, 228, 234, 235, 239–40
anti-humanism, 277
anti-relationality, 165–66, 171–72
apocalypse film. *See* disaster
Aronofsky, Darren, 21–22, 45–46, 246–47, 258–59. See also *Mother!*; *Requiem for a Dream*
Aroonpheng, Phuttiphong, 20–21, 211–12, 238. See also *Kraben Rahu/ Manta Ray*
Arrival, 36–38, 39, 111–12, 140
art cinema (genre), 18, 71–73, 112, 164–66
artificial intelligence, 27, 159–60, 248, 276
art-porn (genre), 164–65
Åsberg, Cecilia, 6–7, 73–74, 108–9
ASL. *See* American sign language
assisted reproductive technologies, 8, 27, 39–41, 47
Audiard, Jacques, 16–17, 32–33. See also *Rust and Bone/De rouille et d'os*
auteur(s), 18–20, 71–72, 150, 176–77
queer auteur(s) 164, 169–70, 172, 176–77
autism, 183–84, 186–87
avatar(s), 159, 160–61, 162, 224
online, 30–31, 162–63
virtual, 7, 36

Bacurau, 1, 17, 66–67, 90–94, 95, 96–97, 101
Badmington, Neil, 2–3, 8–10, 11, 17, 36–37, 58–59

302 INDEX

Barad, Karen, 5–6, 13, 18, 108–9, 149,
  150–51, 245, 249, 258, 262–63
Barker, Jennifer, 214–15, 258–59
Being John Malkovich, 18–20, 150,
  154–64, 176–77
Benjamin, Walter, 226–27
Bennet, Jane, 5–6, 13, 245, 264–65,
  266–67, 270–71
Benshoff, Harry, 151
Bernini, Lorenzo, 164–65, 166, 168–69
Besson, Luc, 41. See also *Lucy*
Biidaaban: First Light, 9, 17, 37–39, 66–67,
  73–80, 101
Biotechnologies, 39–41, 42–43, 46–47
Black Lives Matter, 85–86
Black Mirror, 36, 131
body horror (genre), 160, 162
Bogost, Ian, 5–6, 245
Borden, Lizzie, 18–20, 169–72.
  See also *Born in Flames*
Border/Gräns, 1, 20–21, 211, 216–22,
  226–27, 238
Born in Flames, 18–20, 169–75, 176–77
Bradshaw, Peter, 30–31, 160, 222–23
Braidotti, Rosi, 21–22, 50–51, 55–56, 73–
  74, 100–1, 108–9, 131, 133–34, 151,
  152–53, 173, 183, 244, 245–47, 252,
  259–60, 264–66, 267, 272–73, 277–79
Breton, André, 221–22, 226–27
Briggs, John, 92–93
Brinkema, Eugenie, 164–65
Brody, Richard, 86–88, 89–90, 170–71
Burger, Neil, 16–17. See also *Limitless*
Butler, Judith, 149

capitalism, 68–69, 71, 100–1, 281
  advanced, 11–12, 277–78
  consumer, 15–16, 245
  global, 27, 83–85, 280–81
  late, 17, 67, 73–74, 87
  western, 68
Cartesian, 164–65, 229–30
  dualism, 5–6, 222, 230, 239–40
  subject, 2–3, 9–10
Celle que vous croyez. See *Who You Think I
  Am/Celle que vous croyez*
CGI. *See* computer generated images
Chakravorty, Swagato, 120–21, 132–33

Cheang, Shu Lea, 18–20, 150, 153–54,
  164–65, 169–70, 172–75, 176–77.
  See also *Fluidø*
chthulucene, 11–12, 36
cinema of attractions, 8
climate change, 8–9, 21–22, 64, 83–85,
  89–90, 100–1, 244–45, 246–47,
  254–55, 263
clone(s) and cloning, 3, 8–9, 27, 53–57
cochlear implant, 97, 183, 192–93, 202–5
collective, 18–20, 28–29, 150, 152–54, 167,
  169–75, 176–77
Collisions, 17, 66–67, 73–74, 78–80,
  81–83, 101
colonialism, 27, 38–39, 72, 74–75, 78, 101
comedy (genre), 21–22, 30–31, 48, 49, 50,
  64, 163–64, 253–54
communication technology(ies), 59, 126,
  128–29, 198
computer generated images, 32–33, 41,
  42–43, 175
Congress, The, 7, 109–10, 111–12, 134–35,
  141–44, 145
Cottrell, Adam, 258–59
Covid-19, 17, 85–86, 89–90, 100
crip perspectives, 6–7
  cripping cinema, 196
critical race theory and studies, 4–5, 22–23
critical racial dystopia, 87
Cronenberg, Brandon, 150, 160.
  See also *Possessor*
Cuarón, Alfonso, 8–9, 111–12.
  See also *Gravity*
cybernetics, 27, 32–33
cyber punk (genre), 131
cyborg(s), 11–12, 18–20, 27, 30, 32–34, 36,
  50–51, 59, 107–48, 149, 150–64, 172–
  73, 176–77, 184–86, 202–3, 244
  and gender, 107, 108–9, 138–39,
  150–51
  sexuality of, 109, 125–26, 128–29, 154
  women cyborgs, 18, 108–13, 118–19,
  122–24, 125–26, 132–36, 140–
  41, 143–45
  See also *Cyborg Manifesto, A*;
  Haraway, Donna
Cyborg Manifesto, A, 18, 33–34, 107,
  115–16, 134–35, 172–73

INDEX   303

de Lauretis, Teresa, 170–71
Deleuze, Gilles, 13, 153, 191–92
De rouille et d'os. See *Rust and Bone/De rouille et d'os*
Derrida, Jacques, 69–70, 173
Descartes, Renee, 222
disability, 20, 34, 97, 117, 182–83, 187–88, 190–94, 196–98, 201–3, 204–6
disability studies, 2–3, 4–5, 20, 182–83, 186–87, 196, 204–6, 281–82
disaster (genre), 8–9, 17, 64–65, 66–68, 70–71, 73–74, 77–78, 81, 83–85, 86–88, 92–93, 97, 99, 100–1, 276
Diving Bell and the Butterfly, The, 183–84, 192–93, 196–203, 204–6
Doane, Mary Ann, 111–12, 121, 135–36
documentary (genre), 133, 170–71, 205–6, 210, 224–25, 235–36
Dornelles, Juliano, 1, 66–67.
    See also *Bacurau*
drama (genre), 21–22, 30–31, 78, 131, 163–64, 172, 271–72, 276
    environmental drama, 9
    melodrama, 28–29, 49, 56–57, 58–59, 66–67
drugs, 41, 43–44, 46, 88, 91–92, 142–43
    cognitive and performance enhancing, 27, 39–40, 43–44, 46–47

eco-material posthuman, 21–22, 244–75
embodiment, 2–3, 5, 9–10, 13–14, 28–29, 34, 108–9, 110–11, 124–25, 127–28, 132–34, 151, 156–57, 159, 160–61, 162–63, 166, 172–73, 176–77, 182, 212–13, 225–26, 239, 276
    cyborg, 32–33, 108, 111–12, 122–24, 130, 134–35, 140, 143–44
    female, 107, 110
    nonhuman, 121
    posthuman, 33–34, 109, 110, 141–42, 144–45, 154, 155–56
    transgender, 119–20
enlightenment (movement), 2–3, 52
Enyedi, Ildiko, 1, 50, 211. See also *On Body and Soul/Testről és lélekről*
Epstein, Charlotte, 76–77, 80, 81

Erlingsson, Benedikt, 21–22, 246–47, 253–54. See also *Woman at War/Kona fer í stríð*
ethics, 125–26, 152–53, 237
Ex Machina, 1–2, 9, 15–16, 18, 56–57, 59, 108, 109–10, 112–26, 144–45, 248
exposure scene(s), 110, 119–22, 124
extinction, 1–2, 3, 8–10, 17, 93–94, 99, 244
extraterrestrial experience(s), 18, 111–12, 134–35, 138–39, 141
Ezra, Elizabeth, 15–16

fantasy (genre), 1–2, 16–17, 27, 53–54, 64, 111–12, 131, 216–17, 267
Fast Color, 7, 17, 66–67, 83–88, 89–90, 94–96, 97–99, 101
feminism, 22–23, 170–72, 259–60
    alien feminism, 118–19, 130–31, 133–34, 135, 140
femme fatale, 18, 110, 112–15, 120–21, 124–25, 132–33, 144–45
Ferrando, Francesca, 4, 18, 70–71, 108, 121–22, 144–45, 210
Filho, Kleber Mendonça, 1, 66–67. See also *Bacurau*
film noir (genre), 50, 112–13, 124–25
First Nations people, 74–75, 76–77, 80
First Reformed, 263–73
Fluidø, 18–20, 150, 152, 169–75
Folman, Ari, 7, 109–10. See also *Congress, The*
Frankenstein's monster, 151–52
Fukuyama, Francis, 5, 42–44, 46–47

Galt, Rosalind, 214–15
Garland, Alex, 1, 53–54, 56–57, 108, 193–94, 247–48. See also *Annihilation* and *Ex Machina*
gender, 18, 40–41, 47, 66, 76–77, 83–96, 107, 108–9, 110, 111–12, 119–20, 124, 126, 130–31, 133–34, 144, 150–51, 160, 162–63, 173, 176–77
    binary, 107, 108, 121–22, 151, 176–77
    essentialism, 107
    performativity, 149
    post-gender, 18, 108, 173

304 INDEX

genetics, 249
  biocapitalism, 53–54
  biogenetic, 2–3, 277–78
  engineering, 12–13, 40–41
  experimentation, 53–54
genre, 1–26, 64, 66–67, 90, 117–18, 131,
    132, 140, 163–66, 167, 168–70, 172,
    173, 174, 176–77, 276
Gittel, Noah, 132–33
Glazer, Jonathan, 18, 108. See also
    Under the Skin
González, Jennifer, 122–25
Goodley, Dan, 20, 182, 183–84, 201–2, 205–6
Gräns. See *Border/Gräns*
Gravity, 111–12, 136–37, 140
Grinberg, Daniel, 235
Grosz, Elizabeth, 150, 245
Grusin, Richard, 5–6
Guattari, Félix, 13, 153

Hable con ella. See *Talk to Her/Hable con ella*
Halberstam, Jack, 11, 150–51
Haraway, Donna, 10–12, 17–18, 33–34, 36,
    76–77, 107–9, 115–16, 128–29, 133–
    36, 141–42, 144–45, 150–52, 171–73,
    183, 219, 244, 245–46, 249, 254–55,
    262–63, 264–65, 277–78
Harman, Graham, 5–6, 245
Hart, Julia, 7, 17, 66–67, 87–88.
    See also *Fast Color*
Harvey, Graham, 229–30
hauntology, 173–74
Hayles, N. Katherine, 2–3, 4, 5, 10–11, 18,
    30, 31–32, 34, 55–56, 108–9, 127–28,
    142–43, 153–54, 172–73
Her, 7, 9, 14, 15–16, 18–20, 36, 50, 52, 55–
    56, 132–33, 150, 154–64, 175
Herbrechter, Stefan, 5, 9–11
HIV/AIDS, 167, 173, 174
Hollywood cinema, 47, 112–13
hologram(s), 55–56
horror (genre), 16–17, 18, 21–22, 28–29,
    31–32, 49–50, 53–54, 56–57, 58–59,
    117–18, 121, 131, 151, 160, 162, 163–
    64, 249–51
  eco-horror, 247
human exceptionalism, 20–22, 59, 184–86,
    210–43, 246–47, 258, 272–73, 276–
    77, 281–82

humanism, 3–5, 8–10, 12–17, 18–20, 22–
    23, 28–29, 39, 42–43, 66, 68, 69–71,
    72–73, 74, 77–78, 97, 101, 107, 109,
    118–19, 125–26, 144, 145, 159, 165–
    66, 183, 186–87, 191–92, 205–6, 212–
    13, 230, 232, 245–46, 277–78, 281–82

in vitro fertilization (IVF), 47, 48–49. *See
    also* assisted reproductive technology
independent cinema, 18–20, 111–12, 169–
    70, 176–77
  indie, 16–17, 31–33, 50, 66–67, 83, 276
Indigenous
  experience(s), 73–74, 80
  filmmaker, 9
  futurism, 37–38, 74–75, 77–78, 80
  knowledge, 92–93, 92*f*
  perspective(s), 66–67, 73–74, 77–78, 80
Ingrid Goes West, 30–32, 131, 132, 133–34
intersectionality, 65, 170–72, 182

Jackson, Lisa, 9, 37–38, 66–67, 73–78.
    See also *Biidaaban: First Light*
Jelača, Dijana, 8, 15–16, 118–19, 130–31,
    133, 140
Jenkins, Tamara, 16–17, 47, 48–49.
    See also *Private Life*
Jeunet, Jean-Pierre, 53–54. See also *Alien:
    Resurrection*
Johansson, Scarlett, 41, 50, 108, 122–24, 159
Jonze, Spike, 7, 14, 18–20, 36, 50, 52, 150,
    159, 176–77. See also *Being John
    Malkovich; Her*

Keller, Sarah, 17, 64, 67, 96–97
Kona fer í stríð. See *Woman at War/Kona
    fer í stríð*
Kore-eda, Hirokazu, 8–9, 34–36, 124–25,
    133. See also *Air Doll/Kūki Ningyō*
Kraben Rahu. See *Manta Ray/Kraben Rahu*
Kūki Ningyō. See *Air Doll/Kūki Ningyō*

L.A. Zombie, 9, 18–20, 150, 165–66, 168–69
LaBruce, Bruce, 9, 18–20, 150, 153–54,
    164–71, 172, 173–75, 176–77. See
    also *L.A. Zombie; Otto; or, Up with
    Dead People*,
Lanthimos, Yorgos, 20–21, 50, 211.
    See also *Lobster, The*

LaPensée, Elizabeth, 77–80
Latour, Bruno, 3, 4, 5–6, 277–79
Lawthom, Rebecca, 20, 182, 205–6
Lawtoo, Nidesh, 154, 155, 159
liminality, 151, 164, 166
Limitless, 16–17, 44, 45–47, 55–56
Lobster, The, 20–21, 50, 55–56, 211, 212–
  17, 222, 223–24, 227–28, 238
Lucy, 41–44, 52, 126, 132–33, 159–60

MacCormack, Patricia, 18–20, 69, 151, 153
Manta Ray/Kraben Rahu, 20–21, 211–12,
  228–29, 230, 235–39
Marder, Darius, 20, 183. See also *Sound
  of Metal*
Martu people, 78–80, 81–82
Massumi, Brian, 245, 257–58, 262–63
maternity, 54–55, 111–12, 134–37, 141–
  42, 143–44, 145, 219
Melancholia, 66–67, 68–73, 76–77,
  78, 95–96
mimesis, 155–56
misogyny. See sexism
monster(s) and monstrosity, 11, 18–20,
  53–54, 57, 80, 149, 150, 151–54, 164–
  69, 176–77, 220–21, 232–33
Morgan, Nyarri Nyarri, 78–80, 81–83
Mother!, 21–22, 246–47, 257–63
motherhood, 134–36, 138–39, 140–41. See
  also maternity
Muñoz, José Esteban, 164–66, 171–
  72, 173–74
Murray, Stuart, 182, 198

naturalism, 150, 152–53, 232
Neagu, Adriana-Cecilia, 89–90
Nebbou, Safy, 18, 109–10, 155–56. See
  also *Who You Think I Am/Celle que
  vous croyez*
neo-neorealism (genre), 16–17, 28–29
neuropharmacology, 43–44, 46–47. See
  also drugs
new animism, 20–21, 211–12, 228–30,
  235, 237, 239–40
new materialism, 5–6, 13, 245,
  249, 272–73
new queer cinema, 169–70, 173
Nichols, Jeff, 17, 67. See also *Take Shelter*
Nietzsche, Friedrich, 9–10, 69–70

nomadism, 277–78
Nomadland, 279–82
nonhuman materiality, 110, 112, 120–
  21, 125–26
normativity, 4, 22–23, 165–66
  heteronormativity, 163–64
  homonormativty, 165–66, 167
nostalgia, 5, 8–9, 134–35, 173–74
NQC. See New Queer Cinema

objectification, 112, 132–34, 214–15, 225–
  26, 227–28, 258
Object-Oriented Ontology, 5–6
Oishi, Eve, 172–73, 174–75
On Body and Soul/Teströl és lélekröl, 1–2,
  20–21, 50, 211, 222–28
organ transplant, 12–13
Otto; or, Up with Dead People, 18–20,
  150, 165–66

pharmaceutical technologies, 39–41
porn and pornography, 9, 48, 49, 56–57,
  162–63, 164–66, 167, 168–69, 172,
  174, 175, 224, 225–26
Possessor, 18–20, 150, 154–64, 176–
  77, 187–88
post-anthropocentrism, 210–43
postcolonial
  perspectives, 76–77, 80–81
  theory, 4–5, 65, 72, 74–75
postporn (genre), 18–20, 150, 164, 171–74
Private Life, 16–17, 47, 48–49
prosthetic(s) and prostheses, 2–3, 5, 14,
  20, 30, 31–33, 157, 172–73, 182, 183,
  184–86, 192–93, 216–17
Proxima, 18, 109–10, 111–12, 134–37, 140,
  142–43, 144–45

queer futurity, 164–65, 173–74
queer theory, 2–3, 4–5, 18–20, 22–23, 149–
  51, 163–64, 165–66, 176–77, 281–82

racism, 74, 90, 110
realism, 1–2, 18, 73–74, 83–85, 95–96, 97,
  130–31, 133, 220–21, 232
relationality, 5–6, 20–21, 30, 58–59, 152–
  53, 164–65, 167, 168–70, 171–72,
  173, 176–77, 210, 211–12, 214–15,
  222–23, 235–40, 245, 276–77

306 INDEX

Requiem for a Dream, 45–46
robots and robotics, 1, 2–3, 5, 55–57, 100–1, 110, 113–15, 121–24, 136–37, 248. *See also* androids
Runswick-Cole, Katherine, 20, 182, 205–6
Russworm, TreaAndrea, 87, 88, 96–97. *See also* critical racial dystopia
Rust and Bone/De rouille et d'os, 16–17, 32–34

Satpralat. See *Tropical Malady/Satpralat*
Schnabel, Julian, 183–84. See also *Diving Bell and the Butterfly, The*
Schrader, Paul, 263. See also *First Reformed*
science fiction (genre), 1–2, 18–20, 28–29, 39, 64, 73–75, 94–95, 100–1, 111–12, 124–25, 130–31, 132–33, 160, 163–64, 169–70, 172, 173–74, 248, 276
Sense8, 174–75
sex doll(s), 8–9, 34, 110, 116, 124–25
sexism, 110–11, 133, 171–72
Sharp, Joanne, 92–93
sign language, 196
simulation, 136–37, 142–43, 159
    digital and computer, 142–43, 154
    sexual, 126–27
smartphone(s), 126
    iPhone, 50–51, 138–39
social media, 30–33, 126–27, 130–31, 133
Sontag, Susan, 17, 64, 66, 74–75, 89–90, 94, 100–1
Sound of Metal, 20, 183–84, 192–206
speciesism, 20–21, 210, 239–40
spectacle, 38–39, 43, 57, 66, 67, 86–87, 101, 115–16, 132, 133, 164, 173, 249–51, 265–66, 277–78
speculative fiction, 28–29
Spicer, Matt, 30–31. See also *Ingrid Goes West*
*Still Life/*三峡好人, 9, 21–22, 246–47, 263–73
Stryker, Susan, 152
subjectivity, 11, 16–17, 21–22, 30, 33–34, 76–77, 110–11, 126–27, 130–31, 133–34, 154, 182, 184–86, 190–91, 193–94, 196, 203–4, 236, 246–47, 276–77

cyborg, 133–35, 138–39, 140, 143–44
human, 1–2, 10–11, 152, 183–84, 262–63, 272–73
hybrid, 18, 30, 108–9, 125–26, 184–86
nonhuman, 10–11, 37
normative, 4, 12–13, 190
posthuman, 130–31, 138–39, 145, 191–92
superhero(es), 28–29, 41–42, 66–67, 83, 85–88, 89–90, 95–96, 276
surrealism, 156, 210–14, 216–17, 221–22, 226–27, 228–29, 239–40
surveillance, 256

Take Shelter, 17, 67, 97, 99, 101
Talk to Her/Hable con ella, 20, 183–94, 205–6
technofetishism, 112, 124–25, 141
technophobia, 159–60
technoqueer, 150–51, 162–63, 164
technosexuality, 18, 22–23, 110–11, 125–34, 154
tekhnē, 52
teledildonics, 162–63
Terada, Rei, 49, 56–57, 183–84
Teströl és lélekröl. See *On Body and Soul/Teströl és lélekröl*
transcendentalism, 13
transgender cinema, 119–20
transhumanism, 5, 8–9, 11–12, 14–15, 28–29, 40, 50
Tropical Malady/Satpralat, 20–21, 211–12, 228–29, 230, 231–36, 237
Turing test, 1, 56–57

Under the Skin, 18, 108, 109–11, 112–26, 132–33, 144–45, 202–3

video game(s) and gaming, 87, 160–61, 163–64
Villeneuve, Denis, 36–37. See also *Arrival*
virtual reality (VR), 9, 30, 37–39, 66–67, 73–76, 78–80, 81, 82, 136–37, 142–43, 160–61, 162–63
vital materialism, 2–3, 13, 264–65
von Trier, Lars, 66–67, 69–70, 72–73. See also *Melancholia*

INDEX 307

Wachowski sisters, 174. See also
    Sense8
Wallworth, Lynette, 17, 66–67, 73–74, 78–
    80, 81, 82–83. See also *Collisions*
Watchmen, 85–87, 88–89
Weerasethakul, Apichatpong, 20–21, 211–
    12, 228–30, 231–34, 235–36.
    See also *Tropical Malady/Satpralat*
western (genre), 1–2, 16–17,
    90, 276
    post-Western, 66–67, 93–94
*Who You Think I Am/Celle que vous
    croyez*, 18, 109–11, 125–34, 141, 144–
    45, 155–56

Williams, Evan Calder, 17, 65, 76–77, 89–
    90, 95–96
Williams, Linda, 28–29, 46–47, 49
Wincoeur, Alice, 18, 109–10.
    See also *Proxima*
Wolfe, Cary, 1–3, 4, 5, 10–11, 12–13,
    20–21, 210, 239–40
Woman at War/Kona fer í stríð, 21–22,
    246–57, 272–73

Zhangke, Jia, 9, 246–47. See also *Still Life/
    三峡好人*
zombie, 9, 18–20, 150, 164–70, 172
三峡好人. See *Still Life/*三峡好人

Printed in the USA/Agawam, MA
May 3, 2024

865425.003